DAILY PRAYER 2007

SUNDAY YEAR C
WEEKDAY YEAR I

A BOOK OF PRAYER FOR
EACH DAY OF THE LITURGICAL YEAR

ROBERT C. RABE · DAVID J. CRONAN

LITURGY
TRAINING
PUBLICATIONS

Nihil Obstat
Reverend Louis J. Cameli, STD
Censor Deputatus
April 10, 2006

Imprimatur
Reverence John F. Canary, DMIN
Vicar General
Archdiocese of Chicago
April 18, 2006

DAILY PRAYER 2007 © 2006 Archdiocese of Chicago: Liturgy Training Publications, 1800 N. Hermitage Ave., Chicago IL 60622; 1-800-933-1800; fax 1-800-933-7094; orders@ltp.org; website: www.LTP.org. All rights reserved.

Unless otherwise noted, the reflections and prayers are original works written by Robert C. Rabe and David J. Cronan for *Daily Prayer 2007.*

The publisher is grateful to the copyright holders who granted permission to reprint their texts in this book. Sources are listed beginning on page 395.

This book was edited by Danielle A. Knott. Carol Mycio was the production editor. The design of the interior and icons is by Larry Cope; the cover design is by Anna Manhart. The typesetting was done by Kari Nicholls in Times and Exocet. The editor wishes to thank Suzanne M. Lewis for her assistance.

Printed in Canada.

ISBN-10: 1-56854-569-X
ISBN-13: 978-1-56854-569-1

ADP07

To the monks of Marmion Abbey, Aurora, IL, and the monastic and academic communities of St. John's University School of Theology, Collegeville, MN, for their support, prayers, and tutelage in the Lord's service.

—David J. Cronan

To my mom and dad, Bob and Clare, who nourish me with love and empower me to live God's Word freely and justly.

—Robert C. Rabe

To the Cloud of Witnesses who encircle us with example and prayer.

—Robert C. Rabe and David J. Cronan

TABLE OF CONTENTS

INTRODUCTION

Rejoice always.
Pray without ceasing.
In all circumstances
  give thanks, for this is the
  will of God for you in
  Christ Jesus.

1 Thessalonians 5:16–18

Welcome to *Daily Prayer 2007,* Sunday Year C and Weekday Year I! This edition of the well-loved prayer book provides a familiar order of prayer for each day of the liturgical year, from the First Sunday of Advent, December 3, 2006, to December 31, 2007. This portable prayer book enables further contemplation of and devotion to the mysteries celebrated in the liturgy. The Gospel from daily Mass is provided, and the prayer texts and reflections are in tune with the seasons, solemnities and feasts of the Lord, and the commemoration of saints celebrated during the liturgical year. The prayers within will inspire and bring you to a deeper appreciation for the word that is proclaimed and the Eucharist that is shared in the liturgical life of the Church.

THE ORDER OF PRAYER

Daily Prayer 2007 follows a simple order of prayer: it begins with an opening verse with the sign of the cross; followed by psalmody, a Gospel reading, a brief reflection, the Prayers of the Faithful, the Lord's Prayer, a closing prayer and a closing verse with the sign of the cross. This order remains consistent for each day of the liturgical year,

allowing the repetition to become part of your daily rhythm and routine.

Daily prayer 2007 is organized by season, and the psalter is located in the back of the book (pages 405–421). Everything you need is conveniently contained in this resource! Refer to the table of contents for easy reference.

DAILY HEADING

Daily Prayer is easily navigable. A heading is provided for each day of prayer so you will always know where you are. The heading includes the date and name of the liturgical observance, including solemnities, feasts, and obligatory memorials. All optional memorials have been footnoted when they may occur. These observances are according to the norms prescribed by the United States Conference of Catholic Bishops' Committee on the Liturgy.

OPENING AND CLOSING VERSICLE WITH SIGN OF THE CROSS

The order of prayer begins each day with the sign of the cross and a versicle. The versicles are taken from the refrains proper to particular and seasonal responsorial psalms; antiphons from the Liturgy of the Hours and Roman Missal; and Gospel acclamation verses from the Lectionary. You will notice that the versicles are often repeated throughout individual seasons. This unifies the season with prayer. For some solemnities and special feasts, the repetition is interrupted with a versicle significant to the particular liturgical observance.

PSALMODY

The psalms are an integral part of Catholic prayer. As poetic readings from Sacred Scripture, the psalms reflect upon God's saving work in various modes—praise, thanksgiving, and lamentation. The psalms in *Daily Prayer 2007* have been ordered according to liturgical significance; they follow the liturgical seasons and other observances. Psalms for Advent implore for God to return; psalms for Lent evoke the need for God's mercy and forgiveness; psalms for Easter give praise for his glory and salvation; and psalms for Ordinary Time give thanks for all that is good. On certain days special psalms have been chosen which further enhance the meaning of the liturgical observance.

GOSPEL READING

Each day of prayer includes the Gospel prescribed for the daily Mass. This enables further reflection upon the Word of God proclaimed during the Eucharistic celebration–the "source and summit" of our faith. On some days, excerpts from the Gospel have been selected. For further prayer, or to reference, the complete Gospel texts are listed in the scripture index found on pages 395–404.

REFLECTION

The reflections in *Daily Prayer 2007* are a combination of original compositions, commentary from the Church Fathers, Church documents, papal homilies and addresses, and other spiritual writings. These reflections are meant to direct your prayers in light of the Gospel message, liturgical observance, and season.

PRAYER OF THE FAITHFUL

The Prayer of the Faithful, sometimes referred to as the General Intercessions, is a prayer of the baptized who, through Christ, voice their concerns to God regarding the Church, the world, the downtrodden, local needs, and other concerns. Thus, the prayers in this book connect the individual and small faith groups to the universal Church and those in most need of God's love and mercy. Although specific prayers are provided in this resource, others may be added depending upon local need.

THE LORD'S PRAYER

Jesus taught us to pray to "Our Father." It is fitting to follow the Prayer of the Faithful with this essential Christian prayer for it encapsulates the humility and reverence we give to our God—and neighbor—while asking for God's mercy and forgiveness.

CLOSING PRAYER

The closing prayer follows the form of the traditional collect, "addressed to God the father, through Christ, in the Holy Spirit" *(General Instruction of the Roman Missal, 54)*. Essentially, this prayer "collects" our daily prayer, the prayers found in this book, and those of our hearts and minds—those as individuals or groups—into one Trinitarian prayer, concluded with our assent of "Amen."

USING THE BOOK

These prayers may be used by individuals, families or prayer groups, to begin meetings or catechetical classes, formational and youth ministry events, or as prayer with the aged, sick and homebound. It may be used at any time during the day, and given the convenient size of this book, is easily transported to meet various prayer needs and situations.

The order of prayer may be prayed silently, or, especially for group prayer, prayed out loud. If used for prayer gatherings, it might be helpful to designate someone to open the prayer, lead the Prayer of the Faithful, begin the Lord's Prayer, and to conclude the prayer. Select an additional volunteer to proclaim the Gospel. Allow the faithful to read the psalm together either as an entire group, or divide the stanzas among the faithful for alternating recitation.

Feel free to adapt these prayers for specific needs—intercessions may be added, music may begin and conclude the service, and the psalm, response to the Prayer of the Faithful, and the Lord's Prayer may be chanted.

CUSTOMER FEEDBACK

Daily Prayer 2007 is the sixth edition of an annual publication; *Daily Prayer 2008* is already being prepared. Because it is an annual, it can be changed from year to year to become a better tool for you. As you use this book and adapt it for yourself, you may have ideas about how it can be made more useful for your prayer. Feel free to forward your thoughts to LTP: Editor, Daily Prayer, 1800 North Hermitage Avenue, Chicago IL 60622–1101. Or you may e-mail us at DailyPrayer@ltp.org.

ABOUT THE AUTHORS

This year's authors are Robert C. Rabe and David J. Cronan. In ordering the services, selecting versicles and psalmody; and composing original reflections, Prayers of the Faithful, and closing prayers, they bring to this resource pastoral experience and liturgical sensibilities. Both authors received advanced theological degrees from Saint John's University School of Theology in Collegeville, MN: Robert achieved a Master of Divinity, and David a Master of Arts in Liturgical Studies. A former youth retreat director, Robert currently teaches theology at a Catholic high school in the Chicago area. David is a Catholic youth retreat leader in suburban Chicago.

✝ *Come, O Lord, and set us free.*

PSALM 85 *page 414*

READING *Luke 21:25–28, 34–36*

Jesus said to his disciples: "There will be signs in the sun, the moon and the stars, and on earth nations will be in dismay, perplexed by the roaring of the sea and the waves. People will die of fright in anticipation of what is coming upon the world, for the powers of the heavens will be shaken. And then they will see the Son of Man coming in a cloud with power and great glory. But when these signs begin to happen, stand erect and raise your heads because your redemption is at hand.

"Beware that your hearts do not become drowsy from carousing and drunkenness and the anxieties of daily life, and that day catch you by surprise like a trap. For that day will assault everyone who lives on the face of the earth. Be vigilant at all times and pray that you have the strength to escape the tribulations that are imminent and to stand before the Son of Man."

REFLECTION

As we begin Advent, Jesus strongly warns us to be vigilant and stay focused on actions that are most consistent with the vision of the kingdom of God. There are many distractions preventing us from living the message of the Gospel, especially as we prepare for Christmas celebrations. Let us remember, that during this season we look toward the coming of our glorious redemption in Christ Jesus.

PRAYERS *others may be added*

Confident in the strength of God, we pray:

◆ Rain down your mercy, Lord

For the conversion of those who bring terror into our world, we pray: For those who suffer the effects of terrorism, we pray: ◆ *For those who work for peace and understanding, we pray:* ◆ *For those who watch over us in protective services, we pray:* ◆

Our Father . . .

Lord of all creation,
you fill the universe
with signs and wonders to give
    us confidence
in the strength of your love.
Throughout this season of Advent,
help us to be vigilant
in finding our way on your path
    of redemption.
We ask this through our Lord Jesus
    Christ, your Son,
who lives and reigns with you in the
    unity of the Holy Spirit,
one God, forever and ever. Amen.

✝ *Come, O Lord, and set us free.*

✦ *Come, O Lord, and set us free.*

PSALM 85 *page 414*

READING *Matthew 8:5–11*

When Jesus entered Capernaum, a centurion approached him and appealed to him, saying, "Lord, my servant is lying at home paralyzed, suffering dreadfully." He said to him, "I will come and cure him." The centurion said in reply, "Lord, I am not worthy to have you enter under my roof; only say the word and my servant will be healed. For I too am a man subject to authority, with soldiers subject to me. And I say to one, 'Go,' and he goes; and to another, 'Come here,' and he comes; and to my slave, 'Do this,' and he does it." When Jesus heard this, he was amazed and said to those following him, "Amen, I say to you, in no one in Israel have I found such faith. I say to you, many will come from the east and the west, and will recline with Abraham, Isaac, and Jacob at the banquet in the Kingdom of heaven."

REFLECTION

During this first week of Advent, we are called to make our hearts ready for Christ's Second Coming. Like the centurion in today's Gospel, we come to Jesus and ask for healing—healing for ourselves, for those we love, and for the world. Advent reminds us to have steadfast faith and courage, to rise from our paralysis and darkness, and allow Christ, the hope of the world, to anoint our brokenness.

PRAYERS *others may be added*

Waiting for God's anointing Word of salvation, we pray:

◆ Rain down your mercy, Lord.

For those paralyzed in heart, mind, and body, crying out for healing, we pray: ◆
For those in healing professions, seeking to soothe others' pain, we pray: ◆
For those who are environmentally conscious, laboring to mend the earth, we pray: ◆

Our Father . . .

God of healing,
you touch our hearts
and world with your
     hope-filled words
and saving hands.
May we always be an Advent people,
waiting for your return.
We ask this in the name of Jesus our
     Lord. Amen.

✦ *Come, O Lord, and set us free.*

✦ *Come, O Lord, and set us free.*

PSALM 85 *page 414*

READING *Luke 10:21–24*

Jesus rejoiced in the Holy Spirit and said, "I give you praise, Father, Lord of heaven and earth, for although you have hidden these things from the wise and the learned you have revealed them to the childlike. Yes, Father, such has been your gracious will. All things have been handed over to me by my Father. No one knows who the Son is except the Father, and who the Father is except the Son and anyone to whom the Son wishes to reveal him."

Turning to the disciples in private he said, "Blessed are the eyes that see what you see. For I say to you, many prophets and kings desired to see what you see, but did not see it, and to hear what you hear, but did not hear it."

REFLECTION

The greatest miracle is God's gift of self in Christ Jesus. Jesus is God's love for us, a love, that, although born to us in a specific time and place in history, is always present. God's love for us is timeless! With the openness of the eyes of a child, may we see and hear Christ now, dwelling within us and in each other.

PRAYERS *others may be added*

With hearts wide open, we pray:

◆ Rain down your mercy, Lord.

That we may discover the hidden presence of Christ in our lives, we pray: ◆ *For the courage to be Christ for others, we pray:* ◆ *For the protection of the innocence of children, we pray:* ◆ *For the spirit of joy to fill us all during this Advent season, we pray:* ◆

Our Father . . .

Lord of heaven and earth,
you give us the gift of yourself.
Open our hearts and our eyes
to the joy of your presence today
    and always.
We ask this through Jesus Christ our
    Lord. Amen.

✦ *Come, O Lord, and set us free.*

✦ *Come, O Lord, and set us free.*

PSALM 85   *page 414*

READING   *Matthew 15:32–37*

Jesus summoned his disciples and said, "My heart is moved with pity for the crowd, for they have been with me now for three days and have nothing to eat. I do not want to send them away hungry, for fear they may collapse on the way." The disciples said to him, "Where could we ever get enough bread in this deserted place to satisfy such a crowd?" Jesus said to them, "How many loaves do you have?" "Seven," they replied, "and a few fish." He ordered the crowd to sit down on the ground. Then he took the seven loaves and the fish, gave thanks, broke the loaves, and gave them to the disciples, who in turn gave them to the crowds. They all ate and were satisfied. They picked up the fragments left over—seven baskets full.

REFLECTION

In today's Gospel, we find a hungry crowd waiting to be nourished by the Bread of Life. Advent is a time of waiting, like the crowd, for the heavens to rain down manna that fertilizes and sustains the human heart. We look with expectant hope to a time when there will be enough bread for all to eat—the unexpected guest at our dinner table, the stranger knocking at our door, and those yet to be born.

PRAYERS   *others may be added*

Longing for the Bread of Life,
we pray:

◆ Rain down your mercy, Lord.

For the hungry, may they have their fill, we pray: ◆ *For the lonely, may they come to know you, we pray:* ◆ *For the hopeless, may they know Advent joy, we pray:* ◆ *For the wealthy, may they share their resources, we pray:* ◆

Our Father . . .

Bread of Life,
You feed us and give us salvation
    and peace.
May we be like the crowd in
    today's Gospel:
always waiting,
hungering to feast on your presence.
We ask this through Jesus Christ
    our Lord. Amen.

✦ *Come, O Lord, and set us free.*

✚ *Come, O Lord, and set us free.*

PSALM 85 *page 414*

READING *Matthew 7:21, 24–27*

Jesus said to his disciples: "Not everyone who says to me, 'Lord, Lord,' will enter the Kingdom of heaven, but only the one who does the will of my Father in heaven.

"Everyone who listens to these words of mine and acts on them will be like a wise man who built his house on rock. The rain fell, the floods came, and the winds blew and buffeted the house. But it did not collapse; it had been set solidly on rock. And everyone who listens to these words of mine but does not act on them will be like a fool who built his house on sand. The rain fell, the floods came, and the winds blew and buffeted the house. And it collapsed and was completely ruined."

REFLECTION

Today, Jesus clearly asks us to listen and act. But what do we listen to? We should listen carefully to the teaching of the Church. Life is filled with all kinds of sounds. While some sounds are essential, we need to filter out the noises of sin, commercialism, and self-interest. To act as the wise person in today's parable, we must discern a solid foundation on which to build our actions. St. Ambrose found service to the poor and sound doctrine to be his foundations for a Gospel life. Should we settle for less?

PRAYERS *others may be added*

Trusting in God's word, we pray:

◆ Rain down your mercy, Lord.

For those who build up our Church, we pray: ◆ For cloistered religious who teach us to listen, we pray: ◆ For those who suffer in life, we pray: ◆ For those who increase our wisdom, we pray: ◆

Our Father . . .

Lord of heaven,
you are our hope and salvation.
Fill us with a spirit of discernment
so that we may hear your
   Word wisely
and build your kingdom of love.
We ask this through Christ our Lord.
   Amen.

✚ *Come, O Lord, and set us free.*

✛ *Sing to the Lord a new song for he has done marvelous deeds.*

PSALM 98   *page 416*

READING   *Luke 1:26–35, 38*

The angel Gabriel was sent from God to a town of Galilee called Nazareth, to a virgin betrothed to a man named Joseph, of the house of David, and the virgin's name was Mary. And coming to her, he said, "Hail, full of grace! The Lord is with you." But she was greatly troubled at what was said and pondered what sort of greeting this might be. Then the angel said to her, "Do not be afraid, Mary, for you have found favor with God. Behold, you will conceive in your womb and bear a son, and you shall name him Jesus. He will be great and will be called Son of the Most High, and the Lord God will give him the throne of David his father, and he will rule over the house of Jacob forever, and of his Kingdom there will be no end." But Mary said to the angel, "How can this be, since I have no relations with a man?" And the angel said to her in reply, "The Holy Spirit will come upon you, and the power of the Most High will over-shadow you. Therefore the child to be born will be called holy, the Son of God." Mary said, "Behold, I am the handmaid of the Lord. May it be done to me according to your word." Then the angel departed from her.

REFLECTION   *Suzanne M. Lewis*

Hail Mary, full of grace! God sent an angel to share the great news of his wonderful plan for humanity. Thank you for loving God and for saying, "yes" to his Son, Jesus. Help us to add our "yes" to yours, now and forever.

PRAYERS   *others may be added*

Seeking the courage to say "yes" to God, we pray:

◆ Rain down your mercy, Lord.

That laypeople answer God's call to bring the Gospel message to the workplace, we pray: ◆ That religious answer God's call to be open to transformation and renewal, we pray: ◆ That priests may answer God's call to preach conformity to God's will, we pray: ◆

Our Father . . .

God of the lowly,
you chose Mary
to bear the Light,
which no darkness can overcome.
Following Mary's example,
may we always have the courage
   to say,
"May it be done to me according to
   your word."
We ask this through our Lord Jesus
   Christ, your Son,
who lives and reigns with you in the
   unity of the Holy Spirit,
one God, forever and ever. Amen.

✛ *Come, O Lord, and set us free.*

✚ *Come, O Lord, and set us free.*

PSALM 85   *page 414*

READING   *Matthew 9:35–10:1, 5a, 6–8*

Jesus went around to all the towns and villages, teaching in their synagogues, proclaiming the Gospel of the Kingdom, and curing every disease and illness. At the sight of the crowds, his heart was moved with pity for them because they were troubled and abandoned, like sheep without a shepherd. Then he said to his disciples, "The harvest is abundant but the laborers are few; so ask the master of the harvest to send out laborers for his harvest."

Then he summoned his Twelve disciples and gave them authority over unclean spirits to drive them out and to cure every disease and every illness.

Jesus sent out these twelve after instructing them thus, "Go to the lost sheep of the house of Israel. As you go, make this proclamation: 'The Kingdom of heaven is at hand.' Cure the sick, raise the dead, cleanse lepers, drive out demons. Without cost you have received; without cost you are to give."

REFLECTION

The kingdom of heaven is at hand; it is ours for the taking. All we have to do is respond to Jesus' invitation to share in his authority. The authority Jesus gives the Twelve is not one to foster personal power but rather to heal and to cleanse, for the kingdom of heaven is where all have been nourished and made whole.

PRAYERS   *others may be added*

Awaiting the kingdom of heaven, we pray:

◆ Rain down your mercy, Lord.

For the spiritual, mental, and physical healing of all our dear ones, we pray: ◆ For the selfless use of power by world leaders, we pray: ◆ For those in the healing professions, we pray: ◆ For the elimination of personal demons, we pray: ◆

Our Father . . .

God of power, O Great Physician,
there is no wound you cannot heal.
Cleanse our spirits, mend our bodies,
     and raise us to new life.
Renewed in you, may we spread the
     justice of Christ,
who lives and reigns with you in the
     unity of the Holy Spirit,
one God, forever and ever. Amen.

✚ *Come, O Lord, and set us free.*

✛   *Come, O Lord, and set us free.*

PSALM 85 *page 414*

READING *Luke 3:1–6*

In the fifteenth year of the reign of Tiberius Caesar, when Pontius Pilate was governor of Judea, and Herod was tetrarch of Galilee, and his brother Philip tetrarch of the region of Ituraea and Trachonitis, and Lysanias was tetrarch of Abilene, during the high priesthood of Annas and Caiaphas, the word of God came to John the son of Zechariah in the desert. John went throughout the whole region of the Jordan, proclaiming a baptism of repentance for the forgiveness of sins, as it is written in the book of the words of the prophet Isaiah: *A voice of one crying out in the desert: / "Prepare the way of the Lord, / make straight his paths. / Every valley shall be filled / and every mountain and hill shall be made low. / The winding roads shall be made straight, / and the rough ways made smooth, / and all flesh shall see the salvation of God."*

REFLECTION

A voice cries out! Often we can't hear God's voice beckoning to us because there are so many noises within culture and society, deafening us to the sacred. During this season, let us clear away the clutter and chaos that keeps us from hearing God's announcement that salvation is coming. Echoing the words of the prophet Isaiah, Advent invites us to prepare, clean, and make straight the way for God's gift, Jesus Christ, to come into our hearts, home, and world.

PRAYERS *others may be added*

Preparing the way for the Lord, we pray:

◆   Rain down your mercy, Lord.

To be a repentant people, we pray: ◆
To be a forgiving people, we pray: ◆
To be a listening people, we pray: ◆
To be an Advent people, we pray: ◆

Our Father . . .

God of salvation,
you called the prophets
to announce the coming of your
    kingdom.
May we be like John and Isaiah,
proclaiming your truth
in a world
longing to hear your voice
and see your face.
We ask this through our Lord Jesus
    Christ, your Son,
who lives and reigns with you in the
    unity of the Holy Spirit,
one God, forever and ever. Amen.

✛   *Come, O Lord, and set us free.*

✝ *Come, O Lord, and set us free.*

PSALM 85   page 414

READING   Luke 5:17–26

One day as Jesus was teaching, Pharisees and teachers of the law, who had come from every village of Galilee and Judea and Jerusalem, were sitting there, and the power of the Lord was with him for healing. And some men brought on a stretcher a man who was paralyzed; they were trying to bring him in and set him in his presence. But not finding a way to bring him in because of the crowd, they went up on the roof and lowered him on the stretcher through the tiles into the middle in front of Jesus. When Jesus saw their faith, he said, "As for you, your sins are forgiven."

Then the scribes and Pharisees began to ask themselves, "Who is this who speaks blasphemies? Who but God alone can forgive sins?" Jesus knew their thoughts and said to them in reply, "What are you thinking in your hearts? Which is easier, to say, 'Your sins are forgiven,' or to say, 'Rise and walk'? But that you may know that the Son of Man has authority on earth to forgive sins"—he said to the one who was paralyzed, "I say to you, rise, pick up your stretcher, and go home."

He stood up immediately before them, picked up what he had been lying on, and went home, glorifying God. Then astonishment seized them all and they glorified God, and, struck with awe, they said, "We have seen incredible things today."

REFLECTION   St. Augustine, bishop

Let us do now what he commands. Let us follow in the footsteps of the Lord. Let us throw off the chains that prevent us from following him. Who can throw off these shackles without the aid of the one addressed in these words: You have broken my chains? Another psalm says of him: The Lord frees those in chains, the Lord raises up the downcast.

PRAYERS   others may be added

Glorifying God, we pray:

◆ Rain down your mercy, Lord.

May we be filled with eagerness to do the work of God, we pray: ◆ *May we be open to the surprising ways of God, we pray:* ◆ *May all people promote a spirit of reconciliation, we pray:* ◆ *May we break open the roofs of disbelief, we pray:* ◆

Our Father . . .

Loving Father,
you offer forgiveness to all who sin.
Dispel our disbelief,
carry us with your healing hands,
and raise us to new life by
    your mercy.
We ask this through Christ our Lord.
    Amen.

✝ *Come, O Lord, and set us free.*

✝ *Come, O Lord, and set us free.*

PSALM 40 *page 411*

READING *Luke 1:39–47*

Mary set out and traveled to the hill country in haste to a town of Judah, where she entered the house of Zechariah and greeted Elizabeth. When Elizabeth heard Mary's greeting, the infant leaped in her womb, and Elizabeth, filled with the Holy Spirit, cried out in a loud voice and said, "Most blessed are you among women, and blessed is the fruit of your womb. And how does this happen to me, that the mother of my Lord should come to me? For at the moment the sound of your greeting reached my ears, the infant in my womb leaped for joy. Blessed are you who believed that what was spoken to you by the Lord would be fulfilled." And Mary said:

"My soul proclaims the greatness of the Lord;/my spirit rejoices in God my savior."

REFLECTION

When Elizabeth is greeted by Mary, she immediately knows she is standing in the presence of the Mother of God. Like Elizabeth, we are invited to become aware of God's active presence in our lives—even when darkness and hopelessness envelop us. Recognizing that we are in God's presence is essential if we want our souls to be filled with God's greatness and everlasting mercy.

PRAYERS *others may be added*

Proclaiming the greatness of our Lord and Savior, we pray:

◆ Rain down your mercy, Lord.

For pregnant women, that they may cradle the gift of life within, we pray: ◆ *For health-care workers, that they may cradle the gift of life entrusted to their care, we pray:* ◆ *For all who call themselves Christian, that they may cradle the gift of life with your Word, we pray:* ◆ *For government officials, that they may cradle the gift of life with just laws and policies, we pray:* ◆

Our Father . . .

God of life,
you have revealed yourself
in many ways and many faces.
May we be like Mary,
poor and humble,
willing to become a womb
for your Word of life.
We ask this in the name of Jesus our
Lord. Amen.

✝ *Come, O Lord, and set us free.*

✝ *Come, O Lord, and set us free.*

PSALM 85 *page 414*

READING *Matthew 11:28–30*

Jesus said to the crowds: "Come to me, all you who labor and are burdened, and I will give you rest. Take my yoke upon you and learn from me, for I am meek and humble of heart; and you will find rest for yourselves. For my yoke is easy, and my burden light."

REFLECTION

There is no greater burden than to be hopeless or lost. Working without a sense of purpose and not enjoying the fruits of one's labors is the lot of the slave. Salvation in Christ frees us from the burdens of sin—the burdens of slavery, addictions, and oppression. Our Lord offers us a whole new way of living, a way of hope. Hope uplifts and relieves us from these heavy burdens! The Gospel way is not effortless, but it is an effort that is inspired and supported by Christ. It is a burden that is light; it is a joyful burden.

PRAYERS *others may be added*

In your hope, we pray:

◆ Rain down your mercy, Lord.

For the elimination of all forms of slavery, we pray: ◆ *For the eradication of all forms of addiction, we pray:* ◆ *For better relations between management and labor, we pray:* ◆ *For all those who feel overburdened, we pray:* ◆

Our Father . . .

O Gentle Heart of Jesus,
you relieve our burdens.
Fill our hearts with gentleness
and a thirst for your uplifting ways.
Help us to ease the path of all those
who labor under any constraints.
This we ask of you who reign
in the unity
of the Father and the Holy Spirit,
one God, forever and ever. Amen

✝ *Come, O Lord, and set us free.*

✦ *Come, O Lord, and set us free.*

PSALM 85   *Page 414*

READING   *Matthew 11:11–15*

Jesus said to the crowds: "Amen, I say to you, among those born of women there has been none greater than John the Baptist; yet the least in the Kingdom of heaven is greater than he. From the days of John the Baptist until now, the Kingdom of heaven suffers violence, and the violent are taking it by force. All the prophets and the law prophesied up to the time of John. And if you are willing to accept it, he is Elijah, the one who is to come. Whoever has ears ought to hear."

REFLECTION

Today we celebrate the memorial of St. John of the Cross (1542–+1591), a Carmelite friar who sought to reform abuses within his religious order. He is well known for his mystical writings and poetry which illustrate his profound love for the pervasive light of God. His love relationship with God empowered him to hear truth within the silence of his heart, write words of hope, sing songs that break the shackles of false gods and touch the sacred in the ordinary. May we, like John of the Cross, invite God's love to enlighten the darkest recesses of our hearts.

PRAYERS   *others may be added*

Through the intercession of St. John of the Cross, we pray:

◆ Rain down your mercy, Lord.

That we may hear God's freeing word, we pray: ◆ *That we may see the divine in our midst, we pray:* ◆ *That we may taste the goodness of the Lord, we pray:* ◆ *That we may touch the sacred in humanity, we pray:* ◆

Our Father . . .

Light of God,
you lifted up St. John of the Cross
as a model of sanctity and truth.
May we follow in his footsteps
and seek the light of your love
in our often dark and broken world.
We ask this through Christ our Lord.
    Amen.

✦ *Come, O Lord, and set us free.*

✚ *Come, O Lord, and set us free.*

PSALM 85   *page 414*

READING   *Matthew 11:16–19*

Jesus said to the crowds: "To what shall I compare this generation? It is like children who sit in marketplaces and call to one another, 'We played the flute for you, but you did not dance, we sang a dirge but you did not mourn.' For John came neither eating nor drinking, and they said, 'He is possessed by a demon.' The Son of Man came eating and drinking and they said, 'Look, he is a glutton and a drunkard, a friend of tax collectors and sinners.' But wisdom is vindicated by her works."

REFLECTION

Jesus describes a fickle people in today's Gospel. They reject both the austere John as well as the gregarious Jesus. These two men lived very different manifestations of holiness. We can choose to be frustrated by a world full of opposites or we can revel in the wondrous complement of God's creation. Like pieces of an intricate puzzle, each different shape is necessary to complete the whole. Advent challenges us to wait to see the big picture.

PRAYERS   *others may be added*

In wonder and awe, we pray:

◆ Rain down your mercy, Lord.

That we may be a people of fasting and discipline, we pray: ◆ *That we may be a people appreciative of the joys of life, we pray:* ◆ *That we may be a tolerant people, we pray:* ◆ *That we may be a people ready to wait, we pray:* ◆

Our Father . . .

Loving Creator,
you unfold a magnificent and ever-
    changing pattern
in your wondrous universe.
Help us to take the time
to appreciate the infinite manifesta-
    tions of your love.
We ask this in the name of Jesus our
    Lord. Amen.

✚ *Come, O Lord, and set us free.*

✝ *Come, O Lord, and set us free.*

PSALM 85 *page 414*

READING *Matthew 17:9a, 10–13*

As they were coming down from the mountain, the disciples asked Jesus, "Why do the scribes say that Elijah must come first?" He said in reply, "Elijah will indeed come and restore all things; but I tell you that Elijah has already come, and they did not recognize him but did to him whatever they pleased. So also will the Son of Man suffer at their hands." Then the disciples understood that he was speaking to them of John the Baptist.

REFLECTION *The Cistercian liturgy*

At the coming of the Most High our hearts shall be made clean, and we shall walk worthily in the way of the Lord. The Lord is coming and will not delay.

PRAYERS *others may be added*

Hoping to recognize the Son of Man when he comes, we pray:

◆ Rain down your mercy, Lord.

That we may be a people of awareness, we pray: ◆ *That we may be a people of peace, we pray:* ◆ *That we may be a people of justice, we pray:* ◆ *That we may be a people of prophetic hope, we pray:* ◆

Our Father . . .

God of justice,
you gave us John the Baptist,
the prophetic announcer
of your coming kingdom.
May we be ready for your word
   and kingdom
to be born anew as an inner flame
within our hearts,
burning away the darkness of hatred,
   pain, and suffering.
We ask this in the name of Jesus our
   Lord. Amen.

✝ *Come, O Lord, and set us free.*

✠ *Wisdom, O holy Word of God,*
come and show your people the way
to salvation.

PSALM 85 *page 414*

READING *Luke 3:10–18*

The crowds asked John the Baptist, "What should we do?" He said to them in reply, "Whoever has two cloaks should share with the person who has none. And whoever has food should do likewise." Even tax collectors came to be baptized and they said to him, "Teacher, what should we do?" He answered them, "Stop collecting more than what is prescribed." Soldiers also asked him, "And what is it that we should do?" He told them, "Do not practice extortion, do not falsely accuse anyone, and be satisfied with your wages."

Now the people were filled with expectation, and all were asking in their hearts whether John might be the Christ. John answered them all, saying, "I am baptizing you with water, but one mightier than I is coming. I am not worthy to loosen the thongs of his sandals. He will baptize you with the Holy Spirit and fire. His winnowing fan is in his hand to clear his threshing floor and to gather the wheat into his barn, but the chaff he will burn with unquenchable fire." Exhorting them in many other ways, he preached good news to the people.

REFLECTION

As we enter the final days of Advent, we celebrate the joy of Gaudete Sunday and begin the O Antiphons. Even the usually fiery John the Baptist seems less harsh. In place of prophetic condemnations, John points the way to salvation. He does not demand we change our station in life, but he does exhort us to a radical change of attitude, to a new spirit. John points, in wisdom, to Jesus, the holy Word of God as the way to life.

PRAYERS *others may be added*

Trusting in your tender care, we pray:

◆ Come, O Wisdom, show us the way.

That we may learn to share all that we have, we pray: ◆ *That Church leaders may always point to the Lord, we pray:* ◆ *That we may preach the Good News in our daily lives, we pray:* ◆ *That we may always live in the joy of the Word of God, we pray:* ◆

Our Father . . .

Loving Father,
you sent your Son, the Word
    made flesh,
to free us from sin.
Lead us in your wisdom to embody
    your Son,
who lives and reigns with you in the
    unity of the Holy Spirit,
one God, forever and ever. Amen.

✠ *Wisdom, O holy Word of God,*
come and show your people the way
to salvation.

✝ *O sacred Lord of ancient Israel,*
come, stretch out your mighty hand
to set us free.

PSALM 85 *page 414*

READING *Matthew 1:20–25*

The angel of the Lord appeared to him [Joseph] in a dream and said, "Joseph, son of David, do not be afraid to take Mary your wife into your home. For it is through the Holy Spirit that this child has been conceived in her. She will bear a son and you are to name him Jesus, because he will save his people from their sins." All this took place to fulfill what the Lord had said through the prophet:

Behold, the virgin shall be with child and bear a son,/and they shall name him Emmanuel,

which means "God is with us." When Joseph awoke, he did as the angel of the Lord had commanded him and took his wife into his home. He had no relations with her until she bore a son, and he named him Jesus.

REFLECTION *Stephen Kent*

The people of Israel were becoming tiresome to God with their constant seeking for a sign. And then God offered the sign: His name was Emmanuel, "God-with-us." Today we still look for signs from God, even though we know that God is with us. Let's not take the presence of God, the gift of grace, and the call to holiness for granted. We should moderate our desire for a spectacular sign, and instead look for God's presence in small ways.

PRAYERS *others may be added*

Opening our hearts for the Just One, we pray:

◆ O Sacred Lord, break down the walls of injustice.

That the hungry may feast on your banquet of life, we pray: ◆ *That the homeless may be sheltered in the warmth of your love, we pray:* ◆ *That the weak may be protected by your arm of strength, we pray:* ◆ *That the despairing may find consolation in your word of hope, we pray:* ◆

Our Father . . .

Lord of Israel,
you are love beyond all measure,
challenging us to become
    an instrument
in your symphony of salvation.
Give us the courage
to become a score of music
that sings of your coming
with harmonious sounds of hope
    and justice.
Grant this through Jesus Christ our
    Lord. Amen.

✝ *O sacred Lord of ancient Israel,*
come, stretch out your mighty hand
to set us free.

✚ *O Flower of Jesse's stem, come,*
let nothing keep you from coming to
our aid.

PSALM 85 *page 414*

READING *Luke 1:14–17*

"And you will have joy and gladness, and many will rejoice at his birth, for he will be great in the sight of the Lord. He will drink neither wine nor strong drink. He will be filled with the Holy Spirit even from his mother's womb, and he will turn many of the children of Israel to the Lord their God. He will go before him in the spirit and power of Elijah to turn the hearts of fathers toward children and the disobedient to the understanding of the righteous, to prepare a people fit for the Lord."

REFLECTION

Wondrous events fill this magical season: A virgin gives birth, the barren conceive, the old are given youthful vigor. God has an infinite store of surprises ready for us. We have only to be open to the gifts, to be ready to believe in God's generosity.

PRAYERS *others may be added*

Open to your generosity, we pray:

◆ Come, O Flower of Jesse's stem.

That we may be open to your wondrous ways, we pray: ◆ That we may bring wonder to all we meet, we pray: ◆ That we may speak freely the Word of God, we pray: ◆ That we may blossom into your image, we pray: ◆

Our Father . . .

Loving God,
you bring forth the fruitfulness
    of grace.
Kings are silent in your presence;
nations bow down before you.
Send us your gift of salvation
in the coming of your Son,
    Jesus Christ,
who lives and reigns with you in the
    unity of the Holy Spirit,
one God, forever and ever. Amen.

✚ *O Flower of Jesse's stem, come,*
let nothing keep you from coming to
our aid.

✦ *O Key of David, come, break down the prison walls of death for those who dwell in darkness and the shadow of death; and lead your captive people into freedom.*

PSALM 85   *page 414*

READING   *Luke 1:26–32*

In the sixth month, the angel Gabriel was sent from God to a town of Galilee called Nazareth, to a virgin betrothed to a man named Joseph, of the house of David, and the virgin's name was Mary. And coming to her, he said, "Hail, full of grace! The Lord is with you." But she was greatly troubled at what was said and pondered what sort of greeting this might be. Then the angel said to her, "Do not be afraid, Mary, for you have found favor with God. Behold, you will conceive in your womb and bear a son, and you shall name him Jesus. He will be great and will be called Son of the Most High . . . ."

REFLECTION   *James Chukwuma Okoye, CSSP*

In the Gospel, the angel Gabriel announces the fulfillment of this hope [that the one to come would establish righteousness in the land] through Mary, a virgin betrothed to Joseph, of the house of David. She will give birth to a child who will be given the throne of David. Through him, God will give his people the promised salvation and rest, and "he will rule over the house of Jacob forever, and of his kingdom there will be no end." The child to be born will be "Son of God" in a manner even more miraculous than the promise to David, for conceived of the Holy Spirit, he "will be called holy, the Son of God." God's unconditional attachment to us human beings reaches the highest point—God is to take flesh in a son of David.*

PRAYERS   *others may be added*

Becoming aware of the miracles around us, we pray:

✦ O Key of David, lead your captive people into freedom.

That women who experience unplanned pregnancies may see the possibility of life, we pray: ✦ *That women who cannot conceive children may see the possibility of life, we pray:* ✦ *That the sick may see the possibility of life, we pray:* ✦ *That the dying and grieving may see the possibility of life, we pray:* ✦

Our Father . . .

O Key of David,
you called Mary
to envision the many possibilities
of your love.
May we be like Mary,
able to see a world
touched by your saving hand.
We ask this in the name of Jesus.
   Amen.

✦ *O Key of David, come, break down the prison walls of death for those who dwell in darkness and the shadow of death; and lead your captive people into freedom.*

✦ *O Radiant Dawn, come, shine on those who dwell in darkness and the shadow of death.*

PSALM 85   *page 414*

READING   *Luke 1:39–45*

Mary set out in those days and traveled to the hill country in haste to a town of Judah, where she entered the house of Zechariah and greeted Elizabeth. When Elizabeth heard Mary's greeting, the infant leaped in her womb, and Elizabeth, filled with the Holy Spirit, cried out in a loud voice and said, "Most blessed are you among women, and blessed is the fruit of your womb. And how does this happen to me, that the mother of my Lord should come to me? For at the moment the sound of your greeting reached my ears, the infant in my womb leaped for joy. Blessed are you who believed that what was spoken to you by the Lord would be fulfilled."

REFLECTION   *Suzanne M. Lewis*

Elizabeth's skin is still warm from the loving embrace of her young relative. All the complexities, all the mysteries of this meeting between the two women have flooded Elizabeth's heart in an instant. She stands and stares at Mary. What words could possibly measure up to this moment? She doesn't pause to think or to consider whether to make a speech. Elizabeth's heart simply bubbles over with the most pressing thought in her over-awed mind: Blessed!

PRAYERS   *others may be added*

Looking to your eternal light, we pray:

◆ Come, O Radiant Dawn.

For those who visit the sick and dying, we pray: ◆ *For those who reach out in spite of their own troubles, we pray:* ◆ *For expectant mothers, we pray:* ◆ *For those who are living in darkness, we pray:* ◆

Our Father . . .

God of light,
you illumine all of creation
with the brightness of your Light.
Burn away all the shadows of
    our lives
and fill us with hope of the
    Radiant Dawn,
so we can be light for others.
We ask this through Christ our Lord.
    Amen.

✦ *O Radiant Dawn, come, shine on those who dwell in darkness and the shadow of death.*

Optional memorial of St. Peter Canisius

✝ *O King of all the nations, the only joy of every human heart, come and save the creature you fashioned from the dust.*

PSALM 85   *Page 414*

READING   *Luke 1:46–56*

Mary said:

"My soul proclaims the greatness of the Lord;/my spirit rejoices in God my savior,/for he has looked upon his lowly servant./From this day all generations will call me blessed:/the Almighty has done great things for me,/and holy is his Name./He has mercy on those who fear him/in every generation./He has shown the strength of his arm,/and has scattered the proud in their conceit./He has cast down the mighty from their thrones/and has lifted up the lowly./He has filled the hungry with good things,/and the rich he has sent away empty./He has come to the help of his servant Israel/for he remembered his promise of mercy,/the promise he made to our fathers,/to Abraham and his children for ever."

Mary remained with Elizabeth about three months and then returned to her home.

REFLECTION

As we move closer to Christmas, we are reminded by Mary's great proclamation that the merciful God, through Christ Jesus, is the only path to salvation. The season of Advent gives us time to turn our hearts into fertile ground so that his salvific love can take root and grow. In the spirit of Mary, we seek to find glory in a God who raises up the lowly, fills the hungry, and remembers his promise of mercy. Now is the time to invite the Lord into your life.

PRAYERS   *others may be added*

Preparing our hearts for the merciful Word of God, we pray:

◆ O King of all the nations, encircle us with your compassion.

For an end to hatred, we pray: ◆ *For an end to violence, we pray:* ◆ *For an end to hunger, we pray:* ◆ *For an end to over consumption, we pray:* ◆

Our Father . . .

King of all the nations,
you raised up a lowly virgin
to bear witness to the Word,
which no noise can silence.
Sustain us in our call, like Mary,
to become bearers of your
   liberating Word
so that all generations
will know your mercy.
Grant this through Jesus Christ our
   Lord. Amen.

✝ *O King of all the nations, the only joy of every human heart, come and save the creature you fashioned from the dust.*

✤ *O Emmanuel, desire of the nations, come and set us free.*

PSALM 85 *page 414*

READING *Luke 1:57–66*

When the time arrived for Elizabeth to have her child she gave birth to a son. Her neighbors and relatives heard that the Lord had shown his great mercy toward her, and they rejoiced with her. When they came on the eighth day to circumcise the child, they were going to call him Zechariah after his father, but his mother said in reply, "No. He will be called John." But they answered her, "There is no one among your relatives who has this name." So they made signs, asking his father what he wished him to be called. He asked for a tablet and wrote, "John is his name," and all were amazed. Immediately his mouth was opened, his tongue freed, and he spoke, blessing God. Then fear came upon all their neighbors, and all these matters were discussed throughout the hill country of Judea. All who heard these things took them to heart, saying, "What, then, will this child be? For surely the hand of the Lord was with him."

REFLECTION *Suzanne M. Lewis*

The child is for us. *The son is* given *to us. God is* for *us, his child given* to *us, but we can do nothing* for *God or* to *God.*

God takes the initiative. God is the one who gives. Our giving is, at best, a participation in the larger movement of giving, which is God's action in the world. We
cannot give anything to God, because everything *we have is already a gift: the air we breathe, the hands with which we work, our hearts, the impulse to generosity. Even our sense of gratitude is a gift to us, perhaps one of the greatest gifts we can receive, because the essence of gratitude is grace.*

PRAYERS *others may be added*

Turning to the great lawgiver, we pray:

◆ O Emmanuel, come and set us free.

Make us worthy of the name Christian, we pray: ◆ *Make us aware of the power of our words, we pray:* ◆ *Make us rejoice at your saving works, we pray:* ◆ *Make us ready for your arrival, we pray:* ◆

Our Father . . .

God of our ancestors,
from all eternity you show yourself
worthy of your name, Emmanuel.
Come to us, O desire of the nations,
and fill us with your love and mercy
so that we will be able to celebrate
    the coming of your Son, our Lord
    Jesus Christ,
who lives and reigns with you in the
    unity of the Holy Spirit,
one God forever and ever. Amen.

✤ *O Emmanuel, desire of the nations, come and set us free.*

✠ *Come, O Lord, and set us free.*

PSALM 85 — *Page 414*

READING — *Luke 1:39–45*

Mary set out and traveled to the hill country in haste to a town of Judah, where she entered the house of Zechariah and greeted Elizabeth. When Elizabeth heard Mary's greeting, the infant leaped in her womb, and Elizabeth, filled with the Holy Spirit, cried out in a loud voice and said, "Blessed are you among women, and blessed is the fruit of your womb. And how does this happen to me, that the mother of my Lord should come to me? For at the moment the sound of your greeting reached my ears, the infant in my womb leaped for joy. Blessed are you who believed that what was spoken to you by the Lord would be fulfilled."

REFLECTION

Following in the spirit of Mary's visit to Elizabeth, we have traveled throughout this Advent season preparing our hearts, setting our tables, and adorning our homes for the arrival of the divine guest. We look forward to tomorrow when we will leap, like the infant in Elizabeth's womb, with joy and sing out, "The Great and Holy One is among us." Let us rejoice, for the Light has overcome the darkness, and we are his lanterns guiding all to the humble stable of life.

PRAYERS — *others may be added*

Preparing our lives for Christmas joy, we pray:

◆ Come Emmanuel, fill us with your peace.

For all who travel this holiday season, may they arrive safely to their destinations, we pray: ◆ *For all poor children who will not receive presents this holiday season, may they be clothed in God's gift of eternal life, we pray:* ◆ *For all who have no food at their table this holiday season, may they feast on the Bread of Life, we pray:* ◆ *For all of us this holiday season, may we come to know Christ as true God and true man, we pray:* ◆

Our Father . . .

Emmanuel, God-with-us,
help us to make a world
where all will have a voice and
place at the table of life.
May we be renewed by your coming
    and heed your calling
to build a more just world
so that no one will go hungry,
    be lonely, or
be deprived of the promise
    of Christmas.
Grant this through our Lord Jesus
    Christ, your Son,
who lives and reigns with you in the
    unity of the Holy Spirit,
one God, forever and ever. Amen.

✠ *Come, O Lord, and set us free.*

✝ *A little child is born for us today;*
little and yet called the mighty God,
Alleluia!

PSALM 98 *page 416*

READING *Luke 2:8–11*

Now there were shepherds in that region living in the fields and keeping the night watch over their flock. The angel of the Lord appeared to them and the glory of the Lord shone around them, and they were struck with great fear. The angel said to them, "Do not be afraid; for behold, I proclaim to you good news of great joy that will be for all the people. For today in the city of David a savior has been born for you who is Christ and Lord."

REFLECTION *Suzanne M. Lewis*

Lord Jesus Christ, it was through you that God made each star in the millions of galaxies. You know us each by name and have counted every hair on our heads. Together with the Father and the Holy Spirit, you hold our world, like a small stone, in the palm of your hand! And still, you agreed to become a tiny, helpless baby, so that human beings could hold the mighty God in their very own trembling arms and never ever be the same again. We love you and thank you with all our hearts.

PRAYERS *others may be added*

Looking to the Christ child, we pray:

◆ May your light surround us.

For the powerful, may they be humble like a child, we pray: ◆ *For the lowly, may they be filled with joy and hope, we pray:* ◆ *For all of us, may we be filled with the Good News of great joy, we pray:* ◆ *For peace to all on earth, we pray:* ◆

Our Father . . .

Lord our God,
you break through the darkness of our
    sin and ignorance
and fill us with the light of Christ,
    your Son.
On this great feast of your love,
renew in us the desire to spread
your peace, hope, and love to the
    whole world.
We ask this through our Lord Jesus
    Christ, your Son,
who lives and reigns with you in the
    unity of the Holy Spirit,
one God, forever and ever. Amen.

✝ *A little child is born for us today;*
little and yet called the mighty God,
Alleluia!

✝ *Come, you nations, and adore the Lord. A great light has come upon the earth. Alleluia!*

PSALM 98   *page 416*

READING   *Matthew 10:17–22*

Jesus said to his disciples: "Beware of men, for they will hand you over to courts and scourge you in their synagogues, and you will be led before governors and kings for my sake as a witness before them and the pagans. When they hand you over, do not worry about how you are to speak or what you are to say. You will be given at that moment what you are to say. For it will not be you who speak but the Spirit of your Father speaking through you. Brother will hand over brother to death, and the father his child; children will rise up against parents and have them put to death. You will be hated by all because of my name, but whoever endures to the end will be saved."

REFLECTION

On this, the feast of St. Stephen, the first martyr of the Church, the Gospel reading reminds us that following Jesus is not always easy. Not all of us will be called, like Stephen, to suffer martyrdom for the sake of the Gospel, but we are all called to let go of possessions, break through addictions, promote justice, and serve the poor so that Jesus' message of salvation will be experienced throughout the world. As we trim our homes and gather with family, let us remember that the birth of Christ calls us to be bearers of hope and justice even in the face of adversity.

PRAYERS   *others may be added*

Proclaiming the glorious birth of Christ, we pray:

◆ May your light surround us.

For those struggling with addictions, may they experience courage and healing, we pray: ◆ *For those experiencing persecution for the sake of the Gospel, may they find hope in their pain, we pray:* ◆ *For those serving the poor, may they experience the richness of the kingdom, we pray:* ◆ *For all those bound by material possessions, may they be released, we pray:* ◆

Our Father . . .

God of freedom,
you gave St. Stephen
the inner strength to sacrifice his life
as a witness to your reconciling love.
May we also give our lives
to Christ this Christmas season
and live in the warmth of his light.
We ask this in the name of Jesus our
    Lord. Amen.

✝ *Come, you nations, and adore the Lord. A great light has come upon the earth. Alleluia!*

✦ *Come, you nations, and adore the Lord. A great light has come upon the earth. Alleluia!*

PSALM 98   *page 416*

READING   *John 20:1a, 2–8*

On the first day of the week, Mary Magdalene ran and went to Simon Peter and to the other disciple whom Jesus loved, and told them, "They have taken the Lord from the tomb, and we do not know where they put him." So Peter and the other disciple went out and came to the tomb. They both ran, but the other disciple ran faster than Peter and arrived at the tomb first; he bent down and saw the burial cloths there, but did not go in. When Simon Peter arrived after him, he went into the tomb and saw the burial cloths there, and the cloth that had covered his head, not with the burial cloths but rolled up in a separate place. Then the other disciple also went in, the one who had arrived at the tomb first, and he saw and believed.

REFLECTION

The feast of St. John (+101), the beloved disciple, reminds us that the birth of Jesus is the beginning of his paschal mission. Birth leads to death, death leads to new life. Swaddling clothes give way to discarded burial cloths. John, seeing those cloths, deliberately allows Peter to have the honor of entering the tomb first. The Christmas message is about putting concern for others ahead of concern for ourselves.

PRAYERS   *others may be added*

Through the intercession of St. John the evangelist, we pray:

◆ May your light surround us.

John witnessed the Transfiguration; may we always recognize the glory of the Lord, we pray: ◆ *John stood at the foot of the cross; may we remain steady in times of trouble, we pray:* ◆ *John saw the discarded burial cloths; may we believe in the impossible, we pray:* ◆ *John took Mary into his care; may we safeguard innocence, we pray:* ◆

Our Father . . .

Loving God,
you sent John the evangelist
to instruct us about the divinity
    and fraternal love of Christ.
Give us the same strength of
    character, tender spirit, and
zealous heart to spread the love of
    your Son.
We ask this through Christ our Lord.
    Amen.

✦ *Come, you nations, and adore the Lord. A great light has come upon the earth. Alleluia!*

✦ *Come, you nations, and adore the Lord. A great light has come upon the earth. Alleluia!*

PSALM 98   *page 416*

READING   *Matthew 2:13–16*

When the magi had departed, behold, the angel of the Lord appeared to Joseph in a dream and said, "Rise, take the child and his mother, flee to Egypt, and stay there until I tell you. Herod is going to search for the child to destroy him." Joseph rose and took the child and his mother by night and departed for Egypt. He stayed there until the death of Herod, that what the Lord had said through the prophet might be fulfilled, *"Out of Egypt I called my son."*

When Herod realized that he had been deceived by the magi, he became furious. He ordered the massacre of all the boys in Bethlehem and its vicinity two years old and under, in accordance with the time he had ascertained from the magi.

REFLECTION   *Suzanne M. Lewis*

The magi seek the King of the Jews. Even before they have met him, they recognize his royalty and dominion. Another thirty-three years will pass before [the title of King will once again figure prominently in Jesus' life] and ascends his one earthly throne, when, beneath a sign that reads The King of the Jews, *he dies on the cross.*

How are the magi able to see and recognize his star, and how do they know its significance, when Jerusalem, upon hearing of this new star, grows frightened and has to consult with specialists in order to know what is written in its scrolls?

PRAYERS   *others may be added*

Crying out with joy and gladness, we pray:

◆ May your light surround us.

That we reverence all life from conception to death, we pray: ◆ *That we give witness to the Word of life, we pray:* ◆ *That we nurture faith in children, we pray:* ◆ *That we live Christmas joy throughout the entire year, we pray:* ◆

Our Father . . .

God, flame of hope,
you called Joseph
to carry the Word of God to safety.
Empower us to be a Christmas womb
in which faith, love, and hope
can be birthed anew and
pave the way to peace.
Grant this in the name of Jesus our
    Lord. Amen.

✦ *Come, you nations, and adore the Lord. A great light has come upon the earth. Alleluia!*

✚ *Come, you nations, and adore the Lord. A great light has come upon the earth. Alleluia!*

PSALM 98 page 416

READING Luke 2:25–35

Now there was a man in Jerusalem whose name was Simeon. This man was righteous and devout, awaiting the consolation of Israel, and the Holy Spirit was upon him. It had been revealed to him by the Holy Spirit that he should not see death before he had seen the Christ of the Lord. He came in the Spirit into the temple; and when the parents brought in the child Jesus to perform the custom of the law in regard to him, he took him into his arms and blessed God, saying:

"Lord, now you let your servant go in peace;/your word has been fulfilled:/my own eyes have seen the salvation/which you prepared in the sight of every people,/a light to reveal you to the nations/and the glory of your people Israel."

The child's father and mother were amazed at what was said about him; and Simeon blessed them and said to Mary his mother, "Behold, this child is destined for the fall and rise of many in Israel, and to be a sign that will be contradicted (and you yourself a sword will pierce) so that the thoughts of many hearts may be revealed."

REFLECTION

Christmas is a promise kept. God shows his reliability. Simeon becomes the spokes-person for all people—those of the Old and New Testaments, and everyone else. His words are our words, for we have seen God's promise fulfilled in the birth of Jesus. In this little infant, the greatest promise of the almighty God has completely been fulfilled. Does that not show us then, how much promise can be contained in the smallest of deeds?

PRAYERS others may be added

Relying on God's promises, we pray:

◆ May your light surround us.

That Church leaders may fulfill the promises they make to the Church, we pray: ◆ *That family members may fulfill the promises they make to one another, we pray:* ◆ *That we may cradle the gifts we have been given, we pray:* ◆ *That we may have the courage to reveal the Lord's light to the word, we pray:* ◆

Our Father . . .

God of the prophets,
you revealed your promises in
   various ways.
Help us to recognize the fulfillment of
   your promises,
and lead us to proclaim your
   Christmas glory.
Grant this through Christ our Lord.
   Amen.

✚ *Come, you nations, and adore the Lord. A great light has come upon the earth. Alleluia!*

Optional memorial of St. Thomas Becket

✝ *Come, you nations, and adore the Lord. A great light has come upon the earth. Alleluia!*

PSALM 98   *page 416*

READING   *Luke 2:36–40*

There was a prophetess, Anna, the daughter of Phanuel, of the tribe of Asher. She was advanced in years, having lived seven years with her husband after her marriage, and then as a widow until she was eighty-four. She never left the temple, but worshiped night and day with fasting and prayer. And coming forward at that very time, she gave thanks to God and spoke about the child to all who were awaiting the redemption of Jerusalem.

When they had fulfilled all the prescriptions of the law of the Lord, they returned to Galilee, to their own town of Nazareth. The child grew and became strong, filled with wisdom; and the favor of God was upon him.

REFLECTION

The Christmas season is a time to believe in miracles, dream the impossible, and imagine a renewed humanity. Most of all, it is a time to give thanks and proclaim the Word becoming flesh, like the prophetess Anna does. We find in Anna, a woman of steadfast fidelity to the child of God, the hope of the world. It is easy to remain faithful to Jesus during this season of joy and merriment, but will we remain with our Lord when the peaceful manger becomes a violent, wooden cross?

PRAYERS   *others may be added*

With grateful hearts and prophetic lips, we pray:

◆ May your light surround us.

For married couples, that their love be a sign of God's covenant with us, we pray: ◆ *For widows, that they continue to discern God's call, we pray:* ◆ *For prophets, that their voices may be heard, we pray:* ◆ *For all the baptized, that they hear and live God's call to fidelity, we pray:* ◆

Our Father . . .

God of the prophets
you called Anna to listen to,
    proclaim,
and remain with your Word of life.
May we follow in her footsteps and
ignite the world ablaze
with a burning love for your
    spoken word.
We ask this through Jesus Christ our
    Lord. Amen.

✝ *Come, you nations, and adore the Lord. A great light has come upon the earth. Alleluia!*

✝ *Come, you nations, and adore the Lord. A great light has come upon the earth. Alleluia!*

PSALM 98   *page 416*

READING   *Luke 2:41–49*

Each year Jesus' parents went to Jerusalem for the feast of Passover, and when he was twelve years old, they went up according to festival custom. After they had completed its days, as they were returning, the boy Jesus remained behind in Jerusalem, but his parents did not know it. Thinking that he was in the caravan, they journeyed for a day and looked for him among their relatives and acquaintances, but not finding him, they returned to Jerusalem to look for him. After three days they found him in the temple, sitting in the midst of the teachers, listening to them and asking them questions, and all who heard him were astounded at his understanding and his answers. When his parents saw him, they were astonished, and his mother said to him, "Son, why have you done this to us? Your father and I have been looking for you with great anxiety." And he said to them, "Why were you looking for me? Did you not know that I must be in my Father's house?"

REFLECTION   *Pope John Paul II*

The Holy Family knew poverty, danger, persecution and flight. Hard work provided the repetitive context of daily life. It is not the absence of hardships that is the measure of a happy family life, but the courage and fidelity and love—for one another and for God—with which the family members meet trials, and either overcome them or accept them as expressions of God's will, and as opportunities to share in the redemptive sacrifice of Jesus Christ.

PRAYERS   *others may be added*

Trusting in the gentleness of God, we pray:

◆ May your light surround us.

That all families may be forgiving and patient, we pray: ◆ *That we recognize the wisdom of the young, we pray:* ◆ *That the young strive to be obedient, we pray:* ◆ *That we find God in the ordinary, we pray:* ◆

Our Father . . .

O Trinity of unity,
your very being models the love
    of family.
Help us to embrace that love
and bring Christmas joy to the hearts
    of all.
We ask this through our Lord Jesus
    Christ, your Son,
who lives and reigns with you in the
    unity of the Holy Spirit,
one God, forever and ever. Amen.

✝ *Come, you nations, and adore the Lord. A great light has come upon the earth. Alleluia!*

✝ *Come, you nations, and adore the Lord. A great light has come upon the earth. Alleluia!*

PSALM 98   page 416

READING   Luke 2:16–21

The shepherds went in haste to Bethlehem and found Mary and Joseph, and the infant lying in the manger. When they saw this, they made known the message that had been told them about this child. All who heard it were amazed by what had been told them by the shepherds. And Mary kept all these things, reflecting on them in her heart. Then the shepherds returned, glorifying and praising God for all they had heard and seen, just as it had been told to them.

When eight days were completed for his circumcision, he was named Jesus, the name given him by the angel before he was conceived in the womb.

REFLECTION

Today ends the octave of Christmas. We are given the Christmas story again. However, today's selection focuses upon the humanity of Jesus. He is an infant with a mother; he is named and circumcised just as all other Jewish boys. God has come into human history in a physical form through the cooperation of a young woman. This young woman, Mary, the Mother of God, models for us devoted faithfulness and an attitude of prayer.

PRAYERS   *others may be added*

Following the example of Mary, we pray:

◆ May your light surround us.

That we may always spread Christmas joy, peace, and love, we pray: ◆ *That we may tell others the amazing message of Christ, we pray:* ◆ *That we may always allow Christ to be conceived in our thoughts, words, and actions, we pray:* ◆ *That we may take the time and trouble to ponder all things carefully in our hearts, we pray:* ◆

Our Father . . .

Loving Creator,
your plan of salvation
took flesh in the womb of the
    Virgin Mary.
With your help, may we learn to put
    our trust in others
and accept the call you sound to each
    of us.
Grant this through our Lord Jesus
    Christ, your Son,
who lives and reigns with you in the
    unity of the Holy Spirit,
one God, forever and ever. Amen.

✝ *Come, you nations, and adore the Lord. A great light has come upon the earth. Alleluia!*

✝ *Come, you nations, and adore the Lord. A great light has come upon the earth. Alleluia!*

PSALM 98   *page 416*

READING   *John 1:25–27*

They [the Pharisees] asked him, "Why then do you baptize if you are not the Christ or Elijah or the Prophet?" John answered them, "I baptize with water; but there is one among you whom you do not recognize, the one who is coming after me, whose sandal strap I am not worthy to untie."

REFLECTION

There is one among us whom we do not recognize, one who touches the human story in a unique way. It is easy during the holiday season to see Christ, transformer of humanity, in a child's smile, gifts under a tree, and carols resounding in our churches, but it is difficult to see the Light in a broken relationship, in the beggar on the street, or amid the pain of war. Christmas challenges us to be heralds singing songs of joy even when darkness covers our hearts and world.

PRAYERS   *others may be added*

Singing glad tidings of hope, we pray:

◆ May your light surround us.

That we reconcile broken relationships, we pray: ◆ *That we give to the beggar, we pray:* ◆ *That we heal the pain of war, we pray:* ◆ *That we herald God's Word made flesh, we pray:* ◆

Our Father . . .

Creator God,
you called John the Baptist
from the wilderness of life
to prepare the way
for your saving Word.
Sustain us with your
    empowering spirit
to continually create new paths
    and roads
for your liberating Word to travel.
We ask this in the name of Jesus our
    Lord. Amen.

✝ *Come, you nations, and adore the Lord. A great light has come upon the earth. Alleluia!*

✠ *Come, you nations, and adore the Lord. A great light has come upon the earth. Alleluia!*

PSALM 98   *page 416*

READING   *John 1:29–34*

John the Baptist saw Jesus coming toward him and said, "Behold, the Lamb of God, who takes away the sin of the world. He is the one of whom I said, 'A man is coming after me who ranks ahead of me because he existed before me.' I did not know him, but the reason why I came baptizing with water was that he might be made known to Israel." John testified further, saying, "I saw the Spirit come down like a dove from the sky and remain upon him. I did not know him, but the one who sent me to baptize with water told me, 'On whomever you see the Spirit come down and remain, he is the one who will baptize with the Holy Spirit.' Now I have seen and testified that he is the Son of God."

REFLECTION

John the Baptist echoes our antiphon: "Come, and adore the Lord." John's entire mission is to point to another—the Christ. That is our mission as well. Just as parents put the needs of their children ahead of their own desires, we are asked to point to the Other, to testify to the Son of God. Sometimes that testimony is as dramatic as John's, but more often it is in carrying out the simple duties of everyday life.

PRAYERS   *others may be added*

Baptized in the Spirit, we pray:

◆ May your light surround us.

For those who testify in adversity, we pray: ◆ For those who place others before themselves, we pray: ◆ For those whose work goes unnoticed, we pray: ◆ For those who foster the strengths of others, we pray: ◆

Our Father . . .

Lord God,
you sent your beloved Son for our
    redemption.
May we recognize your saving work
and point the way for others
to know your love and follow
    your way.
We ask this through Jesus Christ,
    your Son. Amen.

✠ *Come, you nations, and adore the Lord. A great light has come upon the earth. Alleluia!*

✦ *Come, you nations, and adore the Lord. A great light has come upon the earth. Alleluia!*

PSALM 98   *page 416*

READING   *John 1:35–41*

John was standing with two of his disciples, and as he watched Jesus walk by, he said, "Behold, the Lamb of God." The two disciples heard what he said and followed Jesus. Jesus turned and saw them following him and said to them, "What are you looking for?" They said to him, "Rabbi" (which translated means Teacher), "where are you staying?" He said to them, "Come, and you will see." So they went and saw where he was staying, and they stayed with him that day. It was about four in the afternoon. Andrew, the brother of Simon Peter, was one of the two who heard John and followed Jesus. He first found his own brother Simon and told him, "We have found the Messiah," which is translated Christ.

REFLECTION

The life of St. Elizabeth Ann Seton (1774–+1821), wife, mother, and foundress of the Sisters of Charity, was a reflection of today's Gospel passage. Her work in educating and caring for the poor and disadvantaged invited those around to find the Messiah in the least expected places. Elizabeth's life, like John the Baptist, was a tapestry of many colors calling others to "Behold, the Lamb of God." In the spirit

of Elizabeth, may our lives always point to the one who redeems the human story.

PRAYERS   *others may be added*

Witnessing to the Lamb of God, we pray:

◆ May your light surround us.

That the laity may share their resources with the impoverished, we pray: ◆
That religious may continue to educate the poor, we pray: ◆ *That priests may always serve the needs of the disadvantaged, we pray:* ◆ *That Church leaders may proclaim just words to the faithful, we pray:* ◆

Our Father . . .

God of all holiness,
you lifted up St. Elizabeth Ann Seton
as a model and witness of
your call to faithfulness.
Continue inspiring men and women
to behold the Lamb of God
in their hearts and lives.
Grant this in the name of Jesus our
   Lord. Amen.

✦ *Come, you nations, and adore the Lord. A great light has come upon the earth. Alleluia!*

✦ *Come, you nations, and adore the Lord. A great light has come upon the earth. Alleluia!*

PSALM 98 *page 416*

READING *John 1:47–51*

Jesus saw Nathanael coming toward him and said of him, "Here is a true child of Israel. There is no duplicity in him." Nathanael said to him, "How do you know me?" Jesus answered and said to him, "Before Philip called you, I saw you under the fig tree." Nathanael answered him, "Rabbi, you are the Son of God; you are the King of Israel." Jesus answered and said to him, "Do you believe because I told you that I saw you under the fig tree? You will see greater things than this." And he said to him, "Amen, amen, I say to you, you will see the sky opened and the angels of God ascending and descending on the Son of Man."

REFLECTION

Jesus consistently condemns duplicity and urges everyone to be his single-hearted followers. Today, Jesus surprises the single-hearted Nathanael with a call and a promise. The promise of the vision of angels is the same vision received by the patriarch Jacob. Just as this vision comforted Jacob with God's promises of protection and fertility, Nathanael is offered the position of giving birth to new people of the promise of God.

PRAYERS *others may be added*

With the angels we offer our petitions and pray:

◆ May your light surround us.

That we may always be single-hearted in following Christ, we pray: ◆ *That we may eagerly answer the call the Lord Jesus extends to us, we pray:* ◆ *That we may trust in the wisdom of God, we pray:* ◆ *That we may be quick to proclaim Jesus as the Son of God, we pray:* ◆

Our Father . . .

God of the patriarchs,
your promises from of old
are fulfilled by the birth of your Son.
Inspire us by the Holy Spirit to
    manifest your greatness,
and proclaim Jesus Christ, your Son,
    as our salvation,
through whom we ask this prayer.
    Amen.

✦ *Come, you nations, and adore the Lord. A great light has come upon the earth. Alleluia!*

✛ *Come, you nations, and adore the Lord. A great light has come upon the earth. Alleluia!*

PSALM 98   *page 416*

READING   *Mark 1:7–11*

This is what John the Baptist proclaimed: "One mightier than I is coming after me. I am not worthy to stoop and loosen the thongs of his sandals. I have baptized you with water; he will baptize you with the Holy Spirit."

It happened in those days that Jesus came from Nazareth of Galilee and was baptized in the Jordan by John. On coming up out of the water he saw the heavens being torn open and the Spirit, like a dove, descending upon him. And a voice came from the heavens, "You are my beloved Son; with you I am well pleased."

REFLECTION

It is important to note that John the Baptist's ministry never draws attention to himself, but is always pointing to the beloved Son of God. John's life and ministry illustrates the fundamental principle of Christianity: to live the Gospel message in a profound and authentic way so that others are drawn into relationship with the Light of the world. We, too, are called to light the way for others to see and experience the all-encompassing radiance of God's love.

PRAYERS   *others may be added*

Proclaiming the glorious birth of Christ, we pray:

◆ May your light surround us.

That our words give witness to the redemptive love of the Son of God, we pray: ◆ *That we renew our baptismal commitment each and every day, we pray:* ◆ *That our ministry and service always points to the one who calls us to the banquet of life, we pray:* ◆ *That we live the promise of Christmas throughout the entire year, we pray:* ◆

Our Father . . .

Light of the world,
you shower us with
Christmas peace and joy.
May we continue to immerse
    ourselves
in the rains of your redemptive
    love so
others will be lead
to you, source of all life.
We ask this in the name of Jesus our
    Lord. Amen.

✛ *Come, you nations, and adore the Lord. A great light has come upon the earth. Alleluia!*

✦ *Come, you nations, and adore the Lord. A great light has come upon the earth. Alleluia!*

PSALM 98 *page 416*

READING *Matthew 2:9b–12*

And behold, the star that they had seen at its rising preceded them, until it came and stopped over the place where the child was. They were overjoyed at seeing the star, and on entering the house they saw the child with Mary his mother. They prostrated themselves and did him homage. Then they opened their treasures and offered him gifts of gold, frankincense, and myrrh. And having been warned in a dream not to return to Herod, they departed for their country by another way.

REFLECTION

Today we celebrate the gift of God's salvation to all peoples. Just as the three kings laid their gifts before the Christ child, so too we bring our gifts to the one who overcame all darkness and sin. We should strive to be an epiphany of God, always revealing the gentle mercy of a king who came in the form of a child. Following the light, like the three kings, let us bring God's gift, Emmanuel, to all the world.

PRAYERS *others may be added*

Bringing our gifts before the Lord, we pray:

◆ May your light surround us.

That we may be like frankincense, burning with the compassion of God, we pray: ◆ That we may be like gold, reflecting the glory of God, we pray: ◆ That we may be like myrrh, reverencing the sacredness of life, we pray: ◆ That we may be gifts for the world, wrapped and adorned in the virtues of faith, hope, and love, we pray: ◆

Our Father . . .

God, giver of all gifts,
you inspired the three kings
to follow a star to your manger
    of salvation.
Give us the courage to use our gifts
to build your kingdom even though
we may traverse the deserts of pain
    and darkness.
We ask this through our Lord Jesus
    Christ, your Son,
who lives and reigns with you in the
    unity of the Holy Spirit,
one God, forever and ever. Amen.

✦ *Come, you nations, and adore the Lord. A great light has come upon the earth. Alleluia!*

✛ *Come, you nations, and adore the Lord. A great light has come upon the earth. Alleluia!*

PSALM 98   *page 416*

READING   *Luke 3:15–16, 21–22*

The people were filled with expectation, and all were asking in their hearts whether John might be the Christ. John answered them all, saying, "I am baptizing you with water, but one mightier than I is coming. I am not worthy to loosen the thongs of his sandals. He will baptize you with the Holy Spirit and fire."

After all the people had been baptized and Jesus also had been baptized and was praying, heaven was opened and the Holy Spirit descended upon him in bodily form like a dove. And a voice came from heaven, "You are my beloved Son; with you I am well pleased."

REFLECTION

As we celebrate the baptism of Jesus, we are reminded of our own Baptism into the Church. For most of us, the choice to be baptized was made by our parents. Therefore, God calls us, especially on this last day of the Christmas season, to renew our commitment to reject Satan and sin, claim God as Father, proclaim Jesus Christ as Lord, believe in the Holy Spirit, and accept the tenants of the Catholic faith. Just as we were baptized with the water of everlasting life, so too must we be water and fire for those who thirst and long for light.

PRAYERS   *others may be added*

Celebrating the baptism of the Lord, we pray:

◆ May your light surround us.

That our faith may be like fire lighting the way for all who are lost, we pray: ◆
That our faith may be like water quenching the parched lives of those who long to know Jesus, we pray: ◆ *That our faith may be like oil poured on the hearts of those who seek the love of God, we pray:* ◆
That our faith may be like a white cloth wrapped around those seeking the purity of God, we pray: ◆

Our Father . . .

Water of life,
you gave us your son, Jesus Christ,
baptizer and redeemer of all creation.
Immerse us with the waters
   of salvation
and sustain us in our commitment
to our baptismal promises.
We ask this through our Lord Jesus
   Christ, your Son,
who lives and reigns with you in the
   unity of the Holy Spirit,
one God, forever and ever. Amen.

✛ *Come, you nations, and adore the Lord. A great light has come upon the earth. Alleluia!*

✝ *Taste and see the goodness of the Lord.*

PSALM 34   *page 410*

READING   *Mark 1:21–28*

Jesus came to Capernaum with his followers, and on the sabbath he entered the synagogue and taught. The people were astonished at his teaching, for he taught them as one having authority and not as the scribes. In their synagogue was a man with an unclean spirit; he cried out, "What have you to do with us, Jesus of Nazareth? Have you come to destroy us? I know who you are—the Holy One of God!" Jesus rebuked him and said, "Quiet! Come out of him!" The unclean spirit convulsed him and with a loud cry came out of him. All were amazed and asked one another, "What is this? A new teaching with authority. He commands even the unclean spirits and they obey him." His fame spread everywhere throughout the whole region of Galilee.

REFLECTION

Today's reading from Mark depicts the early ministry of Jesus. Ironically, it is the unclean spirits who proclaim Jesus as the Holy One of God. Jesus does not want this said openly because he wants to have time to show the people what kind of Holy One he is. He is not what they expect; he is not a political leader using power in the traditional sense. Jesus wants us to understand that his power is for healing and casting out all that keeps us from love.

PRAYERS   *others may be added*

Trusting in God's mercy, we pray:

◆ Bless us, O Lord.

That we may be open to the ways of God rather than following our own will, we pray: ◆ *That we may see and combat the power of evil in our world, we pray:* ◆ *That our Church leaders may speak with authority from God, we pray:* ◆ *That we may spread the fame of the Lord, we pray:* ◆

Our Father . . .

Father of all that is seen and unseen,
we look to you in times of distress
    and times of joy.
We ask you to cast out our
    unclean spirits,
so that we may proclaim your glory
in the name of Jesus Christ,
for he is Lord forever and ever.
    Amen.

✝ *Taste and see the goodness of the Lord.*

✤ *Taste and see the goodness of the Lord.*

PSALM 34   *page 410*

READING   *Mark 1:29–34*

On leaving the synagogue Jesus entered the house of Simon and Andrew with James and John. Simon's mother-in-law lay sick with a fever. They immediately told him about her. He approached, grasped her hand, and helped her up. Then the fever left her and she waited on them.

When it was evening, after sunset, they brought to him all who were ill or possessed by demons. The whole town was gathered at the door. He cured many who were sick with various diseases, and he drove out many demons, not permitting them to speak because they knew him.

REFLECTION

Today's Gospel reading invites us to ask, What demons or sickness do I need purged so I am able to serve God? The Gospel challenges us to name our brokenness in order that we may ask Jesus to mend our pain and restore our spirit. We find in Jesus our medicinal hope to overcome all that binds, severs, and infects. Let us trust in the one who wipes away all pain and sadness.

PRAYERS   *others may be added*

Naming our brokenness and pain, we pray:

◆ Bless us, O Lord.

For the terminally ill, may they find comfort in the promise of eternal life, we pray: ◆ *For the chronically ill, may they find strength to rise each day with renewed hope, we pray:* ◆ *For the addicted, may they find courage to discover a new way of life, we pray:* ◆ *For us, may we find freedom in your saving Word, we pray:* ◆

Our Father . . .

Loving God,
   healer of our every ill,
you touch all of creation
with the balm of your saving grace.
Continue to cast out the demons
in our hearts and in our world.
We ask this in the name of Jesus our
   Lord. Amen.

✤ *Taste and see the goodness of the Lord.*

✠ *Taste and see the goodness of the Lord.*

PSALM 34   *page 410*

READING   *Mark 1:40–45*

A leper came to him and kneeling down begged him and said, "If you wish, you can make me clean." Moved with pity, he stretched out his hand, touched the leper, and said to him, "I do will it. Be made clean." The leprosy left him immediately, and he was made clean. Then, warning him sternly, he dismissed him at once. Then he said to him, "See that you tell no one anything, but go, show yourself to the priest and offer for your cleansing what Moses prescribed; that will be proof for them." The man went away and began to publicize the whole matter. He spread the report abroad so that it was impossible for Jesus to enter a town openly. He remained outside in deserted places, and people kept coming to him from everywhere.

REFLECTION

Although leprosy is not the dreaded disease today as it was in the time of Jesus, every age has its lepers and outcasts. Whether they are people with AIDS, those of other races and ethnicities, the elderly, or anyone who is different from us, we must look to the example of Jesus. He reached out and touched the untouchable and welcomed the sinner. More than physical healing, the miracle in today's reading is the outcast being pulled by the hand into God's circle of love.

PRAYERS   *others may be added*

Depending on the goodness of the Lord, we pray:

◆ Bless us, O Lord.

For the untouchables of the world, may they feel the healing touch of a loving neighbor, we pray: ◆ *For those in need of healing, may they look to the Lord, we pray:* ◆ *For those who tend to the outcasts, may they be encouraged in their work, we pray:* ◆ *For those who provide quiet places of rest, may they know the importance of their ministry, we pray:* ◆

Our Father . . .

Merciful God,
you sent your Son to extend your
    healing hand.
Fill us with your Spirit,
so that we may reach out to touch,
grasp, and hold the ailing of
    the world.
We ask this through Christ our Lord.
    Amen.

✠ *Taste and see the goodness of the Lord.*

✝ *Taste and see the goodness of
the Lord.*

PSALM 34   *page 410*

READING   *Mark 2:3–12*

They [Those who gathered] came
bringing to him a paralytic carried by
four men. Unable to get near Jesus
because of the crowd, they opened up
the roof above him. After they had
broken through, they let down the mat
on which the paralytic was lying.
When Jesus saw their faith, he said to
him, "Child, your sins are forgiven."
Now some of the scribes were sitting
there asking themselves, "Why does
this man speak that way? He is blaspheming. Who but God alone can forgive sins?" Jesus immediately knew in
his mind what they were thinking to
themselves, so he said, "Why are you
thinking such things in your hearts?
Which is easier, to say to the paralytic,
'Your sins are forgiven,' or to say,
'Rise, pick up your mat and walk?'
But that you may know that the Son of
Man has authority to forgive sins on
earth"—he said to the paralytic, "I say
to you, rise, pick up your mat, and go
home." He rose, picked up his mat at
once, and went away in the sight of
everyone. They were all astounded and
glorified God, saying, "We have never
seen anything like this."

REFLECTION

*Each and every day God is working mighty
and wonderful deeds within the human
heart and condition, but so often we are
too busy to recognize or are unable to see
his many acts. We, like the crowd in
today's Gospel, lay paralyzed before Christ,
asking for healing. May we always know
God's saving action in our lives and world
and never miss the astonishing and glorifying presence of the divine.*

PRAYERS   *others may be added*

*Recognizing God's glory in all of
creation, we pray:*

◆ Bless us, O Lord.

*That we may have new eyes to see God's
beauty painted in humanity, we pray: ◆
That we may have new ears to hear God's
voice echoing in the winds of salvation,
we pray: ◆ That we may have new hearts
to love all God's creation, we pray: ◆
That we may have new hands to comfort
all the paralyzed, we pray: ◆*

Our Father . . .

Loving God,
you offer us the grace
to see, hear, love, and touch
all that is born from your
astonishing beauty and enlightening
    glory.
Give us the courage to be renewed
    and healed
from all burdens and divisions
so that we may glorify you in
    the world.
We ask this through Christ our Lord.
    Amen.

✝ *Taste and see the goodness of
the Lord.*

✚ *Taste and see the goodness of the Lord.*

PSALM 34 *page 410*

READING *Mark 2:13–17*

Jesus went out along the sea. All the crowd came to him and he taught them. As he passed by, he saw Levi, son of Alphaeus, sitting at the customs post. Jesus said to him, "Follow me." And he got up and followed Jesus. While he was at table in his house, many tax collectors and sinners sat with Jesus and his disciples; for there were many who followed him. Some scribes who were Pharisees saw that Jesus was eating with sinners and tax collectors and said to his disciples, "Why does he eat with tax collectors and sinners?" Jesus heard this and said to them, "Those who are well do not need a physician, but the sick do. I did not come to call the righteous but sinners."

REFLECTION

Breaking from custom, Jesus associates and eats with some of the most despised people of his time. This was not done specifically to shock or flout traditions. Rather, Jesus looks beyond the barriers of sin and sees the possibility of conversion: the wondrous potential in even the darkest soul. Jesus' rebuke of the Pharisees is meant to be both a solace to "sinners" and a challenge to "the righteous."

PRAYERS *others may be added*

Hoping for conversion, we pray:

◆ Bless us, O Lord.

That we may see a flicker of hope in the darkest corners of life, we pray: ◆
That we may not be prevented by sin from doing good works, we pray: ◆ *That we may recognize our need for healing from the Great Physician, we pray:* ◆ *That we may leave judgment to the Son of Justice, we pray:* ◆

Our Father . . .

Lord God,
you call us from darkness into light.
Remove from us the desire to
    condemn others
and fill us with your tender mercy.
We ask this through Christ, our Lord
    and healer. Amen.

✚ *Taste and see the goodness of the Lord.*

✝ *Taste and see the goodness of the Lord.*

PSALM 34 *page 410*

READING *John 2:1–11*

There was a wedding at Cana in Galilee, and the mother of Jesus was there. Jesus and his disciples were also invited to the wedding. When the wine ran short, the mother of Jesus said to him, "They have no wine." And Jesus said to her, "Woman, how does your concern affect me? My hour has not yet come." His mother said to the servers, "Do whatever he tells you." Now there were six stone water jars there for Jewish ceremonial washings, each holding twenty to thirty gallons. Jesus told them, "Fill the jars with water." So they filled them to the brim. Then he told them, "Draw some out now and take it to the headwaiter." So they took it. And when the headwaiter tasted the water that had become wine, without knowing where it came from—although the servers who had drawn the water knew—, the headwaiter called the bridegroom and said to him, "Everyone serves good wine first, and then when people have drunk freely, an inferior one; but you have kept the good wine until now." Jesus did this as the beginning of his signs at Cana in Galilee and so revealed his glory, and his disciples began to believe in him.

REFLECTION

The miracle of turning water into wine of the finest quality symbolizes the dawning of a new era in which all things will be made new. This miracle signifies the reign of a Messiah who is overflowing with redemption, forgiveness, justice, and compassion. May we drink of the wine that washes away the old, giving way to the new law in which everyone will have a voice.

PRAYERS *others may be added*

Drinking of the Wine of Salvation, we pray:

◆ Bless us, O Lord.

That we may provide drink to those who thirst for justice, we pray: ◆ *That we may nourish those who hunger for compassion, we pray:* ◆ *That we may be filled with God's forgiveness, we pray:* ◆

Our Father . . .

God of hope,
you give us a vineyard of life
filled with your mercy and grace.
Sustain and nourish us
so that your Wine of Salvation
will cleanse, purify, and quench
the thirst of all creation.
We ask this through our Lord Jesus
    Christ, your Son,
who lives and reigns with you in the
    unity of the Holy Spirit,
one God, forever and ever. Amen.

✝ *Taste and see the goodness of the Lord.*

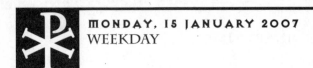
✝ *Taste and see the goodness of the Lord.*

PSALM 34   *page 410*

READING   *Mark 2:18–22*

The disciples of John and of the Pharisees were accustomed to fast. People came to Jesus and objected, "Why do the disciples of John and the disciples of the Pharisees fast, but your disciples do not fast?" Jesus answered them, "Can the wedding guests fast while the bridegroom is with them? As long as they have the bridegroom with them they cannot fast. But the days will come when the bridegroom is taken away from them, and then they will fast on that day. No one sews a piece of unshrunken cloth on an old cloak. If he does, its fullness pulls away, the new from the old, and the tear gets worse. Likewise, no one pours new wine into old wineskins. Otherwise, the wine will burst the skins, and both the wine and the skins are ruined. Rather, new wine is poured into fresh wineskins."

REFLECTION

This question about fasting comes to Jesus directly after he was criticized for eating with sinners. Here again, Jesus asserts that the Pharisees' interpretation of the law is too small and confining to hold his good news and mission. The old ways of the Pharisees cannot stretch enough to contain God's love. Jesus uses common sense examples to show that God's ways are not so complex and limiting. God's love is straightforward and understandable by all.

PRAYERS   *others may be added*

In simple faith, we pray:

◆ Bless us, O Lord.

For the courage to be challenged by God's law, we pray: ◆ *For those who begrudge acts of religiosity, we pray:* ◆ *For those who have become embittered, we pray:* ◆ *For those who yearn to celebrate, we pray:* ◆

Our Father . . .

God of all creation,
you show us your salvation in
   new ways.
Help us to accept your challenge
   to grow
and to look for new ways to spread
   your love.
May we use new wineskins to bring
   your new Wine of Salvation
to a world thirsting to celebrate with
   its bridegroom,
Jesus Christ, who is Lord forever and
   ever. Amen.

✝ *Taste and see the goodness of the Lord.*

✠ *Taste and see the goodness of
the Lord.*

PSALM 34   *page 410*

READING   *Mark 2:23–28*

As Jesus was passing through a field
of grain on the sabbath, his disciples
began to make a path while picking the
heads of grain. At this the Pharisees
said to him, "Look, why are they
doing what is unlawful on the sabbath?" He said to them, "Have you
never read what David did when he
was in need and he and his companions were hungry? How he went into
the house of God when Abiathar was
high priest and ate the bread of offering that only the priests could lawfully
eat, and shared it with his companions?" Then he said to them, "The sabbath was made for man, not man for
the sabbath. That is why the Son of
Man is lord even of the sabbath."

REFLECTION

*All laws must be interpreted according to
God's spirit of love and compassion.
According to Jesus, laws are not meant to
bind, but actually free the human spirit so
they can ultimately serve and reverence
the Lord. By asserting his authority to the
Pharisees, Jesus illustrates the fundamental call to be bearers and animators of a
law that creates a redemptive encounter
between God and his people.*

PRAYERS   *others may be added*

*Hoping to live the spirit of the law,
we pray:*

◆ Bless us, O Lord.

*For legislators, who create the law,
we pray:* ◆ *For police officers, who
enforce the law, we pray:* ◆ *For court
officials, who administer the law,
we pray:* ◆ *For Church leaders, who
interpret the law of Jesus Christ,
we pray:* ◆

Our Father . . .

Holy Spirit of God,
you inspire men and women
throughout the Christian story
to live your loving law in new ways.
May we continue to break open
    your truths
in ways that all are invited
to live your Gospel of life.
We ask this in Jesus' name. Amen.

✠ *Taste and see the goodness of
the Lord.*

✝ *Taste and see the goodness of the Lord.*

PSALM 34   *page 410*

READING   *Mark 3:1–6*

Jesus entered the synagogue. There was a man there who had a withered hand. They watched Jesus closely to see if he would cure him on the sabbath so that they might accuse him. He said to the man with the withered hand, "Come up here before us." Then he said to the Pharisees, "Is it lawful to do good on the sabbath rather than to do evil, to save life rather than to destroy it?" But they remained silent. Looking around at them with anger and grieved at their hardness of heart, Jesus said to the man, "Stretch out your hand." He stretched it out and his hand was restored. The Pharisees went out and immediately took counsel with the Herodians against him to put him to death.

REFLECTION

This healing happens very simply; Jesus merely asks the man to stretch out his hand and it is healed. A simple act of faith resulted in a great reversal of fortune. Today we celebrate St. Anthony of the Desert (251–+356). By the simple, faith-filled act of selling all his property and devoting his life to God, Anthony became the father of all monks and nuns. The tradition of monasticism has enabled a multitude of souls to achieve holiness. What simple, faith-filled act can we perform today?

PRAYERS   *others may be added*

With an openness of heart, we pray:

◆ Bless us, O Lord.

That we may always answer the call of Jesus, we pray: ◆ *That we may extend a helping hand whenever it is needed, we pray:* ◆ *That we may reject anger and hardness of heart, we pray:* ◆ *That monks, nuns, and all religious may continue to be inspired by the example of St. Anthony, we pray:* ◆

Our Father . . .

Loving Father,
you inspired St. Anthony to devote
   his life to you.
May we follow his example and
   change the world
with simple, faith-filled acts
of love and devotion.
We ask this through Christ our Lord.
   Amen.

✝ *Taste and see the goodness of the Lord.*

✝ *Taste and see the goodness of the Lord.*

PSALM 34 *page 410*

READING *Mark 3:7–12*

Jesus withdrew toward the sea with his disciples. A large number of people followed from Galilee and from Judea. Hearing what he was doing, a large number of people came to him also from Jerusalem, from Idumea, from beyond the Jordan, and from the neighborhood of Tyre and Sidon. He told his disciples to have a boat ready for him because of the crowd, so that they would not crush him. He had cured many and, as a result, those who had diseases were pressing upon him to touch him. And whenever unclean spirits saw him they would fall down before him and shout, "You are the Son of God." He warned them sternly not to make him known.

REFLECTION

Like the crowd, we all long to know, touch, and be near Jesus Christ, the one who cures all ills. Just as Jesus warned the crowd, so does he advise us to be discerning when we use his name on our spiritual journey. The name of Jesus should never be used to oppress, enslave, abuse, or bear false witness. Rather, it should liberate, set free, protect, and express truth. Let us shout the name of our Lord authentically so that the prisoner will be freed, the hungry will be fed, and the homeless will be sheltered.

PRAYERS *others may be added*

Proclaiming the wonderful name of our Lord, we pray:

◆ Bless us, O Lord.

For those who have not heard the name Jesus Christ, may they come to experience your grace-filled love, we pray: ◆ For those who have not spoken the name Jesus Christ, may they come to know the importance of proclaiming the truth, we pray: ◆ For those who have used the name Jesus Christ for acts of injustice and hatred, may they come to know the power of divine love, we pray: ◆ For those who have used the name Jesus Christ for acts of peace and compassion, may they shower the earth with your message of hope, we pray: ◆

Our Father . . .

Compassionate God,
you gave us your Son, Jesus,
to illuminate the mystery of
    redemptive love.
May we always use his name
for what is good, right, and just
in order that this life may not
    be a prison
but a freeing road to salvation.
In his name, we pray. Amen.

✝ *Taste and see the goodness of the Lord.*

✚ *Taste and see the goodness of the Lord.*

PSALM 34 *page 410*

READING *Mark 3:13–19*

Jesus went up the mountain and summoned those whom he wanted and they came to him. He appointed Twelve, whom he also named Apostles, that they might be with him and he might send them forth to preach and to have authority to drive out demons: He appointed the Twelve: Simon, whom he named Peter; James, son of Zebedee, and John the brother of James, whom he named Boanerges, that is, sons of thunder; Andrew, Philip, Bartholomew, Matthew, Thomas, James the son of Alphaeus; Thaddeus, Simon the Cananean, and Judas Iscariot who betrayed him.

REFLECTION

This Gospel reading is meant to grab our strictest attention. Jesus goes up a mountain just as Moses did and as Jesus will do again for the Transfiguration. From all his followers, Jesus chooses twelve to be leaders, just as there were twelve tribes of Israel. Summoning familiar images of authority, Jesus names twelve ordinary men to take on extraordinary powers. We too have been chosen for extraordinary things. Will we live up to that call? Will we allow his power to flow through us?

PRAYERS *others may be added*

Following our call, we pray:

◆ Bless us, O Lord.

For the bishops of the Church, successors to the apostles, that they might be worthy of their calling, we pray: ◆ *For priests, that they might be worthy of their calling, we pray:* ◆ *For all laypeople, that they might be worthy of their calling, we pray:* ◆ *For all catechumens, that they might be worthy of their calling, we pray:* ◆

Our Father . . .

Lord our God,
you are the source of all callings.
You have given us ears to hear;
   help us to listen.
You have given us eyes to see;
   help us to perceive.
As you guide us on our path of
   discipleship,
may we be attentive to the
   movements of your Holy Spirit.
We ask this through Christ our Lord.
   Amen.

✚ *Taste and see the goodness of the Lord.*

✚ *Taste and see the goodness of the Lord.*

PSALM 34 *page 410*

READING *Mark 3:20–21*

Jesus came with his disciples into the house. Again the crowd gathered, making it impossible for them even to eat. When his relatives heard of this they set out to seize him, for they said, "He is out of his mind."

REFLECTION

What is our reaction when we hear the word of God? Do we heed with expectation and understand with fidelity, or do we disdain it as crazy and ignore it as untruth? Whether we do or do not understand Jesus' message, we are called as believers to invite the Word made flesh to inform and illuminate the very depths of our hearts and minds. Let us remember, in our lack of understanding and inability to find meaning, that we are to seize the Word so that our lives become vessels of truth in a world longing for peace.

PRAYERS *others may be added*

Seeking understanding and truth, we pray:

◆ Bless us, O Lord.

For teachers, that their spoken words will lead to insight, we pray: ◆ *For preachers, that their proclamations call people to fidelity, we pray:* ◆ *For authors, that their written words challenge others to imagine a renewed humanity, we pray:* ◆ *For lawyers, that they use their words to build a just world, we pray:* ◆

Our Father . . .

Word of life,
you continue to write into the poem
   of creation
words that bring meaning to a world
searching for truth and understanding.
May we always seek you,
even when our hearts
are darkened with doubt and fear.
We ask this in the name of Jesus the
   Lord. Amen.

✚ *Taste and see the goodness of the Lord.*

✠ *Taste and see the goodness of the Lord.*

PSALM 34   *page 410*

READING   *Luke 4:14–21*

Jesus returned to Galilee in the power of the Spirit, and news of him spread throughout the whole region. He taught in their synagogues and was praised by all. He came to Nazareth, where he had grown up, and went according to his custom into the synagogue on the sabbath day. He stood up to read and was handed a scroll of the prophet Isaiah. He unrolled the scroll and found the passage where it was written: / *The Spirit of the Lord is upon me, / because he has anointed me / to bring glad tidings to the poor. / He has sent me to proclaim liberty to captives / and recovery of sight to the blind, / to let the oppressed go free, / and to proclaim a year acceptable to the Lord.*

Rolling up the scroll, he handed it back to the attendant and sat down, and the eyes of all in the synagogue looked intently at him. He said to them, "Today this Scripture passage is fulfilled in your hearing."

REFLECTION

Just as politicians often go to their hometowns to announce their political platforms, Jesus goes to Nazareth to announce his public ministry. Astounding his neighbors, Jesus uses Isaiah's prophecy of the messiah to describe himself. The people look intently at Jesus. However, we are not told their final reaction to this announcement. Certainly this is good news for people in an occupied country; and yet, they reject Jesus and his message. What is our reaction to Jesus?

PRAYERS   *others may be added*

With intent hearts, we pray:

◆ Bless us, O Lord.

That we may listen to God speaking through those who are familiar, we pray: ◆ That we may be anxious to hear the word of God, we pray: ◆ That we may have the courage to face rejection, we pray: ◆ That we may heed the message of Jesus, we pray: ◆

Our Father . . .

God, our Father,
you sent your Son for our salvation.
May we, too, work for freedom,
help the blind to see,
and relieve those who are burdened.
May all that we do be acceptable
   to you.
We ask this in the name of Jesus, our
   Messiah. Amen.

✠ *Taste and see the goodness of the Lord.*

✚ *Taste and see the goodness of the Lord.*

PSALM 34 *page 410*

READING *Mark 3:23–30*

Summoning them [a gathered crowd], he began to speak to them in parables, "How can Satan drive out Satan? If a kingdom is divided against itself, that kingdom cannot stand. And if a house is divided against itself, that house will not be able to stand. And if Satan has risen up against himself and is divided, he cannot stand; that is the end of him. But no one can enter a strong man's house to plunder his property unless he first ties up the strong man. Then he can plunder his house. Amen, I say to you, all sins and all blasphemies that people utter will be forgiven them. But whoever blasphemes against the Holy Spirit will never have forgiveness, but is guilty of an everlasting sin." For they had said, "He has an unclean spirit."

REFLECTION

The key to Jesus' message is that community and relationships characterized by pain and division need to be reconciled and healed in order for the kingdom of God to stand strong against the powers of sin and darkness. Unified hearts, minds, and relationships find their strength in Jesus, the one who builds bridges between all that severs and separates. The beauty of today's Gospel is Jesus' promise of forgiveness and hope to all who reverence the all-pervasive power of the Holy Spirit.

PRAYERS *others may be added*

Seeking to build the kingdom of God, we pray:

◆ Bless us, O Lord.

That we may weave unity in the face of division, we pray: ◆ *That we may sew reconciliation in the face of brokenness, we pray:* ◆ *That we may paint forgiveness in the face of distrust, we pray:* ◆ *That we may sculpt love in the face of hatred, we pray:* ◆

Our Father . . .

Compassionate God,
you encircle us with strength and
forgiveness
to be one family healed of
all division.
May we weave, sew, paint, and sculpt
with our lives
an artistic expression
of your merciful love for all
of creation.
Grant this through Jesus Christ our
Lord. Amen.

✚ *Taste and see the goodness of the Lord.*

✝ *Taste and see the goodness of the Lord.*

PSALM 34 *page 410*

READING *Mark 3:31–35*

The mother of Jesus and his brothers arrived at the house. Standing outside, they sent word to Jesus and called him. A crowd seated around him told him, "Your mother and your brothers and your sisters are outside asking for you." But he said to them in reply, "Who are my mother and my brothers?" And looking around at those seated in the circle he said, "Here are my mother and my brothers. For whoever does the will of God is my brother and sister and mother."

REFLECTION

While Jesus' words about his family may seem harsh, he is making the point that faith has nothing to do with bloodlines. Faith is a gift from God and an active and dynamic force far greater than any other power in the world. Most of us are born into a religion, but that religion does not become our faith until we own it, until we live it. This is Jesus' point; the bonds of faith are stronger than any other bonds, even those of blood.

PRAYERS *others may be added*

Depending on the bonds of faith, we pray:

◆ Bless us, O Lord.

That we may always follow the will of God, we pray: ◆ *That we may always work to strengthen our community of faith, we pray:* ◆ *That we may broaden our circles of concern, we pray:* ◆ *That we may always strive to see the goodness in others, we pray:* ◆

Our Father . . .

God our Father,
you sent your Son to the human
    family.
Through his life, death, and
    Resurrection
he made us members of one body.
Draw us ever closer into this circle
    of love,
where you are Father, Son, and
    Holy Spirit,
one God, forever and ever. Amen.

✝ *Taste and see the goodness of the Lord.*

✝ *Taste and see the goodness of the Lord.*

PSALM 34 *page 410*

READING *Mark 4:2–9*

And he [Jesus] taught them at length in parables, and in the course of his instruction he said to them, "Hear this! A sower went out to sow. And as he sowed, some seed fell on the path, and the birds came and ate it up. Other seed fell on rocky ground where it had little soil. It sprang up at once because the soil was not deep. And when the sun rose, it was scorched and it withered for lack of roots. Some seed fell among thorns, and the thorns grew up and choked it and it produced no grain. And some seed fell on rich soil and produced fruit. It came up and grew and yielded thirty, sixty, and a hundredfold." He added, "Whoever has ears to hear ought to hear."

REFLECTION

Echoing the message of today's parable, the writings and spirituality of St. Francis de Sales (1576–+1622) are seeds yielding much fruit. He invited all people, both lay and religious, to seek the spiritual ground in which their thoughts, beliefs, and convictions could be fertilized and take root in God's reigning mercy. Following Francis de Sales, may our lives be plentiful in faith and prayer so that all people, for all times, will know the glory of God.

PRAYERS *others may be added*

Through the intercession of St. Francis de Sales, we pray:

◆ Bless us, O Lord.

That we are fertile ground for God's word to take root, we pray: ◆ That we are seeds of compassion, falling on the hearts of those in pain, we pray: ◆ That we sow a welcoming Church, we pray: ◆ That we harvest much fruit for the table of life, we pray: ◆

Our Father . . .

Father,
you gave Francis de Sales the spirit
    of compassion
to befriend all men on the way
    to salvation.
By his example, lead us to show your
    gentle love
in the service of our fellow men.
Grant this through our Lord Jesus
    Christ, your Son,
who lives and reigns with you and the
    Holy Spirit,
one God, for ever and ever. Amen.

✝ *Taste and see the goodness of the Lord.*

✝ *Taste and see the goodness of the Lord.*

PSALM 34 *page 410*

READING *Mark 16:15–18*

Jesus appeared to the Eleven and said to them: "Go into the whole world and proclaim the Gospel to every creature. Whoever believes and is baptized will be saved; whoever does not believe will be condemned. These signs will accompany those who believe: in my name they will drive out demons, they will speak new languages. They will pick up serpents with their hands, and if they drink any deadly thing, it will not harm them. They will lay hands on the sick, and they will recover."

REFLECTION

Today we celebrate the conversion of St. Paul (3–+65), apostle of the Gentiles. What better example is there regarding the difference one person can make in the course of the world? Paul was a devout Jew intent on squelching the Christian movement. Instead, as a result of his dramatic conversion, he did more to spread the Christian message than any other person in history. Today's Gospel speaks of the wonders a believer can be known for. How will we be recognized as believers?

PRAYERS *others may be added*

Amazed at the wonders of God, we pray:

◆ Bless us, O Lord.

That we may work tirelessly to drive out the demons of oppression, addiction, and injustice, we pray: ◆ *That we may always strive to speak the gentle, healing language of love, we pray:* ◆ *That we may pick up and remove the serpents of war, hate, and violence, we pray:* ◆ *That we may always use our hands for healing and soothing a broken and ailing world, we pray:* ◆

Our Father . . .

Guiding Father,
you lovingly changed the
    misguided Saul into Paul,
    your missionary to the world.
Take our well-meaning but
    weak spirits
and transform them into the image of
    your Son,
who lives and reigns with you in the
    unity of the Holy Spirit,
one God, for ever and ever. Amen.

✝ *Taste and see the goodness of the Lord.*

✛ *Taste and see the goodness of the Lord.*

PSALM 34 *page 410*

READING *Mark 4:26–29*

Jesus said to the crowds: "This is how it is with the Kingdom of God; it is as if a man were to scatter seed on the land and would sleep and rise night and day and the seed would sprout and grow, he knows not how. Of its own accord the land yields fruit, first the blade, then the ear, then the full grain in the ear. And when the grain is ripe, he wields the sickle at once, for the harvest has come."

REFLECTION

Throughout our spiritual journey, we often try to control God's action in our lives, especially when his responses to our prayers and requests are challenging and difficult to comprehend. We are like the sleeping farmer who rises day and night, trying to understand how his crops sprout. But he does not understand and easily becomes frustrated. Likewise, we often try desperately to understand the ways of God and often give up. Let us not become discouraged and disheartened, for we are called to be people of awareness who trust in God's moving and stirring within the created order.

PRAYERS *others may be added*

Trusting in God's saving action, we pray:

◆ Bless us, O Lord.

For the laity, that they may be witnesses to God in their homes and workplace, we pray: ◆ *For religious sisters and brothers, that they may heed the call to be community, we pray:* ◆ *For priests, that they may see the longings within the hearts of those they serve, we pray:* ◆ *For bishops, that they may be authentic shepherds of the Gospel message, we pray:* ◆

Our Father . . .

God of mystery,
you chisel our hearts of stone
into beautiful images of
    your kingdom.
May we always trust
in your providential action,
even when we do not see or
    understand your ways
within our lives and world.
We ask this in the name of Jesus the
    Lord. Amen.

✛ *Taste and see the goodness of the Lord.*

SATURDAY, 27 JANUARY 2007
WEEKDAY

✝ *Taste and see the goodness of the Lord.*

PSALM 34   *page 410*

READING   *Mark 4:35–41*

On that day, as evening drew on, Jesus said to his disciples: "Let us cross to the other side." Leaving the crowd, they took Jesus with them in the boat just as he was. And other boats were with him. A violent squall came up and waves were breaking over the boat, so that it was already filling up. Jesus was in the stern, asleep on a cushion. They woke him and said to him, "Teacher, do you not care that we are perishing?" He woke up, rebuked the wind, and said to the sea, "Quiet! Be still!" The wind ceased and there was great calm. Then he asked them, "Why are you terrified? Do you not yet have faith?" They were filled with great awe and said to one another, "Who then is this whom even wind and sea obey?"

REFLECTION

Today we celebrate the life of a strong, courageous woman who changed the face of the Church and education, St. Angela Merici (1474–+1540), foundress of the Ursuline Sisters. Just as Jesus calmed the winds and quieted the sea, so too did St. Angela calm the winds of individualism by choosing to live in community and quieted the sea of poverty by empowering marginalized, young girls through education. Angela and her sisters gave witness through their vowed life that a peaceful world will only exist when we love inclusively, give abundantly, and listen openly.

PRAYERS   *others may be added*

Through the intercession of St. Angela Merici, we pray:

◆ Bless us, O Lord.

For Ursuline Sisters, that they may live St. Angela's message in today's Church and world, we pray: ◆*For women discerning religious life, that they may consider living St. Angela's vision as an Ursuline, we pray:* ◆ *For all men and women educated by Ursulines, that they may emulate St. Angela's strength and courage, we pray:* ◆ *For the Church, that she may model St. Angela's mission and empower young women through the Gospel message, we pray:* ◆

Our Father . . .

Lord,
may St. Angela commend us to
    your mercy;
may her charity and wisdom help us
to be faithful to your teaching
and to follow it in our lives.
We ask this through our Lord Jesus
    Christ, your Son,
who lives and reigns with you and the
    Holy Spirit,
one God, for ever and ever. Amen.

✝ *Taste and see the goodness of the Lord.*

✚ *Taste and see the goodness of the Lord.*

PSALM 34   *page 410*

READING   *Luke 4:24–30*

And he [Jesus] said, "Amen, I say to you, no prophet is accepted in his own native place. Indeed, I tell you, there were many widows in Israel in the days of Elijah when the sky was closed for three and a half years and a severe famine spread over the entire land. It was to none of these that Elijah was sent, but only to a widow in Zarephath in the land of Sidon. Again, there were many lepers in Israel during the time of Elisha the prophet; yet not one of them was cleansed, but only Naaman the Syrian." When the people in the synagogue heard this, they were all filled with fury. They rose up, drove him out of the town, and led him to the brow of the hill on which their town had been built, to hurl him down headlong. But Jesus passed through the midst of them and went away.

REFLECTION

Jesus was not only sent for the Jewish people, but for all who are able and willing to hear his message of forgiveness and salvation. As a matter of fact, many of his own townspeople rejected him; therefore, he had to set out for other towns and communities where ears and hearts were receptive and heard his message of reconciling love. In the spirit of Elijah, Elisha, and Jesus, let us leave our comfort zone and embark on a journey to foreign lands, proclaiming God's word to all people.

PRAYERS   *others may be added*

Setting out on the journey to preach God's word, we pray:

◆ Bless us, O Lord.

That we are open to God's diversity in creation, we pray: ◆ *That we are open to hear God's call, we pray:* ◆ *That we are open to be missionaries of the word, we pray:* ◆ *That we are open to the least among us, we pray:* ◆

Our Father . . .

God of all people,
you called Elijah and Elisha
to set out on roads and avenues
where their gift of prophecy would
    be embraced.
May we emulate them in our
    Christian journey,
always willing to venture on
    new travels
so that your word will be spread
throughout all of creation.
We ask this through our Lord Jesus
    Christ, your Son,
who lives and reigns with you in the
    unity of the Holy Spirit,
one God, forever and ever. Amen.

✚ *Taste and see the goodness of the Lord.*

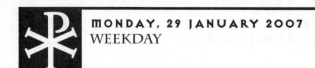
✝ *Taste and see the goodness of
the Lord.*

PSALM 34   *page 410*

READING   *Mark 5:1–3, 5–7*

Jesus and his disciples came to the
other side of the sea, to the territory of
the Gerasenes. When he got out of the
boat, at once a man from the tombs
who had an unclean spirit met him.
The man had been dwelling among the
tombs, and no one could restrain him
any longer, even with a chain. Night
and day among the tombs and on the
hillsides he was always crying out and
bruising himself with stones. Catching
sight of Jesus from a distance, he ran
up and prostrated himself before him,
crying out in a loud voice, "What have
you to do with me, Jesus, Son of the
Most High God?"

REFLECTION

*Today, Jesus is outside of Israel, speaking
to a Gentile who lived among tombs and
who was possessed by unclean spirits—
very drastic for people who lived by laws
of ritual cleanliness. Jesus reaches into the
depths of evil to rescue someone, and this
someone is us.*

PRAYERS   *others may be added*

Reaching out to God in love, we pray:

◆ Bless us, O Lord.

*That you may help us to reach out
beyond ourselves to those in most need
of healing, we pray:* ◆ *That you may
help us consider no work too unclean,
we pray:* ◆ *That you may help us to
look beyond our differences, we pray:* ◆
*That you may help us to not count the
cost of serving you, we pray:* ◆

Our Father . . .

Lord our God,
we are afflicted with demons.
Fill us with faith in the saving power
of your Son,
so that we may leave the tombs of
self pity
and embrace your way of love.
We ask this in the name of Jesus our
Lord. Amen.

✝ *Taste and see the goodness of
the Lord.*

✚ *Taste and see the goodness of the Lord.*

PSALM 34   *page 410*

READING   *Mark 5:21–24, 38–42*

When Jesus had crossed again in the boat to the other side, a large crowd gathered around him, and he stayed close to the sea. One of the synagogue officials, named Jairus, came forward. Seeing him he fell at his feet and pleaded earnestly with him, saying, "My daughter is at the point of death. Please, come lay your hands on her that she may get well and live." He went off with him and a large crowd followed him.

When they arrived at the house of the synagogue official, he caught sight of a commotion, people weeping and wailing loudly. So he went in and said to them, "Why this commotion and weeping? The child is not dead but asleep." And they ridiculed him. Then he put them all out. He took along the child's father and mother and those who were with him and entered the room where the child was. He took the child by the hand and said to her, *"Talitha koum,"* which means, "Little girl, I say to you, arise!" The girl, a child of twelve, arose immediately and walked around. At that they were utterly astounded.

REFLECTION

Following Jesus Christ in today's world is not always easy, and there may be times when we are ready to throw in the towel.

Today's Gospel tells us to arise, get up from our pain, discouragement, and struggles and embrace the dawning of a new day, for it is on that day when we will be able to walk in the light of God's radiating love. We are called to leave the commotion and weeping behind so that the message of Jesus can rise and heal our pangs of sadness and hopelessness."

PRAYERS   *others may be added*

Rising with hope and joy, we pray:

◆ Bless us, O Lord.

For those suffering from depression, we pray: ◆ *For those struggling to overcome disease and illness, we pray:* ◆ *For those dealing with the pain and grief of death, we pray:* ◆ *For those who work with and minister to the sick and dying, we pray:* ◆

Our Father . . .

Healing God,
you are always present,
even amid strife and discord.
You beckon us to move beyond
    despair and desolation
to serenity and hope.
Give us the strength and power
to arise and carry
your redeeming message of love
to the street and marketplace.
We ask this through Christ our Lord.
    Amen.

✚ *Taste and see the goodness of the Lord.*

✚ *Taste and see the goodness of the Lord.*

PSALM 34   *page 410*

READING   *Mark 6:1–6*

Jesus departed from there and came to his native place, accompanied by his disciples. When the sabbath came he began to teach in the synagogue, and many who heard him were astonished. They said, "Where did this man get all this? What kind of wisdom has been given him? What mighty deeds are wrought by his hands! Is he not the carpenter, the son of Mary, and the brother of James and Joseph and Judas and Simon? And are not his sisters here with us?" And they took offense at him. Jesus said to them, "A prophet is not without honor except in his native place and among his own kin and in his own house." So he was not able to perform any mighty deed there, apart from curing a few sick people by laying his hands on them. He was amazed at their lack of faith.

REFLECTION

The Gospels recount very few instances where Jesus is amazed. What infamy to cause the Son of God to be amazed about faithlessness! St. John Bosco (1815–+1888) knew rejection from his townspeople. He began his work of rescuing and educating children from the streets during a time of extreme anticlericalism. Bosco was not daunted by this rejection, but went on to found two religious communities while earning the title of Apostle of Youth. May

we also amaze and inspire others by our faith.

PRAYERS   *others may be added*

Through the intercession of St. John Bosco, we pray:

◆ Bless us, O Lord.

For those who follow Christ in the face of opposition, we pray: ◆ For those who care for and educate the young, we pray: ◆ For religious followers of St. John Bosco, we pray: ◆ For all those taught in schools under the charism of St. John Bosco, we pray: ◆

Our Father . . .

Wisdom on high,
you summoned St. John Bosco
to spend his life educating children.
Give us the faith to surmount
   all obstacles
so that we may accomplish your will
and bring amazement to the
   entire world.
We ask this through Christ our Lord.
   Amen.

✚ *Taste and see the goodness of the Lord.*

✝ *Taste and see the goodness of the Lord.*

PSALM 34   *page 410*

READING   *Mark 6:7–13*

Jesus summoned the Twelve and began to send them out two by two and gave them authority over unclean spirits. He instructed them to take nothing for the journey but a walking stick—no food, no sack, no money in their belts. They were, however, to wear sandals but not a second tunic. He said to them, "Wherever you enter a house, stay there until you leave from there. Whatever place does not welcome you or listen to you, leave there and shake the dust off your feet in testimony against them." So they went off and preached repentance. The Twelve drove out many demons, and they anointed with oil many who were sick and cured them.

REFLECTION

Jesus' instructions to the Twelve show the urgency he felt about the message of God's love. There was no time or energy to waste. In Jewish law, two witnesses were required to prove a fact, and so the chosen Twelve were sent two by two, carrying as little as possible. And, most importantly, they were to show God's love by curing the sick. If one town wouldn't listen, then they must quickly move on to the next. This message is still urgent and the best method is still to lead by example.

PRAYER   *others may be added*

Trusting in God's providence, we pray:

◆ Bless us, O Lord.

For missionaries, we pray: ◆
For preachers, we pray: ◆ For teachers, we pray: ◆ For lay ministers, we pray: ◆
For the ordained, we pray: ◆

Our Father . . .

O God,
Provider of all,
we place our trust in you.
Feed us with the Bread of Life,
clothe us with your sanctifying
   grace, and
supply us with the richness of
   your mercy.
Grant this through Christ our Lord.
   Amen.

✝ *Taste and see the goodness of the Lord.*

✚ *Christis the light of the nations and the glory of Israel his people.*

PSALM 27 *page 408*

READING *Luke 2:22–32*

When the days were completed for their purification according to the law of Moses, Mary and Joseph took Jesus up to Jerusalem to present him to the Lord, just as it is written in the law of the Lord, *Every male that opens the womb shall be consecrated to the Lord,* and to offer the sacrifice of *a pair of turtledoves or two young pigeons,* in accordance with the dictate in the law of the Lord.

Now there was a man in Jerusalem whose name was Simeon. This man was righteous and devout, awaiting the consolation of Israel, and the Holy Spirit was upon him. It had been revealed to him by the Holy Spirit that he should not see death before he had seen the Christ of the Lord. He came in the Spirit into the temple; and when the parents brought in the child Jesus to perform the custom of the law in regard to him, he took him into his arms and blessed God, saying:

"Now, Master, you may let your servant go / in peace, according to your word, / for my eyes have seen your salvation, / which you prepared in the sight of all the peoples, / a light for revelation to the Gentiles, / and glory for your people Israel."

REFLECTION

It has been 40 days since Christmas when the true Light came into the world. On this day we celebrate that Light being brought into the temple to be ritually dedicated to God's service. For this reason it is customary on this feast (also known as Candlemas) to bless candles that will be used in the Church's rituals throughout the year. Just as the light of a single candle is a great consolation in the darkness, so too each simple act of service becomes hope for a weary world.

PRAYERS *others may be added*

Looking to the Light of the world, we pray:

◆ Bless us, O Lord.

That we may be burning beacons of light in a world dark with sin and fear, we pray: ◆ *That we may have the eyes to see your salvation in all its manifestations, we pray:* ◆ *That we may have a spirit willing to wait for the fullness of God's time, we pray:* ◆

Our Father . . .

Hope of the nations,
you are the promise of salvation.
Help us to be beacons of light
for all those who wait for the return
    of your Son,
who lives and reigns with you and the
    Holy Spirit,
one God, forever and ever. Amen.

✚ *Christ is the light of the nations and the glory of Israel his people.*

✚ *Taste and see the goodness of
the Lord.*

PSALM 34 *page 410*

READING *Mark 6:30–34*

The Apostles gathered together with Jesus and reported all they had done and taught. He said to them, "Come away by yourselves to a deserted place and rest a while." People were coming and going in great numbers, and they had no opportunity even to eat. So they went off in the boat by themselves to a deserted place. People saw them leaving and many came to know about it. They hastened there on foot from all the towns and arrived at the place before them.

When Jesus disembarked and saw the vast crowd, his heart was moved with pity for them, for they were like sheep without a shepherd; and he began to teach them many things.

REFLECTION

Throughout scripture, the desert is often portrayed as a deeply spiritual place. In today's passage, Jesus invites the apostles to venture into the desert alone to rest. Whether in solitude or with a vast crowd, the desert is a place to encounter God. It is to God we should look for nourishment and rest. Christ leads us to the desert, to encounters with the Father through the power of the Holy Spirit. May we always be willing to follow Christ into the desert.

PRAYERS *others may be added*

Resting in the Lord, we pray:

◆ Bless us, O Lord.

Lead us to places of solitude, that we may grow in prayer, we pray: ◆ *Lead us to teachers, that we may learn your ways, we pray:* ◆ *Lead us to physical healing through the intercession of Saint Blase, we pray:* ◆ *Lead us to concern for missionaries through the intercession of Saint Ansgar, we pray:* ◆

Our Father . . .

God of our journeys,
you have sent your Son to guide us
through the desert.
Help us to be strengthened,
fed, taught,
and tempered by your Spirit.
Grant this through Christ our Lord.
Amen.

✚ *Taste and see the goodness of
the Lord.*

✠ *We are his people, the sheep of
his flock.*

PSALM 100   *page 417*

READING   *Luke 5:3a–11*

Then he [Jesus] sat down and taught
the crowds from the boat. After he had
finished speaking, he said to Simon,
"Put out into deep water and lower
your nets for a catch." Simon said in
reply, "Master, we have worked hard
all night and have caught nothing, but
at your command I will lower the
nets." When they had done this, they
caught a great number of fish and their
nets were tearing. They signaled to
their partners in the other boat to come
to help them. They came and filled
both boats so that the boats were in
danger of sinking. When Simon Peter
saw this, he fell at the knees of Jesus
and said, "Depart from me, Lord, for I
am a sinful man." For astonishment at
the catch of fish they had made seized
him and all those with him, and likewise James and John, the sons of
Zebedee, who were partners of Simon.
Jesus said to Simon, "Do not be afraid;
from now on you will be catching
men." When they brought their boats
to the shore, they left everything and
followed him.

REFLECTION

*On this day of sabbath, we are reminded
that the call to be fishers of men requires
that we leave everything behind so that
nothing hinders or prevents us from spreading the Good News of Jesus Christ. For*
*many of us, it is very difficult to let go of
our possessions, attachments, and ideolo-
gies because we are convinced that they
give meaning to our existence. Jesus proclaimed from the crèche to the cross that
our meaning exists only in our Father in
heaven who calls us out of darkness into
his wonderful light.*

PRAYERS   *others may be added*

*Leaving everything behind to follow
Jesus Christ, we pray:*

◆ Hear us, O Shepherd.

*That we are able to shed material things
from our lives, we pray: ◆ That we are
able to detach from all that obstructs
and hinders, we pray: ◆ That we find
meaning in the cross of salvation,
we pray: ◆*

Our Father . . .

God of all creation,
you sent your Son, Jesus,
to summon us into the vast sea of life
to catch the hearts of humanity.
Help us to leave all behind so that we
    may continue to dive
into the seas and rivers of
    your creation
within your net of salvific love.
Grant this through our Lord Jesus
    Christ, your Son,
who lives and reigns with you in the
    unity of the Holy Spirit,
one God, forever and ever. Amen.

✠ *We are his people, the sheep of
his flock.*

✚ *We are his people, the sheep of his flock.*

PSALM 100   page 417

READING   Mark 6:53–56

After making the crossing to the other side of the sea, Jesus and his disciples came to land at Gennesaret and tied up there. As they were leaving the boat, people immediately recognized him. They scurried about the surrounding country and began to bring in the sick on mats to wherever they heard he was. Whatever villages or towns or countryside he entered, they laid the sick in the marketplaces and begged him that they might touch only the tassel on his cloak; and as many as touched it were healed.

REFLECTION

We are physical and spiritual beings. However, we often become so preoccupied with the physical that our spiritual self is neglected. Today's Gospel shows Jesus being swarmed by people looking for physical healing. Meanwhile, did they have any sense that they were in the presence of the Son of God? St. Agatha, whom today we honor, stands in stark contrast to these people. She suffered physical mutilation and death rather than deny her spiritual identity as a Christian. May we rush to Christ for the healing of our entire being— body and soul.

PRAYERS   *others may be added*

Rushing to Christ, we pray:

◆ Hear us, O Shepherd.

For those who heal the mind, we pray: ◆
For those who heal the spirit, we pray: ◆
For those who heal physical ailments, we pray: ◆ For those who suffer for the faith, we pray: ◆

Our Father . . .

Loving Creator,
you formed us in your image.
Heal our sufferings,
and raise us to new life in
    Christ Jesus,
who lives with you and the
    Holy Spirit
forever and ever. Amen.

✚ *We are his people, the sheep of his flock.*

✚ *We are his people, the sheep of his flock.*

PSALM 100   page 417

READING   Mark 7:5–13

So the Pharisees and scribes questioned him [Jesus], "Why do your disciples not follow the tradition of the elders but instead eat a meal with unclean hands?" He responded, "Well did Isaiah prophesy about you hypocrites, as it is written:

This people honors me with their lips, / but their hearts are far from me; / in vain do they worship me, / teaching as doctrines human precepts.

You disregard God's commandment but cling to human tradition." He went on to say, "How well you have set aside the commandment of God in order to uphold your tradition! For Moses said, *Honor your father and your mother,* and *Whoever curses father or mother shall die.* Yet you say, 'If someone says to father or mother, "Any support you might have had from me is *qorban*"' (meaning, dedicated to God), you allow him to do nothing more for his father or mother. You nullify the word of God in favor of your tradition that you have handed on. And you do many such things."

REFLECTION

Jesus is quite clear that it is not how or what people eat that makes them unclean but inconsistency between their words and what is truly in their heart. Jesus breaks through tradition, custom, and law and demands that our words and actions truly reflect our beliefs and feelings. Summoned by the word, we are called to throw confining and limiting human precepts into the wind of God's grace, inviting the divine to transform them into breezes of truth and justice.

PRAYERS   others may be added

Seeking singleness of mind and heart, we pray:

◆ Hear us, O Shepherd.

For teachers, that their words may reflect their truthful hearts, we pray: ◆ *For police officers, that their enforcement of the law may be consistent with their beliefs, we pray:* ◆ *For priests, that they may live the word they preach, we pray:* ◆ *For Church leaders, that their lives may be living examples of the truths they espouse, we pray:* ◆

Our Father . . .

Holy Spirit of God,
you shatter sinful barriers
that inhibit your saving action
from filling the human heart.
Empower us to live what we believe
so that we may be authentic witnesses
   to your redeeming love.
We ask this in the name of Jesus our
   Lord. Amen.

✚ *We are his people, the sheep of his flock.*

✝ *We are his people, the sheep of his flock.*

PSALM 100   *page 417*

READING   *Mark 7:14–23*

Jesus summoned the crowd again and said to them, "Hear me, all of you, and understand. Nothing that enters one from outside can defile that person; but the things that come out from within are what defile."

When he got home away from the crowd his disciples questioned him about the parable. He said to them, "Are even you likewise without understanding? Do you not realize that everything that goes into a person from outside cannot defile, since it enters not the heart but the stomach and passes out into the latrine?" (Thus he declared all foods clean.) "But what comes out of the man, that is what defiles him. From within the man, from his heart, come evil thoughts, unchastity, theft, murder, adultery, greed, malice, deceit, licentiousness, envy, blasphemy, arrogance, folly. All these evils come from within and they defile."

REFLECTION

Here Jesus lays out a basic premise of discipleship—what is in each person's heart is the measuring stick of that person's Christianity. Our faithfulness is measured by the attitudes of our heart. Let us always be mindful that if it does not come from the heart, our actions are empty.

PRAYERS   *others may be added*

In deepest sincerity, we pray:

◆ Hear us, O Shepherd.

For all Church leaders, that they may respond to the Holy Spirit, we pray: ◆ *For the People of God, that we may be the heart of Jesus, we pray:* ◆ *For world leaders, that they may be concerned for the powerless, we pray:* ◆ *For the faithful departed, that they may enjoy the company of Christ, we pray:* ◆

Our Father . . .

Loving God,
you sent your Son
to free humanity from the bondage
     of sin.
Grant us sincere hearts producing
     the finest fruit
for the nourishment of a world
     hungry for truth.
We ask this through Christ our Lord.
     Amen.

✝ *We are his people, the sheep of his flock.*

✝ *We are his people, the sheep of his flock.*

PSALM 100 *page 417*

READING *Mark 7:24–30*

Jesus went to the district of Tyre. He entered a house and wanted no one to know about it, but he could not escape notice. Soon a woman whose daughter had an unclean spirit heard about him. She came and fell at his feet. The woman was a Greek, a Syrophoenician by birth, and she begged him to drive the demon out of her daughter. He said to her, "Let the children be fed first. For it is not right to take the food of the children and throw it to the dogs." She replied and said to him, "Lord, even the dogs under the table eat the children's scraps." Then he said to her, "For saying this, you may go. The demon has gone out of your daughter." When the woman went home, she found the child lying in bed and the demon gone.

REFLECTION

The woman in today's Gospel passage reveals the fundamental truth of the Christian story: Jesus came so that all might believe and have the fullness of life. We are called, like the Gentile woman, to stand strong before our Lord and the world declaring our fidelity to the truth and faith in the message of Christ. Then we will be able to cast the demons from our hearts and world in the name of the one who liberates the human spirit from the darkness of sin and snare of evil.

PRAYERS *others may be added*

Confessing our faith before our sisters and brothers, we pray:

◆ Hear us, O Shepherd.

That all may have access to the message of Jesus Christ, we pray: ◆ *That all may confess their faith in Jesus Christ with freedom and righteousness, we pray:* ◆ *That all may name and cast out the demons preying on the People of God, we pray:* ◆ *That all may seek liberation in the temple of God's love, we pray:* ◆

Our Father . . .

Sanctifying God,
you wipe away all sin and evil
with your protective hand and
    guiding spirit.
Give us the courage to name
    our demons
so that we may stand strong in
    the presence
of your radiating and encircling love.
We ask this in the name of Jesus.
    Amen.

✝ *We are his people, the sheep of his flock.*

✠ *We are his people, the sheep of his flock.*

PSALM 100 *page 417*

READING *Mark 7:31–37*

Jesus left the district of Tyre and went by way of Sidon to the Sea of Galilee, into the district of the Decapolis. And people brought to him a deaf man who had a speech impediment and begged him to lay his hand on him. He took him off by himself away from the crowd. He put his finger into the man's ears and, spitting, touched his tongue; then he looked up to heaven and groaned, and said to him, *"Ephphatha!"* (that is, "Be opened!") And immediately the man's ears were opened, his speech impediment was removed, and he spoke plainly. He ordered them not to tell anyone. But the more he ordered them not to, the more they proclaimed it. They were exceedingly astonished and they said, "He has done all things well. He makes the deaf hear and the mute speak."

REFLECTION

This healing of the deaf man with the speech impediment comes after numerous instances where the people do not understand what Jesus is saying to them. It's as if the Gospel writer is saying to us, don't be like them! They are unable to hear, to understand, or articulate the Good News of salvation. We must speak plainly of the truth of Jesus Christ and be opened to hearing and seeing where the spirit of Christ is being manifested today.

PRAYERS *others may be added*

Proclaiming the wonders of God, we pray:

◆ Hear us, O Shepherd.

That our ears may be opened to cries of those in need of our care, we pray: ◆ *That our eyes may be opened to the victims of oppression, we pray:* ◆ *That our mouths may be opened to utter the prophetic words of Good News, we pray:* ◆ *That our hearts may be opened to those who are hardest for us to love, we pray:* ◆

Our Father . . .

O God,
you speak in all languages at
    all times.
We yearn to hear your word.
Lift the barriers that keep us from
    understanding
your universal language of love,
and change our groaning into
    eloquent praise of your name.
We ask this through Christ our Lord.
    Amen.

✠ *We are his people, the sheep of his flock.*

✛ *We are his people, the sheep of his flock.*

PSALM 100   *page 417*

READING   *Mark 8:1–10*

In those days when there again was a great crowd without anything to eat, Jesus summoned the disciples and said, "My heart is moved with pity for the crowd, because they have been with me now for three days and have nothing to eat. If I send them away hungry to their homes, they will collapse on the way, and some of them have come a great distance." His disciples answered him, "Where can anyone get enough bread to satisfy them here in this deserted place?" Still he asked them, "How many loaves do you have?" They replied, "Seven." He ordered the crowd to sit down on the ground. Then, taking the seven loaves he gave thanks, broke them, and gave them to his disciples to distribute, and they distributed them to the crowd. They also had a few fish. He said the blessing over them and ordered them distributed also. They ate and were satisfied. They picked up the fragments left over—seven baskets. There were about four thousand people.

He dismissed the crowd and got into the boat with his disciples and came to the region of Dalmanutha.

REFLECTION

St. Scholastica (480–+543), a Benedictine nun and twin sister of St. Benedict, lived a monastic life of hospitality, simplicity, and contemplation. Echoing today's Gospel passage, her contemplative love of God was like a single loaf of bread that multiplied into numerous loaves of divine understanding and insight on which men and women of faith throughout the centuries have been able to feast. St. Scholastica's life inspires us to seek God with open ears and hearts so that we may become bread for the spiritual hunger of all those around us and those yet to come.

PRAYERS   *others may be added*

Seeking God with contemplative eyes, we pray:

◆ Hear us, O Shepherd.

May we welcome all into our lives and homes, we pray: ◆ *May we remain unattached and live simply, we pray:* ◆ *May we be bread and water for all who hunger and thirst, we pray:* ◆ *May we live stable, faithful lives filled with compassion and prayer, we pray:* ◆

Our Father . . .

Gracious God,
you called your daughter,
   St. Scholastica,
to become an icon of contemplation
   and hospitality.
May we, too, welcome your Word
   into our lives
so that we become spiritual food
for a starving world.
We ask this through Jesus Christ our
   Lord. Amen.

✛ *We are his people, the sheep of his flock.*

✦ *We are his people, the sheep of his flock.*

PSALM 100   *page 417*

READING   *Luke 6:17, 20–26*

Jesus came down with the Twelve and stood on a stretch of level ground with a great crowd of his disciples and a large number of the people from all Judea and Jerusalem and the coastal region of Tyre and Sidon. And raising his eyes toward his disciples he said:/ "Blessed are you who are poor,/for the kingdom of God is yours./Blessed are you who are now hungry,/for you will be satisfied./Blessed are you who are now weeping,/for you will laugh./ Blessed are you when people hate you,/and when they exclude and insult you,/and denounce your name as evil/ on account of the Son of Man. Rejoice and leap for joy on that day! Behold, your reward will be great in heaven. For their ancestors treated the prophets in the same way. But woe to you who are rich,/for you have received your consolation./Woe to you who are filled now, for you will be hungry./Woe to you who laugh now,/for you will grieve and weep./Woe to you when all speak well of you,/for their ancestors treated the false prophets in this way."

REFLECTION

The Gospel message is not all warm fuzzies. It is consoling and comforting at times, but it is also prodding and challenging. It is too easy to see comforting words directed at me and challenging words directed at others. *We are told that scripture is a two-edged sword. The same blade that removes our oppressors is also there to prod us out of our comfort zone into loving action. May we listen to all the words of the Gospel.*

PRAYERS   *others may be added*

Trusting in the word of God, we pray:

◆ Hear us, O Shepherd.

That the poor may be assisted in their need, we pray: ◆ *That the hungry may be nourished, we pray:* ◆ *That the sorrowful will be consoled, we pray:* ◆ *That the persecuted may be relieved of their burdens, we pray:* ◆

Our Father . . .

God who heals all suffering,
your compassion exceeds all
    expectations.
Make us true disciples of your Son.
Show us the way,
strengthen our resolve, and
help us to be your compassion to all.
We ask this through our Lord Jesus
    Christ, your Son,
who lives and reigns with you in the
    unity of the Holy Spirit,
one God, forever and ever. Amen.

✦ *We are his people, the sheep of his flock.*

✝ *We are his people, the sheep of his flock.*

PSALM 100 *page 417*

READING *Mark 8:11–13*

The Pharisees came forward and began to argue with Jesus, seeking from him a sign from heaven to test him. He sighed from the depth of his spirit and said, "Why does this generation seek a sign? Amen, I say to you, no sign will be given to this generation." Then he left them, got into the boat again, and went off to the other shore.

REFLECTION

So often we look to the heavens for signs and proof of God's existence; that the Word became flesh. We become frustrated or skeptical because we do not see visions of a transfigured Christ in the clouds or the Virgin Mary clothed in the sun. Yet God also appears to us in the beauty of creation, a child's laughter, or the comforting voice of a friend. Today's Gospel passage challenges us to look for God's signs and wonders in the ordinary, the everyday.

PRAYERS *others may be added*

Recognizing God's presence in our daily lives, we pray:

◆ Hear us, O Shepherd.

For the oppressed, that they may see God's miracles of hope, we pray: ◆ *For the sick, that they may see God's miracles of healing, we pray:* ◆ *For the dying, that they may see God's miracles of new life, we pray:* ◆ *For the mourning, that they may see God's miracles of joy, we pray:* ◆

Our Father . . .

Redeeming God,
you continue to drench the earth
with signs and symbols
of your radiating presence
    and existence.
May we always recognize
    your beauty
encircling us in the ordinary routines
    of life.
Grant this through Christ our Lord.
    Amen.

✝ *We are his people, the sheep of his flock.*

✚ *We are his people, the sheep of his flock.*

PSALM 100   *page 417*

READING   *Mark 8:14–21*

The disciples had forgotten to bring bread, and they had only one loaf with them in the boat. Jesus enjoined them, "Watch out, guard against the leaven of the Pharisees and the leaven of Herod." They concluded among themselves that it was because they had no bread. When he became aware of this he said to them, "Why do you conclude that it is because you have no bread? Do you not yet understand or comprehend? Are your hearts hardened? Do you have eyes and not see, ears and not hear? And do you not remember, when I broke the five loaves for the five thousand, how many wicker baskets full of fragments you picked up?" They answered him, "Twelve." "When I broke the seven loaves for the four thousand, how many full baskets of fragments did you pick up?" They answered him, "Seven." He said to them, "Do you still not understand?"

REFLECTION

Today, Jesus offers rather challenging words. He is rather exasperated with the apostles and asks, "Do you not understand?" By highlighting the numbers 12 (the number of the tribes of Israel) and 7 (the number associated with completeness, fullness), Jesus is reminding us that we are the new people of God and he, Jesus, is the fullness of the kingdom of God. Our Lord wants to make sure that we understand and that our hearts have not hardened to his message.

PRAYERS   *others may be added*

Looking to the Lord, we pray:

◆ Hear us, O Shepherd.

That we may truly see Christ among us, we pray: ◆ *That we may truly hear the word of God, we pray:* ◆ *That we may have open hearts and minds, we pray:* ◆ *That we may always shun those things that drive us away from lives of love, we pray:* ◆

Our Father . . .

Loving God,
Provider of all our needs,
you gave the people of Israel manna
   in the desert.
Feed us with your Bread of Life,
and raise us to new life with
   your Son.
Grant this through Christ our Lord.
   Amen.

✚ *We are his people, the sheep of his flock.*

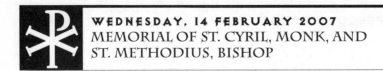

✚ *We are his people, the sheep of his flock.*

PSALM 100   *page 417*

READING   *Mark 8:22–26*

When Jesus and his disciples arrived at Bethsaida, people brought to him a blind man and begged Jesus to touch him. He took the blind man by the hand and led him outside the village. Putting spittle on his eyes he laid his hands on the man and asked, "Do you see anything?" Looking up the man replied, "I see people looking like trees and walking." Then he laid hands on the man's eyes a second time and he saw clearly; his sight was restored and he could see everything distinctly. Then he sent him home and said, "Do not even go into the village."

REFLECTION

We live in a time and culture of immediate gratification where so much of the world is at our fingertips. When embarking on the Christian journey, it can be rather tedious and difficult. We want a messiah who is going to tell us exactly where we are going and how we will get there. Yet, it is not that easy. Like the blind man, Jesus' touch is a compass that gradually reveals our path and destination. Let us be a people of patience and hope, always looking through transition lenses for the next piece in the divine puzzle of redemption.

PRAYERS   *others may be added*

Trusting in Jesus' revealing touch, we pray:

◆ Hear us, O Shepherd.

That we may be healed of spiritual blindness, we pray: ◆ *That we may remain faithful in our Christian journey, we pray:* ◆ *That we may trust God's saving action in our lives, we pray:* ◆ *That we may continue to serve and minister to the poor, sick, and dying, we pray:* ◆

Our Father . . .

Enlightening God,
you touched humanity by
    becoming flesh
and carrying the cross of salvation.
May we always look to you
with patience and expectation
as a moral guide and compass
on the spiritual journey.
Grant this through your Son, Jesus
    Christ our Lord. Amen.

✚ *We are his people, the sheep of his flock.*

✝ *We are his people, the sheep of his flock.*

PSALM 100   *page 417*

READING   *Mark 8:27–33*

Jesus and his disciples set out for the villages of Caesarea Philippi. Along the way he asked his disciples, "Who do people say that I am?" They said in reply, "John the Baptist, others Elijah, still others one of the prophets." And he asked them, "But who do you say that I am?" Peter said to him in reply, "You are the Christ." Then he warned them not to tell anyone about him.

He began to teach them that the Son of Man must suffer greatly and be rejected by the elders, the chief priests, and the scribes, and be killed, and rise after three days. He spoke this openly. Then Peter took him aside and began to rebuke him. At this he turned around and, looking at his disciples, rebuked Peter and said, "Get behind me, Satan. You are thinking not as God does, but as human beings do."

REFLECTION

For the first time in Mark's Gospel, Peter finally gets it right. He recognizes that Jesus is the Christ, the Messiah, but immediately Jesus tries to make the disciples understand that he is not the political leader that most expect the Messiah to be. His role as suffering servant is not what Peter wants to believe about Jesus. What about us? Who is Jesus for us? Are we willing to accept the sufferings of Jesus along with his healings?

PRAYERS   *others may be added*

Acknowledging Jesus as the Christ, we pray:

◆ Hear us, O Shepherd.

That we may always accept Jesus as our Lord and Savior, we pray: ◆ *That we may graciously accept the hardships of life, we pray:* ◆ *That we may learn to love those who perpetrate evil, we pray:* ◆ *That we may assist others through times of turmoil, we pray:* ◆

Our Father . . .

Lord of all creation,
you sent your Son to suffer and die
    for us.
Help us to understand the role of pain
    and suffering,
to accept the inevitable,
to change the changeable,
and to proclaim your Son, Jesus,
    as Lord.
We ask this through Christ our Lord.

✝ *We are his people, the sheep of his flock.*

✠ *We are his people, the sheep of his flock.*

PSALM 100 *page 417*

READING *Mark 8:34—9:1*

Jesus summoned the crowd with his disciples and said to them, "Whoever wishes to come after me must deny himself, take up his cross, and follow me. For whoever wishes to save his life will lose it, but whoever loses his life for my sake and that of the Gospel will save it. What profit is there for one to gain the whole world and forfeit his life? What could one give in exchange for his life? Whoever is ashamed of me and of my words in this faithless and sinful generation, the Son of Man will be ashamed of when he comes in his Father's glory with the holy angels." He also said to them, "Amen, I say to you, there are some standing here who will not taste death until they see that the Kingdom of God has come in power."

REFLECTION

We are told by Jesus that if we want to inherit the kingdom of God we must lose our life! These words may be rather difficult for a twenty-first-century disciple to hear because we live in a time when winning is for the strong-hearted and losing is for the weak and undetermined. Our value system is based on monetary achievements and productivity rather than the innate dignity of the human person. Jesus calls us to divest and let go of all that devalues the human person so that we may experience the richness and opulence of God's mansion of salvation.

PRAYERS *others may be added*

Laying down our life for the sake of the Gospel, we pray:

◆ Hear us, O Shepherd.

That we are willing to lose in order to gain, we pray: ◆ *That our values and morals are grounded in Jesus' message, we pray:* ◆ *That we reverence the gift of life, we pray:* ◆ *That more people will answer the call to ministry, teaching, and other helping professions, we pray:*◆

Our Father . . .

God of truth,
you called your Son, Jesus,
to forfeit his life
for the redemption of your holy
    family on earth.
Give us the strength to lose our lives
so that we may walk in the rain of
    your saving love.
Grant this in Jesus' name. Amen.

✠ *We are his people, the sheep of his flock.*

✚ *We are his people, the sheep of
his flock.*

PSALM 100   *page 417*

READING   *Mark 9:2–9*

Jesus took Peter, James, and John and
led them up a high mountain apart by
themselves. And he was transfigured
before them, and his clothes became
dazzling white, such as no fuller on
earth could bleach them. Then Elijah
appeared to them along with Moses,
and they were conversing with Jesus.
Then Peter said to Jesus in reply,
"Rabbi, it is good that we are here! Let
us make three tents: one for you, one
for Moses, and one for Elijah." He
hardly knew what to say, they were so
terrified. Then a cloud came, casting a
shadow over them; then from the cloud
came a voice, "This is my beloved
Son. Listen to him." Suddenly, looking
around, the disciples no longer saw
anyone but Jesus alone with them.

As they were coming down from
the mountain, he charged them not to
relate what they had seen to anyone,
except when the Son of Man had risen
from the dead.

REFLECTION

*How do we react to the high points in our
lives? The disciples wanted to enshrine
their high point, a vision, by erecting tents
at the site. The temptation is usually to try
to capture the moment. The seven founders
of the Servites began their religious life as
austere hermits, but their bishop asked
them to modify their life and accept new*
*recruits. In doing so, they transfigured
their world. We are given special moments
to spur us on to great deeds.*

PRAYERS   *others may be added*

Turning our hearts to God, we pray:

◆ Hear us, O Shepherd.

*That our hearts may be burning torches
of love, we pray: ◆ That our world may
be transfigured into a place of beauty
and peace, we pray: ◆ That we may
be inspired by all the mystical moments
that we receive, we pray: ◆ That we may
always listen to the Son of God, we pray: ◆*

Our Father . . .

Lord of the law and the prophets,
you sent your Son to live,
    die, and rise for us.
Bring us to the top of your mountain,
and guide us on to deeds of greatness,
transfigured by your glory.
We ask this through Christ our Lord.
    Amen.

✚ *We are his people, the sheep of
his flock.*

✛ *We are his people, the sheep of his flock.*

PSALM 100 *page 417*

READING *Luke 6:27–33*

Jesus said to his disciples: "To you who hear I say, love your enemies, do good to those who hate you, bless those who curse you, pray for those who mistreat you. To the person who strikes you on one cheek, offer the other one as well, and from the person who takes your cloak, do not withhold even your tunic. Give to everyone who asks of you, and from the one who takes what is yours do not demand it back. Do to others as you would have them do to you. For if you love those who love you, what credit is that to you? Even sinners love those who love them. And if you do good to those who do good to you, what credit is that to you? Even sinners do the same."

REFLECTION

Jesus' message to the disciples is quite clear: Choose love in the face of adversity and hatred. The message may be clear, but it is not always easy to love those who hate, curse, hurt, and rob us. Even though Jesus never says this is a simple task, he maintains that forgiving and reconciling love is the disciple's call and the only pathway to salvation. Following in his footsteps, let us wash away hatred with love, bandage pain with consoling hope, encircle hurt with forgiveness, and dismantle violence with healing gratitude.

PRAYERS *others may be added*

Heeding Jesus' call to live reconciling love, we pray:

◆ Hear us, O Shepherd.

That all hatred and violence will end, we pray: ◆ *That we choose mutuality and understanding in the place of intolerance, we pray:* ◆ *That forgiveness can heal our broken relationships and hearts, we pray:* ◆ *That we share our resources with the less fortunate, we pray:* ◆

Our Father . . .

Compassionate and gracious Father,
your hand heals the wounds of
   this world.
Expand our ability to love and give
in ways that transform hearts of stone
into living, pumping vessels of
   redeeming grace.
Grant this through our Lord, Jesus
   Christ, your Son,
who lives and reigns with you in the
   unity of the Holy Spirit,
one God, forever and ever. Amen.

✛ *We are his people, the sheep of his flock.*

✚ *We are his people, the sheep of his flock.*

PSALM 100   *page 417*

READING   *Mark 9:16–18, 23–29*

He [Jesus] asked them [a large crowd], "What are you arguing about with them?" Someone from the crowd answered him, "Teacher, I have brought to you my son possessed by a mute spirit. Wherever it seizes him, it throws him down; he foams at the mouth, grinds his teeth, and becomes rigid. I asked your disciples to drive it out, but they were unable to do so." Jesus said to him, "'If you can!' Everything is possible to one who has faith." Then the boy's father cried out, "I do believe, help my unbelief!" Jesus, on seeing a crowd rapidly gathering, rebuked the unclean spirit and said to it, "Mute and deaf spirit, I command you: come out of him and never enter him again!" Shouting and throwing the boy into convulsions, it came out. He became like a corpse, which caused many to say, "He is dead!" But Jesus took him by the hand, raised him, and he stood up. When he entered the house, his disciples asked him in private, "Why could we not drive the spirit out?" He said to them, "This kind can only come out through prayer."

REFLECTION

Faith makes anything possible. Jesus repeats this throughout the Gospels. The disciples were unable to heal the boy because of their lack of faith and prayer.

However, the boy's father had absolute faith in the power of Jesus and the boy was healed. We are asked to place our absolute trust in God who has all power—even the power to raise the dead. Through our prayer, trust, and faith in God, all things are possible.

PRAYERS   *others may be added*

Placing our hope in the Lord, we pray:

◆ Hear us, O Shepherd.

That Church leaders may make prayer the center of their lives, we pray: ◆
That contemplative religious may continue to model lives of deep prayer, we pray: ◆
That families may incorporate prayer into their daily life, we pray: ◆ *That the dead may be raised to new life in Christ, we pray:* ◆

Our Father . . .

Lord God,
Master of life and death,
Help us to trust and have faith in you.
Continue to send us your Holy Spirit
to inspire our prayer
and to help us live through
    difficult times.
We ask this through Christ our Lord.
    Amen.

✚ *We are his people, the sheep of his flock.*

✦ *We are his people, the sheep of his flock.*

PSALM 100 *page 417*

READING *Mark 9:33–37*

They came to Capernaum and, once inside the house, He began to ask them, "What were you arguing about on the way?" But they remained silent. For they had been discussing among themselves on the way who was the greatest. Then he sat down, called the Twelve, and said to them, "If anyone wishes to be first, he shall be the last of all and the servant of all." Taking a child, he placed it in their midst, and putting his arms around it, he said to them, "Whoever receives one child such as this in my name, receives me; and whoever receives me, receives not me but the One who sent me."

REFLECTION

In today's Gospel, the disciples are arguing about who is the greatest among them. Jesus shocks them and proclaims that the last shall be first and the first shall be last. So often we are like the disciples—seeking the limelight and center stage in the hope that we will gain recognition, importance, and prestige within our social circles and other areas of life. Jesus challenges us to become humble servants and move to the back of the line so that we will be able to stand in the light on God's stage of salvation.

PRAYERS *others may be added*

Striving to be servants of all, we pray:

◆ Hear us, O Shepherd.

That we feed the hungry, we pray: ◆
That we clothe the naked, we pray: ◆
That we shelter the homeless, we pray: ◆
That we care for the sick, we pray: ◆

Our Father . . .

God of humility,
you sent your Son, Jesus,
to become a servant of the lowly.
May we model his example of
modesty and meekness
by serving and ministering to all
who enter the woven fabric of
our lives.
Grant this through Jesus Christ
our Lord. Amen.

✦ *We are his people, the sheep of his flock.*

✚ *With the Lord there is mercy and fullness of redemption.*

PSALM 130   *page 420*

READING   *Matthew 6:16–18*

[Jesus said,] "When you fast, do not look gloomy like the hypocrites. They neglect their appearance, so that they may appear to others to be fasting. Amen, I say to you, they have received their reward. But when you fast, anoint your head and wash your face, so that you may not appear to be fasting, except to your Father who is hidden. And your Father who sees what is hidden will repay you."

REFLECTION

We enter the Lenten season signed with ashes, symbolizing the dust from which we came, our choice to turn away from sin and commitment to remain faithful to the Gospel message. The ashes call us to enter a period of repentance for 40 days and nights, confessing our sin and asking for forgiveness from the fountain of redemption, Jesus Christ. Let us place ourselves at the foot of the cross, giving alms in secret, praying behind closed doors, and fasting with joy.

PRAYERS   *others may be added*

Marked with the ashes of salvation, we pray:

◆ Come and save us, Lord.

That we give alms to all those in need, we pray: ◆ *That we heed God's call to prayer and contemplation during this Lenten season, we pray:* ◆ *That we fast from all that separates us from the message of Calvary, we pray:* ◆ *That we enter Lent with faithful and repentant hearts, we pray:* ◆

Our Father . . .

Forgiving Father,
you are the source of redemption
   and mercy.
As we journey through this
   Lenten season,
walking with the sacrificial Lamb,
who shed his blood for the salvation
   of humanity,
hold us in your loving arms,
as we call out our sin and cry
   for forgiveness
so that our lives and hearts may
   become pure and holy.
Grant this through our Lord Jesus
   Christ, your Son,
who lives and reigns with you in the
   unity of the Holy Spirit,
one God, forever and ever. Amen.

✚ *With the Lord there is mercy and fullness of redemption.*

✝ *With the Lord there is mercy and fullness of redemption.*

PSALM 130   page 420

READING   Matthew 16:13–19

When Jesus went into the region of Caesarea Philippi he asked his disciples, "Who do people say that the Son of Man is?" They replied, "Some say John the Baptist, others Elijah, still others Jeremiah or one of the prophets." He said to them, "But who do you say that I am?" Simon Peter said in reply, "You are the Christ, the Son of the living God." Jesus said to him in reply, "Blessed are you, Simon son of Jonah. For flesh and blood has not revealed this to you, but my heavenly Father. And so I say to you, you are Peter, and upon this rock I will build my Church, and the gates of the netherworld shall not prevail against it. I will give you the keys to the Kingdom of heaven. Whatever you bind on earth shall be bound in heaven; and whatever you loose on earth shall be loosed in heaven."

REFLECTION

Today we celebrate a promise that Christ has given to us—the promise that we may put our trust and faith in the teaching authority of Peter and his successors. Peter is the rock and foundation upon which God has built his "house." What confidence our Lord has in Peter! If the Son of God is willing to place his confidence in poor, weak Peter, should we be any less willing to trust in this promise of Christ?

PRAYERS   *others may be added*

Trusting in the promise of Christ, we pray:

◆ Come and save us, Lord.

For the Pope, that he may be the rock and foundation for our time, we pray: ◆
For the bishops, as successors to the apostles, that they may listen to the promptings of the Holy Spirit, we pray: ◆
For priests, that they may faithfully preach the word of God, we pray: ◆
For those who teach the faith, that they may build solid foundations for those whom they instruct, we pray: ◆

Our Father . . .

Loving Father,
you sent your Son to teach us of your love for us.
Through the intercession of St. Peter,
may we always remain faithful to the message of your Son,
worship you with clean hearts,
and one day join you in glory.
We ask this through Christ our Lord.
Amen.

✝ *With the Lord there is mercy and fullness of redemption.*

✠ *With the Lord there is mercy and fullness of redemption.*

PSALM 130 *page 420*

READING *Matthew 9:14–15*

The disciples of John approached Jesus and said, "Why do we and the Pharisees fast much, but your disciples do not fast?" Jesus answered them, "Can the wedding guests mourn as long as the bridegroom is with them? The days will come when the bridegroom is taken away from them, and then they will fast."

REFLECTION

These are new days, Jesus says. While the Messiah is in their presence, there is no need to fast. The old traditions of waiting are over. Jesus is the fulfillment of all the promises of God; he is the long-awaited one. But Jesus also predicts his suffering and death; he foretells of the time to come when the bridegroom (Jesus) will be "taken away" and all will need to repent and do penance. That time is now; Lent is the appropriate time to mourn the sins that caused our Savior to suffer.

PRAYERS *others may be added*

Through the intercession of St. Polycarp, we pray:

◆ Come and save us, Lord.

For a spirit of true repentance, we pray: ◆
For cheerful hearts and faces during this time of fast, we pray: ◆ *For the acceptance of our sufferings as salvific, we pray:* ◆

Our Father . . .

Compassionate Father,
you sent your Son for our salvation.
Through his Passion, death,
    and Resurrection,
we have been set free from sin
    and death.
By our acts of penance, may we
    become open
to your grace and mercy.
We ask this through Christ our Lord.
    Amen.

✠ *With the Lord there is mercy and fullness of redemption.*

✠ *With the Lord there is mercy, and
fullness of redemption.*

PSALM 130 *page 420*

READING *Luke 5:27–32*

Jesus saw a tax collector named Levi
sitting at the customs post. He said to
him, "Follow me." And leaving everything behind, he got up and followed
him. Then Levi gave a great banquet
for him in his house, and a large crowd
of tax collectors and others were at
table with them. The Pharisees and
their scribes complained to his disciples, saying, "Why do you eat and
drink with tax collectors and sinners?"
Jesus said to them in reply, "Those
who are healthy do not need a physician, but the sick do. I have not come
to call the righteous to repentance but
sinners."

REFLECTION

*Lent invites us to name the sin that plagues
our souls and hearts. Jesus, our Great
Physician, brings health and life to all that
hurts, hinders, and divides us by stretching out his arms on the cross of salvation.
Leaving all behind, we approach this time
of sorrow, repentance, and sacrifice in
hopes that Jesus, our Lord, will touch our
lives and turn all despair and death into
joy and resurrection.*

PRAYERS *others may be added*

*Asking for healing for our spiritual
sickness, we pray:*

◆ Come and save us, Lord.

*For those struggling with addiction,
we pray:* ◆ *For those fighting disease
and illness, we pray:* ◆ *For those
facing the darkness of death, we pray:* ◆
*For those seeking forgiveness and
reconciliation, we pray:*◆

Our Father . . .

Father of love,
source of all blessing,
you offer us
the renewing and healing power
    of your salvation.
Open our broken and sinful lives
to the power of the Great Physician,
who carries the pangs of creation
to the cross of hope and redemption.
We ask this in the name of Jesus our
    Lord. Amen.

✠ *With the Lord there is mercy and
fullness of redemption.*

✦ *With the Lord there is mercy and fullness of redemption.*

PSALM 130   *page 420*

READING   *Luke 4:1–12*

Filled with the Holy Spirit, Jesus returned from the Jordan and was led by the Spirit into the desert for forty days, to be tempted by the devil. He ate nothing during those days, and when they were over he was hungry. The devil said to him, "If you are the Son of God, command this stone to become bread." Jesus answered him, "It is written, *One does not live on bread alone.*" Then he took him up and showed him all the kingdoms of the world in a single instant. The devil said to him, "I shall give to you all this power and glory; for it has been handed over to me, and I may give it to whomever I wish. All this will be yours, if you worship me." Jesus said to him in reply, "It is written: / *You shall worship the Lord, your God, / and him alone shall you serve.*" Then he led him to Jerusalem, made him stand on the parapet of the temple, and said to him, "If you are the Son of God, throw yourself down from here, for it is written: / *He will command his angels concerning you, to guard you, /* and: / *With their hands they will support you, / lest you dash your foot against a stone.*" Jesus said to him in reply, "It also says, / *You shall not put the Lord, your God, to the test.*"

REFLECTION

After tempting Jesus with food and power, the devil cleverly appeals to Jesus' sense of mission. Jesus, newly baptized in the Jordan, is now aware of his mission. The devil tempts Jesus with a "quick fix mission," a highly dramatic jump off the roof of the temple. But Jesus realizes his mission requires time and patience and the cross. The way of Jesus is the only "fix"; we, too, must face our crosses this Lent and always.

PRAYERS   *others may be added*

With repentant hearts, we pray:

◆ Come and save us, Lord.

For those tempted by sins of the senses, we pray: ◆ *For those tempted by sins of pride, we pray:* ◆ *For those tempted by messiah complexes, we pray:* ◆ *For those tempted in any way, we pray:* ◆

Our Father . . .

Father,
you know our weaknesses.
Help us to become strengthened in
    our Lenten resolutions,
    and give us your patience.
We ask this through our Lord Jesus
    Christ, your Son,
who lives and reigns with you in the
    unity of the Holy Spirit,
one God, forever and ever. Amen.

✦ *With the Lord there is mercy and fullness of redemption.*

✝ *With the Lord there is mercy and fullness of redemption.*

PSALM 130   page 420

READING   Matthew 25:31–40

Jesus said to his disciples: "When the Son of Man comes in his glory, and all the angels with him, he will sit upon his glorious throne, and all the nations will be assembled before him. And he will separate them one from another, as a shepherd separates the sheep from the goats. He will place the sheep on his right and the goats on his left. Then the king will say to those on his right, 'Come, you who are blessed by my Father. Inherit the kingdom prepared for you from the foundation of the world. For I was hungry and you gave me food, I was thirsty and you gave me drink, a stranger and you welcomed me, naked and you clothed me, ill and you cared for me, in prison and you visited me.' Then the righteous will answer him and say, 'Lord, when did we see you hungry and feed you, or thirsty and give you drink? When did we see you a stranger and welcome you, or naked and clothe you? When did we see you ill or in prison, and visit you?' And the king will say to them in reply, 'Amen, I say to you, whatever you did for one of these least brothers of mine, you did for me.' "

REFLECTION

Feed the hungry. Give drink to the thirsty. Welcome the stranger. Care for the ill. Visit the imprisoned. Jesus is quite clear that when we serve the least among us we are actually serving him. And, those who follow this prescription for discipleship will find an eternal home with the King. Before we can serve others and pitch a tent with the King, we need to give voice to our hungers, find water for our thirsting, rid ourselves of sin, hang our illness upon the cross of life, and break through the chains of darkness.

PRAYERS   others may be added

With heart-felt sorrow and repentance, we pray:

◆ Come and save us, Lord.

For all of us, parched by darkness and sadness, we pray: ◆ *For all of us, excluded by our sinful choices, we pray:* ◆ *For all of us, weighed down by illness and disease, we pray:* ◆ *For all of us, bound by the darkness of hatred, we pray:* ◆

Our Father . . .

God of the lowly,
you gave us your Son, Jesus,
who was scourged, crowned with
     thorns, and crucified,
so that we might have eternal life.
Empower us to take up our cross
so that we may be raised to new life.
Grant this through Jesus Christ our
     Lord. Amen.

✝ *With the Lord there is mercy and fullness of redemption.*

✛ *With the Lord there is mercy and fullness of redemption.*

PSALM 130 *page 420*

READING *Matthew 6:7–15*

Jesus said to his disciples: "In praying, do not babble like the pagans, who think that they will be heard because of their many words. Do not be like them. Your Father knows what you need before you ask him.

"This is how you are to pray:

Our Father who art in heaven, / hallowed be thy name, / thy Kingdom come, / thy will be done, / on earth as it is in heaven. / Give us this day our daily bread; / and forgive us our trespasses, / as we forgive those who trespass against us; / and lead us not into temptation, / but deliver us from evil.

"If you forgive men their transgressions, your heavenly Father will forgive you. But if you do not forgive men, neither will your Father forgive your transgressions."

REFLECTION

The three traditional Lenten practices are prayer, fasting, and almsgiving. Today, Jesus teaches us to pray. All prayer should be like the Our Father: short, direct, and simple. This is how Jesus tells us to pray, with words spoken from the heart in the manner one would speak to a confidante or parent. Prayer (as all Lenten practices) is about strengthening our relationship with God. In the words of Jesus, or in our own, let us continue to build this most important relationship.

PRAYERS *others may be added*

With sincere hearts, we turn to our God:

◆ Come and save us, Lord.

That our prayers may be both simple and direct, we pray: ◆ *That our forgiveness toward others may be unending, we pray:* ◆ *That we may always desire to deepen our relationship with God, we pray:* ◆ *That we reach out to others in prayer, we pray:* ◆

Our Father . . .

Loving Father,
even as we struggle,
you reach out to us in loving and
     wondrous ways.
Teach us to pray so that we may
     know you
and grow in our love for you and
     each other.
We ask this through Christ our Lord.
     Amen.

✛ *With the Lord there is mercy and fullness of redemption.*

✝ *With the Lord there is mercy and fullness of redemption.*

PSALM 130   page 420

READING   Luke 11:29–32

While still more people gathered in the crowd, Jesus said to them, "This generation is an evil generation; it seeks a sign, but no sign will be given it, except the sign of Jonah. Just as Jonah became a sign to the Ninevites, so will the Son of Man be to this generation. At the judgment the queen of the south will rise with the men of this generation and she will condemn them, because she came from the ends of the earth to hear the wisdom of Solomon, and there is something greater than Solomon here. At the judgment the men of Nineveh will arise with this generation and condemn it, because at the preaching of Jonah they repented, and there is something greater than Jonah here."

REFLECTION

There are numerous Gospel accounts of people seeking signs of Jesus' authority. Like the questioning crowd in today's passage, we are skeptical people who only believe in realities that can be scientifically proven or immediately seen. We continue our journey through the Lenten season—a season which challenges us to see proof of God's reconciling and redeeming love through ashes, water, blood, thorns, nails, and ultimately a wooden tree. During this sacred season, may our skepticism be diminished by the abundant signs of God's mysterious gift of salvation.

PRAYERS   others may be added

Laying our skepticism and disbelief at the foot of the cross, we pray:

◆ Come and save us, Lord.

For those preparing for the sacrament of Baptism, we pray: ◆ *For those preparing for the sacrament of Confirmation, we pray:* ◆ *For those preparing to enter into full communion with the Church, we pray:* ◆ *For all of us, may we be strengthened as we live out our Lenten promises, we pray:* ◆

Our Father . . .

God of all creation,
you flood our lives with signs
of your saving action within
   the world.
Give us the courage to remove
   the nails
of sin and evil from our hearts
so that we may bow humbly
before the cross of forgiveness.
We ask this in the name of Jesus.
   Amen.

✝ *With the Lord there is mercy and fullness of redemption.*

✚   *With the Lord there is mercy and
    fullness of redemption.*

PSALM 130   *page 420*

READING   *Matthew 7:7–12*

Jesus said to his disciples: "Ask and it will be given to you; seek and you will find; knock and the door will be opened to you. For everyone who asks, receives; and the one who seeks, finds; and to the one who knocks, the door will be opened. Which one of you would hand his son a stone when he asked for a loaf of bread, or a snake when he asked for a fish? If you then, who are wicked, know how to give good gifts to your children, how much more will your heavenly Father give good things to those who ask him.

"Do to others whatever you would have them do to you. This is the law and the prophets."

REFLECTION

A common saying is "Be careful what you ask for." Rather, Jesus says, "Don't be afraid to ask." Take the risk, go to prayer, rely on God. There is no greater reality to be aware of than that we are dependent on God. We cannot do it on our own. We need God. But Jesus reassures us that we should not be afraid of the Father; no one knows better what we need and how to give it to us. Rely on God, pray!

PRAYERS   *others may be added*

Relying on the Father's love, we pray:

◆ Come and save us, Lord.

That we may bring our true needs to God, we pray: ◆ That we may remember to pray for a broken world, we pray: ◆ That we may pray sincerely for our Church and civic leaders, we pray: ◆ That we may always remember to pray for the dead, we pray: ◆

Our Father . . .

Father of all life,
you are the giver of all good things.
Help us to be heedful of your
      constant care
and our ever-present need for you.
During our Lenten observances,
may we be filled with a spirit
      of prayer.
Grant this through Jesus Christ our
      Lord. Amen.

✚   *With the Lord there is mercy and
    fullness of redemption.*

✚ *With the Lord there is mercy and fullness of redemption.*

PSALM 130 page 420

READING Matthew 5:22–24

"But I [Jesus] say to you, whoever is angry with his brother will be liable to judgment, and whoever says to his brother, *Raqa,* will be answerable to the Sanhedrin, and whoever says, 'You fool,' will be liable to fiery Gehenna. Therefore, if you bring your gift to the altar, and there recall that your brother has anything against you, leave your gift there at the altar, go first and be reconciled with your brother, and then come and offer your gift."

REFLECTION

For many people, Lent is not their favorite liturgical season because it involves the difficult work of naming sin, making sacrifices, experiencing pain, reconciling relationships, and asking for mercy. In order to live the message of today's Gospel passage, we must let go of grudges, unforgiving attitudes, and needless guilt. It is only then that we will be able stand in awe before God's altar and offer our gifts of fidelity, commitment, and love.

PRAYERS others may be added

Approaching God's altar of grace, we pray:

◆ Come and save us, Lord.

That we forgive those who have sinned against us, we pray: ◆ *That we are willing to make sacrifices to grow in our relationship with God, we pray:* ◆ *That we turn away from the power of evil and sin, we pray:* ◆ *That we let go of enslaving guilt so we can gaze upon God's mighty and wondrous throne of salvation, we pray:* ◆

Our Father . . .

God of mystery,
you travel with us during this
    Lenten season,
beckoning us to behold the wood of
    the cross.
Give us the strength to hold, touch,
    and kiss the cross of salvation
so that our hearts may be released
from all sin and despair.
Grant this through Jesus Christ our
    Lord. Amen.

✚ *With the Lord there is mercy and fullness of redemption.*

✛ *With the Lord there is mercy and fullness of redemption.*

PSALM 130   *page 420*

READING   *Matthew 5:43–48*

Jesus said to his disciples: "You have heard that it was said, Y*ou shall love your neighbor and hate your enemy.* But I say to you, love your enemies, and pray for those who persecute you, that you may be children of your heavenly Father, for he makes his sun rise on the bad and the good, and causes rain to fall on the just and the unjust. For if you love those who love you, what recompense will you have? Do not the tax collectors do the same? And if you greet your brothers and sisters only, what is unusual about that? Do not the pagans do the same? So be perfect, just as your heavenly Father is perfect."

REFLECTION

St. Katharine was a living example of the Christian call to love all, even the enemy: those despised, rejected, and considered worthless by society. She founded a religious community to empower Native and African Americans through education and the Gospel message during a time when they were viewed as undeserving of equal rights and, in many instances, were considered enemies of the cultural norm. St. Katharine and her sisters model the Lenten challenge to break through the barriers of pain and sin so that the cross of salvation can become a wooden bridge between all peoples.

PRAYERS   *others may be added*

Through the intercession of St. Katharine, we pray:

◆ Come and save us, Lord.

That the cross of Jesus Christ may become a sign of equality within the world, we pray: ◆ That the cross of Jesus Christ may inspire reconciliation within the world, we pray: ◆ That the cross of Jesus Christ may foster unity within the world, we pray: ◆ That the cross of Jesus Christ may motivate God's justice within the world, we pray: ◆

Our Father . . .

Loving God,
you raised the cross
as a compass for the journey
to your saving arms of compassion
    and peace.
Make us true icons of a life
    devoted to
penance, compunction,
    and repentance.
Grant this in the name of Jesus our
    Lord. Amen.

✛ *With the Lord there is mercy and fullness of redemption.*

✝   *With the Lord there is mercy and*
    fullness of redemption.

PSALM 130   *page 420*

READING   *Luke 9:28b–36*

Jesus took Peter, John, and James and went up the mountain to pray. While he was praying his face changed in appearance and his clothing became dazzling white. And behold, two men were conversing with him, Moses and Elijah, who appeared in glory and spoke of his exodus that he was going to accomplish in Jerusalem. Peter and his companions had been overcome by sleep, but becoming fully awake, they saw his glory and the two men standing with him. As they were about to part from him, Peter said to Jesus, "Master, it is good that we are here; let us make three tents, one for you, one for Moses, and one for Elijah." But he did not know what he was saying. While he was still speaking, a cloud came and cast a shadow over them, and they became frightened when they entered the cloud. Then from the cloud came a voice that said, "This is my chosen Son; listen to him." After the voice had spoken, Jesus was found alone. They fell silent and did not at that time tell anyone what they had seen.

REFLECTION

This is one of the most dramatic scenes in scripture. Moses and Elijah, Old Testament figures of the law and the prophets, appear; Jesus is transfigured; and God, the Father, speaks. For such drama, the audience is limited to three leading apostles. It can only be that this episode was meant to fortify them for the events of Holy Week. May we look to our peak moments of faith when we experience the valleys of doubt and uncertainty.

PRAYERS   *others may be added*

   Looking to the cross, we pray:

◆ Come and save us, Lord.

For those preparing for Baptism,
we pray: ◆ *For those preparing for full*
communion with the Church, we pray: ◆
For those experiencing doubt, we pray: ◆
For all of us as we continue our Lenten
journey, we pray: ◆

Our Father . . .

God of the patriarchs,
in creation you gave light to
   the world.
Send us moments of inspiration
so that we may know you even in our
   darkest moments.
We ask this through Christ our Lord.
   Amen.

✝   *With the Lord there is mercy and*
    fullness of redemption.

✝ *With the Lord there is mercy and fullness of redemption.*

PSALM 130   *page 420*

READING   *Luke 6:36–38*

Jesus said to his disciples: "Be merciful, just as your Father is merciful.

"Stop judging and you will not be judged. Stop condemning and you will not be condemned. Forgive and you will be forgiven. Give and gifts will be given to you; a good measure, packed together, shaken down, and overflowing, will be poured into your lap. For the measure with which you measure will in return be measured out to you."

REFLECTION

These short and simple directives of Jesus are anything but easy. The difficulty lies not in complexity but in our fallen nature. Unlike complex recipes often found in gourmet cooking, with measurements needing to be exact, the recipe for the Gospel way of life is simple; no half measures of goodness. Jesus asks that our mercy and forgiveness be as overflowing as the Father's. We can only be this generous if we allow the Holy Spirit to fill us with grace.

PRAYERS   *others may be added*

Recognizing our needfulness, we pray:

◆ Come and save us, Lord.

That Christians may stop judging one another, we pray: ◆ *That Christians may give without counting the cost, we pray:* ◆ *That we may persevere in our Lenten practices, we pray:* ◆ *That all the faithful departed may rest in peace, we pray:* ◆

Our Father . . .

Merciful God,
you offer forgiveness without limit.
On the cross of our salvation
your Son gave the supreme example
    of forgiveness.
Through the power of the Holy Spirit,
may we learn to be more like you.
We ask this through Christ our Lord.
    Amen.

✝ *With the Lord there is mercy and fullness of redemption.*

TUESDAY, 6 MARCH 2007
LENTEN WEEKDAY

✦ *With the Lord there is mercy and
fullness of redemption.*

PSALM 130   page 420

READING   *Matthew 23:1–12*

Jesus spoke to the crowds and to his
disciples, saying, "The scribes and the
Pharisees have taken their seat on the
chair of Moses. Therefore, do and
observe all things whatsoever they tell
you, but do not follow their example.
For they preach but they do not practice. They tie up heavy burdens hard to
carry and lay them on people's shoulders, but they will not lift a finger to
move them. All their works are performed to be seen. They widen their
phylacteries and lengthen their tassels.
They love places of honor at banquets,
seats of honor in synagogues, greetings in marketplaces, and the salutation 'Rabbi.' As for you, do not be called
'Rabbi.' You have but one teacher, and
you are all brothers. Call no one on
earth your father; you have but one
Father in heaven. Do not be called
'Master'; you have but one master, the
Christ. The greatest among you must
be your servant. Whoever exalts himself will be humbled; but whoever
humbles himself will be exalted."

REFLECTION

*Today's Gospel reading challenges us to
examine whether there is consistency
between our words and actions. The key to
Jesus' message of discipleship is living
authentically to who we say we are and*
*what we believe. Lent offers us an oppor-
tunity to draw back from the chaos and
business of life to ask our compassionate
and reconciling God to weave our words
and actions together so they may form a
tapestry of his glory and splendor.*

PRAYERS

*Seeking to live as authentic witnesses
to Christ, we pray:*

◆ Come and save us, Lord.

*That laypeople may attract others to
Jesus' message through their actions,
we pray:* ◆ *That religious brothers and
sisters may draw people to God's saving
message through their works of mercy,
we pray:* ◆ *That priests may call people
to conversion through the word they
preach, we pray:* ◆ *That bishops may
shepherd the souls of all with God's staff
of redemption, we pray:* ◆

Our Father . . .

Forgiving God,
you call us to live
words of peace and actions of mercy.
Sustain us in our commitment
to live genuinely the Lenten journey
    of fasting and abstinence
so that our words and actions
will meet on the road to salvation.
We ask this through Jesus Christ our
    Lord. Amen.

✦ *With the Lord there is mercy and
fullness of redemption.*

✠ *With the Lord there is mercy and fullness of redemption.*

PSALM 130 — page 420

READING — Matthew 20:17–23

As Jesus was going up to Jerusalem, he took the Twelve disciples aside by themselves, and said to them on the way, "Behold, we are going up to Jerusalem, and the Son of Man will be handed over to the chief priests and the scribes, and they will condemn him to death, and hand him over to the Gentiles to be mocked and scourged and crucified, and he will be raised on the third day."

Then the mother of the sons of Zebedee approached Jesus with her sons and did him homage, wishing to ask him for something. He said to her, "What do you wish?" She answered him, "Command that these two sons of mine sit, one at your right and the other at your left, in your kingdom." Jesus said in reply, "You do not know what you are asking. Can you drink the chalice that I am going to drink?" They said to him, "We can." He replied, "My chalice you will indeed drink, but to sit at my right and at my left, this is not mine to give but is for those for whom it has been prepared by my Father."

REFLECTION

The disciples are so stuck in their own way of thinking; they won't accept what Jesus tells them. Using the Old Testament image of drinking the chalice of God's wrath,

Jesus foretells his suffering and death—a fate the disciples will share with Jesus along with St. Perpetua and St. Felicity. These two women martyrs, a mother and her slave, so inspired early Christians that their names are included in Eucharistic Prayer I. Lent is a time to get out of our own way of thinking and drink the chalice of Christ.

PRAYERS — others may be added

Through the intercession of St. Perpetua and St. Felicity, we pray:

◆ Come and save us, Lord.

For the powerful, we pray: ◆ *For the suffering, we pray:* ◆ *For mothers, we pray:* ◆ *For domestic workers, we pray:* ◆

Our Father . . .

King of the universe,
you are the mighty one.
All power resides in you.
Help us to be servants to all,
so that we may follow in the steps of
   your Son,
who leads us to the cross of salvation.
We ask this through Christ our Lord.
   Amen.

✠ *With the Lord there is mercy and fullness of redemption.*

✠ *With the Lord there is mercy and fullness of redemption.*

PSALM 130   *page 420*

READING   *Luke 16:19–25*

Jesus said to the Pharisees: "There was a rich man who dressed in purple garments and fine linen and dined sumptuously each day. And lying at his door was a poor man named Lazarus, covered with sores, who would gladly have eaten his fill of the scraps that fell from the rich man's table. Dogs even used to come and lick his sores. When the poor man died, he was carried away by angels to the bosom of Abraham. The rich man also died and was buried, and from the netherworld, where he was in torment, he raised his eyes and saw Abraham far off and Lazarus at his side. And he cried out, 'Father Abraham, have pity on me. Send Lazarus to dip the tip of his finger in water and cool my tongue, for I am suffering torment in these flames.' Abraham replied, 'My child, remember that you received what was good during your lifetime while Lazarus likewise received what was bad; but now he is comforted here, whereas you are tormented.' "

REFLECTION

Disillusioned by wealth and the violence of war, St. John of God, founder of the Brothers Hospitallers, experienced God's call to nurse the dying and care for the sick. Like the rich man in today's Gospel, St. John knew a life of comfort; unlike the rich man, he turned away from worldly ways so that others would know God's healing love. St. John's life calls us to turn away from sin and be faithful to the Gospel so we do not end up like the rich man enveloped by the flames of suffering in the netherworld.

PRAYERS   *others may be added*

In the spirit of St. John of God, we pray:

◆ Come and save us, Lord.

For nurses, that they may be signs of God's compassion, we pray: ◆ *For hospital administrators, that they may advocate policy that protects their patients, we pray:* ◆ *For those discerning vocations, that they may consider religious communities who minister to the sick and dying, we pray:* ◆

Our Father . . .

God of all healing,
you gave St. John of God
the fortitude and wisdom
to lay down his life and become a
    humble servant
of the broken, lost, and dying.
Support us during this Lenten season
as we deny the world's promise of
    happiness and
embrace your cross of salvation.
We ask this through Jesus Christ our
    Lord. Amen.

✠ *With the Lord there is mercy and fullness of redemption.*

✦ *With the Lord there is mercy and fullness of redemption.*

PSALM 130 *page 420*

READING   *Matthew 21:42–43, 45–46*

Jesus said to them, "Did you never read in the Scriptures:

The stone that the builders rejected/ has become the cornerstone; / by the Lord has this been done, / and it is wonderful in our eyes?

Therefore, I say to you, the Kingdom of God will be taken away from you and given to a people that will produce its fruit." When the chief priests and the Pharisees heard his parables, they knew that he was speaking about them. And although they were attempting to arrest him, they feared the crowds, for they regarded him as a prophet.

REFLECTION

Jesus was not afraid of speaking the truth, even when it hurt, angered, or upset others. It's not that Jesus didn't care about the feelings of his listeners, but he knew that to live in deception, untruth, or ignorance hurts far more than the pain of being told the truth. Today, Jesus warns us that the kingdom will be taken away from those who won't speak or listen to the truth. Will we listen? Will we heed Jesus?

PRAYERS *others may be added*

Turning to the Lord, we pray:

◆ Come and save us, Lord.

That we, like St. Frances of Rome, may find holiness in our everyday existence, we pray: ◆ *That we may not be afraid to speak the truth, we pray:* ◆ *That all religious may be encouraged in their vocation, we pray:* ◆

Our Father . . .

Heavenly Father,
during these Lenten days,
guide us with your mercy and grace
so that we may always speak
   the truth,
live it in our daily lives, and
be raised to glory with you.
We ask this through Christ our Lord.

✦ *With the Lord there is mercy and fullness of redemption.*

✦ *With the Lord there is mercy and fullness of redemption.*

PSALM 130   *page 420*

READING   *Luke 15:29–32*

"He [the good son] said to his father in reply, 'Look, all these years I served you and not once did I disobey your orders; yet you never gave me even a young goat to feast on with my friends. But when your son returns who swallowed up your property with prostitutes, for him you slaughter the fattened calf.' He said to him, 'My son, you are here with me always; everything I have is yours. But now we must celebrate and rejoice, because your brother was dead and has come to life again; he was lost and has been found.' "

REFLECTION

Today we hear the conclusion to the parable of the prodigal son. The beauty of this narrative is the illustration of God's willingness to accept us with unconditional love, even when we have turned away. Lent invites us to let go of sin and all we have squandered to return to our Father, the one who is waiting to celebrate because we have found the path to eternal life. Let us embark on this Lenten road of sacrifice and penance so that we may be reunited with our Father who is ready and willing to slaughter the fattened calf with joy.

PRAYERS   *others may be added*

Approaching our Father with a repentant heart, we pray:

◆ Come and save us, Lord.

That we turn to God when we sin, we pray: ◆*That we turn to God when we squander the riches of the kingdom, we pray:* ◆ *That we turn to God when we do not love, we pray:* ◆ *That we turn to God when we fail to live the Gospel message, we pray:* ◆

Our Father . . .

God of acceptance,
you wait with open and loving arms
    for us to come home and
find refuge in your saving Word.
May we continue to renounce the
    evils in this world
through penance and reconciliation,
ultimately leading to a joyous and
everlasting reunion with you.
Grant this in the name of Jesus, the
    Lord. Amen.

✦ *With the Lord there is mercy and fullness of redemption.*

✦ *Be with me, Lord, when I am in trouble.*

PSALM 91   *page 415*

READING   *Luke 13:1–9*

Some people told Jesus about the Galileans whose blood Pilate had mingled with the blood of their sacrifices. Jesus said to them in reply, "Do you think that because these Galileans suffered in this way they were greater sinners than all other Galileans? By no means! But I tell you, if you do not repent, you will all perish as they did! Or those eighteen people who were killed when the tower at Siloam fell on them—do you think they were more guilty than everyone else who lived in Jerusalem? By no means! But I tell you, if you do not repent, you will all perish as they did!"

And he told them this parable: "There once was a person who had a fig tree planted in his orchard, and when he came in search of fruit on it but found none, he said to the gardener, 'For three years now I have come in search of fruit on this fig tree but have found none. So cut it down. Why should it exhaust the soil?' He said to him in reply, 'Sir, leave it for this year also, and I shall cultivate the ground around it and fertilize it; it may bear fruit in the future. If not you can cut it down.'"

REFLECTION

Today, Jesus uses events current to the biblical narrative to sternly call all people to repentance. Bad things happen to everyone; however, we are not always the cause of our problems. Jesus promises that a refusal to repent will certainly cause our doom. He is not trying to instill fear of a vengeful God, but rather to emphasize that the consequence of sin is more sin, more disaster. God is not trying to spoil our fun; he is trying to bring us to Easter joy!

PRAYERS   *others may be added*

With repentant hearts, we pray:

◆ By your cross, set us free.

That Lent may be a time for true repentance, we pray: ◆ *That those preparing for Baptism or full communion will be blessed by God and strengthened by our support, we pray:* ◆ *That those afflicted by catastrophes will be strengthened in their faith, we pray:* ◆

Our Father . . .

O patient God,
you give us time to repent,
open our ears to your word,
turn our hearts to your way,
and bring us to the salvation
    offered by your Son, Jesus Christ,
who lives and reigns with you in the
    unity of the Holy Spirit,
one God, forever and ever. Amen.

✦ *Be with me, Lord, when I am in trouble.*

✝ *Be with me, Lord, when I am
in trouble.*

PSALM 91   page 415

READING   Luke 4:24–30

Jesus said to the people in the synagogue at Nazareth: "Amen, I say to
you, no prophet is accepted in his own
native place. Indeed, I tell you, there
were many widows in Israel in the days
of Elijah when the sky was closed for
three and a half years and a severe
famine spread over the entire land. It
was to none of these that Elijah was
sent, but only to a widow in Zarephath
in the land of Sidon. Again, there were
many lepers in Israel during the time
of Elisha the prophet; yet not one of
them was cleansed, but only Naaman
the Syrian." When the people in the
synagogue heard this, they were all
filled with fury. They rose up, drove
him out of the town, and led him to the
brow of the hill on which their town
had been built, to hurl him down headlong. But he passed through the midst
of them and went away.

REFLECTION

*Many times we are unable to hear God's
call because our ears are deafened to the
sacred, our eyes are blind to God's beauty,
and our hearts are hardened to his word.
Today's Gospel passage beckons us to ask,
Would we recognize and heed the voice of
Jesus if he were here? Lent is a time to rid
ourselves of all that keeps us from hearing,*
*seeing, and loving Jesus Christ, the pro-
claimer of God's saving word through the
power of the cross.*

PRAYERS   *others may be added*

*Beholding the wood of the cross,
we pray:*

◆ By your cross, set us free.

*That we may listen to the voice of Jesus
spoken through the Church, we pray:* ◆
*That God will continue to lift up more
people to speak of his saving love,
we pray:* ◆ *That God will inspire more
people to sacrifice their lives for the
sake of the Gospel, we pray:* ◆

Our Father . . .

God of our Lenten journey,
you remain faithful and steadfast,
even though our hearts are darkened
    by sin and evil.
Cleanse our lives of selfishness
    and pride,
enabling us to carry the cross of
    Jesus Christ,
through whom we ask this prayer.
    Amen.

✝ *Be with me, Lord, when I am
in trouble.*

✚ *Be with me, Lord, when I am in trouble.*

PSALM 91   *page 415*

READING   *Matthew 18:21–24, 27–35*

Peter approached Jesus and asked him, "Lord, if my brother sins against me, how often must I forgive him? As many as seven times?" Jesus answered, "I say to you, not seven times but seventy-seven times. That is why the Kingdom of heaven may be likened to a king who decided to settle accounts with his servants. When he began the accounting, a debtor was brought before him who owed him a huge amount. Moved with compassion the master of that servant let him go and forgave him the loan. When that servant had left, he found one of his fellow servants who owed him a much smaller amount. He seized him and started to choke him, demanding, 'Pay back what you owe.' Falling to his knees, his fellow servant begged him, 'Be patient with me, and I will pay you back.' But he refused. Instead, he had him put in prison until he paid back the debt. Now when his fellow servants saw what had happened, they were deeply disturbed, and went to their master and reported the whole affair. His master summoned him and said to him, 'You wicked servant! I forgave you your entire debt because you begged me to. Should you not have had pity on your fellow servant, as I had pity on you?' Then in anger his master handed him over to the torturers until he should pay back the whole debt. So will my heavenly Father do to you, unless each of you forgives your brother from your heart."

REFLECTION

Are we really forgiving someone if we count how many times we do it? Instead, aren't we just biding our time until we can seek revenge? That seems to be what Jesus is saying to Peter. God expects us to offer forgiveness without reserve. In fact, the one instance where God may appear to limit his bounty is when we refuse to forgive. As we look at those things for which we need forgiveness, let us not forget to offer forgiveness to others.

PRAYERS   *others may be added*

With forgiving hearts, we pray:

◆ By your cross, set us free.

For those who harm us, we pray: ◆
For those in serious debt, we pray: ◆
For those who show us forgiveness, we pray: ◆ *For those imprisoned, we pray:* ◆

Our Father . . .

God of mercy,
you reach out in forgiveness to all.
Help us to accept your saving
    actions and
to spread your forgiving love.
We ask this through Christ our Lord.
    Amen.

✚ *Be with me, Lord, when I am in trouble.*

✝ *Be with me, Lord, when I am*
  in trouble.

PSALM 91 *page 415*

READING *Matthew 5:17–19*

Jesus said to his disciples: "Do not think that I have come to abolish the law or the prophets. I have come not to abolish but to fulfill. Amen, I say to you, until heaven and earth pass away, not the smallest letter or the smallest part of a letter will pass from the law, until all things have taken place. Therefore, whoever breaks one of the least of these commandments and teaches others to do so will be called least in the Kingdom of heaven. But whoever obeys and teaches these commandments will be called greatest in the Kingdom of heaven."

REFLECTION

One of the foundational doctrines within the Catholic tradition is the belief in the communion of saints: the holy men and women raised to the altar of God who encircle and support us with their prayers. They embody the message of today's Gospel not only by supporting us, but also by leading us to God through their lives of fidelity, recognition of Jesus as the fulfillment of the Old Testament, and innate ability to follow God's commandments of love. These models of sanctity encourage us during this Lenten fast to live the message of Christ with our whole hearts, minds, and bodies.

PRAYERS *others may be added*

Seeking to remain faithful to God's commandments, we pray:

◆ By your cross, set us free.

That we give witness to Jesus Christ as the fulfillment of the Old Testament, we pray: ◆ *That we follow God's laws of compassion and justice, we pray:* ◆ *That we call upon the saints when we are in need of help, we pray:* ◆ *That we contemplate the mystery of God's gift of redemption, we pray:* ◆

Our Father . . .

Saving God,
you give us the communion of saints
to light the way to your Word of life.
In the spirit of these holy men
    and women,
may we journey to your altar of
    reconciliation,
giving witness to the cross of glory.
We ask this in the name of Jesus our
    Lord. Amen.

✝ *Be with me, Lord, when I am*
  in trouble.

✝ *Be with me, Lord, when I am*
   in trouble.

PSALM 91 page 415

READING Luke 11:14–23

Jesus was driving out a demon that was mute, and when the demon had gone out, the mute man spoke and the crowds were amazed. Some of them said, "By the power of Beelzebul, the prince of demons, he drives out demons." Others, to test him, asked him for a sign from heaven. But he knew their thoughts and said to them, "Every kingdom divided against itself will be laid waste and house will fall against house. And if Satan is divided against himself, how will his kingdom stand? For you say that it is by Beelzebul that I drive out demons. If I, then, drive out demons by Beelzebul, by whom do your own people drive them out? Therefore they will be your judges. But if it is by the finger of God that I drive out demons, then the Kingdom of God has come upon you. When a strong man fully armed guards his palace, his possessions are safe. But when one stronger than he attacks and overcomes him, he takes away the armor on which he relied and distributes the spoils. Whoever is not with me is against me, and whoever does not gather with me scatters."

REFLECTION

People were trying to use Jesus' good deeds against him. They were ascribing evil intent to his acts of healing, to his attempts to bring about the reign of God. Do we ever stand in their shoes? Do we tear down the good deeds of others out of jealousy or malice? Jesus worked his deeds through the power of the Father and Holy Sprit, from whom all goodness flows—no matter who is the agent. Jesus warns us, if we are against his agents, we are against him.

PRAYERS others may be added

In sincerity, we pray:

◆ By your cross, set us free.

For those haunted by the demons of addiction, we pray: ◆ *For those possessed by the evil spirit of malice, we pray:* ◆ *For those afflicted with diseases, we pray:* ◆ *For those in opposition to the Gospel, we pray:* ◆

Our Father . . .

God of unity,
you bind all things together in
   your love,
gather our hearts, minds, and spirits
in union with your Son,
who beckons to us to drive out
the demons of division and discord.
May we all share in your presence.
We ask this through Christ our Lord.
   Amen.

✝ *Be with me, Lord, when I am*
   in trouble.

✝ *Be with me, Lord, when I am
in trouble.*

PSALM 91 *page 415*

READING *Mark 12:28–34*

One of the scribes came to Jesus and asked him, "Which is the first of all the commandments?" Jesus replied, "The first is this: *Hear, O Israel! The Lord our God is Lord alone! You shall love the Lord your God with all your heart, with all your soul, with all your mind, and with all your strength.* The second is this: *You shall love your neighbor as yourself.* There is no other commandment greater than these." The scribe said to him, "Well said, teacher. You are right in saying, *He is One and there is no other than he.* And *to love him with all your heart, with all your understanding, with all your strength, and to love your neighbor as yourself* is worth more than all burnt offerings and sacrifices." And when Jesus saw that he answered with understanding, he said to him, "You are not far from the Kingdom of God." And no one dared to ask him any more questions.

REFLECTION

In the Gospel passage we find an honest and sincere scribe approaching Jesus with questions regarding God's commandments of love and salvation. Like the trusting and heartfelt scribe, we are called to bring our questions, concerns, and feelings before the Lord, seeking to gain understanding and insight into the Gospel message. Lent is a time to seek spiritual clarity, reconciliation,

and forgiveness so that we may love our one, true God and reverence our neighbor.

PRAYERS *others may be added*

Longing to know and live God's commandments, we pray:

♦ By your cross, set us free.

That we lay our worries and anxieties before our crucified Lord, we pray: ♦ *That we worship and love God alone, we pray:* ♦ *That we love our neighbor as ourself, we pray:* ♦ *That we live all of God's laws with joy, we pray:* ♦

Our Father . . .

God of truth,
you give us your commandments
    and laws
to guide our footsteps in the ways
    of righteousness.
May we always be eager, like
    the scribe,
seeking to know and understand
the freedom that comes in following
    your precepts.
Grant this through Christ our Lord.
    Amen.

✝ *Be with me, Lord, when I am
in trouble.*

✛ *Be with me, Lord, when I am
in trouble.*

PSALM 91   *page 415*

READING   *Luke 18:9–14*

Jesus addressed this parable to those who were convinced of their own righteousness and despised everyone else. "Two people went up to the temple area to pray; one was a Pharisee and the other was a tax collector. The Pharisee took up his position and spoke this prayer to himself, 'O God, I thank you that I am not like the rest of humanity—greedy, dishonest, adulterous—or even like this tax collector. I fast twice a week, and I pay tithes on my whole income.' But the tax collector stood off at a distance and would not even raise his eyes to heaven but beat his breast and prayed, 'O God, be merciful to me a sinner.' I tell you, the latter went home justified, not the former; for everyone who exalts himself will be humbled, and the one who humbles himself will be exalted."

REFLECTION

The word humility *comes from the Latin word* humilis, *meaning near to the ground. The typical image of humility is a person bending low, but it is probably better to think of a person who is close to the ground of one's existence; or one who knows his or her foundation. Ultimately, to be humble is to know the truth about oneself. St. Patrick was well aware that he was not a very learned man, but his cooperation with*

God's grace led him to become one of the most popular saints of all time.

PRAYERS   *others may be added*

Recognizing God as our foundation, we pray:

◆ *By your cross, set us free.*

For bishops and pastors, that they may lead us in humility, we pray: ◆
For world leaders, that they may work to eliminate all forms of slavery, we pray: ◆
For the end of religious strife and discord in Northern Ireland, we pray: ◆
For the grace to look to the cross for encouragement in our Lenten practices, we pray: ◆

Our Father . . .

O God of the most high,
you reign from your throne of glory.
Help us to truly know ourselves
and accept our need for your grace.
We ask this through Christ our Lord.
Amen.

✛ *Be with me, Lord, when I am
in trouble.*

Optional memorial of St. Patrick   **105**

✠ *Be with me, Lord, when I am
in trouble.*

PSALM 91   page 415

READING   Luke 15:20b–24a

"While he [the younger son] was still a long way off, his father caught sight of him, and was filled with compassion. He ran to his son, embraced him and kissed him. His son said to him, 'Father, I have sinned against heaven and against you; I no longer deserve to be called your son.' But his father ordered his servants, 'Quickly bring the finest robe and put it on him; put a ring on his finger and sandals on his feet. Take the fattened calf and slaughter it. Then let us celebrate with a feast, because this son of mine was dead, and has come to life again; he was lost, and has been found.'"

REFLECTION

The Fourth Sunday of Lent is known as Laetare Sunday, *marking the midpoint between the beginning of Lent and Easter Sunday. It is a day of celebration because we have been living our Lenten promises and are beginning to see the light of Easter joy. Traditionally, this was the day to give the catechumens the Apostles' Creed, which signified their final step in preparing for Baptism. Let us rejoice, like the father in today's parable and the catechumens approaching the waters of life, that we will be immersed in the radiance of Easter glory.*

PRAYERS   *others may be added*

*Rejoicing with our catechumens,
we pray:*

◆ By your cross, set us free.

That we remain steadfast in our penitential practices, we pray: ◆ *That the catechumens may courageously continue their journey to God's font of salvation, we pray:* ◆ *That more people may know the freedom in following Jesus to the cross, we pray:* ◆ *That people everywhere may know and understand the truth embodied in the Catholic Church, we pray:* ◆

Our Father . . .

Source of life,
you give us this special day,
    Laetare Sunday,
to celebrate your wonderful work
in and through our Lenten fast.
Sustain us during the remainder of
    our Lenten observance
as we prepare to walk the road
    to Calvary,
finding a cross, an empty tomb,
and the glory of your redeeming love.
We ask this through our Lord Jesus
    Christ, your Son,
who lives and reigns with you in the
    unity of the Holy Spirit,
one God, forever and ever. Amen.

✠ *Be with me, Lord, when I am
in trouble.*

✙ *Blessed are those who dwell in your house, O Lord. They never cease to praise you.*

PSALM 145   page 421

READING   Matthew 1:16, 18–21, 24a

Jacob was the father of Joseph, the husband of Mary. Of her was born Jesus who is called the Christ.

Now this is how the birth of Jesus Christ came about. When his mother Mary was betrothed to Joseph, but before they lived together, she was found with child through the Holy Spirit. Joseph her husband, since he was a righteous man, yet unwilling to expose her to shame, decided to divorce her quietly. Such was his intention when, behold, the angel of the Lord appeared to him in a dream and said, "Joseph, son of David, do not be afraid to take Mary your wife into your home. For it is through the Holy Spirit that this child has been conceived in her. She will bear a son and you are to name him Jesus, because he will save his people from their sins." When Joseph awoke, he did as the angel of the Lord had commanded him and took his wife into his home.

REFLECTION

Usually, we are least willing to trust when life seems to make no sense at all. We become wary of everything and everyone, almost to the point of paranoia. We find in St. Joseph a different reaction. Understandably distressed at Mary's unexpected pregnancy, he accepts God's message, choosing trust over fear and faith over failure. St. Joseph is a model of letting go of fear and placing our trust in God, especially when it seems most difficult.

PRAYERS   *others may be added*

Through the intercession of St. Joseph, we pray:

◆ Lord, make us holy.

That you may help us trust in your saving power, we pray: ◆ *That you may help us to care for expectant parents, we pray:* ◆ *That you may help us to be open to the messages of angels, we pray:* ◆ *That you may help us to provide for all in our care, we pray:* ◆

Our Father . . .

God of all holiness,
you revealed your plan of salvation to
    St. Joseph.
Help us to understand your ways,
to trust in your providence, and
to be holy and humble in your sight.
We ask this through our Lord Jesus
    Christ, your Son,
who lives and reigns with you in the
    unity of the Holy Spirit,
one God, forever and ever. Amen.

✙ *Blessed are those who dwell in your house, O Lord. They never cease to praise you.*

✝ *Be with me, Lord, when I am*
in trouble.

PSALM 91 *page 415*

READING *John 5:9b–16*

Now that day was a sabbath. So the Jews said to the man who was cured, "It is the sabbath, and it is not lawful for you to carry your mat." He answered them, "The man who made me well told me, 'Take up your mat and walk.'" They asked him, "Who is the man who told you, 'Take it up and walk'?" The man who was healed did not know who it was, for Jesus had slipped away, since there was a crowd there. After this Jesus found him in the temple area and said to him, "Look, you are well; do not sin any more, so that nothing worse may happen to you." The man went and told the Jews that Jesus was the one who had made him well. Therefore, the Jews began to persecute Jesus because he did this on a sabbath.

REFLECTION

The sick man in today's Gospel did not understand God's miracle and sign of healing even though he directly benefited from the saving action of Jesus. Quite often, we are like the sick man, receiving God's curing grace and healing forgiveness, but not comprehending the power and authority of the one from whom all truth flows. We are called to recognize God's extraordinary action in our lives so that we may be able to take up our mat and walk in a
world longing to know a Messiah who lives and reigns forever.

PRAYERS *others may be added*

Recognizing God's healing powers, we pray:

◆ By your cross, set us free.

That all may know your mercy and forgiveness, we pray: ◆ *That all may know your compassion and love, we pray:* ◆ *That all may know your might and authority, we pray:* ◆ *That all may know your justice and peace, we pray:* ◆

Our Father . . .

God of redemption,
you continually paint and color
   our lives
with words and actions of hope.
May we see through
our blindness and uncertainty
the miracle of your overflowing
grace and truth.
Grant this through Jesus Christ our
   Lord. Amen.

✝ *Be with me, Lord, when I am*
in trouble.

✝ *Be with me, Lord, when I am*
in trouble.

PSALM 91   *page 415*

READING   *John 5:17–24*

Jesus answered the Jews: "My Father is at work until now, so I am at work." For this reason they tried all the more to kill him, because he not only broke the sabbath but he also called God his own father, making himself equal to God.

Jesus answered and said to them, "Amen, amen, I say to you, the Son cannot do anything on his own, but only what he sees the Father doing; for what he does, the Son will do also. For the Father loves the Son and shows him everything that he himself does, and he will show him greater works than these, so that you may be amazed. For just as the Father raises the dead and gives life, so also does the Son give life to whomever he wishes. Nor does the Father judge anyone, but he has given all judgment to the Son, so that all may honor the Son just as they honor the Father. Whoever does not honor the Son does not honor the Father who sent him. Amen, amen, I say to you, whoever hears my word and believes in the one who sent me has eternal life and will not come to condemnation, but has passed from death to life."

REFLECTION

Jesus identifies his power and authority with that of the Father. And, just as the Father is the source of life, the Son, too, is full of life. That life is shared with all who become sons and daughters of God. Each act of love, each act of belief, each act of faith is life growing within us, so that when physical death occurs, our life is unconquerable. Christ will judge us on how truly alive we are as we appear at the judgment seat.

PRAYERS   *others may be added*

Looking to the living God, we pray:

◆ By your cross, set us free.

That the clergy may strive to be life for the Church, we pray: ◆ *That we may act in life-giving ways, we pray:* ◆ *That we may respect life in all its forms, we pray:* ◆ *That the dead may have life eternal, we pray:* ◆

Our Father . . .

Father, source of all life,
through our Baptism
we were buried and brought to new
    life with your Son.
When we are discouraged by
    our weakness,
help us to rely on your saving power.
We ask this through Christ our Lord.
    Amen.

✝ *Be with me, Lord, when I am*
in trouble.

✢ *Be with me, Lord, when I am
in trouble.*

PSALM 91   *page 415*

READING   *John 5:32–38*

[Jesus said,] "But there is another who
testifies on my behalf, and I know that
the testimony he gives on my behalf is
true. You sent emissaries to John, and
he testified to the truth. I do not accept
human testimony, but I say this so that
you may be saved. He was a burning
and shining lamp, and for a while you
were content to rejoice in his light. But
I have testimony greater than John's.
The works that the Father gave me to
accomplish, these works that I perform
testify on my behalf that the Father has
sent me. Moreover, the Father who sent
me has testified on my behalf. But you
have never heard his voice nor seen his
form, and you do not have his word
remaining in you, because you do not
believe in the one whom he has sent."

REFLECTION

*Woven throughout scripture are images of
light: the separation of day and night, the
vision of a burning bush, a pillar of fire
guiding the Hebrews to the Promised Land,
a fiery furnace manifesting God's salvation, a lamp for all to see, and tongues of
flame signifying the presence of the Holy
Spirit. Light is used as a symbol of that
which is good, holy, and true. Jesus testifies before the Jews and all of us today his
authority as the one, true lamp burning
with God's mission and lighting the way
to salvation.*

PRAYERS   *others may be added*

*Professing our faith in the one, true
Light, we pray:*

◆ By your cross, set us free.

*That we may see Jesus, our pillar of fire,
guiding us through the darkness of life,
we pray:* ◆ *That we may be cleansed from
sin by God's fiery furnace of purification,
we pray:* ◆ *That we may be a lamp
enflamed with the love of God, we pray:* ◆
*That our faith may be like tongues
of flame, igniting the world ablaze with
God's freeing word, we pray:* ◆

Our Father . . .

God of life,
you call us out of the darkness of sin
    and pain
to wash us with your forgiveness,
clothe us with your cloth of
    compassion,
and anoint us with the oil of
    salvation.
Renew in us our Lenten promises
so that we may recognize the wisdom
    and light
revealed in the cross of redemption.
We ask this through Jesus Christ our
    Lord. Amen.

✢ *Be with me, Lord, when I am
in trouble.*

✚ *Be with me, Lord, when I am*
in trouble.

PSALM 91   *page 415*

READING   *John 7:1–2, 10, 25–30*

Jesus moved about within Galilee; he did not wish to travel in Judea, because the Jews were trying to kill him. But the Jewish feast of Tabernacles was near.

But when his brothers had gone up to the feast, he himself also went up, not openly but as it were in secret.

Some of the inhabitants of Jerusalem said, "Is he not the one they are trying to kill? And look, he is speaking openly and they say nothing to him. Could the authorities have realized that he is the Christ? But we know where he is from. When the Christ comes, no one will know where he is from." So Jesus cried out in the temple area as he was teaching and said, "You know me and also know where I am from. Yet I did not come on my own, but the one who sent me, whom you do not know, is true. I know him, because I am from him, and he sent me." So they tried to arrest him, but no one laid a hand upon him, because his hour had not yet come.

REFLECTION

The people are wondering, who is this Jesus? But how can they know Jesus, when they do not know God the Father? Their skepticism about Jesus is based on their notions of the Father. Jesus is challenging the very foundations of their beliefs. This challenge is also given to us. Do we have shallow images of God? This Lent, let us *take the time to see if our image of God is faulty when held up to the light of Jesus' message.*

PRAYERS   *others may be added*

Through the intercession of St. Toribio, we pray:

◆ By your cross, set us free.

That we may have an image of God that spurs us into concern for oppressed peoples, we pray: ◆ *That we may speak openly of our faith in the true God, we pray:* ◆ *That we may never wish harm to others, we pray:* ◆ *That we may have a zeal for souls, we pray:* ◆

Our Father . . .

Loving God,
you make yourself known through all
    your works.
Open our eyes that we may see your
    majesty,
open our ears that we may hear of
    your wondrous deeds,
and open our mouths that we may
    sing your praises
in the company of all the saints.
Grant this through Christ our Lord.
    Amen.

✚ *Be with me, Lord, when I am*
in trouble.

✚ *Be with me, Lord, when I am in trouble.*

PSALM 91 page 415

READING John 7:40–46

Some in the crowd who heard these words of Jesus said, "This is truly the Prophet." Others said, "This is the Christ." But others said, "The Christ will not come from Galilee, will he? Does not Scripture say that the Christ will be of David's family and come from Bethlehem, the village where David lived?" So a division occurred in the crowd because of him. Some of them even wanted to arrest him, but no one laid hands on him.

So the guards went to the chief priests and Pharisees, who asked them, "Why did you not bring him?" The guards answered, "Never before has anyone spoken like this man."

REFLECTION

Tension is rising within the crowd regarding the identity and authority of Jesus. Some believe he is a prophet, while others believe he is the Christ! Many individuals can't grasp the idea that the Messiah could come from Galilee. Lent challenges us to name our sin of complacency and proclaim the identity of the true Christ to a world filled with other gods—idols of materialism, consumerism, and power. In the spirit of the guards in today's reading, may we tell the Pharisees of this world that no other man has ever spoken the words of salvation in the way Jesus Christ did—for he is salvation!

PRAYERS *others may be added*

Claiming Jesus Christ as Lord and Savior, we pray:

◆ By your cross, set us free.

That you may give us strength to overcome sin in our lives, we pray: ◆
That you may give us strength to rid our world of false gods, we pray: ◆
That you may give us courage to stand up for what is right and good, we pray: ◆
That you may give us courage to proclaim the greatness of our Messiah from Galilee, we pray: ◆

Our Father . . .

O God, source of every blessing,
you gave us your Son, Jesus,
to enlighten our sinful minds
    and hearts.
Raise us as models of sacrifice
    and repentance
so that we may witness to your Word
    made flesh,
crucified on a tree for the salvation
    of humanity.
We ask this through Jesus Christ our
    Lord. Amen.

✚ *Be with me, Lord, when I am in trouble.*

✝ *Be with me, Lord, when I am
in trouble.*

PSALM 91   *page 415*

READING   *John 8:3–11*

Then the scribes and the Pharisees brought a woman who had been caught in adultery and made her stand in the middle. They said to him, "Teacher, this woman was caught in the very act of committing adultery. Now in the law, Moses commanded us to stone such women. So what do you say?" They said this to test him, so that they could have some charge to bring against him. Jesus bent down and began to write on the ground with his finger. But when they continued asking him, he straightened up and said to them, "Let the one among you who is without sin be the first to throw a stone at her." Again he bent down and wrote on the ground. And in response, they went away one by one, beginning with the elders. So he was left alone with the woman before him. Then Jesus straightened up and said to her, "Woman, where are they? Has no one condemned you?" She replied, "No one, sir." Then Jesus said, "Neither do I condemn you. Go, and from now on do not sin any more."

REFLECTION

The woman caught in adultery is saved by Jesus: saved from death, saved from sin. Without asking, she is forgiven. The only condition is that she go and sin no more. We are that woman. We are saved from sin, from death, without even asking to be saved. We too have been given this great gift of forgiveness. We cannot not earn this gift, we can only offer thanksgiving. Acts of penance serve as reminders to offer our sorrow and thanks to God.

PRAYERS   *others may be added*

Claiming Jesus Christ as Lord and Savior, we pray:

◆ By your cross, set us free.

For those committing public sin, we pray: ◆ *For those who condemn others, we pray:* ◆ *For those who find it difficult to forgive, we pray:* ◆ *For those preparing for Baptism and full communion, we pray:* ◆

Our Father . . .

Father in heaven,
your Son accepted the cross out of
    love for us.
May we look to the cross, the sign of
    your forgiveness,
and live lives of holiness.
We ask this through our Lord Jesus
    Christ, your Son,
who lives and reigns with you in the
    unity of the Holy Spirit,
one God, forever and ever. Amen.

✝ *Be with me, Lord, when I am
in trouble.*

✦ *Here am I, Lord; I come to do your will.*

PSALM 40 *page 411*

READING *Luke 1:38*

Mary said, "Behold, I am the handmaid of the Lord. May it be done to me according to your word." Then the angel departed from her.

REFLECTION

Today is the solemnity of the Annunciation of the Lord. The Gospel for this solemnity proclaims the story of a poor and humble virgin, Mary, who said "yes" to God's plan of salvation, even though she might be scorned or cast aside to the margins of society. Mary announced the reign of God by offering her entire self to house and nourish God's Word become flesh. Venerating Mary as a model of discipleship, may we emulate her and say "yes" to God in every way. Then, like Mary, we can change and transform the human story!

PRAYERS *others may be added*

Following in the footsteps of Mary, we pray:

◆ By your cross, set us free.

That we embrace God's will with open hearts, we pray: ◆ *That we may be sincere and merciful disciples drawing others to Christ, we pray:* ◆ *That we renew humanity with our simple "yes" to God, we pray:* ◆ *That we embody the humility of Mary, our Mother, we pray:* ◆

Our Father . . .

God of the poor and lowly,
you called your daughter, Mary,
to bear your Word of life to the world.
Enkindle in us the desire this
    Lenten season
to be authentic disciples,
giving witness to your reconciling
    action
within our lives and throughout
    history.
We ask this through our Lord Jesus
    Christ, your Son,
who lives and reigns with you and the
    Holy Spirit,
one God, forever and ever. Amen.

✦ *Here am I, Lord; I come to do your will.*

✝ *Be with me, Lord, when I am in trouble.*

PSALM 91   *page 415*

READING   *John 8:25–30*

So they [the Pharisees] said to him, "Who are you?" Jesus said to them, "What I told you from the beginning. I have much to say about you in condemnation. But the one who sent me is true, and what I heard from him I tell the world." They did not realize that he was speaking to them of the Father. So Jesus said to them, "When you lift up the Son of Man, then you will realize that I AM, and that I do nothing on my own, but I say only what the Father taught me. The one who sent me is with me. He has not left me alone, because I always do what is pleasing to him." Because he spoke this way, many came to believe in him.

REFLECTION

Once again Jesus is turning our expectations on their heads. He says that his glory will be fully apparent when he is lifted up on the cross. This can only be understood if we know the Father, the great I AM, as the one who offers us his Son on the cross as the great sign of his love for us. Jesus will not be alone on the cross because the Father is there; likewise, we are never alone.

PRAYERS   *others may be added*

With understanding hearts, we pray:

◆ By your cross, set us free.

That we may be open to the surprising ways of God, we pray: ◆ That we may turn to Jesus to learn of the Father's love, we pray: ◆ That we may glory in the cross of Christ, we pray: ◆ That the world may see God's love in the crucified Christ, we pray: ◆

Our Father . . .

Father of love,
your tender compassion is
   without end.
You sent your Son to anoint creation
   with your love.
Help us to look to your Son for
   example and strength
as we carry our own burdening cross.
Grant this through Christ our Lord.
   Amen.

✝ *Be with me, Lord, when I am in trouble.*

✝ *Be with me, Lord, when I am
in trouble.*

PSALM 91   *page 415*

READING   *John 8:31–37*

Jesus said to those Jews who believed in him, "If you remain in my word, you will truly be my disciples, and you will know the truth, and the truth will set you free." They answered him, "We are descendants of Abraham and have never been enslaved to anyone. How can you say, 'You will become free'?" Jesus answered them, "Amen, amen, I say to you, everyone who commits sin is a slave of sin. A slave does not remain in a household forever, but a son always remains. So if the Son frees you, then you will truly be free. I know that you are descendants of Abraham. But you are trying to kill me, because my word has no room among you."

REFLECTION

During this Lenten season we are fasting, abstaining, giving, and repenting so that our souls will be filled with the body and blood of eternal life. As we approach Holy Week, let us make room in our lives to remain with the Word made flesh who will be scourged, crucified, and left to die on a cross.

PRAYERS   *others may be added*

Creating room for the Word made flesh, we pray:

◆ By your cross, set us free.

That our fasting frees our heart from sin, we pray: ◆ *That our abstaining frees our heart from evil, we pray:* ◆ *That our giving frees our hearts from injustice, we pray:* ◆ *That our repenting frees us to love God and his saving Word, we pray:* ◆

Our Father . . .

God of all wisdom,
you scatter the seeds of freedom,
    truth, and hope
upon our desolate and sinful lives.
Journey with us as we try to make
    room and space
in our hearts for your
    reconciling message
to take root and grow.
We ask this in your name. Amen.

✝ *Be with me, Lord, when I am
in trouble.*

✝ *Be with me, Lord, when I am in trouble.*

PSALM 91   *page 415*

READING   *John 8:51–59*

Jesus said to the Jews: "Amen, amen, I say to you, whoever keeps my word will never see death." So the Jews said to him, "Now we are sure that you are possessed. Abraham died, as did the prophets, yet you say, 'Whoever keeps my word will never taste death.' Are you greater than our father Abraham, who died? Or the prophets, who died? Who do you make yourself out to be?" Jesus answered, "If I glorify myself, my glory is worth nothing; but it is my Father who glorifies me, of whom you say, 'He is our God.' You do not know him, but I know him. And if I should say that I do not know him, I would be like you a liar. But I do know him and I keep his word. Abraham your father rejoiced to see my day; he saw it and was glad." So the Jews said to him, "You are not yet fifty years old and you have seen Abraham?" Jesus said to them, "Amen, amen, I say to you, before Abraham came to be, I AM." So they picked up stones to throw at him; but Jesus hid and went out of the temple area.

REFLECTION

Jesus is making bolder and bolder claims. He is fully aware of his identity. He is trying to be clear to those who believe in the unity Jesus shares with the Father. He even uses the very name of God for himself:
I AM, the meaning of Yahweh! Jesus' message has an urgency that reflects the nearness of the events of Holy Week. May we be bold in our faith in Christ and throw away the stones of cynicism.

PRAYERS   *others may be added*

Standing boldly before our God, we pray:

◆ By your cross, set us free.

Free us from cynicism, we pray: ◆
Free the world from slavery to sin, we pray: ◆ *Free us from our preconceived notions of God, we pray:* ◆ *Free the dead from their sins, we pray:* ◆

Our Father . . .

Saving God,
you give us this Lenten season
to know the urgency of your love.
Send your Holy Spirit to inspire us
to lead lives worthy of your
    generosity.
We ask this through Christ our Lord.
    Amen.

✝ *Be with me, Lord, when I am in trouble.*

✝ *Be with me, Lord, when I am*
in trouble.

PSALM 91   *page 415*

READING   *John 10:31–39*

The Jews picked up rocks to stone Jesus. Jesus answered them, "I have shown you many good works from my Father. For which of these are you trying to stone me?" The Jews answered him, "We are not stoning you for a good work but for blasphemy. You, a man, are making yourself God." Jesus answered them, "Is it not written in your law, 'I said, "You are gods" '? If it calls them gods to whom the word of God came, and Scripture cannot be set aside, can you say that the one whom the Father has consecrated and sent into the world blasphemes because I said, 'I am the Son of God'? If I do not perform my Father's works, do not believe me; but if I perform them, even if you do not believe me, believe the works, so that you may realize and understand that the Father is in me and I am in the Father." Then they tried again to arrest him; but he escaped from their power.

REFLECTION

As we prepare our hearts to walk with Jesus on the harsh and cold road to Golgatha during Holy Week, we need to remove the stones of anger and injustice from our lives. By ridding ourselves of sin and evil, we will no longer be like those who tried to stone Jesus with their hardened and disbelieving hearts. Lent calls us to let go of everything that weighs us down and hinders us from carrying the cross of Jesus, wiping his bleeding face, and remaining with him during his final hour of death.

PRAYERS   *others may be added*

Finding hope in the power of the cross, we pray:

◆ By your cross, set us free.

That the Church may be a living sign of reconciliation, we pray: ◆ *That the Church may renew her commitment to the poor, we pray:* ◆ *That the Church may heal the world of division and pain, we pray:* ◆ *That the Church may challenge all people to live a life of repentance, we pray:* ◆

Our Father . . .

God in heaven,
you deliver and redeem us
from the terror of evil.
Help us cast the stones from our lives
so that we may know
your promise of eternal life.
We ask this through Jesus Christ our
     Lord. Amen.

✝ *Be with me, Lord, when I am*
in trouble.

✝ *Be with me, Lord, when I am*
in trouble.

PSALM 91 *page 415*

READING *John 11:45–53*

Many of the Jews who had come to Mary and seen what Jesus had done began to believe in him. But some of them went to the Pharisees and told them what Jesus had done. So the chief priests and the Pharisees convened the Sanhedrin and said, "What are we going to do? This man is performing many signs. If we leave him alone, all will believe in him, and the Romans will come and take away both our land and our nation." But one of them, Caiaphas, who was high priest that year, said to them, "You know nothing, nor do you consider that it is better for you that one man should die instead of the people, so that the whole nation may not perish." He did not say this on his own, but since he was high priest for that year, he prophesied that Jesus was going to die for the nation, and not only for the nation, but also to gather into one the dispersed children of God. So from that day on they planned to kill him.

REFLECTION

Today we see why the actions of Jesus lead to so much anxiety in the local leaders. The Sanhedrin's fear of losing more to the Romans leads directly to their desire to kill Jesus. What are we afraid of? What holds us back from following the Lord? The bold actions of Jesus teach us that living out of fear and anxiety is actually a form of slavery. Ironically, all the anxious plans of the Sanhedrin did not prevent the Romans from later destroying Jerusalem and their great temple.*

PRAYERS *others may be added*

Boldly bringing our petitions before the Lord, we pray:

◆ By your cross set us free.

That world leaders may work for peace among nations, we pray: ◆ That Church leaders may bravely live and teach the Gospel, we pray: ◆ That we may live in freedom as sons and daughters of God, we pray: ◆ That we may work for an end to all forms of slavery, we pray: ◆

Our Father . . .

Father,
your loving ways set us free.
May our Lenten observances
    unshackle our fearful hearts,
prepare us to embrace the Paschal
    Mystery, and
lead us to new life in your Son,
who is Lord forever and ever. Amen.

✝ *Be with me, Lord, when I am*
in trouble.

✚ *My God, my God, why have you abandoned me?*

PSALM 22 *page 406*

READING *Luke 19:36–40*

As he [Jesus] rode along, the people were spreading their cloaks on the road; and now as he was approaching the slope of the Mount of Olives, the whole multitude of his disciples began to praise God aloud with joy for all the mighty deeds they had seen. They proclaimed: "Blessed is the king who comes / in the name of the Lord. / Peace in heaven / and glory in the highest." Some of the Pharisees in the crowd said to him, "Teacher, rebuke your disciples." He said in reply, "I tell you, if they keep silent, the stones will cry out!"

REFLECTION

Here is Jesus at the height of his popularity: he triumphantly enters Jerusalem with the crowds waving palm branches and lining his path with their cloaks. We can hear the shouting. But the shouts will change. The cross is only a few days away. It's as if we need to hear the hosannahs of today in order to fully appreciate the sound of the whip ripping flesh and the crowd crying, "Crucify him!" What sounds do we make in the presence of Christ?

PRAYERS *others may be added*

Adoring the Lord, we pray:

◆ Lord, bring us your salvation.

That the Church may proclaim Jesus our Lord, we pray: ◆ That those about to be baptized and brought into full communion with the Church may shout the praises of the Lord, we pray: ◆ That world leaders may follow the example of servant leadership of Jesus, we pray: ◆ That the sound of peace may be heard throughout the earth, we pray: ◆

Our Father . . .

Almighty God,
you gave us your Son as a model
    of humility.
He emptied himself of glory and
    dwelt among us.
May we always sing his praises,
remember his sacrifice on the
    cross, and
be raised with him on the last day.
We ask this through our Lord Jesus
    Christ, your Son,
who lives and reigns with you in the
    unity of the Holy Spirit,
one God, forever and ever. Amen.

✚ *My God, my God, why have you abandoned me?*

✚ *My God, my God, why have you abandoned me?*

PSALM 22 *page 406*

READING *John 12:1–8*

Six days before Passover Jesus came to Bethany, where Lazarus was, whom Jesus had raised from the dead. They gave a dinner for him there, and Martha served, while Lazarus was one of those reclining at table with him. Mary took a liter of costly perfumed oil made from genuine aromatic nard and anointed the feet of Jesus and dried them with her hair; the house was filled with the fragrance of the oil. Then Judas the Iscariot, one of his disciples, and the one who would betray him, said, "Why was this oil not sold for three hundred days' wages and given to the poor?" He said this not because he cared about the poor but because he was a thief and held the money bag and used to steal the contributions. So Jesus said, "Leave her alone. Let her keep this for the day of my burial. You always have the poor with you, but you do not always have me."

REFLECTION

As we journey through Holy Week, we are reminded that we have little time to prepare ourselves to witness the greatest act of love: Jesus handing his life over so that we might know God's saving mercy and forgiveness. We need to live our penitential practices with even greater fidelity and commitment, enabling us to leave behind the many ways we have betrayed our Lord, like Judas the Iscariot. Let us move forward during this sacred week and ask God to anoint our brokenness; thus, empowering us to remain with Jesus in his darkest hour.

PRAYERS *others may be added*

Turning away from a life of sin, we pray:

◆ Lord, bring us your salvation.

That we continue our fast from the empty promises of this world with eagerness and joy, we pray: ◆ *That we renounce sin and evil in our lives, we pray:* ◆ *That we recognize God's great act of salvation, we pray:* ◆ *That we vow to proclaim the message of the cross, we pray:* ◆

Our Father . . .

Word of God,
you call us to walk with you
as you lay down your life
for the salvation of humanity.
Give us the strength and power
to approach your redeeming cross
with repentant hearts.
We ask this in your name. Amen.

✚ *My God, my God, why have you abandoned me?*

✝ *My God, my God, why have you abandoned me?*

PSALM 22   page 406

READING   *John 13:21–30*

Reclining at table with his disciples, Jesus was deeply troubled and testified, "Amen, amen, I say to you, one of you will betray me." The disciples looked at one another, at a loss as to whom he meant. One of his disciples, the one whom Jesus loved, was reclining at Jesus' side. So Simon Peter nodded to him to find out whom he meant. He leaned back against Jesus' chest and said to him, "Master, who is it?" Jesus answered, "It is the one to whom I hand the morsel after I have dipped it." So he dipped the morsel and took it and handed it to Judas, son of Simon the Iscariot. After Judas took the morsel, Satan entered him. So Jesus said to him, "What you are going to do, do quickly." Now none of those reclining at table realized why he said this to him. Some thought that since Judas kept the money bag, Jesus had told him, "Buy what we need for the feast," or to give something to the poor. So Judas took the morsel and left at once. And it was night.

REFLECTION

Today we hear a portion of the Last Supper narrative. Jesus is quite clear that he is aware of Judas's betrayal. Although Judas leaves before he can partake of the Bread of Life, Jesus still makes sure to feed him. Who are we in this scene? Judas, the betrayer? The apostle reclining with Christ? The confused disciples? Or, Jesus who nourishes even those who betray him?

PRAYERS   *others may be added*

Looking to Christ, we pray:

◆ Lord, bring us your salvation.

For those who have turned their backs on Christ, we pray: ◆ For those who have been betrayed, we pray: ◆ For those who nourish our hearts and minds, we pray: ◆ For those who nourish our bodies, we pray: ◆

Our Father . . .

All-powerful God,
you sustain us with your Holy Spirit.
May we always look to your Son, the
    Bread of Life,
for nourishment and inspiration,
so that our lives may be strengthened
    by the cross of Christ.
Grant this in the name of Jesus the
    Lord. Amen.

✝ *My God, my God, why have you abandoned me?*

✟ *My God, my God, why have you abandoned me?*

PSALM 22   *page 406*

READING   *Matthew 26:19–25*

The disciples then did as Jesus had ordered, and prepared the Passover.

When it was evening, he reclined at table with the Twelve. And while they were eating, he said, "Amen, I say to you, one of you will betray me." Deeply distressed at this, they began to say to him one after another, "Surely it is not I, Lord?" He said in reply, "He who has dipped his hand into the dish with me is the one who will betray me. The Son of Man indeed goes, as it is written of him, but woe to that man by whom the Son of Man is betrayed. It would be better for that man if he had never been born." Then Judas, his betrayer, said in reply, "Surely it is not I, Rabbi?" He answered, "You have said so."

REFLECTION

What would Jesus find if he were to look into our hearts? Would he find a heart tainted by evil ready to hand him over or a repentant heart ready to remain with him at the foot of the cross? As we enter the Triduum, the three high holy days of the liturgical year, let us ask God to cleanse and purify our hearts so that when we drink of the blood of salvation, Jesus Christ, our Rabbi, will not find a betrayer, like Judas, ready to orchestrate his death.

PRAYERS   *others may be added*

Renouncing the glamour of evil, we pray:

◆ Lord, bring us your salvation.

For us, may we remain faithful on our journey to the cross, we pray: ◆
For priests, may they lift high the cross of Jesus Christ through word and deed, we pray: ◆ *For bishops, may they embody the message of the cross, we pray:* ◆
For the Pope, may he proclaim the cross to a world in need of light and peace, we pray: ◆

Our Father . . .

God of mercy,
you call us into the Passion of
    your Son.
May we embark on this journey of
    pain and suffering,
gaining insight and understanding
into your amazing gift of love
    and redemption.
We ask this through Jesus Christ
    our Lord. Amen.

✟ *My God, my God, why have you abandoned me?*

✝ *Love one another as I have loved you.*

PSALM 116 *page 418*

READING *John 13:4–9, 12b–15*

He [Jesus] rose from supper and took off his outer garments. He took a towel and tied it around his waist. Then he poured water into a basin and began to wash the disciples' feet and dry them with the towel around his waist. He came to Simon Peter, who said to him, "Master, are you going to wash my feet?" Jesus answered and said to him, "What I am doing, you do not understand now, but you will understand later." Peter said to him, "You will never wash my feet." Jesus answered him, "Unless I wash you, you will have no inheritance with me." Simon Peter said to him, "Master, then not only my feet, but my hands and head as well."

"Do you realize what I have done for you? You call me 'teacher' and 'master,' and rightly so, for indeed I am. If I, therefore, the master and teacher, have washed your feet, you ought to wash one another's feet. I have given you a model to follow, so that as I have done for you, you should also do."

REFLECTION

Teach by example, lead by serving, live by dying, first shall be last, the humble shall be exalted—Jesus always does the unexpected and commands the outrageous. Peter has just been given the Bread of Life and the Wine of Salvation, yet he still has trouble understanding what Jesus wants. Peter is not confused because Jesus is unclear. Peter is confused because Jesus clearly wants what Peter is not expecting. Are we ready to follow Jesus' lead? Will we serve, feed, wash, and die? Or will we simply be confused?

PRAYERS *others may be added*

Cleansed and fed by Christ, we pray:

◆ Lord, bring us your salvation.

May the Church continue to feed and wash both body and soul, we pray: ◆
May bishops, priests, and deacons lead by example and service, we pray: ◆
May the Body and Blood of Christ strengthen us on our journey, we pray: ◆
May we receive the grace to do God's will in all our actions, we pray: ◆

Our Father . . .

Ever-loving Father,
you welcome us as sons
and daughters
in the cleansing waters of Baptism.
May the Bread of Life and the Cup
of Salvation
strengthen us for the
cleansing service
commanded by your Son,
who lives and reigns with you in
the unity
of the Holy Spirit, one God, forever
and ever. Amen.

✝ *Love one another as I have loved you.*

✚ *Christ became obedient to the point of death, even death on a cross.*

PSALM 22 *page 406*

READING *John 19:16b–19, 23, 28–30*

So they took Jesus, and, carrying the cross himself, he went out to what is called the Place of the Skull, in Hebrew, Golgotha. There they crucified him, and with him two others, one on either side, with Jesus in the middle. Pilate also had an inscription written and put on the cross. It read, "Jesus the Nazorean, the King of the Jews."

When the soldiers had crucified Jesus, they took his clothes and divided them into four shares, a share for each soldier.

After this, aware that everything was now finished, in order that the Scripture might be fulfilled, Jesus said, "I thirst." There was a vessel filled with common wine. So they put a sponge soaked in wine on a sprig of hyssop and put it up to his mouth. When Jesus had taken the wine, he said, "It is finished." And bowing his head, he handed over the spirit.

REFLECTION

Stripped. Scourged. Bleeding. Ridiculed. Crucified. This is our Good Friday story: the story of one man, Jesus Christ, who changed the course of salvation by loving us so much that he died a horrific, painful death, witnessing to the glory and power of our all-forgiving God. Let us claim this story! Let us live this story! Let us weep for our Lamb was slaughtered and left to die! But, most of all, let us lift high the cross for all to see God's salvific action and kneel before our bruised and beaten Messiah who loved, bowed, prayed, died, and redeemed.

PRAYERS *others may be added*

With great sorrow and sadness, we pray:

◆ Lord, bring us your salvation.

For the Church, that she may be guided by God's saving power, we pray: ◆ For the clergy and laity, that they may remain faithful to their vocation, we pray: ◆ For the catechumens, that they may find peace in the waters of new life, we pray; ◆ For nonbelievers, that their hearts may be turned toward the cross of salvation, we pray: ◆

Our Father . . .

Crucified Lord,
you call us to the foot of your cross
to witness God's saving action.
Give us the courage to wait with you
so that we may see reconciling
    love manifested
in your beaten, bruised, and
    broken body.
We ask this in your name. Amen.

✚ *Christ became obedient to the point of death, even death on a cross.*

✠ *Come, let us worship Christ,*
who for our sake suffered death and
was buried.

PSALM 22   *page 406*

READING   *Luke 23:50–56**

Now there was a virtuous and righteous man named Joseph who, though he was a member of the council, had not consented to their plan of action. He came from the Jewish town of Arimathea and was awaiting the kingdom of God. He went to Pilate and asked for the body of Jesus. After he had taken the body down, he wrapped it in a linen cloth and laid him in a rock-hewn tomb in which no one had yet been buried. It was the day of preparation, and the sabbath was about to begin. The women who had come from Galilee with him followed behind, and when they had seen the tomb and the way in which his body was laid in it, they returned and prepared spices and perfumed oils. Then they rested on the sabbath according to the commandment.

REFLECTION

Today Christ the Lord lies in the tomb. The Lord of all has descended to hell. The one who was betrayed in a garden, who was crucified in a garden, and was buried in a garden has descended to hell to save those who sinned in a garden. Humans were not created to be slaves to sin and prisoners of hell. Our Lord prepares the way for us into freedom. May we rise tomorrow to new life in Christ.

PRAYERS   *others may be added*

Turning to our Savior, we pray:

◆ Lord, bring us your salvation.

That all who mourn the loss of loved ones may be comforted, we pray: ◆ *That all those about to be baptized and brought into full communion may receive new life in Christ, we pray:* ◆ *That we all may die to sin and live in the goodness of the Lord, we pray:* ◆ *That all the dead may be raised on the last day, we pray:* ◆

Our Father . . .

All-powerful and ever-living God,
your Son descended to hell
to rescue those caught in the grip
   of death.
May we who have risen to new life
   in Baptism
help to release this world caught in
   the grip of sin
and give you glory through Christ
   our Lord. Amen.

✠ *Come, let us worship Christ,*
who for our sake suffered death and
was buried.

*Today's Gospel text is an excerpt from Luke's account of the Passion and death of our Lord Jesus Christ, proclaimed during Palm Sunday. Although not the prescribed reading for Holy Saturday (Luke 24:1–12 for the Vigil in the Holy Night of Easter), it is fitting for this day of mourning to reflect further upon Jesus' Passion and death.

✛ *This is the day the Lord has made;*
let us rejoice and be glad. Alleluia.

PSALM 118 *page 419*

READING *John 20:1–9*

On the first day of the week, Mary of Magdala came to the tomb early in the morning, while it was still dark, and saw the stone removed from the tomb. So she ran and went to Simon Peter and to the other disciple whom Jesus loved, and told them, "They have taken the Lord from the tomb, and we don't know where they put him." So Peter and the other disciple went out and came to the tomb. They both ran, but the other disciple ran faster than Peter and arrived at the tomb first; he bent down and saw the burial cloths there, but did not go in. When Simon Peter arrived after him, he went into the tomb and saw the burial cloths there, and the cloth that had covered his head, not with the burial cloths but rolled up in a separate place. Then the other disciple also went in, the one who had arrived at the tomb first, and he saw and believed. For they did not yet understand the Scripture that he had to rise from the dead.

REFLECTION

Let us sing with joy for our Lord has risen! On this Easter Sunday, we are invited to approach the empty tomb, see the burial cloths, and proclaim to all the earth that Christ, our Light, has burned away the darkness of sin and death so that all might know the promise of salvation. We are an

Easter people, a holy people, redeemed by God's saving action in the Resurrection of our Lord and Messiah, Jesus Christ. Today, God calls us to the glorious tomb to see what wonderful things he has done for us. Do we understand? Do we believe?

PRAYERS *others may be added*

Recognizing the Lord Jesus in our midst, we pray:

◆ Risen Lord, clothe us in your glory. Alleluia.

May we see your saving presence in each other, we pray: ◆ *May we see your redeeming love in our Church, we pray:* ◆ *May we see the hope of salvation in the lives of the newly baptized and those brought into full communion, we pray:* ◆ *May we see your life-giving promise fulfilled in our beloved dead, we pray:* ◆

Our Father . . .

Lord of life,
you raised your Son in glory,
revealing the wonder of your love.
Enliven our hearts, restore our hope,
   and renew our faith
so that all may know your gift of
   redemption
and live in Easter joy.
We ask this through our Lord Jesus
   Christ, your Son,
who lives and reigns with you in the
   unity of the Holy Sprit,
one God, forever and ever. Amen.

✛ *This is the day the Lord has made;*
let us rejoice and be glad. Alleluia.

✝ *This is the day the Lord has made;*
let us rejoice and be glad. Alleluia.

PSALM 118   *page 419*

READING   *Matthew 28:8–10*

Mary Magdalene and the other Mary went away quickly from the tomb, fearful yet overjoyed, and ran to announce the news to his disciples. And behold, Jesus met them on their way and greeted them. They approached, embraced his feet, and did him homage. Then Jesus said to them, "Do not be afraid. Go tell my brothers to go to Galilee, and there they will see me."

REFLECTION

The custom of celebrating Easter for eight days (an octave) dates from the early days of Christianity. The Easter event is the culmination of the Paschal Mystery: the life, death, and Resurrection of Jesus Christ. One day is not enough to celebrate this central belief of our faith. During this time let us ponder the meaning of the Paschal Mystery in our lives.

PRAYERS   *others may be added*

Recognizing the Lord Jesus in our midst, we pray:

◆ Risen Lord, clothe us in your glory. Alleluia.

You conquered sin; help us to overcome trials and tribulations, we pray: ◆
You rose from the dead; help us to live your life-giving message, we pray: ◆
You raised the just from the shackles of death; help us to throw off the bindings of skepticism and disbelief, we pray: ◆
You come to us with new life; help us to live Easter joy and hope, we pray: ◆

Our Father . . .

Lord of life,
you raised your Son in glory,
revealing the wonder of your love.
Enliven our hearts, restore our hope,
    and renew our faith
so that all may know your gift
    of redemption
and live in Easter joy.
We ask this through our Lord Jesus
    Christ, your Son,
who lives and reigns with you in the
    unity of the Holy Spirit,
one God, forever and ever. Amen.

✝ *This is the day the Lord has made;*
let us rejoice and be glad. Alleluia.

✛ *This is the day the Lord has made;*
let us rejoice and be glad. Alleluia.

PSALM 118   *page 419*

READING   *John 20:11–18*

Mary Magdalene stayed outside the tomb weeping. And as she wept, she bent over into the tomb and saw two angels in white sitting there, one at the head and one at the feet where the Body of Jesus had been. And they [two angels] said to her, "Woman, why are you weeping?" She said to them, "They have taken my Lord, and I don't know where they laid him." When she had said this, she turned around and saw Jesus there, but did not know it was Jesus. Jesus said to her, "Woman, why are you weeping? Whom are you looking for?" She thought it was the gardener and said to him, "Sir, if you carried him away, tell me where you laid him, and I will take him." Jesus said to her, "Mary!" She turned and said to him in Hebrew, "Rabbouni," which means Teacher. Jesus said to her, "Stop holding on to me, for I have not yet ascended to the Father. But go to my brothers and tell them, 'I am going to my Father and your Father, to my God and your God.'" Mary went and announced to the disciples, "I have seen the Lord," and then reported what he had told her.

REFLECTION

When Jesus first appears to Mary Magdalene she thinks he is a gardener, but once Jesus calls her by name she recognizes him! Although the Lord's physical appearance has changed, his voice remains the same. Easter challenges us, like Mary Magdalene, to know and heed our risen Shepherd's voice. Although he may appear in unexpected places and at unforeseen times, we are invited by the waters of Easter to see with new eyes, hear with new ears, and speak with new words.

PRAYERS   *others may be added*

Recognizing the Lord Jesus in our midst, we pray:

◆ Risen Lord, clothe us in your glory. Alleluia.

That we may see your saving presence in each other, we pray: ◆ That we may see the hope of salvation written in the lives of the newly baptized, we pray: ◆ That we may see your life-giving promise fulfilled in our beloved dead, we pray: ◆

Our Father . . .

Lord of life,
you raised your Son in glory,
revealing the wonder of your love.
Enliven our hearts, restore our hope,
    and renew our faith
so that all may know your gift
    of redemption
and live in Easter joy.
We ask this through our Lord Jesus
    Christ, your Son,
who lives and reigns with you in the
    unity of the Holy Sprit,
one God, forever and ever. Amen.

✛ *This is the day the Lord has made;*
let us rejoice and be glad. Alleluia.

✝ *This is the day the Lord has made;*
let us rejoice and be glad. Alleluia.

PSALM 118 *page 419*

READING *Luke 24:13–16, 28–32*

That very day, the first day of the week, two of Jesus' disciples were going to a village seven miles from Jerusalem called Emmaus, and they were conversing about all the things that had occurred. And it happened that while they were conversing and debating, Jesus himself drew near and walked with them, but their eyes were prevented from recognizing him. As they approached the village to which they were going, he gave the impression that he was going on farther. But they urged him, "Stay with us, for it is nearly evening and the day is almost over." So he went in to stay with them. And it happened that, while he was with them at table, he took bread, said the blessing, broke it, and gave it to them. With that their eyes were opened and they recognized him, but he vanished from their sight. Then they said to each other, "Were not our hearts burning within us while he spoke to us on the way and opened the Scriptures to us?"

REFLECTION

There is a world of difference between being lonely and being alone. Today the disciples are struggling with feelings of loneliness and abandonment over the death of Jesus. Yet, the Lord becomes present to them in the breaking of the bread, and their hearts are filled with burning love and joy!

This encounter with the Lord should be encouragement that, even though we may not see him physically, the risen Lord is always with us throughout all our times of loneliness, estrangement, and isolation.

PRAYERS *others may be added*

Recognizing the Lord Jesus in our midst, we pray:

◆ Risen Lord, clothe us in your glory. Alleluia.

You conquered sin; help us to overcome trials and tribulations, we pray: ◆
You rose from the dead; help us to live your life-giving message, we pray: ◆
You raised the just from the shackles of death; help us to throw off the bindings of skepticism and disbelief, we pray: ◆
You come to us with new life; help us to live Easter joy and hope, we pray: ◆

Our Father . . .

Lord of life,
you raised your Son in glory,
revealing the wonder of your love.
Enliven our hearts, restore our hope,
    and renew our faith
so that all may know your gift
    of redemption
and live in Easter joy.
We ask this through our Lord Jesus
    Christ, your Son,
who lives and reigns with you in the
    unity of the Holy Spirit,
one God, forever and ever. Amen.

✝ *This is the day the Lord has made;*
let us rejoice and be glad. Alleluia.

✠ *This is the day the Lord has made;*
let us rejoice and be glad. Alleluia.

PSALM 118 *page 419*

READING *Luke 24:35–40*

The disciples of Jesus recounted what had taken place along the way, and how they had come to recognize him in the breaking of bread.

While they were still speaking about this, he stood in their midst and said to them, "Peace be with you." But they were startled and terrified and thought that they were seeing a ghost. Then he said to them, "Why are you troubled? And why do questions arise in your hearts? Look at my hands and my feet, that it is I myself. Touch me and see, because a ghost does not have flesh and bones as you can see I have." And as he said this, he showed them his hands and his feet.

REFLECTION

Every Sunday we are invited to gather as a community around the altar so that we may, like the disciples on the road to Emmaus, recognize and celebrate the presence of Jesus Christ in the breaking of the bread. During Easter, we are reminded that Jesus Christ has not abandoned us, but is always present, offering himself in the Eucharist: the "source and summit" of all healing, forgiveness, and reconciliation. As our hearts rejoice, let us never forget to come to the banquet of life to touch, see, and taste the bread of salvation.

PRAYERS *others may be added*

Recognizing the Lord Jesus in our midst, we pray:

◆ Risen Lord, clothe us in your glory. Alleluia.

May we see your saving presence in each other, we pray: ◆ *May we see your redeeming love in our Church, we pray:* ◆ *May we see the hope of salvation written in the lives of the newly baptized, we pray:* ◆ *May we see your life-giving promise fulfilled in our beloved dead, we pray:* ◆

Our Father . . .

Lord of life,
you raised your Son in glory,
revealing the wonder of your love.
Enliven our hearts, restore our hope,
    and renew our faith
so that all may know your gift
    of redemption
and live in Easter joy.
We ask this through our Lord Jesus
    Christ, your Son,
who lives and reigns with you in the
    unity of the Holy Sprit,
one God, forever and ever. Amen.

✠ *This is the day the Lord has made;*
let us rejoice and be glad. Alleluia.

✝ *This is the day the Lord has made;*
let us rejoice and be glad. Alleluia.

PSALM 118   *page 419*

READING   *John 21:4–7, 12–14*

When it was already dawn, Jesus was standing on the shore; but the disciples did not realize that it was Jesus. Jesus said to them, "Children, have you caught anything to eat?" They answered him, "No." So he said to them, "Cast the net over the right side of the boat and you will find something." So they cast it, and were not able to pull it in because of the number of fish. So the disciple whom Jesus loved said to Peter, "It is the Lord." Jesus said to them, "Come, have breakfast." And none of the disciples dared to ask him, "Who are you?" because they realized it was the Lord. Jesus came over and took the bread and gave it to them, and in like manner the fish. This was now the third time Jesus was revealed to his disciples after being raised from the dead.

REFLECTION

In this Gospel the disciples have caught nothing all night. When they see Jesus, they are nearly overwhelmed with their catch. Nothing is possible without Christ. It is Christ who empowers us to do the good that we do. As the Risen Lord, Jesus is always present to us; we just need to recognize him. As Risen Lord, he is always ready to nourish us; we only need to accept his offer to feed us.

PRAYERS   *others may be added*

Recognizing the Lord Jesus in our midst, we pray:

◆ Risen Lord, clothe us in your glory. Alleluia.

You conquered sin; help us to overcome trials and tribulations, we pray: ◆
You rose from the dead; help us to live your life-giving message, we pray: ◆
You raised the just from the shackles of death; help us to throw off the bindings of skepticism and disbelief, we pray: ◆
You come to us with new life; help us to live Easter joy and hope, we pray: ◆

Our Father . . .

Lord of life,
you raised your Son in glory,
revealing the wonder of your love.
Enliven our hearts, restore our hope,
    and renew our faith
so that all may know your gift
    of redemption
and live in Easter joy.
We ask this through our Lord Jesus
    Christ, your Son,
who lives and reigns with you in the
    unity of the Holy Spirit,
one God, forever and ever. Amen.

✝ *This is the day the Lord has made;*
let us rejoice and be glad. Alleluia.

✛ *This is the day the Lord has made;*
let us rejoice and be glad. Alleluia.

PSALM 118 *page 419*

READING *Mark 16:9–15*

When Jesus had risen, early on the first day of the week, he appeared first to Mary Magdalene, out of whom he had driven seven demons. She went and told his companions who were mourning and weeping. When they heard that he was alive and had been seen by her, they did not believe.

After this he appeared in another form to two of them walking along on their way to the country. They returned and told the others; but they did not believe them either.

But later, as the Eleven were at table, he appeared to them and rebuked them for their unbelief and hardness of heart because they had not believed those who saw him after he had been raised. He said to them, "Go into the whole world and proclaim the Gospel to every creature."

REFLECTION

When we have a profound experience, we often want to keep it to ourselves rather than share it with others. Can you imagine being Mary Magdalene or the other companions who encountered the risen Christ? They, too, probably wanted to hold onto their experience of Jesus, the Christ, but he instructed them to take their sacred encounter, their holy awakening, to the world. Easter calls us not to own or possess our knowledge or experiences of the
Christ, but to spread them so that others will have the faith to say "yes" to God's gift of salvation.

PRAYERS *others may be added*

Recognizing the Lord Jesus in our midst, we pray:

◆ Risen Lord, clothe us in your glory. Alleluia.

That we may see your saving presence in each other, we pray: ◆ *That we may see your redeeming love in our Church, we pray:* ◆ *That we may see the hope of salvation written in the lives of the newly baptized, we pray:* ◆ *That we may see your life-giving promise fulfilled in our beloved dead, we pray:* ◆

Our Father . . .

Lord of life,
you raised your Son in glory,
revealing the wonder of your love.
Enliven our hearts, restore our hope,
    and renew our faith
so that all may know your gift
    of redemption
and live in Easter joy.
We ask this through our Lord Jesus
    Christ, your Son,
who lives and reigns with you in the
    unity of the Holy Sprit,
one God, forever and ever. Amen.

✛ *This is the day the Lord has made;*
let us rejoice and be glad. Alleluia.

✠ *This is the day the Lord has made;*
let us rejoice and be glad. Alleluia.

PSALM 118   *page 419*

READING   *John 20:24–29*

Thomas, called Didymus, one of the Twelve, was not with them when Jesus came. So the other disciples said to him, "We have seen the Lord." But he said to them, "Unless I see the mark of the nails in his hands and put my finger into the nailmarks and put my hand into his side, I will not believe."

Now a week later his disciples were again inside and Thomas was with them. Jesus came, although the doors were locked, and stood in their midst and said, "Peace be with you." Then he said to Thomas, "Put your finger here and see my hands, and bring your hand and put it into my side, and do not be unbelieving, but believe." Thomas answered and said to him, "My Lord and my God!" Jesus said to him, "Have you come to believe because you have seen me? Blessed are those who have not seen and have believed."

REFLECTION

"Doubting Thomas" is a familiar phrase. It is unfortunate that St. Thomas is known for his doubt. Rather, he should be known for his firm belief; he is the first person in the Gospels to acknowledge Jesus Christ as God. On this last day of the octave of Easter, Jesus, our Lord and God, speaks out to us: "Blessed are those who have not seen and have believed."

PRAYERS   *others may be added*

Recognizing the Lord Jesus in our midst, we pray:

◆ Risen Lord, clothe us in your glory. Alleluia.

You conquered sin; help us to overcome trials and tribulations, we pray: ◆
You rose from the dead; help us to live your life-giving message, we pray: ◆
You raised the just from the shackles of death; help us to throw off the bindings of skepticism and disbelief, we pray: ◆
You come to us with new life; help us to live Easter joy and hope, we pray: ◆

Our Father . . .

Lord of life,
you raised your Son in glory,
revealing the wonder of your love.
Enliven our hearts, restore our hope,
     and renew our faith
so that all may know your gift
     of redemption
and live in Easter joy.
We ask this through our Lord Jesus
     Christ, your Son,
who lives and reigns with you in the
     unity of the Holy Spirit,
one God, forever and ever. Amen.

✠ *This is the day the Lord has made;*
let us rejoice and be glad. Alleluia.

✝ *Let all the earth cry out to God with joy, alleluia.*

PSALM 66   *page 413*

READING   *John 3:4–8*

Nicodemus said to him, "How can a man once grown old be born again? Surely he cannot reenter his mother's womb and be born again, can he?" Jesus answered, "Amen, amen, I say to you, unless one is born of water and Spirit he cannot enter the Kingdom of God. What is born of flesh is flesh and what is born of spirit is spirit. Do not be amazed that I told you, 'You must be born from above.' The wind blows where it wills, and you can hear the sound it makes, but you do not know where it comes from or where it goes; so it is with everyone who is born of the Spirit."

REFLECTION

Easter is a time to renew our baptismal promises. Even though these promises, for many of us, were made many years ago, we are called to profess our faith and renew our commitment to Christ. Let us take this opportunity to profess our fidelity to Jesus Christ, be faithful to the Gospel message, and live the teachings of the Catholic Church so that the waters of Baptism flow throughout our lives and the Holy Spirit lives in our hearts.

PRAYERS   *others may be added*

Renewing our baptismal promises, we pray:

◆ Risen Lord, make all things new.

To live Easter joy, so others may know the peace of God's forgiveness, we pray: ◆
To live Easter hope, so others may know the compassion of God, we pray: ◆
To live Easter faith, so others may know the saving message of Jesus Christ, we pray: ◆ *To live Easter gratitude, so others may know the gift of the empty tomb, we pray:* ◆

Our Father . . .

God of faithfulness,
you wash your people in saving water
and anoint them with your
    Holy Spirit.
May we be a people born from above,
always living anew your promise
    of redemption.
We ask this through Jesus Christ
    our Lord.

✝ *Let all the earth cry out to God with joy, alleluia.*

✦ Let all the earth cry out to God with joy, alleluia.

PSALM 66   *page 413*

READING   *John 3:7b–15*

Jesus said to Nicodemus: "You must be born from above. The wind blows where it wills, and you can hear the sound it makes, but you do not know where it comes from or where it goes; so it is with everyone who is born of the Spirit." Nicodemus answered and said to him, "How can this happen?" Jesus answered and said to him, "You are the teacher of Israel and you do not understand this? Amen, amen, I say to you, we speak of what we know and we testify to what we have seen, but you people do not accept our testimony. If I tell you about earthly things and you do not believe, how will you believe if I tell you about heavenly things? No one has gone up to heaven except the one who has come down from heaven, the Son of Man. And just as Moses lifted up the serpent in the desert, so must the Son of Man be lifted up, so that everyone who believes in him may have eternal life."

REFLECTION

Certainly, the ways of God are mysterious, yet today Jesus says that they are not completely inscrutable. We may not see or understand the wind, but we can hear and feel it. So it is with the ways of God. We don't know all of God's purposes or every detail of providence. However, those of us who have been born of the Holy Spirit, *baptized, have been given the Son of Man, the one lifted up, so that God's plan may be revealed.*

PRAYERS   *others may be added*

Looking to the Son of Man, we pray:

◆ Risen Lord, make all things new.

That all the clergy may point to Christ as the one who saves, we pray: ◆ *That all teachers of your word may seek truth with a sincere heart, we pray:* ◆ *That all the faithful may accept the testimony of Jesus Christ, we pray:* ◆ *That all the dead may be welcomed into eternal life by Christ our Lord, we pray:* ◆

Our Father . . .

Eternal Father,
you fill us with hope by the
    Paschal Mystery.
Through our faith in your Son,
assist us to see the glory of your
    divine plan,
and may we live in Easter joy both
    here and in eternity.
We ask this through Christ our Lord.
    Amen.

✦ Let all the earth cry out to God with joy, alleluia.

✝ *Let all the earth cry out to God with joy, alleluia.*

PSALM 66   *page 413*

READING   *John 3:16–21*

God so loved the world that he gave his only-begotten Son, so that everyone who believes in him might not perish but might have eternal life. For God did not send his Son into the world to condemn the world, but that the world might be saved through him. Whoever believes in him will not be condemned, but whoever does not believe has already been condemned, because he has not believed in the name of the only-begotten Son of God. And this is the verdict, that the light came into the world, but people preferred darkness to light, because their works were evil. For everyone who does wicked things hates the light and does not come toward the light, so that his works might not be exposed. But whoever lives the truth comes to the light, so that his works may be clearly seen as done in God.

REFLECTION

Live the truth and love the light! This is our call and challenge. As Easter people, we are to live life disdaining darkness and sin and embracing the truth and light revealed in Jesus Christ, the Savior of the world. We should be filled with elation and joy, knowing that Jesus, our Lord and Messiah, came so that we would not fall to the clutches of sin and perish, but have eternal life, gazing upon the glorious throne of God. Let us be a people of the Resurrection, always walking in the light and proclaiming the truth throughout creation.

PRAYERS   *others may be added*

Living the truth and loving the light, we pray:

◆ Risen Lord, make all things new.

For those who spread the Gospel, we pray: ◆ *For those who promote vocations to religious life and priesthood, we pray:* ◆ *For those working to create a culture of life, we pray:* ◆ *For those who minister to the hungry and homeless, we pray:* ◆

Our Father . . .

Risen Christ,
you call us to be children of light
and models of truth.
May we continue to labor in the fields of life
and give witness to your saving love.
In your name we pray. Amen.

✝ *Let all the earth cry out to God with joy, alleluia.*

✝ *Let all the earth cry out to God with joy, alleluia.*

PSALM 66   *page 413*

READING   *John 3:31–36*

The one who comes from above is above all. The one who is of the earth is earthly and speaks of earthly things. But the one who comes from heaven is above all. He testifies to what he has seen and heard, but no one accepts his testimony. Whoever does accept his testimony certifies that God is trustworthy. For the one whom God sent speaks the words of God. He does not ration his gift of the Spirit. The Father loves the Son and has given everything over to him. Whoever believes in the Son has eternal life, but whoever disobeys the Son will not see life, but the wrath of God remains upon him.

REFLECTION

We live after the Resurrection. If we believe the testimony of those who came before us, we can see with the eyes of faith the fulfillment of God's promises. Jesus has been raised from the dead. He has won for us life eternal. It is time for us to give testimony to what we have seen and heard. And, we need not worry; God does not ration his gift of the Spirit.

PRAYERS   *others may be added*

Depending on God, we pray:

◆ Risen Lord, make all things new.

For those who minister in the Church, we pray: ◆ *For those who testify to the truth in the world, we pray:* ◆ *For those who have been newly baptized and brought into full communion, we pray:* ◆ *For those who do not believe, we pray:* ◆

Our Father . . .
All-knowing Father,
you sent us your Son to give
    testimony to your love.
May we be filled with your Spirit
so that we may have hearts born
    from above,
overflowing with desire to spread
    the word
of the salvation won for all.
We ask this in the name of the risen
    Lord. Amen.

✝ *Let all the earth cry out to God with joy, alleluia.*

✚ *Let all the earth cry out to God with joy, alleluia.*

PSALM 66 *page 413*

READING *John 6:5–10a, 10b–13*

When Jesus raised his eyes and saw that a large crowd was coming to him, he said to Philip, "Where can we buy enough food for them to eat?" He said this to test him, because he himself knew what he was going to do. Philip answered him, "Two hundred days' wages worth of food would not be enough for each of them to have a little." One of his disciples, Andrew, the brother of Simon Peter, said to him, "There is a boy here who has five barley loaves and two fish; but what good are these for so many?" Jesus said, "Have the people recline." So the men reclined, about five thousand in number. Then Jesus took the loaves, gave thanks, and distributed them to those who were reclining, and also as much of the fish as they wanted. When they had had their fill, he said to his disciples, "Gather the fragments left over, so that nothing will be wasted." So they collected them, and filled twelve wicker baskets with fragments from the five barley loaves that had been more than they could eat.

REFLECTION

Just as the loaves were multiplied to feed the many, so must our Easter faith increase and grow, witnessing to the Bread of Life, Jesus Christ. Our faith is not to be hidden or disguised, but should be set before all, like a feast, so that all will know the God who longs to fill our hunger and quench our thirst. Living the miracle of the multiplication of the loaves, let us move forward this Easter season, seeking to be, to give, and to live our faith.

PRAYERS *others may be added*

With fervent faith and joyful hearts, we pray:

◆ Risen Lord, make all things new.

For laypeople, that they may live the Gospel with zeal, we pray: ◆
For religious, that they may remain faithful to their vows, we pray: ◆
For priests, that they may proclaim faith with their words, we pray: ◆

Our Father . . .

God of new life,
you call us to have ardent faith
and unwavering fidelity to your
　　Gospel message.
Multiply and increase our faith
so that others will know
　　and understand
the salvific promise of Easter.
We ask this through Christ our Lord.
　　Amen.

✚ *Let all the earth cry out to God with joy, alleluia.*

✦ *Let all the earth cry out to God with joy, alleluia.*

PSALM 66   *page 413*

READING   *John 6:16–21*

When it was evening, the disciples of Jesus went down to the sea, embarked in a boat, and went across the sea to Capernaum. It had already grown dark, and Jesus had not yet come to them. The sea was stirred up because a strong wind was blowing. When they had rowed about three or four miles, they saw Jesus walking on the sea and coming near the boat, and they began to be afraid. But he said to them, "It is I. Do not be afraid." They wanted to take him into the boat, but the boat immediately arrived at the shore to which they were heading.

REFLECTION

There are all kinds of things to be afraid of: illness, unemployment, terrorism, failure, death. Jesus has come to calm all our fears, to calm the storms in our lives, to bring us to the shore of salvation by conquering sin and death. Nothing is impossible for Christ. Just as Christ stood by St. Anselm (1033–+1109), a Benedictine monk, during his exile from England due to struggles with political leaders of his time, our Lord is walking with us now through every wave that rocks our boat.

PRAYERS   *others may be added*

Relying on Christ, we pray:

◆ Risen Lord, make all things new.

For those who defend the Church against worldly powers, we pray: ◆ For those who are afflicted with any kind of fear, we pray: ◆ For those who must brave stormy seas, we pray: ◆ For all monks and nuns of the Order of St. Benedict, we pray: ◆

Our Father . . .

God of life,
you called St. Anselm to brave
     the waters
of political strife and inspire us by
     his wisdom.
Be with us through all our struggles,
and help us to be your
     calming presence
in a world longing to be brought to
     the shores of salvation.
We ask this through Christ our Lord.
     Amen.

✦ *Let all the earth cry out to God with joy, alleluia.*

✛ *Let all the earth cry out to God with joy, alleluia.*

PSALM 66   *page 413*

READING   *John 21:1–7a*

At that time, Jesus revealed himself again to his disciples at the Sea of Tiberias. He revealed himself in this way. Together were Simon Peter, Thomas called Didymus, Nathanael from Cana in Galilee, Zebedee's sons, and two others of his disciples. Simon Peter said to them, "I am going fishing." They said to him, "We also will come with you." So they went out and got into the boat, but that night they caught nothing. When it was already dawn, Jesus was standing on the shore; but the disciples did not realize that it was Jesus. Jesus said to them, "Children, have you caught anything to eat?" They answered him, "No." So he said to them, "Cast the net over the right side of the boat and you will find something." So they cast it, and were not able to pull it in because of the number of fish. So the disciple whom Jesus loved said to Peter, "It is the Lord."

REFLECTION

We set out on the journey and cast our nets into the deep ocean of life, hoping to draw others to Christ, our Redeemer. But often we become discouraged and frustrated when we catch nothing or can't see the fruits of our labor. We want to give up and put our nets away. Easter hope challenges us to continue our efforts, to press on, because Jesus, the Christ, is always present, offering new direction and giving new life.

PRAYERS   *others may be added*

Casting our nets into the sea of life, we pray:

◆ Risen Lord, make all things new.

For those who work to heal our earth, may they remain steadfast in their call, we pray: ◆ *For those who labor to end violence, may they remain steadfast in their call, we pray:* ◆ *For those who minister to the disabled, may they remain steadfast in their call, we pray:* ◆ *For those who catechize about the faith, may they remain steadfast in their call, we pray:* ◆

Our Father . . .

God of all peoples,
you call us to draw others
into your plan of salvation.
Help us to empty our nets of pride
so that they may overflow with your
    words of life.
We ask this through our Lord Jesus
    Christ, your Son,
who lives and reigns with you in the
    unity of the Holy Spirit,
one God, forever and ever. Amen.

✛ *Let all the earth cry out to God with joy, alleluia.*

✚ *Let all the earth cry out to God with joy, alleluia.*

PSALM 66 *page 413*

READING *John 6:25–29*

And when they [the disciples] found him across the sea they said to him, "Rabbi, when did you get here?" Jesus answered them and said, "Amen, amen, I say to you, you are looking for me not because you saw signs but because you ate the loaves and were filled. Do not work for food that perishes but for the food that endures for eternal life, which the Son of Man will give you. For on him the Father, God, has set his seal." So they said to him, "What can we do to accomplish the works of God?" Jesus answered and said to them, "This is the work of God, that you believe in the one he sent."

REFLECTION

How can we accomplish the works of God? How did St. George (+304), an obscure soldier in the Roman army, become one of the best-known and most revered figures in history? St. George, a person about whom very little historical fact is known, has become the valiant dragon slayer of legends and a saint venerated throughout Christianity. And, how did a young worldly noble, St. Adalbert (957–+997), become a bishop and martyr? Both St. George and St. Adalbert believed firmly in Christ. Will we do the same?

PRAYERS *others may be added*

Believing in Christ, we pray:

◆ Risen Lord, make all things new.

Lord Jesus Christ, you slew the dragon of death; bring us to new life, we pray: ◆ *Lord Jesus Christ, you sacrificed yourself for us; give us thankful hearts, we pray:* ◆ *Lord Jesus Christ, you humbled yourself; show us how to follow your example, we pray:* ◆ *Lord Jesus Christ, you rose to new life; fill us with your spirit, we pray:* ◆

Our Father . . .

Almighty God,
all glory, honor, and praise belong
    to you.
Great works are possible only
    through you.
Give us the faith and strength to
    follow your Son
who slays the dragon of sin
and rescues a world caught
    in darkness.
Grant this through Christ our Lord.
    Amen.

✚ *Let all the earth cry out to God with joy, alleluia.*

✚ *Let all the earth cry out to God with joy, alleluia.*

PSALM 66   *page 413*

READING   *John 6:30–35*

The crowd said to Jesus: "What sign can you do, that we may see and believe in you? What can you do? Our ancestors ate manna in the desert, as it is written:

He gave them bread from heaven to eat."

So Jesus said to them, "Amen, amen, I say to you, it was not Moses who gave the bread from heaven; my Father gives you the true bread from heaven. For the bread of God is that which comes down from heaven and gives life to the world."

So they said to Jesus, "Sir, give us this bread always." Jesus said to them, "I am the bread of life; whoever comes to me will never hunger, and whoever believes in me will never thirst."

REFLECTION

Nourishment for the soul, manna for the heart, food for the hungry, bread for the world. Jesus Christ, our Messiah, is all these things and more. He breaks open his life, proclaiming, "I am the bread of life," the bread which feeds all with the gift of salvation. In Christ, we find the sustenance for life—the very source of all creatures that move and have being. Our world longs, our lives hunger, and our spirits groan for the Christ who feeds us with his sacrament of everlasting peace. What more do we need?

PRAYERS   *others may be added*

Feasting on the manna from heaven, we pray:

◆ Risen Lord, make all things new.

That the hungry may taste of the Bread of Life, we pray: ◆ *That the poor may have their fill, we pray:* ◆ *That the homeless may taste of the Bread of Life, we pray:* ◆ *That the powerless may have their fill, we pray:* ◆

Our Father. . .

Christ, our Bread of Life,
you nourish and sustain us
with your broken body and
    freeing words.
May we always gather around the
    table of life,
seeking sacramental food for our
    spiritual journey.
We ask this in your name. Amen.

✚ *Let all the earth cry out to God with joy, alleluia.*

✙ *Let all the earth cry out to God with joy, alleluia.*

PSALM 66 *page 413*

READING *Mark 16:15–20*

Jesus appeared to the Eleven and said to them: "Go into the whole world and proclaim the Gospel to every creature. Whoever believes and is baptized will be saved; whoever does not believe will be condemned. These signs will accompany those who believe: in my name they will drive out demons, they will speak new languages. They will pick up serpents with their hands, and if they drink any deadly thing, it will not harm them. They will lay hands on the sick, and they will recover."

Then the Lord Jesus, after he spoke to them, was taken up into heaven and took his seat at the right hand of God. But they went forth and preached everywhere, while the Lord worked with them and confirmed the word through accompanying signs.

REFLECTION

St. Mark (+68), whose feast we celebrate today, presents us with a Gospel written to those who were persecuted and endured hardships for their faith. In this passage we see Jesus giving his disciples the power to remain unharmed in the presence of demons, serpents, and poisons. The resurrected Christ has won for us all that we need in order to face the perils of our time. May we go forth in the power of Christ.

PRAYERS *others may be added*

Called by Christ, we pray:

◆ Risen Lord, make all things new.

That the baptized may give witness to the Gospel, we pray: ◆ That we may be healed from the demons of pride, gluttony, and envy, we pray: ◆ That we may ward off the serpents of greed and lust, we pray: ◆ That we may be unharmed by the poisons of anger and sloth, we pray: ◆

Our Father . . .

All-powerful and ever-living God,
our Son has won the victory over sin
   and death.
Fortify us with the power of your
   Holy Spirit
so that we may work signs of
   your wonder
for the glory of your name.
We ask this through Christ our Lord.
   Amen.

✙ *Let all the earth cry out to God with joy, alleluia.*

✦ *Let all the earth cry out to God with joy, alleluia.*

PSALM 66   *page 413*

READING   *John 6:44–51*

Jesus said to the crowds: "No one can come to me unless the Father who sent me draw him, and I will raise him on the last day. It is written in the prophets:

They shall all be taught by God.

Everyone who listens to my Father and learns from him comes to me. Not that anyone has seen the Father except the one who is from God; he has seen the Father. Amen, amen, I say to you, whoever believes has eternal life. I am the bread of life. Your ancestors ate the manna in the desert, but they died; this is the bread that comes down from heaven so that one may eat it and not die. I am the living bread that came down from heaven; whoever eats this bread will live forever; and the bread that I will give is my Flesh for the life of the world."

REFLECTION

Throughout the Easter season, the Lectionary readings often show Jesus describing himself as the "bread of life." Bread, as food, is a basic need for human life. It sustains, nourishes, and prolongs life! As a religious image, bread becomes a powerful and multivalent symbol. When Jesus refers to himself as the bread of life, he is identifying himself as the source of salvation, the nourishment for our souls, and the giver of eternal life. Let us always remember that we encounter Jesus Christ, the word made flesh, in the sacrament of the Eucharist, the true bread of life.

PRAYERS   *others may be added*

Nourished by the Bread of Life, we pray:

◆ Risen Lord, make all things new.

Let us work for peace during turbulent times; we pray: ◆ *Let us show reverence to the sacred in a culture of death; we pray:* ◆ *Let us be humble in a power-hungry world; we pray:* ◆ *Let us embrace simple lives in a materialistic society; we pray:* ◆

Our Father . . .

Lamb of God,
you are food for the journey.
Fill our hearts with
your everlasting love
   and compassion.
Give us the courage to be bread
in a world that hungers to know you.
We ask this in your name. Amen.

✦ *Let all the earth cry out to God with joy, alleluia.*

✚ *Let all the earth cry out to God with joy, alleluia.*

PSALM 66 *page 413*

READING *John 6:52–59*

The Jews quarreled among themselves, saying, "How can this man give us his Flesh to eat?" Jesus said to them, "Amen, amen, I say to you, unless you eat the Flesh of the Son of Man and drink his Blood, you do not have life within you. Whoever eats my Flesh and drinks my Blood has eternal life, and I will raise him on the last day. For my Flesh is true food, and my Blood is true drink. Whoever eats my Flesh and drinks my Blood remains in me and I in him. Just as the living Father sent me and I have life because of the Father, so also the one who feeds on me will have life because of me. This is the bread that came down from heaven. Unlike your ancestors who ate and still died, whoever eats this bread will live forever." These things he said while teaching in the synagogue in Capernaum.

REFLECTION

This is not the manna of the desert. Moses ate manna and yet he died. This is bread from heaven, not a gift from God, but a gift of God. This bread, this wine is more than nourishment for the journey; it is a fore-taste of the heavenly banquet. How often do we realize that when we partake in the celebration of the Eucharist we are gathered with all the angels and saints, brought to the brink of heaven, and given our very God to eat?

PRAYERS *others may be added*

With the angels and saints, we pray:

◆ Risen Lord, make all things new.

That missionaries may continue to carry your Body and Blood to those who hunger for you, we pray: ◆ *That we may urgently build our relationships with you and each other, we pray:* ◆ *That your Church may live in Easter joy, we pray:* ◆ *That our dearly departed may enjoy the heavenly banquet, we pray:* ◆

Our Father . . .

Heavenly Father,
you lay out a banquet for all to enjoy.
Your Son invites us to partake in
    your love
with all the angels and saints.
May we become one with you,
our Bread of Life,
so that we may nourish a
    broken world.
We ask this through Christ our Lord.
    Amen.

✚ *Let all the earth cry out to God with joy, alleluia.*

✛ *Let all the earth cry out to God with joy, alleluia.*

PSALM 66   *page 413*

READING   *John 6:60–69*

Many of the disciples of Jesus who were listening said, "This saying is hard; who can accept it?" Since Jesus knew that his disciples were murmuring about this, he said to them, "Does this shock you? What if you were to see the Son of Man ascending to where he was before? It is the Spirit that gives life, while the flesh is of no avail. The words I have spoken to you are Spirit and life. But there are some of you who do not believe." Jesus knew from the beginning the ones who would not believe and the one who would betray him. And he said, "For this reason I have told you that no one can come to me unless it is granted him by my Father."

As a result of this, many of his disciples returned to their former way of life and no longer walked with him. Jesus then said to the Twelve, "Do you also want to leave?" Simon Peter answered him, "Master, to whom shall we go? You have the words of eternal life. We have come to believe and are convinced that you are the Holy One of God."

REFLECTION

There are numerous accounts in scripture in which Jesus is described as the keeper, giver, and animator of the words of eternal life. Words and language are one of the most powerful tools we have as human beings. With our words, we can influence the heart, change the mind, and direct the soul. Let us become a language of love, freeing all to see and know the risen Christ, our path to salvation.

PRAYERS   *others may be added*

Seeking to be transformed by the words of eternal life, we pray:

◆ Risen Lord, make all things new.

That we may proclaim words that free the heart, we pray: ◆ *That we may speak a language that changes the mind, we pray:* ◆ *That we may profess words that transform the soul, we pray:* ◆ *That we may articulate a language that empowers people to hear and understand the Gospel message, we pray:* ◆

Our Father . . .

Word of life,
you call us to be a language
of faith, hope, and love.
Help us to speak your truth
with sincerity of heart, clarity
    of mind,
and fidelity of soul.
We ask this through Christ our Lord.
    Amen.

✛ *Let all the earth cry out to God with joy, alleluia.*

Optional memorials of St. Peter Chanel; St. Louis Mary de Montfort   **147**

✠ *Let all the earth cry out to God with joy, alleluia.*

PSALM 66   *page 413*

READING   *John 10:27–30*

Jesus said: "My sheep hear my voice; I know them, and they follow me. I give them eternal life, and they shall never perish. No one can take them out of my hand. My Father, who has given them to me, is greater than all, and no one can take them out of the Father's hand. The Father and I are one."

REFLECTION

In today's world there are so many reasons to be plagued by insecurity: economic uncertainty, terrorism, lack of family stability, etc. Jesus echoes his familiar refrain: do not be afraid—no one can take you from my grasp. There is no power or uncertainty—nothing—that can separate us from the love of God. As we are tempted to despair, let us be comforted by the Good Shepherd who will never let us perish.

PRAYERS   *others may be added*

Following the Good Shepherd, we pray:

◆ Risen Lord, make all things new.

That he may lead bishops, priests, and deacons on your path of service to all, we pray: ◆ *That he may lead government officials onto the road to fostering peace, we pray:* ◆ *That he may lead the insecure into your pastures of comfort and solace, we pray:* ◆ *That he may lead those who doubt into the joy of Easter certainty, we pray:* ◆

Our Father . . .

Loving Father,
we are no longer lost sheep without
   a shepherd.
Your Son, the Good Shepherd,
   has found us
and has shown us the path to
   your salvation.
Help us to hear his voice as he
   beckons to us, and
follow his steps as he leads us
to unity with you and all your people.
We ask this through our Lord Jesus
   Christ, your Son,
who lives and reigns with you in the
   unity of the Holy Spirit,
one God, forever and ever. Amen.

✠ *Let all the earth cry out to God with joy, alleluia.*

✝ *Let all the earth cry out to God with joy, alleluia.*

PSALM 66 — page 413

READING — John 10:7–10

So Jesus said: "Amen, amen, I say to you, I am the gate for the sheep. All who came before me are thieves and robbers, but the sheep did not listen to them. I am the gate. Whoever enters through me will be saved, and will come in and go out and find pasture. A thief comes only to steal and slaughter and destroy; I came so that they might have life and have it more abundantly."

REFLECTION

We live in a time of gated communities, exclusive clubs, and private memberships. The questions become: What are we keeping in? and, Whom are we keeping out? Jesus turns this modern paradigm of exclusivity upside down. He speaks of a gate, a portal, that all are invited to enter through. The only requirement is that we, like sheep, know and heed our Shepherd's voice. We must enter the one, true and holy Gate so that we might have abundant life. We are challenged this Easter to open our restricted and privileged lives, becoming thresholds and doorways to the sacred.

PRAYERS — *others may be added*

Entering the gate of salvation, we pray:

◆ Risen Lord, make all things new.

That social workers become doorways of mercy, we pray, ◆ That teachers become gateways of wisdom, we pray: ◆ That nurses and doctors become doorways of healing, we pray: ◆ That ministers become gateways of God's saving word, we pray: ◆

Our Father . . .

O God,
Gate of eternal life,
you are the portal of
healing forgiveness and
    redeeming grace.
Dismantle the exclusivity
in our hearts and world
so that we may invite all to
glory in your saving cross.
Grant this through Christ our Lord.
    Amen.

✝ *Let all the earth cry out to God with joy, alleluia.*

✝ *Let all the earth cry out to God with joy, alleluia.*

PSALM 66   *page 413*

READING   *John 10:22–30*

The feast of the Dedication was taking place in Jerusalem. It was winter. And Jesus walked about in the temple area on the Portico of Solomon. So the Jews gathered around him and said to him, "How long are you going to keep us in suspense? If you are the Christ, tell us plainly." Jesus answered them, "I told you and you do not believe. The works I do in my Father's name testify to me. But you do not believe, because you are not among my sheep. My sheep hear my voice; I know them, and they follow me. I give them eternal life, and they shall never perish. No one can take them out of my hand. My Father, who has given them to me, is greater than all, and no one can take them out of the Father's hand. The Father and I are one."

REFLECTION

In this scene, which is a foretaste of Jesus' trial before the Sanhedrin, certain Jews are being smug with Jesus. Here, Jesus responds boldly and bluntly. It would be too easy for us to shake our heads in disdain at the Jews' treatment of Jesus. The real challenge is to ask ourselves how often we are smug with Christ. Do we see and believe the works Christ performs for and through us? Do we recognize his voice today?

PRAYERS   *others may be added*

Through the intercession of St. Joseph, we pray:

◆ Risen Lord, make all things new.

That you may work wonders through our belief in you, we pray: ◆ *That you may work out growth in meaningful employment for all, we pray:* ◆ *That you may work on increasing our attentiveness to you, we pray:* ◆ *That you may work our hearts into compassionate vehicles for your love, we pray:* ◆

Our Father . . .

Lord of all creation,
through your goodness we have
   the dignity
of being your children.
May all that we do give you glory,
may our labors bring prosperity
   and equity to the world, and
may your will be done.
We ask this through Christ our Lord.
   Amen.

✝ *Let all the earth cry out to God with joy, alleluia.*

✠ *Let all the earth cry out to God with joy, alleluia.*

PSALM 66   *page 413*

READING   *John 12:44–50*

Jesus cried out and said, "Whoever believes in me believes not only in me but also in the one who sent me, and whoever sees me sees the one who sent me. I came into the world as light, so that everyone who believes in me might not remain in darkness. And if anyone hears my words and does not observe them, I do not condemn him, for I did not come to condemn the world but to save the world. Whoever rejects me and does not accept my words has something to judge him: the word that I spoke, it will condemn him on the last day, because I did not speak on my own, but the Father who sent me commanded me what to say and speak. And I know that his commandment is eternal life. So what I say, I say as the Father told me."

REFLECTION

St. Athanasius (295–+373) lived in a time when there was doctrinal controversy regarding the divinity of the Son of God. St. Athanasius was persecuted because he defended the belief that Jesus Christ was both truly divine and truly human. Along with his great defense of orthodoxy, St. Athanasius was known as a spiritual teacher of the ascetic and monastic life, and writer of the Life of Antony of Egypt. *In his fervor and fidelity to the spiritual life, St. Athanasius is a model of sanctity*

and witness to the Light which no darkness overcomes.

PRAYERS   *others may be added*

Through the intercession of St. Athanasius, we pray:

◆ Risen Lord, make all things new.

For lay men and women, that they may proclaim the true identity of Christ to the secular world, we pray: ◆ *For religious sisters and brothers, that they may be the truth of Christ within their communities and apostolates, we pray:* ◆ *For priests, that they may preach both the divinity and humanity of Jesus Christ, we pray:* ◆ *For Church leaders, that they may be a living testimony of faith, we pray:* ◆

Our Father . . .

Almighty God,
you sent your servant, St. Athanasius,
to defend the identity of your Son,
    Jesus Christ,
and dispense wisdom regarding the
    spiritual life.
Following in his footsteps, may our
    lives declare
the light and truth of your Word
    made flesh.
We ask this in the name of Jesus,
    the Lord. Amen.

✠ *Let all the earth cry out to God with joy, alleluia.*

✝ *Let all the earth cry out to God with joy, alleluia.*

PSALM 66   *page 413*

READING   *John 14:8–14*

Philip said to him [Jesus], "Master, show us the Father, and that will be enough for us." Jesus said to him, "Have I been with you for so long a time and you still do not know me, Philip? Whoever has seen me has seen the Father. How can you say, 'Show us the Father'? Do you not believe that I am in the Father and the Father is in me? The words that I speak to you I do not speak on my own. The Father who dwells in me is doing his works. Believe me that I am in the Father and the Father is in me, or else, believe because of the works themselves. Amen, amen, I say to you, whoever believes in me will do the works that I do, and will do greater ones than these, because I am going to the Father. And whatever you ask in my name, I will do, so that the Father may be glorified in the Son. If you ask anything of me in my name, I will do it."

REFLECTION

What a promise! We will do greater works than even Jesus did! Is that possible? It seems so. A band of 12, mostly unremarkable men, spread the word about Jesus to the ends of their world. St. James and St. Philip were two of those people who laid the foundation of the Church that has lasted for over two thousand years. What a promise we have been given. And what greatness we can build upon through the name of Jesus.

PRAYERS   *others may be added*

In the name of Jesus, we pray:

◆ Risen Lord, make all things new.

For bishops, the successors to the apostles, that they may continue to build up the Church, we pray: ◆
For teachers, that they may work wonders in the minds of their students, we pray: ◆
For missionaries, that they may rely on the Father in their work, we pray: ◆
For the faithful departed, that they may share in the Resurrection of Christ, we pray: ◆

Our Father . . .

Loving Father,
you give us new life through your
    Risen Son.
Purify our hearts with your truth,
show us the way to holiness, and
strengthen us to do wonders in
    your sight.
We ask this in the name of Jesus the
    Lord. Amen.

✝ *Let all the earth cry out to God with joy, alleluia.*

✛ *Let all the earth cry out to God with joy, alleluia.*

PSALM 66 — page 413

READING — John 14:1–6

Jesus said to his disciples: "Do not let your hearts be troubled. You have faith in God; have faith also in me. In my Father's house there are many dwelling places. If there were not, would I have told you that I am going to prepare a place for you? And if I go and prepare a place for you, I will come back again and take you to myself, so that where I am you also may be. Where I am going you know the way." Thomas said to him, "Master, we do not know where you are going; how can we know the way?" Jesus said to him, "I am the way and the truth and the life. No one comes to the Father except through me."

REFLECTION

I am the bread of life . . . light of the world . . . gate . . . good shepherd . . . resurrection and life . . . vine . . . way, truth and life. Hearkening back to God's revelation to Moses in the burning bush, the Gospel of John uses "I am" statements to explicate the role and authority of Jesus as the Messiah. It is precisely in the "I am" statements that we are led to realize Jesus is our path to salvation, our Christ. There is no other bread, shepherd, light, gate, resurrection, life, vine, way, or truth other than Jesus who reveals the very face of God within the human condition.

PRAYERS — *others may be added*

Bowing before the Great "I AM," we pray:

◆ Risen Lord, make all things new.

To be bread for a world hungering to hear the Good News, we pray: ◆ *To be light for those who long to see the Word, we pray:* ◆ *To be a gate leading others to Christ, we pray:* ◆ *To be truth pointing the way to eternal life, we pray:* ◆

Our Father . . .

Risen Christ,
you are the way of salvation,
the truth of the kingdom, and the
    life of the world.
Grant us the wisdom to follow
    you faithfully
so that there may be a dwelling place
    for us
in our Father's house.
grant this in your name. Amen.

✛ *Let all the earth cry out to God with joy, alleluia.*

✝ *Let all the earth cry out to God with joy, alleluia.*

PSALM 66 *page 413*

READING *John 14:7–11*

Jesus said to his disciples: "If you know me, then you will also know my Father. From now on you do know him and have seen him." Philip said to Jesus, "Master, show us the Father, and that will be enough for us." Jesus said to him, "Have I been with you for so long a time and you still do not know me, Philip? Whoever has seen me has seen the Father. How can you say, 'Show us the Father'? Do you not believe that I am in the Father and the Father is in me? The words that I speak to you I do not speak on my own. The Father who dwells in me is doing his works. Believe me that I am in the Father and the Father is in me, or else, believe because of the works themselves."

REFLECTION

We are more than halfway through the Easter season. Have we taken the time to try and appreciate the meaning of Easter in our lives this year? In today's Gospel, taken from the Last Supper, Philip still has not grasped the connection between Jesus and the Father. Will we wait too long? May we take all the opportunities given to us to appreciate, learn, and grow in our faith in the risen Lord Jesus.

PRAYERS *others may be added*

Calling on Christ, we pray:

◆ Risen Lord, make all things new.

That we may show the world the face of the Father through our faith, we pray: ◆ That we may be shown the path of new life, we pray: ◆ That the dead may be shown the glory of your kingdom, we pray: ◆

Our Father . . .

Father of all,
you spoke your love to us
through the life, death, and
   Resurrection of your Son.
May we who have been given the
   gift of faith
reflect your radiance to a world
   darkened by doubt.
Grant this through Christ our Lord.
   Amen.

✝ *Let all the earth cry out to God with joy, alleluia.*

✚ *Let all the earth cry out to God with joy, alleluia.*

PSALM 66 *page 413*

READING *John 13:31–33a, 34–35*

When Judas had left them, Jesus said, "Now is the Son of Man glorified, and God is glorified in him. If God is glorified in him, God will also glorify him in himself, and God will glorify him at once. My children, I will be with you only a little while longer. I give you a new commandment: love one another. As I have loved you, so you also should love one another. This is how all will know that you are my disciples, if you have love for one another."

REFLECTION

The goal of the Christian journey is to be love, give love, and walk with love. Jesus tells us that mutual love is our story and our path to salvation. According to Jesus, if we want people to know who our Messiah is all we have to do is love as he loved his own disciples. It sounds like an easy prescription for inheriting the kingdom of God, but the reality is we even have to love those who hate, hurt, or wrong us. Let us move forward this Easter season loving as Jesus loved, forgiving as Jesus forgave, and giving as Jesus gave.

PRAYERS *others may be added*

Loving our neighbors as ourselves, we pray:

◆ Risen Lord, make all things new, we pray:

That we may sow love in the face of hatred, we pray: ◆ *That we may weave peace in the face of violence, we pray:* ◆ *That we may sow understanding in the face of prejudice and racism, we pray:* ◆ *That we may weave justice in the face of poverty, hunger, and homelessness, we pray:* ◆

Our Father . . .

God of compassion,
you call us to spread your
 merciful love
throughout all of creation.
Instill in us a love that invites all
to share in the saving promise of
 your Resurrection.
We ask this through our Lord Jesus
 Christ, your Son,
who lives and reigns with you in the
 unity of the Holy Spirit,
one God, forever and ever. Amen.

✚ *Let all the earth cry out to God with joy, alleluia.*

✢ *Let all the earth cry out to God with joy, alleluia.*

PSALM 66 *page 413*

READING *John 14:21–26*

Jesus said to his disciples: "Whoever has my commandments and observes them is the one who loves me. Whoever loves me will be loved by my Father, and I will love him and reveal myself to him." Judas, not the Iscariot, said to him, "Master, then what happened that you will reveal yourself to us and not to the world?" Jesus answered and said to him, "Whoever loves me will keep my word, and my Father will love him, and we will come to him and make our dwelling with him. Whoever does not love me does not keep my words; yet the word you hear is not mine but that of the Father who sent me.

"I have told you this while I am with you. The Advocate, the Holy Spirit whom the Father will send in my name—he will teach you everything and remind you of all that I told you."

REFLECTION

God does not force us to believe in him. Instead, he opens his arms and invites us to respond to his gift of self as revealed in Jesus Christ—God's polite invitation to the kingdom. What Judas didn't realize is that Jesus reveals himself to all, but not everyone responds. The invitation is gentle. The response is love. And we are promised the Holy Spirit to continue to show us the way.

PRAYERS *others may be added*

In love and trust, we pray:

◆ Risen Lord, make all things new.

For all who work for peace, we pray: ◆ *For those who toil for a just workplace, we pray:* ◆ *For those who comfort the ailing, we pray:* ◆ *For those who build up our spirits, we pray:* ◆

Our Father . . .

Bountiful God,
your gentle presence
revealed by your Son
is sustained in us through the
   Holy Spirit.
Help us to accept your invitation to
   your kingdom
so that we may celebrate with all the
   angels and saints
and be brought to the glory of
   new life.
We ask this through Christ our Lord.
   Amen.

✢ *Let all the earth cry out to God with joy, alleluia.*

✦ *Let all the earth cry out to God with joy, alleluia.*

PSALM 66 — *page 413*

READING — *John 14:27–31a*

Jesus said to his disciples: "Peace I leave with you; my peace I give to you. Not as the world gives do I give it to you. Do not let your hearts be troubled or afraid. You heard me tell you, 'I am going away and I will come back to you.' If you loved me, you would rejoice that I am going to the Father; for the Father is greater than I. And now I have told you this before it happens, so that when it happens you may believe. I will no longer speak much with you, for the ruler of the world is coming. He has no power over me, but the world must know that I love the Father and that I do just as the Father has commanded me."

REFLECTION

The Easter season is a time to celebrate God's gift of peace to the world through Jesus Christ. Now that we have experienced the peace of the risen Christ, it is our responsibility to bring about harmony and tranquility throughout creation. We are called to be the hands and feet of Christ, sharing God's great gift of saving peace. Let not our hearts be troubled, for the gift of peace has been given; now we must spread it to all!

PRAYERS — *others may be added*

Stewarding God's gift of peace, we pray:

◆ Risen Lord, make all things new.

That we experience the peace of forgiveness, we pray: ◆ *That we share the peace of compassion, we pray:* ◆ *That we sense the peace of humility, we pray:* ◆ *That we proclaim the peace of salvation, we pray:* ◆

Our Father . . .

God of peace,
you gave us your Son, Jesus Christ,
to show us the path
of sacred serenity and divine
   harmony.
May our hearts always know
   the stillness
of your freeing love and
   redeeming mercy.
We ask this through Jesus Christ our
   Lord. Amen.

✦ *Let all the earth cry out to God with joy, alleluia.*

✛ *Let all the earth cry out to God with joy, alleluia.*

PSALM 66   *page 413*

READING   *John 15:1–8*

Jesus said to his disciples: "I am the true vine, and my Father is the vine grower. He takes away every branch in me that does not bear fruit, and everyone that does he prunes so that it bears more fruit. You are already pruned because of the word that I spoke to you. Remain in me, as I remain in you. Just as a branch cannot bear fruit on its own unless it remains on the vine, so neither can you unless you remain in me. I am the vine, you are the branches. Whoever remains in me and I in him will bear much fruit, because without me you can do nothing. Anyone who does not remain in me will be thrown out like a branch and wither; people will gather them and throw them into a fire and they will be burned. If you remain in me and my words remain in you, ask for whatever you want and it will be done for you. By this is my Father glorified, that you bear much fruit and become my disciples."

REFLECTION

There is no such thing as a solitary Christian. Jesus tells us we must remain in him, our true vine, and be linked to one another in order to be truly alive. Just as a light bulb is totally useless when not connected to electricity, if we are not connected to our source we have no hope of being light for the world. We maintain our connection with Christ and each other through worship, prayer, and acts of love and support.

PRAYERS   *others may be added*

Looking to the true vine, we pray:

◆ Risen Lord, make all things new.

That we may remain united in faith with our Pope and bishops, we pray: ◆ That our worship and prayer may be sincere expressions of our love for Christ and each other, we pray: ◆ That we may reach out to the lonely, we pray: ◆ That the grieving may know that the bonds of love are not broken by death, we pray: ◆

Our Father . . .

Ever-living God,
you are the source of all life.
Keep us united with your Risen Son,
unfettered by the shackles of sin
    and death,
so that we may be together in your
    kingdom forever.
We ask this through Christ our Lord.
    Amen.

✛ *Let all the earth cry out to God with joy, alleluia.*

✤ *Let all the earth cry out to God with joy, alleluia.*

PSALM 66 *page 413*

READING *John 15:9–11*

Jesus said to his disciples: "As the Father loves me, so I also love you. Remain in my love. If you keep my commandments, you will remain in my love, just as I have kept my Father's commandments and remain in his love.

"I have told you this so that my joy might be in you and your joy might be complete."

REFLECTION

Bl. Damien (1840 – +1889) remained in Christ's love by ministering to the lepers on the Hawaiian island of Moloka'i. At a time when leprosy was rampant and fear darkened the hearts of most people, Bl. Damien worked tirelessly to instill a sense of dignity and self-worth in those suffering from this dreaded disease. He loved the victims of leprosy so much that he spent his entire life creating support systems and structures that reverenced their experiences, feelings, thoughts, and basic needs. He eventually died of leprosy himself. The life of Bl. Damien challenges us to move beyond our comfort zone so that all people will know and remain in God's love.

PRAYERS *others may be added*

Remaining joyful in God's love, we pray:

◆ Risen Lord, make all things new.

That we may be signs of God's healing for those addicted to drugs and alcohol, we pray: ◆ *That we may be symbol's of God's hope to those struggling with depression, we pray:* ◆ *That we may be images of God's compassion to those physically or emotionally abused, we pray:* ◆ *That we may be metaphors of God's love to the world, we pray:* ◆

Our Father . . .

God of mercy,
you lifted up your servant,
    Bl. Damien,
as a model of your
    compassionate love.
Give us the courage to minister to
the lepers in our world,
giving witness to your healing
    gift of grace.
We ask this through Jesus our Lord.
    Amen.

✤ *Let all the earth cry out to God with joy, alleluia.*

Optional memorial of Bl. Damien Joseph de Veuster of Moloka'i

✝ *Let all the earth cry out to God with joy, alleluia.*

PSALM 66   *page 413*

READING   *John 15:12–17*

Jesus said to his disciples: "This is my commandment: love one another as I love you. No one has greater love than this, to lay down one's life for one's friends. You are my friends if you do what I command you. I no longer call you slaves, because a slave does not know what his master is doing. I have called you friends, because I have told you everything I have heard from my Father. It was not you who chose me, but I who chose you and appointed you to go and bear fruit that will remain, so that whatever you ask the Father in my name he may give you. This I command you: love one another."

REFLECTION

Here we have the commandment to love. A commandment is more than just a law; a commandment can come only from the Creator. A commandment is a direction about how to be human. Its force is that it comes from the Creator, the one who determined what it means to be truly human. Jesus is not "legislating" behavior; he is describing how we can be more like what the Creator intended us to be. Will we listen?

PRAYERS   *others may be added*

In obedience, we pray:

◆ Risen Lord, make all things new.

For Church leaders, that they may lay down their lives in service, we pray: ◆
For those in the armed services, that they may work for peace, we pray: ◆ *For all who enforce the law, that they may serve all equally, we pray:* ◆ *For firefighters, that they may be safe in their duties, we pray:* ◆

Our Father . . .

God of all creation,
in this Easter season
we celebrate the Resurrection of
    your Son.
Help us to live by his example,
and sacrifice our lives
to be loving brothers and sisters
    in Christ.
We ask this through Christ our Lord.
    Amen.

✝ *Let all the earth cry out to God with joy, alleluia.*

✠ *Let all the earth cry out to God with joy, alleluia.*

PSALM 66   *page 413*

READING   *John 15:18–21*

Jesus said to his disciples: "If the world hates you, realize that it hated me first. If you belonged to the world, the world would love its own; but because you do not belong to the world, and I have chosen you out of the world, the world hates you. Remember the word I spoke to you, 'No slave is greater than his master.' If they persecuted me, they will also persecute you. If they kept my word, they will also keep yours. And they will do all these things to you on account of my name, because they do not know the one who sent me."

REFLECTION

Following Jesus in today's world can be very difficult and sometimes painful. Being a disciple involves walking a path and proclaiming a message that many will not understand, recognize, or heed. Our choice to follow the way of our Messiah may lead to rejection, hatred, and non-acceptance. Even so, Jesus maintains that if we want to reside in the Father's house, then we must not belong to this world—a world that persecutes light and truth. We must be faithful witnesses willing to keep the word of God and follow the risen Lord, even when the cost is extremely high.

PRAYERS   *others may be added*

Willing to pay the cost of discipleship, we pray:

◆ Risen Lord, make all things new.

To be faithful followers of Jesus Christ, we pray: ◆ *To be compassionate ministers of the Word, we pray:* ◆ *To be forgiving servants of God's saving message, we pray:* ◆ *To be joyful witnesses of the Resurrection, we pray:* ◆

Our Father . . .

God of redemption,
you call us to follow you
by letting go of the promises of
    this world.
Instill in us the strength to love and
proclaim your name even when others
    despise us.
We ask this in your name. Amen.

✠ *Let all the earth cry out to God with joy, alleluia.*

Optional memorials of St. Nereus and St. Achilleus; St. Pancras   **161**

✚ *Let all the earth cry out to God with joy, alleluia.*

PSALM 66 page 413

READING John 14:23–29

Jesus said to his disciples: "Whoever loves me will keep my word, and my Father will love him, and we will come to him and make our dwelling with him. Whoever does not love me does not keep my words; yet the word you hear is not mine but that of the Father who sent me.

"I have told you this while I am with you. The Advocate, the Holy Spirit, whom the Father will send in my name, will teach you everything and remind you of all that I told you. Peace I leave with you; my peace I give to you. Not as the world gives do I give it to you. Do not let your hearts be troubled or afraid. You heard me tell you, 'I am going away and I will come back to you.' If you loved me, you would rejoice that I am going to the Father; for the Father is greater than I. And now I have told you this before it happens, so that when it happens you may believe."

REFLECTION

Today, Jesus promises us the Holy Spirit. He knows that his task will not be easy for us to accomplish. Think of it, for all the wonders that the apostles saw, when Jesus was taken from them, they hid like frightened children. We all need support. We need someone to be present and give us strength. Our Lord wants us to succeed in *our mission. And so Jesus sends us his Holy Spirit. We have all the help we need.*

PRAYERS others may be added

In peace, we pray:

◆ Risen Lord, make all things new.

That all artists may draw their inspiration from the Holy Spirit, we pray: ◆ *That fathers and mothers may be honored for their loving acts, we pray:* ◆ *That diplomats may use all their skills for peace, we pray:* ◆ *That all the baptized may live in joy and hope, we pray:* ◆

Our Father . . .

Father of our Lord Jesus Christ,
you have shown your favor upon
 your Son
by raising him from the dead.
Grant us the peace
that comes from loving you,
and help us to share it with the
 entire world.
We ask this through our Lord Jesus
 Christ, your Son,
who lives and reigns with you in the
 unity of the Holy Spirit,
one God, forever and ever. Amen.

✚ *Let all the earth cry out to God with joy, alleluia.*

✚ *Let all the earth cry out to God with joy, alleluia.*

PSALM 66   *page 413*

READING   *John 15:12–17*

"This is my commandment: love one another as I love you. No one has greater love than this, to lay down one's life for one's friends. You are my friends if you do what I command you. I no longer call you slaves, because a slave does not know what his master is doing. I have called you friends, because I have told you everything I have heard from my Father. It was not you who chose me, but I who chose you and appointed you to go and bear fruit that will remain, so that whatever you ask the Father in my name he may give you. This I command you: love one another."

REFLECTION

Chosen by the apostles to replace Judas after his death, St. Matthias (+80) was well known for his insistence on the importance of mortification, great love of others, and willingness to lay down his life for the sake of the Gospel. We celebrate St. Matthias, a faithful follower of Christ, because his life and wisdom witness to the demands and expectations of Christian love—a love that is not always easy, but ever rewarding. May we follow in his footsteps, loving all and willing to sacrifice anything for our God!

PRAYERS   *others may be added*

Through the intercession of St. Matthias, we pray:

◆ Risen Lord, make all things new.

For the local Church, that it may be a vibrant and tangible sign of God's redemption, we pray: ◆ For all who live the works of mercy, that they may be the healing hands of Christ, we pray: ◆ For the foreign missions, that more men and women may feel called to spread the Gospel, we pray: ◆ For ourselves, that we may profess Gospel values in all areas of our world, we pray: ◆

Our Father . . .

God of all creation,
you called St. Matthias
to preach and teach your saving
    mission of love.
Enliven our hearts with the faith
    and truth
you poured into the souls of
    the apostles
so that your Gospel reaches the ends
    of the earth.
We ask this in the name of Jesus our
    Lord. Amen.

✚ *Let all the earth cry out to God with joy, alleluia.*

✠ Let all the earth cry out to God with joy, alleluia.

PSALM 66   page 413

READING   John 16:5–11

Jesus said to his disciples: "Now I am going to the one who sent me, and not one of you asks me, 'Where are you going?' But because I told you this, grief has filled your hearts. But I tell you the truth, it is better for you that I go. For if I do not go, the Advocate will not come to you. But if I go, I will send him to you. And when he comes he will convict the world in regard to sin and righteousness and condemnation: sin, because they do not believe in me; righteousness, because I am going to the Father and you will no longer see me; condemnation, because the ruler of this world has been condemned."

REFLECTION

Jesus says he must go to the Father in order to send us the Holy Spirit. He can do more good away from the world than within it. St. Isidore (1070–+1130) is an example of how this can happen. Known as the "farmer," this saint was a little-known married layman during his life. His biography, written after his death, brought him much more notoriety and devotees than he ever knew in life. Do we have the faith to wait on the action of the Holy Spirit?

PRAYERS   *others may be added*

Through the intercession of St. Isidore, we pray:

◆ Risen Lord, make all things new.

That farmers may be examples of hope-filled trust and faithful expectancy, we pray: ◆ That the poor may find assistance in the Church, we pray: ◆ That reconciliation may be embraced by all faith traditions, we pray: ◆ That the faithful departed may find Easter joy in the Lord, we pray: ◆

Our Father . . .

Father of the humble,
you are glorified by your saints.
Fill us with your Spirit
so that we may follow in the steps of
    your Son
and live in Easter holiness.
We ask this through Christ our Lord.
    Amen.

✠ Let all the earth cry out to God with joy, alleluia.

✠ *Let all the earth cry out to God with joy, alleluia.*

PSALM 66 *page 413*

READING *John 16:12–15*

Jesus said to his disciples: "I have much more to tell you, but you cannot bear it now. But when he comes, the Spirit of truth, he will guide you to all truth. He will not speak on his own, but he will speak what he hears, and will declare to you the things that are coming. He will glorify me, because he will take from what is mine and declare it to you. Everything that the Father has is mine; for this reason I told you that he will take from what is mine and declare it to you."

REFLECTION

Having faith in something we cannot see or touch is difficult in a culture that values material proof and scientific evidence. We find it hard to follow Jesus because he is not present in his human, bodily form, but there is great hope and consolation in today's Gospel. Even though Jesus is not tangible in body, the Paraclete, Spirit of truth, will always be with us guiding in the ways of mercy. Easter challenges us to not live in fear and skepticism, for God's spirit is within and around helping us make right choices to live faithfully and follow the path of life.

PRAYERS *others may be added*

Trusting in the help and guidance of the Holy Spirit, we pray:

◆ Risen Lord, make all things new.

For scientists, that their work may be informed by God's saving knowledge, we pray: ◆ *For doctors, that their work may be rooted in God's healing Word, we pray:* ◆ *For lawyers, that their work may be embedded in God' redeeming law, we pray:* ◆ *For politicians, that their work may be centered in God's spirit of truth, we pray:* ◆

Our Father . . .

Holy Spirit,
you guide us on the path
to peace and redemption.
Grant us the courage to believe
 and trust
in your saving presence
so that we may sing of your glory
throughout all the earth.
Grant this through Jesus Christ our
 Lord. Amen.

✠ *Let all the earth cry out to God with joy, alleluia.*

✠ *God mounts his throne to shouts of joy.*

PSALM 47 *page 412*

READING *Luke 24:46–53*

Jesus said to his disciples: "Thus it is written that the Christ would suffer and rise from the dead on the third day and that repentance, for the forgiveness of sins, would be preached in his name to all the nations, beginning from Jerusalem. You are witnesses of these things. And behold I am sending the promise of my Father upon you; but stay in the city until you are clothed with power from on high."

Then he led them out as far as Bethany, raised his hands, and blessed them. As he blessed them he parted from them and was taken up to heaven. They did him homage and then returned to Jerusalem with great joy, and they were continually in the temple praising God.

REFLECTION

Today's solemnity is more about the ending of Jesus' earthly ministry than it is about where Jesus has gone. The Gospel focuses upon the disciples—upon us. We are to be witnesses, those who offer testimony to the forgiveness of sins accomplished in Christ Jesus. We are not to work on our own; we have been promised power from on high. Great things have been asked of us, and even greater things have been promised.

PRAYERS *others may be added*

Doing homage to the Lord, we pray:

◆ Fill us with your Spirit.

That we may give witness to the wondrous things the Lord has done, we pray: ◆ *That we may be a blessing upon the earth, we pray:* ◆ *That we may always be open and ready for the workings of the Holy Spirit, we pray:* ◆ *That we may always offer praise to God with joy, we pray:* ◆

Our Father . . .

Almighty God,
today your Son returns to your
   right hand.
Direct our gaze outward
to a world yearning
to hear your message of forgiveness
so that we may go out to all
   the nations,
forever singing your praise.
We ask this through our Lord Jesus
   Christ, your Son,
who lives and reigns with you in the
   unity of the Holy Spirit,
one God, forever and ever. Amen.

✠ *God mounts his throne to shouts of joy.*

✛ *Let all the earth cry out to God with joy, alleluia.*

PSALM 66   *page 413*

READING   *John 16:20–23*

Jesus said to his disciples: "Amen, amen, I say to you, you will weep and mourn, while the world rejoices; you will grieve, but your grief will become joy. When a woman is in labor, she is in anguish because her hour has arrived; but when she has given birth to a child, she no longer remembers the pain because of her joy that a child has been born into the world. So you also are now in anguish. But I will see you again, and your hearts will rejoice, and no one will take your joy away from you. On that day you will not question me about anything. Amen, amen, I say to you, whatever you ask the Father in my name he will give you."

REFLECTION

The Resurrection of Jesus has turned our weeping and mourning into joy and peace. The grief and pain we experienced at the foot of the cross is difficult to remember because we have witnessed the glory of the empty tomb. From the sorrow of Good Friday to the splendor of Easter morning, we are reminded that Jesus is always there holding, supporting, and prodding us to be light in a world that dances in the darkness.

PRAYERS   *others may be added*

Living the joy and wonder of Easter, we pray:

◆ Fill us with your Holy Spirit.

That we may turn our hearts into living vessels of compassion, we pray: ◆
That we may turn our minds into basins of holy knowledge, we pray: ◆ *That we may turn our souls into images of your divine work, we pray:* ◆ *That we may turn our lives into tapestries of your saving story, we pray:* ◆

Our Father . . .

God of joy,
you have turned our sadness
   and mourning
into the peace and hope of Easter.
May we always be a living sign
   and symbol
of your light and truth in the world.
Grant this through Jesus Christ
   our Lord. Amen.

✛ *Let all the earth cry out to God with joy, alleluia.*

Optional memorial of St. John I   **167**

✜ *Let all the earth cry out to God with joy, alleluia.*

PSALM 66 *page 413*

READING *John 16:23b–28*

Jesus said to his disciples: "Amen, amen, I say to you, whatever you ask the Father in my name he will give you. Until now you have not asked anything in my name; ask and you will receive, so that your joy may be complete.

"I have told you this in figures of speech. The hour is coming when I will no longer speak to you in figures but I will tell you clearly about the Father. On that day you will ask in my name, and I do not tell you that I will ask the Father for you. For the Father himself loves you, because you have loved me and have come to believe that I came from God. I came from the Father and have come into the world. Now I am leaving the world and going back to the Father."

REFLECTION

Where are we going? Where does all of this end? Does the confusion ever end? These are questions that humanity has pondered since the beginning of time. Certainly the apostles also wondered about these things. Today, Jesus reminds us that he did not disappear at the Ascension, but rather, has led the way to our final destination. He shows us that our ultimate destiny is to dwell with God. Christ no longer speaks in riddles; he simply asks us to follow him home.

PRAYERS *others may be added*

In the name of Jesus, we pray:

◆ Fill us with your Holy Spirit.

For philosophers and educators, that they may coax our minds to ponder the deeper questions, we pray: ◆ *For preachers and catechists, that they may properly help inform our consciences, we pray:* ◆ *For storytellers, that they may open our imaginations to the wonders of God, we pray:* ◆ *For linguists, that they may help us to express our inner most thoughts and feelings, we pray:* ◆

Our Father . . .

Heavenly Father,
you are the beginning and end of
    all creation.
May our hearts and minds be
    attentive to your word
so that we will be brought together
in our heavenly homeland.
We ask this through Christ our Lord.
    Amen.

✜ *Let all the earth cry out to God with joy, alleluia.*

✦ *Let all the earth cry out to God with joy, alleluia.*

PSALM 66 *page 413*

READING *John 17:20–23*

Lifting up his eyes to heaven, Jesus prayed saying: "Holy Father, I pray not only for them, but also for those who will believe in me through their word, so that they may all be one, as you, Father, are in me and I in you, that they also may be in us, that the world may believe that you sent me. And I have given them the glory you gave me, so that they may be one, as we are one, I in them and you in me, that they may be brought to perfection as one, that the world may know that you sent me, and that you loved them even as you loved me."

REFLECTION

The Word became flesh to dismantle the barriers and obstacles of sin and darkness among the children of God. To be Christian, a follower of Jesus, is to live in community. Claiming Jesus as Lord and Messiah is a proclamation of one's willingness to work for the unity of all people. We seek to create a world, a family, where the voices and prayers of many are heard as one melodious song announcing God's salvific action in the world.

PRAYERS *others may be added*

Working to build one community of love, we pray:

◆ Fill us with your Spirit.

That we may fan the flame of courage within our lives, we pray: ◆ *That we may fan the flame of reverence within our Church, we pray:* ◆ *That we may fan the flame of right judgment within our government, we pray:* ◆ *That we may fan the flame of wonder and awe within our world, we pray:* ◆

Our Father . . .

God the Father of our Lord
    Jesus Christ,
you sent your only-begotten Son
to reconcile the world to yourself
and free it from all sin and division.
Give us the wisdom and knowledge
    to build
a resurrected community
    profoundly shaped
by the message of the cross.
We ask this through Jesus Christ, our
    Messiah. Amen.

✦ *Let all the earth cry out to God with joy, alleluia.*

✚ *Let all the earth cry out to God with joy, alleluia.*

PSALM 66 *page 413*

READING *John 16:29–33*

The disciples said to Jesus, "Now you are talking plainly, and not in any figure of speech. Now we realize that you know everything and that you do not need to have anyone question you. Because of this we believe that you came from God." Jesus answered them, "Do you believe now? Behold, the hour is coming and has arrived when each of you will be scattered to his own home and you will leave me alone. But I am not alone, because the Father is with me. I have told you this so that you might have peace in me. In the world you will have trouble, but take courage, I have conquered the world."

REFLECTION

Scattered, alone, and troubled—this sounds like the life of so many people—the homeless, the unemployed, the destitute. Even if our lives are not so dramatically afflicted, we have all felt distressed. Today, Jesus tells us to take courage and believe that he has conquered all that harms us. St. Christopher Magallanes and his companions were martyred for practicing their faith in nineteenth-century Mexico when religious activities were outlawed. Their courage came from the sure belief that Christ has conquered all.

PRAYERS *others may be added*

In the faith of the martyrs, we pray:

◆ Fill us with your Holy Spirit.

When we are afflicted with doubt, we pray: ◆ *When we are in need of your strength, we pray:* ◆ *When the Church is persecuted, we pray:* ◆ *When we breathe our last breath, we pray:* ◆

Our Father . . .

God of compassion,
you desire us to live in your peace.
Send us the Holy Spirit,
   the Comforter,
to breath new life into our
   weakened souls
and gather us into the strength of your
   loving embrace
so that we may be the risen body of
   your Son in the world.
Grant this through Christ our Lord.
   Amen.

✚ *Let all the earth cry out to God with joy, alleluia.*

✠ *Let all the earth cry out to God with joy, alleluia.*

PSALM 66   *page 413*

READING   *John 17:4–8*

[Jesus said] "I glorified you on earth by accomplishing the work that you gave me to do. Now glorify me, Father, with you, with the glory that I had with you before the world began.

"I revealed your name to those whom you gave me out of the world. They belonged to you, and you gave them to me, and they have kept your word. Now they know that everything you gave me is from you, because the words you gave to me I have given to them, and they accepted them and truly understood that I came from you, and they have believed that you sent me."

REFLECTION

St. Rita of Cascia (1377–+1457) at an early age longed to be a nun, but her parents would not support her in this vocational pursuit and forced her to marry a man who proved to be violent and unfaithful. After the death of her husband and two sons, St. Rita was able to follow her dream and become an Augustinian nun. Bearing the stigmata on her forehead, St. Rita was well known for her contemplative spirituality, devoted care of sick nuns, and counseling skills. St. Rita is a model of holiness: always glorifying God, keeping the word, and revealing the name of Jesus Christ.

PRAYERS   *others may be added*

Through the intercession of St. Rita of Cascia, we pray:

◆ Fill us with your Holy Spirit.

That married men and women remain faithful to their vows, we pray: ◆
That marriage becomes a symbol of mutual love and respect, we pray: ◆
That mothers nurture the spirituality of their children, we pray: ◆ *That more men and women answer the call to religious life, we pray:* ◆

Our Father . . .

God of fidelity,
you called your servant, St. Rita
    of Cascia,
to live a life of sanctity
through marriage, motherhood, and
    religious life.
May her example inspire us to remain
    faithful and unwavering
in our vocation, even when others
disapprove and are unsupportive.
We ask this through Jesus our Lord.
    Amen.

✠ *Let all the earth cry out to God with joy, alleluia.*

✠ *Let all the earth cry out to God with joy, alleluia.*

PSALM 66   *page 413*

READING   *John 17:11b–19*

Lifting up his eyes to heaven, Jesus prayed, saying: "Holy Father, keep them in your name that you have given me, so that they may be one just as we are one. When I was with them I protected them in your name that you gave me, and I guarded them, and none of them was lost except the son of destruction, in order that the Scripture might be fulfilled. But now I am coming to you. I speak this in the world so that they may share my joy completely. I gave them your word, and the world hated them, because they do not belong to the world any more than I belong to the world. I do not ask that you take them out of the world but that you keep them from the Evil One. They do not belong to the world any more than I belong to the world. Consecrate them in the truth. Your word is truth. As you sent me into the world, so I sent them into the world. And I consecrate myself for them, so that they also may be consecrated in truth."

REFLECTION

This is Jesus' prayer for us. It is deeply personal and touching. He does not want us to be alone or unprotected from those who reject God and godly ways. Jesus knew he could not remain on earth forever in his human body, nor could he personally keep watch over all those who would follow him. So he turns to the Father and asks him to send his Holy Spirit to hold, protect, and strengthen us. We are very dearly loved by God. Are we ready to spread that love?

PRAYERS   *others may be added*

To our loving God, we pray:

◆ Fill us with your Holy Spirit.

That we may be strengthened for the journey, we pray: ◆ *That we may always share in Easter joy, we pray:* ◆ *That the truth may always be a mark of the Church, we pray:* ◆ *That those who live in disbelief may find their way to Christ, we pray:* ◆

Our Father . . .

Loving Father,
your compassion for us knows
    no bounds.
In your infinite wisdom you created
a multitude of gifts in humanity.
Send us your Holy Spirit to ignite us
into lanterns, leading the way to your
    heavenly kingdom.
We ask this through Christ our Lord.
    Amen.

✠ *Let all the earth cry out to God with joy, alleluia.*

✜ *Let all the earth cry out to God with joy, alleluia.*

PSALM 66 *page 413*

READING *John 17:20–23*

Lifting up his eyes to heaven, Jesus prayed saying: "I pray not only for these, but also for those who will believe in me through their word, so that they may all be one, as you, Father, are in me and I in you, that they also may be in us, that the world may believe that you sent me. And I have given them the glory you gave me, so that they may be one, as we are one, I in them and you in me, that they may be brought to perfection as one, that the world may know that you sent me, and that you loved them even as you loved me. Father, they are your gift to me."

REFLECTION

We too, like Jesus, are called to lift our eyes and voices to our heavenly Father in prayer. Prayer is an essential element of the Christian journey. It is our nourishment, our food for the soul. Prayer affords us the opportunity to intimately pursue, seek, and know the mind and ways of God. Living Easter faith requires that we approach our saving God in prayer, offering blessing and adoration, lifting up our petitions, interceding for others, giving thanks, proclaiming praise, and asking forgiveness.

PRAYERS *others may be added*

Approaching God with contemplative hearts, we pray:

◆ Fill us with your Holy Spirit.

That we offer blessing and adoration to the divine, we pray: ◆ *That we place our needs and the needs of others before the Lord on a daily basis, we pray:* ◆ *That we give thanks to God for the many blessings he has bestowed upon us, we pray:* ◆ *That we ask for forgiveness when we have hurt someone or have not lived the Gospel message, we pray:* ◆

Our Father . . .

God of mercy,
you gave us your Son, Jesus Christ,
to teach us how to pray and live
    contemplatively.
May we remain faithful to a life of
    silence and prayer
so that all will know your ways of
    mercy and forgiveness.
Grant this through Christ our Lord.
    Amen.

✜ *Let all the earth cry out to God with joy, alleluia.*

✚ *Let all the earth cry out to God with joy, alleluia.*

PSALM 66 *page 413*

READING *John 21:15–18*

[Jesus] said to Simon Peter, "Simon, son of John, do you love me more than these?" Simon Peter answered him, "Yes, Lord, you know that I love you." Jesus said to him, "Feed my lambs." He then said to Simon Peter a second time, "Simon, son of John, do you love me?" Simon Peter answered him, "Yes, Lord, you know that I love you." He said to him, "Tend my sheep." He said to him the third time, "Simon, son of John, do you love me?" Peter was distressed that he had said to him a third time, "Do you love me?" and he said to him, "Lord, you know everything; you know that I love you." Jesus said to him, "Feed my sheep. Amen, amen, I say to you, when you were younger, you used to dress yourself and go where you wanted; but when you grow old, you will stretch out your hands, and someone else will dress you and lead you where you do not want to go."

REFLECTION

The parallel between these three questions of Jesus to Peter and the three denials of Peter is hard to miss. Is Jesus trying rub salt into Peter's wound? Not unless the salt is healing balm! Jesus is giving Peter the opportunity to repent for his awful denials of Holy Thursday. This is the entire message of the Gospels: forgiveness is offered to each of us for our every failing. The way of forgiveness is not easy, but it is the path that Christ invites us to be on.

PRAYERS *others may be added*

Stretching out our hands, we pray:

◆ Fill us with your Holy Spirit.

In the spirit of St. Bede, that we may always have a deep love of scripture, we pray: ◆ In the spirit of St. Gregory, that the Church may grow in integrity, we pray: ◆ In the spirit of St. Mary Magdalene de'Pazzi, that our desire for union with God in prayer may burn brighter, we pray: ◆

Our Father . . .

God,
your forgiveness is unending.
May we follow your Son
   in righteousness
to build your kingdom.
We ask this through Christ our Lord.
   Amen.

✚ *Let all the earth cry out to God with joy, alleluia.*

✝ *Let all the earth cry out to God with joy, alleluia.*

PSALM 66   *page 413*

READING   *John 21:20–25*

Peter turned and saw the disciple following whom Jesus loved, the one who had also reclined upon his chest during the supper and had said, "Master, who is the one who will betray you?" When Peter saw him, he said to Jesus, "Lord, what about him?" Jesus said to him, "What if I want him to remain until I come? What concern is it of yours? You follow me." So the word spread among the brothers that that disciple would not die. But Jesus had not told him that he would not die, just "What if I want him to remain until I come? What concern is it of yours?"

It is this disciple who testifies to these things and has written them, and we know that his testimony is true. There are also many other things that Jesus did, but if these were to be described individually, I do not think the whole world would contain the books that would be written.

REFLECTION

As we approach Pentecost Sunday, it seems fitting to celebrate the life and witness of St. Philip Neri (1515–+1595), founder of the Oratorians. Having had a mystical experience where the power and love of the Holy Spirit enflamed his body and heart, he felt called to light people on fire with the desire to pray, participate in the sacraments frequently, and perform works

of charity. May we follow in the footsteps of St. Philip Neri, a beloved disciple of Jesus, who was esteemed for his sensitivity, common sense, and ability to humanize religion.

PRAYERS   *others may be added*

Through the intercession of St. Philip Neri, we pray:

◆ Fill us with your Holy Spirit.

That we may live a life of prayer and contemplation, we pray: ◆ *That we may recognize sacraments as graced moments, opportunities, we pray:* ◆ *That we may extend the charity of Christ to all those in need, we pray:* ◆ *That all may come to know the beauty of the Catholic faith, we pray:* ◆

Our Father . . .

Almighty and ever-present Father,
you called St. Philip Neri
to found a community of men
to pray, preach, teach, and guide.
May our lives be an oratory where all
can come to hear and accept the word
    of salvation.
We ask this through Jesus Christ our
    Lord. Amen.

✝ *Let all the earth cry out to God with joy, alleluia.*

✠ *Lord, send out your Spirit, and renew the face of the earth.*

PSALM 66 *page 413*

READING *John 20:19–23*

On the evening of that first day of the week, when the doors were locked, where the disciples were, for fear of the Jews, Jesus came and stood in their midst and said to them, "Peace be with you." When he had said this, he showed them his hands and his side. The disciples rejoiced when they saw the Lord. Jesus said to them again, "Peace be with you. As the Father has sent me, so I send you." And when he had said this, he breathed on them and said to them, "Receive the Holy Spirit. Whose sins you forgive are forgiven them, and whose sins you retain are retained."

REFLECTION

We are people of the Holy Spirit! We are a Church bound together by the Holy Spirit! Our very life comes from the Spirit of God living within us. Just as we are not aware of the blood coursing through our body, we are not usually attentive to the Holy Spirit flowing within. We need Pentecost, a great reminder of the source of our peace, the source of our goodness. May we be like the apostles on fire with the Holy Spirit—living, loving, forgiving, and proclaiming the risen Christ.

PRAYERS *others may be added*

Celebrating the birth of the Church, we pray:

◆ Fill us with your Holy Spirit.

That you may enflame our hearts with the fire of your love and compassion, we pray: ◆ That you may light our souls on fire with the courage to follow Jesus Christ, we pray: ◆ That you may enlighten our minds with the knowledge and wisdom to build a unified community of faith, we pray: ◆ That you may enkindle in us fidelity to the apostolic mission of the Church, we pray: ◆

Our Father . . .

Come, Holy Spirit, come!
And from your celestial home
    Shed a ray of light divine! . . .
Heal our wounds, our strength renew;
On our dryness pour your dew;
    Wash the stains of guilt away: . . .
On the faithful, who adore
And confess you, evermore
    In your sevenfold gift descend;
Give them virtue's sure reward;
Give them your salvation, Lord;
    Give them joys that never end.
    Amen. Alleluia

✠ *Lord, send out your Spirit, and renew the face of the earth.*

✤ *Your words, Lord, are Spirit and life.*

PSALM 19   *page 405*

READING   *Mark 10:17–22*

As Jesus was setting out on a journey, a man ran up, knelt down before him, and asked him, "Good teacher, what must I do to inherit eternal life?" Jesus answered him, "Why do you call me good? No one is good but God alone. *You know the commandments: You shall not kill; you shall not commit adultery; you shall not steal; you shall not bear false witness; you shall not defraud; honor your father and your mother."* He replied and said to him, "Teacher, all of these I have observed from my youth." Jesus, looking at him, loved him and said to him, "You are lacking in one thing. Go, sell what you have, and give to the poor and you will have treasure in heaven; then come, follow me." At that statement, his face fell, and he went away sad, for he had many possessions.

REFLECTION

Jesus gives us a rule of life, a prescription on how to be a holy disciple and inherit the kingdom of God. We are told not to kill, commit adultery, steal, bear false witness, and defraud. We are also told to love and honor our mother and father. According to Jesus, living and observing these commandments is not enough; we must also sell everything we have and give to the poor. This may sound like a heavy load to bear, but following Jesus, our Messiah, *requires that we rid ourselves of the trappings and wealth that keep us from the love of God.*

PRAYERS   *others may be added*

Living and following your saving commandments, we pray:

◆ Show us the path of everlasting life.

That we respect and love our neighbors, we pray: ◆ *That we honor our mothers and fathers in word and deed, we pray:* ◆ *That we sell everything and give to the poor, we pray:* ◆ *That we continually seek the face of God, we pray:* ◆

Our Father . . .

God of truth,
you call us to be a people
rooted in your loving commandments
    and saving Word.
Give us the courage and wisdom
to live your rules and way of life
    authentically
so that all may know your
    merciful name.
We ask this through Jesus Christ, our
    Savior and Lord. Amen.

✤ *Your words, Lord, are Spirit and life.*

✦ *Your words, Lord, are Spirit and life.*

PSALM 19   page 405

READING   Mark 10:28–31

Peter began to say to Jesus, "We have given up everything and followed you." Jesus said, "Amen, I say to you, there is no one who has given up house or brothers or sisters or mother or father or children or lands for my sake and for the sake of the Gospel who will not receive a hundred times more now in this present age: houses and brothers and sisters and mothers and children and lands, with persecutions, and eternal life in the age to come. But many that are first will be last, and the last will be first."

REFLECTION

The Gospel of Mark presents us with a realistic Jesus. Today, Jesus promises that although we may have to give up many good things that stand in the way of our discipleship, we will be given many rewards. But we are not getting a "candy-coated" promise; we are also promised persecutions. Can we face hardships even after having sacrificed certain comforts for the Lord?

PRAYERS   *others may be added*

Depending on the Lord, we pray:

◆ Show us the path of everlasting life.

That your Church may be guided by you, especially during difficult times, we pray: ◆ *That you may guide us to know and let go of those things that stand in the way of following Christ, we pray:* ◆ *That you may guide world leaders to find the path of peace and harmony, we pray:* ◆ *That you may guide religious and all those who have made special sacrifices for the sake of the Gospel to continue their cheerful giving, we pray:* ◆

Our Father . . .

Lord, source of all life,
you have filled creation with
   innumerable wonders.
Help us to live in joyful appreciation
   of all your gifts,
to accept the hardships we
   cannot avoid,
and bless your name in all that we do.
We ask this through Christ our Lord.
   Amen.

✦ *Your words, Lord, are Spirit and life.*

✛ *Your words, Lord, are Spirit and life.*

PSALM 19 *page 405*

READING *Mark 10:39b–45*

Jesus said to them, "The chalice that I drink, you will drink, and with the baptism with which I am baptized, you will be baptized; but to sit at my right or at my left is not mine to give but is for those for whom it has been prepared." When the ten heard this, they became indignant at James and John. Jesus summoned them and said to them, "You know that those who are recognized as rulers over the Gentiles lord it over them, and their great ones make their authority over them felt. But it shall not be so among you. Rather, whoever wishes to be great among you will be your servant; whoever wishes to be first among you will be the slave of all. For the Son of Man did not come to be served but to serve and to give his life as a ransom for many."

REFLECTION

We, like James and John, long to be with our God, to sit with him in the heavenly paradise. Being with God does not involve an earthly life of glory and recognition, but a life of humble servitude. If we wish to be great and worthy, we must align ourselves with the least in our world. To be Christian is to seek to follow in the footsteps of the Son of Man, the one who came to serve and free the many. Let us go into the world breaking open our lives so that all may know the richness and opulence of God's heavenly home.

PRAYERS *others may be added*

Living a life of humble servitude, we pray:

◆ Show us the path of everlasting life.

For the impoverished, that they may know what it means to be great in God's sight, we pray: ◆ For the neglected, that they may experience God's unconditional love and compassion, we pray: ◆ For victims of war, that they may experience the peace of God's reconciling hand, we pray: ◆ For us, that we may only seek the splendor and glory of heaven, we pray: ◆

Our Father . . .

O Christ,
servant of all,
you modeled a life
of humility, mercy, and self-giving.
Sustain us in our Christian vocation
to love what lies before us, to
    sacrifice personal gain,
and to serve all of creation.
In your name we pray. Amen.

✛ *Your words, Lord, are Spirit and life.*

✛   *Your words, Lord, are Spirit and life.*

PSALM 19   *page 405*

READING   *Luke 1:39–45*

Mary set out and traveled to the hill country in haste to a town of Judah, where she entered the house of Zechariah and greeted Elizabeth. When Elizabeth heard Mary's greeting, the infant leaped in her womb, and Elizabeth, filled with the Holy Spirit, cried out in a loud voice and said, "Most blessed are you among women, and blessed is the fruit of your womb. And how does this happen to me, that the mother of my Lord should come to me? For at the moment the sound of your greeting reached my ears, the infant in my womb leaped for joy. Blessed are you who believed that what was spoken to you by the Lord would be fulfilled."

REFLECTION

The power of belief—the power of faith— has the ability to turn the world upside down. Here, Elizabeth, pregnant long after she hoped to be, and Mary, pregnant far sooner than she expected to be, meet and sing the praises of God. Elizabeth easily could have been resentful and Mary understandably could have hidden herself away, but these women did not respond so negatively. Their faith enabled them to see the wondrous possibilities and rejoice in each others blessings.

PRAYERS   *others may be added*

Rejoicing in God, our Savior, we pray:

◆   Show us the path of everlasting life.

That we may always reach out to those in need, we pray: ◆ *That through faith we may strive to see the potential for good in all the twists and turns of life, we pray:* ◆ *That we may value life in all its stages, we pray:* ◆ *That we may turn to Mary in our times of need, we pray:* ◆

Our Father . . .

Almighty Father,
you filled Mary and Elizabeth with
    the Holy Spirit,
and they responded to your plan
    of salvation.
Give us the same openness to your
    workings in our lives
so that we may bring about
    your kingdom
now and always.
Grant this through Christ our Lord.
    Amen.

✛   *Your words, Lord, are Spirit and life.*

✝ *Your words, Lord, are Spirit and life.*

PSALM 19   *page 405*

READING   *Mark 11:15–17*

They [Jesus and the Twelve] came to Jerusalem, and on entering the temple area he began to drive out those selling and buying there. He overturned the tables of the money changers and the seats of those who were selling doves. He did not permit anyone to carry anything through the temple area. Then he taught them saying, "Is it not written:

My house shall be called a house of prayer for all peoples? / But you have made it a den of thieves."

REFLECTION

Jesus put himself on a collision course with the authorities by his actions in the temple. He was not trying to foster a rebellion or political turmoil. Jesus was ushering in a new way to approach the Father. No longer were the old ways working; they were full of corruption and almost empty of sincerity. In the new way of Jesus, having temple currency and the proper animals for sacrifice are not needed for prayer. Instead, the true temple offering is a forgiving heart filled with sincere faith.

PRAYERS   *others may be added*

With sincere hearts, we pray:

◆ Show us the path of everlasting life.

Like St. Justin and all the martyrs, may we be willing to give all for the Gospel, we pray: ◆ *As Jesus cleansed the temple, may we cleanse our hearts of sin and corruption, we pray:* ◆ *Like the apostles, may we be ever ready to listen to the Lord, we pray:* ◆ *Like the early Christians, may we be filled with a brilliant fervor for our faith, we pray:* ◆

Our Father . . .

Father of all knowledge,
you called St. Justin to teach
    your wisdom
by word and example.
May we always approach you with
    forgiving and sincere hearts
so that our example may lead others
    to you.
We ask this through Christ our Lord.
    Amen.

✝ *Your words, Lord, are Spirit and life.*

✝ *Your words, Lord, are Spirit and life.*

PSALM 19   *page 405*

READING   *Mark 11:27–33*

Jesus and his disciples returned once more to Jerusalem. As he was walking in the temple area, the chief priests, the scribes, and the elders approached he and said to him, "By what authority are you doing these things? Or who gave you this authority to do them?" Jesus said to them, "I shall ask you one question. Answer me, and I will tell you by what authority I do these things. Was John's baptism of heavenly or of human origin? Answer me." They discussed this among themselves and said, "If we say, 'Of heavenly origin,' he will say, 'Then why did you not believe him?' But shall we say, 'Of human origin'?"—they feared the crowd, for they all thought John really was a prophet. So they said to Jesus in reply, "We do not know." Then Jesus said to them, "Neither shall I tell you by what authority I do these things."

REFLECTION

St. Marcellinus (+320) and St. Peter (+304) were imprisoned and beheaded during the persecutions of Diocletian because they converted many souls and hearts to the faith. St. Marcellinus, a prominent priest in the city of Rome, and St. Peter, a well-know exorcist, were esteemed for their strong convictions, charismatic personalities, and innate ability to proclaim the Word of God. Through their martyrdom, they witnessed to the authority of Jesus Christ, the Messiah, who shed his blood for the redemption of humanity. We, too, are called to sacrifice, to shed our lives, pointing all to the true author of salvation.

PRAYERS   *others may be added*

Through the intercession of St. Marcellinus and St. Peter, we pray:

◆ Show us the path of everlasting life.

That more men answer the call to the priesthood, we pray: ◆ That more people cast the demons of materialism and extreme individualism out of society, we pray: ◆ That more men and women are willing to sacrifice their lives for the Gospel, we pray: ◆ That all those suffering from persecution may know your comforting Word, we pray: ◆

Our Father . . .

God of strength,
you lifted up St. Marcellinus
    and St. Peter
as martyrs for the faith.
Stir in us the courage to declare
your message of truth and peace,
even in the face of adversity
    and disbelief.
Grant this through Christ our Lord.
    Amen.

✝ *Your words, Lord, are Spirit and life.*

✠ *Glory to you, O Trinity, one God in three equal Persons, as in the beginning, so now, and for ever.*

PSALM 145
page 421

READING
John 16:12–15

Jesus said to his disciples: "I have much more to tell you, but you cannot bear it now. But when he comes, the Spirit of truth, he will guide you to all truth. He will not speak on his own, but he will speak what he hears, and will declare to you the things that are coming. He will glorify me, because he will take from what is mine and declare it to you. Everything that the Father has is mine; for this reason I told you that he will take from what is mine and declare it to you."

REFLECTION

Today's celebration gives us the opportunity to appreciate the revelation of the three persons of the Trinity. We have the Old Testament, all of creation, and the testimony of Jesus showing us the Father. We have the Gospels and the example of the saints to see and hear the Son. And, we have the words of Jesus, all the movements of grace, and the quiet whispers in our soul to learn about the Holy Spirit. Our God yearns to be known and loved; our God waits to be met in every sacramental moment.

PRAYERS
others may be added

Turning to our triune God, we pray:

◆ Show us the path of everlasting life.

Father, send us the Holy Spirit, so that we may learn how to pray for that which will truly benefit your people, we pray: ◆
Christ Jesus, you implored the Father to send us the Holy Spirit; may we never reject that gift of life, we pray: ◆
Holy Spirit, inspire our every thought, desire, word, and action; may we follow the example of Christ and bring the knowledge of the Father to all, we pray: ◆

Our Father . . .

Father of all,
you sent your Son to reveal yourself
    to us
and your Holy Spirit to bind
    us together.
May we live in your unity and
    love forever.
We ask this through our Lord Jesus
    Christ, your Son,
who lives and reigns with you in the
    unity of the Holy Spirit,
one God, forever and ever. Amen.

✠ *Glory to you, O Trinity, one God in three equal Persons, as in the beginning, so now, and for ever.*

✠ *Your words, Lord, are Spirit and life.*

PSALM 19   *page 405*

READING   *Mark 12:1b–8*

[Jesus said,] "A man planted a vineyard, put a hedge around it, dug a wine press, and built a tower. Then he leased it to tenant farmers and left on a journey. At the proper time he sent a servant to the tenants to obtain from them some of the produce of the vineyard. But they seized him, beat him, and sent him away empty-handed. Again he sent them another servant. And that one they beat over the head and treated shamefully. He sent yet another whom they killed. So, too, many others; some they beat, others they killed. He had one other to send, a beloved son. He sent him to them last of all, thinking, 'They will respect my son.' But those tenants said to one another, 'This is the heir. Come, let us kill him, and the inheritance will be ours.' So they seized him and killed him, and threw him out of the vineyard."

REFLECTION

We often fail to see Christ, the beloved Son, in our midst. We move through life rushing through the work day, consumed with paying bills and planning for tomorrow, but missing the extraordinary presence and action of Jesus Christ within the vineyard of life. We are unable to set aside expectations and plans, hoping to find time tomorrow or next week to enjoy family, reverence the earth, and contemplate the mysteries of God. We are called to carve time out of each day to acknowledge and recognize Jesus Christ, the foundation and cornerstone of our lives.

PRAYERS   *others may be added*

Acknowledging the presence of God in our lives, we pray:

◆ Show us the path of everlasting life.

That we express gratitude for our families, we pray: ◆ *That we reverence the beauty of creation, we pray:* ◆ *That we contemplate the mysteries of faith, we pray:* ◆ *That we live lives recognizing Jesus Christ's saving action in the world, we pray:* ◆

Our Father . . .

Jesus Christ,
you paint our lives with
    beautiful images
of your forgiving love and
    saving presence.
Give us eyes to see and ears to hear
the many ways you appear and speak
    to us
within our daily lives.
In your name we pray. Amen.

✠ *Your words, Lord, are Spirit and life.*

✤ *Your words, Lord, are Spirit and life.*

PSALM 19 page 405

READING *Mark 12:13–17*

Some Pharisees and Herodians were sent to Jesus to ensnare him in his speech. They came and said to him, "Teacher, we know that you are a truthful man and that you are not concerned with anyone's opinion. You do not regard a person's status but teach the way of God in accordance with the truth. Is it lawful to pay the census tax to Caesar or not? Should we pay or should we not pay?" Knowing their hypocrisy he said to them, "Why are you testing me? Bring me a denarius to look at." They brought one to him and he said to them, "Whose image and inscription is this?" They replied to him, "Caesar's." So Jesus said to them, "Repay to Caesar what belongs to Caesar and to God what belongs to God." They were utterly amazed at him.

REFLECTION

Where is our allegiance? What are our priorities? St. Boniface (673/680–+754) clearly allied himself with God and his Church. He gave up a promising educational career in England to devote himself to missionary work among the German people. St. Boniface is best known for cutting down an oak tree sacred to the pagans and feared for its evil powers. He became an archbishop and built many churches and monasteries on former pagan sites. Eventually he resigned his position as archbishop and returned to missionary work. Boniface gave to God what belonged to God. Do we?

PRAYERS *others may be added*

Through the intercession of St. Boniface, we pray:

◆ Show us the path of everlasting life.

For missionaries, that they may be zealous about the work of God, we pray: ◆
For religious, that they may continue to model a life of prayer, we pray: ◆
For government leaders, that they may use lawful revenues for the uplifting of society, we pray: ◆ *For all of us, that we may chop down the empty symbols of sin in our lives, we pray:* ◆

Our Father . . .

Almighty God,
your power extends through
    all creation.
The nations bow down at your name.
May we follow the example of
    St. Boniface
and devote our gifts to the spread of
    your reign.
We ask this through Christ our Lord.
    Amen.

✤ *Your words, Lord, are Spirit and life.*

✚ *Your words, Lord, are Spirit and life.*

PSALM 19   *page 405*

READING   *Mark 12:18–27*

Some Sadducees, who say there is no resurrection, came to Jesus and put this question to him, saying, "Teacher, Moses wrote for us, *If someone's brother dies, leaving a wife but no child, his brother must take the wife and raise up descendants for his brother.* Now there were seven brothers. The first married a woman and died, leaving no descendants. So the second brother married her and died, leaving no descendants, and the third likewise. And the seven left no descendants. Last of all the woman also died. At the resurrection when they arise whose wife will she be? For all seven had been married to her." Jesus said to them, "Are you not misled because you do not know the Scriptures or the power of God? When they rise from the dead, they neither marry nor are given in marriage, but they are like the angels in heaven. As for the dead being raised, have you not read in the Book of Moses, in the passage about the bush, how God told him, *I am the God of Abraham, the God of Isaac, and the God of Jacob?* He is not God of the dead but of the living. You are greatly misled."

REFLECTION

After having a conversion experience similar to St. Paul, St. Norbert (1080–+1134) founded the Canons Regular of Prémontré, a religious community of men, to preach, engage in pastoral work, and live an austere life marked by strict poverty. St. Norbert was well known for his dynamic preaching, clerical reform, and commitment to the mission of the Church. The life of St. Norbert calls us to give witness through simplicity and fidelity to the freeing message of God—a God of the living, not of the dead.

PRAYERS   *others may be added*

Living simply and faithfully, we pray:

◆ Show us the path of everlasting life.

That more people will feel drawn to the charism of St. Norbert, we pray: ◆
That Norbertines throughout the world will be renewed in their vocation, we pray: ◆ *That Norbertines will challenge our wealthy world by living lives of austerity and poverty, we pray:* ◆
That we proclaim the word of God and minister to those in need, we pray: ◆

Our Father . . .

God of grace,
you called St. Norbert
to renew religious life.
Inspired by his example,
may we live simply, love freely,
and give witness to the Gospel.
We ask this through Christ our
    Lord. Amen.

✚ *Your words, Lord, are Spirit and life.*

✝ *Your words, Lord, are Spirit and life.*

PSALM 19   page 405

READING   Mark 12:28–34

One of the scribes came to Jesus and asked him, "Which is the first of all the commandments?" Jesus replied, "The first is this: *Hear, O Israel! The Lord our God is Lord alone! You shall love the Lord your God with all your heart, with all your soul, with all your mind, and with all your strength.* The second is this: *You shall love your neighbor as yourself.* There is no other commandment greater than these." The scribe said to him, "Well said, teacher. You are right in saying, *He is One and there is no other than he. And to love him with all your heart, with all your understanding, with all your strength, and to love your neighbor as yourself* is worth more than all burnt offerings and sacrifices." And when Jesus saw that he answered with understanding, he said to him, "You are not far from the Kingdom of God." And no one dared to ask him any more questions.

REFLECTION

Jesus is the fulfillment of the old law and the expression of the new law. This passage is a perfect example. Jesus quotes two different commandments from the old law. However, these two commandments had never been united. Here, Jesus declares that it is impossible to show love for God without loving one's neighbor and vice versa. Jesus, the God-man, who in himself unites heaven and earth, tells us that true love is a cross of two directions, the vertical and the horizontal.

PRAYERS   *others may be added*

Seeking the kingdom, we pray:

◆ Show us the path of everlasting life.

For the clergy, that they may always preach the kingdom, we pray: ◆
For teachers, that they may lead their students closer to the kingdom, we pray: ◆
For legislators, that they may enact laws that are expressions of the kingdom, we pray: ◆ *For us, that we may always reach out to our neighbors in love of our God, we pray:* ◆

Our Father . . .

God of the universe,
you guide all creation by your
    commandment of love.
May we love you with all our hearts,
    minds, souls, and strength.
And may we love our neighbors
    as ourselves.
We ask this through Christ our Lord.
    Amen.

✝ *Your words, Lord, are Spirit and life.*

✛ *Your words, Lord, are Spirit and life.*

PSALM 19   *page 405*

READING   *Mark 12:35–37*

As Jesus was teaching in the temple area he said, "How do the scribes claim that the Christ is the son of David? David himself, inspired by the Holy Spirit, said:

The Lord said to my lord, / 'Sit at my right hand / until I place your enemies under your feet.'

David himself calls him 'lord'; so how is he his son?" The great crowd heard this with delight.

REFLECTION

Jesus uses riddles, questions, and parables to declare his authority as the Messiah: the one who came so that all might have life. In this particular passage, Jesus does not negate his Davidic lineage, but challenges the crowd to ponder his true identity. David himself calls his son, his descendant, Lord. The crowd does not understand, but Jesus is slowly revealing and unveiling his identity as the Christ who will die to bring about the true kingdom. He will not only bring about salvation as David's son, but as David's Lord!

PRAYERS   *others may be added*

Announcing the authority of our Messiah, we pray:

◆ Show us the path of everlasting life.

For those who do not know the love of God, we pray: ◆ For those who do not know the forgiveness of God, we pray: ◆ For those who do not know the peace of God, we pray: ◆ For those who do not know God's freeing Word, we pray: ◆

Our Father . . .

Lord of all creation,
you call us to reveal your light
    and truth
in a world immersed in the darkness
of sin and disbelief.
May we be like David, courageous
    and strong,
proclaiming your divine name
so that all will know your
    true identity.
We ask this in your name. Amen.

✛ *Your words, Lord, are Spirit and life.*

✝ *Your words, Lord, are Spirit and life.*

PSALM 19
page 405

READING
Mark 12:38–44

In the course of his teaching Jesus said, "Beware of the scribes, who like to go around in long robes and accept greetings in the marketplaces, seats of honor in synagogues, and places of honor at banquets. They devour the houses of widows and, as a pretext, recite lengthy prayers. They will receive a very severe condemnation."

He sat down opposite the treasury and observed how the crowd put money into the treasury. Many rich people put in large sums. A poor widow also came and put in two small coins worth a few cents. Calling his disciples to himself, he said to them, "Amen, I say to you, this poor widow put in more than all the other contributors to the treasury. For they have all contributed from their surplus wealth, but she, from her poverty, has contributed all she had, her whole livelihood."

REFLECTION

Jesus loves to teach by using contrasting images. Today we see people of power and honor contrasted with a powerless outcast. We see those who take and demand alongside those who give generously. Without hesitation Jesus declares that as our models we should take the outcast, the powerless, and those who give generously. To what extent have we succeeded in following this directive of our Lord?

PRAYERS
others may be added

Through the intercession of St. Ephrem, we pray:

◆ Show us the path of everlasting life.

That we may give all of our being to the service of the Gospel, we pray: ◆ That we may wear the long robe of generosity, we pray: ◆ That we may sit in the seat of service to others, we pray: ◆ That we may willingly accept greetings of disdain for the sake of Christ, we pray: ◆

Our Father . . .

Lord God,
our very life is your gift to us.
When we see others in need,
    may we give generously;
when we desire power,
    may we look to your Son's cross;
and when we feel our utter poverty,
    may we simply say, yes,
so that all will glory in your might.
We ask this through Christ our Lord.
    Amen.

✝ *Your words, Lord, are Spirit and life.*

✛ *I am the living bread that comes down from heaven; whoever eats this bread will live forever.*

PSALM 116 — page 418

READING — Luke 9:12–17

The Twelve approached him [Jesus] and said, "Dismiss the crowd so that they can go to the surrounding villages and farms and find lodging and provisions; for we are in a deserted place here." He said to them, "Give them some food yourselves." They replied, "Five loaves and two fish are all we have, unless we ourselves go and buy food for all these people." Now the men there numbered about five thousand. Then he said to his disciples, "Have them sit down in groups of about fifty." They did so and made them all sit down. Then taking the five loaves and the two fish, and looking up to heaven, he said the blessing over them, broke them, and gave them to the disciples to set before the crowd. They all ate and were satisfied. And when the leftover fragments were picked up, they filled twelve wicker baskets.

REFLECTION

Today we celebrate the sacrificial gift of Jesus Christ in bread and wine—not just any bread and wine, but the very bread of his flesh and wine of his blood, broken and poured out so that all might taste God's saving love. Jesus, our life, our sweetness, our hope, calls us to the banquet of salvation to feast on the Eucharist, the source of eternal joy. Following Melchizedek in the Old Testament, we bring the bread of our lives to God's table, seeking, like Elijah, to be fed by the bread of angels. Let us celebrate, for we are invited every day to eat, drink, and savor the Body and Blood of Christ, our medicine for immortality.

PRAYERS — others may be added

Rejoicing in the Body and Blood of Christ, we pray:

◆ May we taste your presence.

That we approach the table of life with humble and pure hearts, we pray: ◆
That we receive Holy Communion worthily and frequently, we pray: ◆
That we express gratitude for the gift of the Eucharist by sharing your saving Word, we pray: ◆ *That all will recognize you in the breaking of the bread, we pray:* ◆

Our Father . . .

O Christ,
our Bread of Life,
you nourish and sustain us
    with your Body and Blood.
Transform our hearts
so we are able to proclaim
your Eucharistic gift for the world.
We ask this through our Lord Jesus
    Christ, your Son,
who lives and reigns with you in the
    unity of the Holy Spirit,
one God, forever and ever. Amen.

✛ *I am the living bread that comes down from heaven; whoever eats this bread will live forever.*

✝ *Your words, Lord, are Spirit and life.*

PSALM 19   *page 405*

READING   *Matthew 10:7–13**

Jesus said to the Twelve: "As you go, make this proclamation: 'The Kingdom of heaven is at hand.' Cure the sick, raise the dead, cleanse the lepers, drive out demons. Without cost you have received; without cost you are to give. Do not take gold or silver or copper for your belts; no sack for the journey, or a second tunic, or sandals, or walking stick. The laborer deserves his keep. Whatever town or village you enter, look for a worthy person in it, and stay there until you leave. As you enter a house, wish it peace. If the house is worthy, let your peace come upon it; if not, let your peace return to you."

REFLECTION

Jesus' mission method flies in the face of what most of us would expect to do if we were sent on a journey. The message is this: Rely on the goodness of others; rely on the goodness of God. Our faith, our very life is a gift from God. We did nothing to earn it; it cost us nothing. In the same way, we are to give witness freely, give of ourselves freely, give all we have freely. God will not let us down; God and his people will provide.

PRAYERS   *others may be added*

Through the intercession of St. Barnabas, we pray:

◆ Show us the path of everlasting life.

That the sick may be strengthened in body and spirit, we pray: ◆ *That those who live with deadened spirits may be uplifted, we pray:* ◆ *That those who are outcast like lepers may be welcomed within our midst, we pray:* ◆ *That the demons of addiction and abuse be cast out of our homes, we pray:* ◆

Our Father . . .

Generous God,
you summoned St. Barnabas to be a
    co-worker
of your first apostles.
May we emulate Barnabas,
and be of help to all who require it,
    never counting the cost,
so that all may come to know your
    bountiful love.
Grant this through Christ our Lord.
    Amen.

✝ *Your words, Lord, are Spirit and life.*

*Today's Gospel is from the memorial of St. Barnabus, Lectionary #580. The alternate Gospel for the day is from the Monday of the Tenth Week in Ordinary Time, Matthew 5:1–12, Lectionary #359.

✚ *Your words, Lord, are Spirit and life.*

PSALM 19 *page 405*

READING *Matthew 5:13–16*

Jesus said to his disciples: "You are the salt of the earth. But if salt loses its taste, with what can it be seasoned? It is no longer good for anything but to be thrown out and trampled underfoot. You are the light of the world. A city set on a mountain cannot be hidden. Nor do they light a lamp and then put it under a bushel basket; it is set on a lampstand, where it gives light to all in the house. Just so, your light must shine before others, that they may see your good deeds and glorify your heavenly Father."

REFLECTION

To be salt—To be light! This is our mantra as disciples on the journey proclaiming the saving message of Jesus Christ. We are to be salt, seasoning the souls of humanity with God's message of love. We are to be light, illuminating the recesses of the human heart with God's saving Word. When the salt of our faith becomes tasteless and the light of our beliefs become dim, we are not to hide but to place ourselves in the arms of Jesus Christ, the savory salt of truth and bright light of hope, so that we can become a lamp, giving glory to our Father in heaven.

PRAYERS *others may be added*

Seasoning and enlightening the hearts of nonbelievers, we pray:

◆ Show us the path of everlasting life.

To be salt for the earth, we pray: ◆
To be light for the world, we pray: ◆
To be reconciliation for creation,
we pray: ◆ *To give glory to our Father*
in heaven, we pray: ◆

Our Father . . .

God of peace,
you gave us your Son, Jesus,
as the one, true lamp,
giving light to all in the house.
May we be faithful in our
    Christian vocation
so that we may become salt and light
    in a world
longing for the flavor of your love
and light of your salvation.
We ask this through Jesus our Lord.
    Amen.

✚ *Your words, Lord, are Spirit and life.*

✝ *Your words, Lord, are Spirit and life.*

PSALM 19 *page 405*

READING *Matthew 5:17–19*

Jesus said to his disciples: "Do not think that I have come to abolish the law or the prophets. I have come not to abolish but to fulfill. Amen, I say to you, until heaven and earth pass way, not the smallest letter or the smallest part of a letter will pass from the law, until all things have taken place. Therefore, whoever breaks one of the least of these commandments and teaches others to do so will be called least in the Kingdom of heaven. But whoever obeys and teaches these commandments will be called greatest in the Kingdom of heaven."

REFLECTION

St. Anthony (1195–+1231) began his religious life as an Augustinian canon, engaged in scriptural studies. Later, being enthralled with the humility and missionary zeal of the Franciscans, he joined them and, although poor health kept him from the missions, he became a kitchen worker. When Anthony's superiors learned about his talent for preaching and teaching, they ordered him to leave the kitchen and spread the word of God to the thousands who were drawn to his sermons. As one of the most familiar saints, Anthony clearly fulfills Jesus' words in today's Gospel.

PRAYERS *others may be added*

In obedience, we pray:

◆ Show us the path of everlasting life.

To be humble as St. Anthony was humble, we pray: ◆ *To be zealous for preaching and teaching the word of God, we pray:* ◆ *To care for those who persecute us, we pray:* ◆ *To be grateful to those who offer us hospitality, we pray:* ◆

Our Father . . .

God of power,
in the Holy Spirit you give us
gifts and graces to accomplish
    your will.
Through the example and intercession
    of St. Anthony,
may we find your will in our lives,
use our gifts generously,
and proclaim your glory.
We ask this through Christ our Lord.
    Amen.

✝ *Your words, Lord, are Spirit and life.*

✝ *Your words, Lord, are Spirit and life.*

PSALM 19 *page 405*

READING *Matthew 5:22–24*

[Jesus said,] "But I say to you [the disciples], whoever is angry with his brother will be liable to judgment, and whoever says to his brother, *Raqa,* will be answerable to the Sanhedrin, and whoever says, 'You fool,' will be liable to fiery Gehenna. Therefore, if you bring your gift to the altar, and there recall that your brother has anything against you, leave your gift there at the altar, go first and be reconciled with your brother, and then come and offer your gift."

REFLECTION

There are so many signs of unresolved anger in our world. We live in an age characterized by road rage, monetary competition, abusive language, and physical exploitation. This anger stems from our inability to forgive, to reverence the sacredness of life, and to find peace within the reign of God. If we want a more peaceful, merciful, and reconciled world we must invite God to transform our everyday experiences of hurt and loss into moments of grace and redemption so that we will be ready, along with our brothers and sisters, to offer our gift at the altar.

PRAYERS *others may be added*

Seeking the peace of Christ, we pray:

◆ Show us the path of everlasting life.

For the times when we have hurt someone with our words and actions, we pray: ◆
For the times when we have been hurt by our brothers and sisters, we pray: ◆
For unresolved anger that has resulted in abuse and violence, we pray: ◆
For a more forgiving and merciful world, we pray: ◆

Our Father . . .

God of reconciliation,
your Son was nailed to a tree
to rid the world of anger and sin.
Give us compassionate and
     forgiving hearts
so we may let go of the grudges
     and guilt
that hinder us from experiencing
     your love.
Grant this through Christ our Lord.
     Amen.

✝ *Your words, Lord, are Spirit and life.*

✦ *In you is the fountain of life; we drink from the streams of your goodness.*

PSALM 33 *page 409*

READING *Luke 15:3–7*

Jesus addressed this parable to the Pharisees and scribes: "What man among you having a hundred sheep and losing one of them would not leave the ninety-nine in the desert and go after the lost one until he finds it? And when he does find it, he sets it on his shoulders with great joy and, upon his arrival home, he calls together his friends and neighbors and says to them, 'Rejoice with me because I have found my lost sheep.' I tell you, in just the same way there will be more joy in heaven over one sinner who repents than over ninety-nine righteous people who have no need of repentance."

REFLECTION

The heart is the seat of deepest emotions—the core of our being—the physical centerpiece. Poets and artists through the centuries have celebrated the heart in all its many meanings. Is it any surprise that from the earliest of times devotions to the heart of Jesus have developed and flourished? From Christ's heart pierced by a lance to the visions of St. Margaret Mary Alacoque (1647–+1690), authentic devotions to the Sacred Heart always celebrate the merciful love of God as manifest in Jesus Christ.

PRAYERS *others may be added*

Appealing to the Sacred Heart of Christ, we pray:

◆ Show us the path of everlasting life.

Divine love of the pre-existing Word, animate our love; we pray: ◆ *Perfect love of Jesus for God and humankind, enflame our love; we pray:* ◆ *Natural affections of Jesus, stretch our hearts to reach out to all; we pray:* ◆ *Good Shepherd, find the hearts that are lost and restore them to your flock; we pray:* ◆

Our Father . . .

Father,
we celebrate the love you show us
in the heart of your Son, Jesus Christ.
May your Spirit enflame our hearts
so that in our joy we may spread your
    forgiving love.
We ask this through our Lord Jesus
    Christ, your Son,
who lives and reigns with you and the
    Holy Spirit,
one God, forever and ever. Amen.

✦ *In you is the fountain of life; we drink from the streams of your goodness.*

✠ *Here I am, Lord; I come to do your will.*

PSALM 40   *page 411*

READING   *Luke 2:41–43, 46–51*

Each year Jesus' parents went to Jerusalem for the feast of Passover, and when he was twelve years old, they went up according to festival custom. After they had completed its days, as they were returning, the boy Jesus remained behind in Jerusalem, but his parents did not know it. After three days they found him in the temple, sitting in the midst of the teachers, listening to them and asking them questions, and all who heard him were astounded at his understanding and his answers. When his parents saw him, they were astonished, and his mother said to him, "Son, why have you done this to us? Your father and I have been looking for you with great anxiety." And he said to them, "Why were you looking for me? Did you not know that I must be in my Father's house?" But they did not understand what he said to them. He went down with them and came to Nazareth, and was obedient to them; and his mother kept all these things in her heart.

REFLECTION

The first traces of a devotion to the Immaculate Heart of Mary can be found in the sermons of St. Bernard of Clairvaux (1090–+1153), but the devotion became well known and popular under the leadership and witness of St. John Eudes (1601–+1680). St. John Eudes and his religious community, the Congregation of Jesus and Mary, invited people to contemplate Mary's interior life, her joys and sorrows, virtues and hidden perfections, but above all her virginal love of God. May we find in the Most Holy Heart of Mary a simple but pure pathway to the Sacred Heart of Jesus.

PRAYERS   *others may be added*

Through the intercession of the Immaculate Heart of Mary, we pray:

◆ Show us the path of everlasting life.

That we may be humble, we pray: ◆ That our lives may be pure and chaste, we pray: ◆ That we may ponder the word of God in our hearts, we pray: ◆ That we may say "yes" to God's will, we pray: ◆

Our Father . . .

Holy One,
you called the Blessed Virgin Mary
to hold and keep your Word
within the purity of her heart.
Grant us the humility and simplicity
to bear your saving message to
    the world.
Grant this through Jesus Christ our
    Lord. Amen.

✠ *Here I am, Lord; I come to do your will.*

✠ *Your words, Lord, are Spirit and life.*

PSALM 19   page 405

READING   *Luke 7:44–50*

Then he turned to the woman and said to Simon, "Do you see this woman? When I entered your house, you did not give me water for my feet, but she has bathed them with her tears and wiped them with her hair. You did not give me a kiss, but she has not ceased kissing my feet since the time I entered. You did not anoint my head with oil, but she anointed my feet with ointment. So I tell you, her many sins have been forgiven because she has shown great love. But the one to whom little is forgiven, loves little." He said to her, "Your sins are forgiven." The others at table said to themselves, "Who is this who even forgives sins?" But he said to the woman, "Your faith has saved you; go in peace."

REFLECTION

Today's Gospel is about self-sufficiency, or the myth of self-sufficiency. The "sinful woman" empties her heart, her tears, and her vial of oil and asks for Christ's forgiveness and love. On the other hand, the host of the dinner feels not even the slightest need to offer Jesus the common courtesies of hospitality. The host is full of his own importance and self-righteousness; he believes himself to be self-sufficient. If we are so full of our own importance, there will never be room for the saving love of Christ.

PRAYERS   *others may be added*

With open hearts, we pray:

◆ Show us the path of everlasting life.

That we may empty our hearts of all self-importance and self-righteousness, we pray: ◆ *That we may turn from self-indulgence to self-giving, we pray:* ◆ *That we may welcome all guests to the Lord's banquet with the same respect and love, we pray:* ◆ *That peace may reign in our world, we pray:* ◆

Our Father . . .

Lord of the banquet,
you invite us to partake of
   your bounty
at the table of love.
Help us to empty our hearts and
   our lives
of all that stands in the way of
   receiving and accepting
your call to peace and forgiveness.
We ask this through our Lord Jesus
   Christ, your Son,
who lives and reigns with you in the
   unity of the Holy Spirit,
one God, forever and ever. Amen.

✠ *Your words, Lord, are Spirit and life.*

✝ *Your words, Lord, are Spirit and life.*

PSALM 19   page 405

READING   Matthew 5:38–42

Jesus said to his disciples: "You have heard that it was said, *An eye for an eye and a tooth for a tooth.* But I say to you, offer no resistance to one who is evil. When someone strikes you on your right cheek, turn the other one to him as well. If anyone wants to go to law with you over your tunic, hand him your cloak as well. Should anyone press you into service for one mile, go with him for two miles. Give to the one who asks of you, and do not turn your back on one who wants to borrow."

REFLECTION

Jesus challenges his disciples to eliminate retaliation and vengeance from their lives. Even though the Old Testament law allows some forms of retaliation, Jesus wants us, his followers, to be different. Rather than adopting the attitudes and actions of our enemies, we are to be a people of mercy, sacrifice, and forgiveness. We are to give what we have and ask for nothing in return, even to those who hate and hurt us. Let us wear the tunic of understanding and the cloak of compassion, witnessing to Jesus Christ, fulfillment of the old law and giver of the new.

PRAYERS   others may be added

Living the law of Jesus Christ, we pray:

◆ Show us the path of everlasting life.

That we extend the mercy of God to all those in need, we pray: ◆ *That we are willing to make the necessary sacrifices for God's reign to abound, we pray:* ◆ *That we forgive those who have wronged or hurt us, we pray:* ◆ *That we graciously share what we have, expecting nothing in return, we pray:* ◆

Our Father. . .

O Christ,
the anointed one,
you institute laws that empower the
    human spirit
to soar with your message of
    everlasting life.
Instill in us forgiving hearts
so that all will know the peace of
    a world
no longer ruled by vengeance.
We ask this in your name. Amen.

✝ *Your words, Lord, are Spirit and life.*

✛ *Your words, Lord, are Spirit and life.*

PSALM 19   page 405

READING   *Matthew 5:43–48*

Jesus said to his disciples: "You have heard that it was said, *You shall love your neighbor and hate your enemy.* But I say to you, love your enemies and pray for those who persecute you, that you may be children of your heavenly Father, for he makes his sun rise on the bad and the good, and causes rain to fall on the just and the unjust. For if you love those who love you, what recompense will you have? Do not the tax collectors do the same? And if you greet your brothers and sisters only, what is unusual about that? Do not the pagans do the same? So be perfect, just as your heavenly Father is perfect."

REFLECTION

But, Lord, it's hard enough to love my neighbor. Do I have to love my enemies too? We know the answer: Love knows no boundaries; it is truly free-range. St. Romuald (950–+1027) knew no boundaries in his devotion to God. Dissatisfied with the monastic life of his day, he took greater and greater steps toward solitude and prayer, ultimately founding the Camaldolese Congregation. St. Romuald, in his harsh and restless ways, may not have been the easiest man to love, but his many followers saw in his heart a perfect love of God.

PRAYERS   *others may be added*

Through the intercession of St. Romuald, we pray:

◆ Show us the path of everlasting life.

That we may love those who are most difficult to love, we pray: ◆ *That we may fight all temptations to judge others, we pray:* ◆ *That we may learn to appreciate and grow in solitude and prayer, we pray:* ◆ *That more people will answer the call to the contemplative life, we pray:* ◆

Our Father . . .

Gentle God,
your word is most often found
in the quiet stirrings of the soul.
Give us the patience to stop and listen
    to your soft voice
so that we may have the courage to
    love our enemies
and the strength to pray for those who
    persecute us.
We ask this through Christ our Lord.
    Amen.

✛ *Your words, Lord, are Spirit and life.*

✦ *Your words, Lord, are Spirit and life.*

PSALM 19 *page 405*

READING *Matthew 6:1–6,16–18*

Jesus said to his disciples: "Take care not to perform righteous deeds in order that people may see them; otherwise, you will have no recompense from your heavenly Father. When you give alms, do not blow a trumpet before you, as the hypocrites do in the synagogues and in the streets to win the praise of others. Amen, I say to you, they have received their reward. But when you give alms, do not let your left hand know what your right is doing, so that your almsgiving may be secret. And your Father who sees in secret will repay you.

"When you pray, do not be like the hypocrites, who love to stand and pray in the synagogues and on street corners so that others may see them. Amen, I say to you, they have received their reward. But when you pray, go to your inner room, close the door, and pray to your Father in secret. And your Father who sees in secret will repay you.

"When you fast, do not look gloomy like the hypocrites. They neglect their appearance, so that they may appear to others to be fasting. Amen, I say to you, they have received their reward. But when you fast, anoint your head and wash your face, so that you may not appear to be fasting, except to your Father who is hidden. And your Father who sees what is hidden will repay you."

REFLECTION

The wisdom of Jesus is clear here. He understands the way we work. We need motivation. He tells us to undertake acts of piety: prayer, fasting, and almsgiving— with the right motivation—to please God. He is not asking for us to look for no return, for he promises rewards from God. He is asking us to do these acts in secret— to please God, not others. The mission of Jesus is to reveal the Father's love. It is this love that should push us to pray, fast, and give alms.

PRAYERS *others may be added*

In response to God's love, we pray:

◆ Show us the path of everlasting love.

That we may give quietly, we pray: ◆
That we may pray humbly, we pray: ◆
That we may sacrifice cheerfully, we pray: ◆ *That we may love always, we pray:* ◆

Our Father . . .

Father,
your love is unbounded.
Give us generous souls that respond
    only to you
so that our lives may be
    quiet witnesses
to your kingdom.
Grant this through Christ our Lord.
    Amen.

✦ *Your words, Lord, are Spirit and life.*

✝ *Your words, Lord, are Spirit and life.*

Psalm 19 *page 405*

Reading *Matthew 6:7–15*

Jesus said to his disciples: "In praying, do not babble like the pagans, who think that they will be heard because of their many words. Do not be like them. Your Father knows what you need before you ask him.

"This is how you are to pray:

Our Father who art in heaven, / hallowed be thy name, / thy Kingdom come, / thy will be done, / on earth as it is in heaven. / Give us this day our daily bread; / and forgive us our trespasses, / as we forgive those who trespass against us; / and lead us not into temptation, / but deliver us from evil.'

"If you forgive men their transgressions, your heavenly Father will forgive you. But if you do not forgive men, neither will your Father forgive your transgressions."

Reflection

St. Aloysius Gonzaga (1568–+1591), a Jesuit, was known for his ability to teach by example, purvey words that all could understand, and live fully for others. Having died at the young age of 23, people could not believe the heights this child prodigy reached in the areas of asceticism and contemplation. St. Aloysius's faith and spirituality were like fire—lighting the world ablaze with God's love and burning with the mystery of the incarnation. Let us be like St. Aloysius, never babbling like the pagans, but always on fire, longing to know the heavenly Father.

Prayers *others may be added*

Through the intercession of St. Aloysius, we pray:

◆ Show us the path of everlasting life.

For young people, that they may consider a life of service as a religious priest, brother, or sister, we pray: ◆ *For Jesuits, that they may live the Ignatian charism with great zeal and authenticity, we pray:* ◆ *For Jesuit institutions of learning, that they may faithfully pursue God through study and prayer, we pray:* ◆ *For people everywhere, that they may long to know the heavenly father, we pray:* ◆

Our Father . . .

God of life,
you called St. Aloysius
to teach your word and humbly
    serve others.
Ignite in us a youthful flame
    that burns
with ardent zeal, unconditional love,
    and enduring hope.
Grant this through Jesus our Lord.
    Amen.

✝ *Your words, Lord, are Spirit and life.*

✠ *Your words, Lord, are Spirit and life.*

PSALM 19   page 405

READING   *Matthew 6:19–23*

Jesus said to his disciples: "Do not store up for yourselves treasures on earth, where moth and decay destroy, and thieves break in and steal. But store up treasures in heaven, where neither moth nor decay destroys, nor thieves break in and steal. For where your treasure is, there also will your heart be.

"The lamp of the body is the eye. If your eye is sound, your whole body will be filled with light; but if your eye is bad, your whole body will be in darkness. And if the light in you is darkness, how great will the darkness be."

REFLECTION

Both St. John Fisher (1469–+1535) and St. Thomas More (1478–+1535) were beheaded because they would not take an oath sanctioning the royal supremacy of King Henry VIII and repudiating papal authority. As avid defenders of the faith during the Reformation, they were known for their intelligence, integrity, and deep spirituality. When one glances at the lives of St. John Fisher and St. Thomas More, it becomes quite apparent that these two men did not store up treasures on earth, but in heaven. Following their example, may we live our faith with sincerity and be willing to sacrifice anything, even our lives, for the kingdom of God.

PRAYERS   *others may be added*

Willing to give our lives for the sake of the Gospel, we pray:

◆ Show us the path of everlasting life.

That the word of God may never be used for political manipulation and gain, we pray: ◆ That those facing persecution for their faith will know the comfort of God's saving message, we pray: ◆ That we may always follow the teachings of the Church, we pray: ◆ That people may recognize the beauty, truth, and wisdom of the Church, we pray: ◆

Our Father . . .

O God,
You are the strength of the martyrs.
You continually call men and women to shed their blood for the kingdom.
Instill in us sacrificial faith and
    profound conviction
so that all will know your Son, our
    saving Lamb.
Grant this through Christ our Lord.
    Amen.

✠ *Your words, Lord, are Spirit and life.*

✝ *Your words, Lord, are Spirit and life.*

PSALM 19   *page 405*

READING   *Matthew 6:26–34a*

[Jesus said:] "Look at the birds in the sky; they do not sow or reap, they gather nothing into barns, yet your heavenly Father feeds them. Are not you more important than they? Can any of you by worrying add a single moment to your life-span? Why are you anxious about clothes? Learn from the way the wild flowers grow. They do not work or spin. But I tell you that not even Solomon in all his splendor was clothed like one of them. If God so clothes the grass of the field, which grows today and is thrown into the oven tomorrow, will he not much more provide for you, O you of little faith? So do not worry and say, 'What are we to eat?' or 'What are we to drink?' or 'What are we to wear?' All these things the pagans seek. Your heavenly Father knows that you need them all. But seek first the Kingdom of God and his righteousness, and all these things will be given you besides. Do not worry about tomorrow; tomorrow will take care of itself."

REFLECTION

Here we see the happy Jesus, the one who delights in the wonders of the Father's creation. He invites us to do the same. Take in the beauty that surrounds us everywhere. Stuck in traffic? Look at things you can't usually see as you drive past. Bringing out the garbage? Enjoy the early morning stillness or the stars in the sky. Trouble sleeping? Watch the moon's slow dance across the sky. All these and more are constant reminders of the Father's love for us. Don't worry, God is taking care of you.

PRAYERS   *others may be added*

    With delight, we pray:

◆ Show us the path of everlasting life.

That the goods of the earth may be distributed justly, we pray: ◆ That all the baptized may be clothed with the garment of holiness, we pray: ◆ That we may honor, preserve, and take delight in the beauty of nature, we pray: ◆ That joy may be our hallmark, we pray: ◆

Our Father . . .

God of all creation,
your care extends through all
    the universe.
We turn to you and depend on you for
    your life-giving Spirit;
Help us to live in your delight.
We ask this through Christ our Lord.
    Amen.

✝ *Your words, Lord, are Spirit and life.*

✚ *The Lord is my light and my salvation.*

PSALM 27
page 408

READING
Luke 1:57–63

When the time arrived for Elizabeth to have her child she gave birth to a son. Her neighbors and relatives heard that the Lord had shown his great mercy toward her, and they rejoiced with her. When they came on the eighth day to circumcise the child, they were going to call him Zechariah after his father, but his mother said in reply, "No. He will be called John." But they answered her, "There is no one among your relatives who has this name." So they made signs, asking his father what he wished him to be called. He asked for a tablet and wrote, "John is his name," and all were amazed."

REFLECTION

It seems rather fitting to celebrate the birth of St. John the Baptist during this time of year when daylight is beginning to be overshadowed by darkness. As days become shorter and daylight becomes a distant memory, the world longs for someone to be born to announce the coming Light. John the Baptist is that person—the one who declares, heralds, and makes straight the way for God's true Light, which no darkness can overcome. We are reminded by his birth to decrease like the setting sun so that Jesus Christ can increase in our hearts and world.

PRAYERS
others may be added

Rejoicing in the birth of St. John the Baptist, we pray:

◆ Lord, graciously hear us.

For lay men and women, that they may announce the salvation of God at work and home, we pray: ◆ *For religious, that they may herald the Good News to all those in darkness, we pray:* ◆ *For priests and deacons, that they may preach God's message of forgiveness and reconciliation to their people, we pray:* ◆ *For bishops, that they may declare the Gospel of life in a culture of death, we pray:* ◆

Our Father . . .

God of light,
you called St. John the Baptist
to prepare the way for your
    redeeming Word made flesh.
May our lives be a living testimony
    and pronouncement
of your salvific love and action in
    the world.
We ask this through our Lord Jesus
    Christ, your Son,
who lives and reigns with you in the
    unity of the Holy Spirit,
one God, forever and ever. Amen.

✚ *The Lord is my light and my salvation.*

✦ *Praise the Lord for he is good.*

PSALM 33   page 409

READING   *Matthew 7:1–5*

Jesus said to his disciples: "Stop judging, that you may not be judged. For as you judge, so will you be judged, and the measure with which you measure will be measured out to you. Why do you notice the splinter in your brother's eye, but do not perceive the wooden beam in your own eye? How can you say to your brother, 'Let me remove that splinter from your eye,' while the wooden beam is in your eye? You hypocrite, remove the wooden beam from your eye first; then you will see clearly to remove the splinter from your brother's eye."

REFLECTION

"Stop judging." Jesus is very direct. And yet, it is one of the most difficult directions to follow. It is so much easier to judge others than to look at ourselves honestly. The problem is, we can only see the actions of others; we cannot see into their hearts and souls. Only God can look into those deepest places and truly understand the motivations behind human actions. Judgment of character is reserved to God alone. Let's work on removing the beams from our eyes, so that we can see into our own hearts and let God take care of the rest.

PRAYER   *others may be added*

Trusting in God, we pray:

◆ Lord, graciously hear us.

That we may always walk in the way of mercy, we pray: ◆ *That peace and harmony may prevail in our world, we pray:* ◆ *That all forms of prejudice may be rejected by the Christian community, we pray:* ◆ *That the dead may rest in peace, we pray:* ◆

Our Father . . .

Almighty God,
you give without measure.
May we learn your mercy,
may we live your love in our lives,
and may all know the saving power
    of your Son.
We ask this through Christ our Lord.
    Amen.

✦ *Praise the Lord for he is good.*

✦ *Praise the Lord for he is good.*

PSALM 33   *page 409*

READING   *Matthew 7:6, 12–14*

Jesus said to his disciples: "Do not give what is holy to dogs, or throw your pearls before swine, lest they trample them underfoot, and turn and tear you to pieces.

"Do to others whatever you would have them do to you. This is the Law and the Prophets.

"Enter through the narrow gate; for the gate is wide and the road broad that leads to destruction, and those who enter through it are many. How narrow the gate and constricted the road that leads to life. And those who find it are few."

REFLECTION

We are given yet another principle to follow in living a life pleasing to our God: "Do to others as you would have them do to you." It seems basic and simple, but in reality it can be very difficult and challenging. Jesus tells us that if we want to pass through the narrow gate to salvation we must reverence all life, forgive all hurt, and love all people. Seeking to pass through the constricted road to eternal life, we must treat others as priceless pearls, rare gems, valued in the eyes of God.

PRAYERS   *others may be added*

Respecting the dignity of all life, we pray:

◆ Lord, graciously hear us.

For an end to abortion, that we may know and understand God's gift of life, we pray: ◆ *For an end to capital punishment, that we may find new ways to help people make retribution for their crimes and find healing, we pray:* ◆ *For an end to violence, that we may follow God's ways of reconciliation and forgiveness, we pray:* ◆ *For an end to hunger, that we may distribute goods with fairness and equity, we pray:* ◆

Our Father . . .

God of life,
you call us to reverence all
    of creation.
Give us the courage to speak
    out against
the many ways in which we
denigrate and abuse your gift of life.
Grant this through Jesus Christ our
    Lord. Amen.

✦ *Praise the Lord for he is good.*

✚ *Praise the Lord for he is good.*

PSALM 33 *page 409*

READING *Matthew 7:15–20*

Jesus said to his disciples: "Beware of false prophets, who come to you in sheep's clothing, but underneath are ravenous wolves. By their fruits you will know them. Do people pick grapes from thornbushes, or figs from thistles? Just so, every good tree bears good fruit, and a rotten tree bears bad fruit. A good tree cannot bear bad fruit, nor can a rotten tree bear good fruit. Every tree that does not bear good fruit will be cut down and thrown into the fire. So by their fruits you will know them."

REFLECTION

Today we commemorate St. Cyril of Alexandria (376–+444). St. Cyril lived through a time of great theological controversies. He defended the true humanity of Christ, and Mary as Mother of God. St. Cyril's ability to discern the fruit of the arguments of his time earned him the title of doctor of the Church. We, too, must examine what we see, hear, and do to determine if it will bear good fruit to give sustenance to the faith of all.

PRAYERS *others may be added*

Through the intercession of St. Cyril, we pray:

◆ Lord, graciously hear us.

For bishops, priests, and deacons, that they may faithfully preach the word of God, we pray: ◆ *For all the faithful, that they may accurately discern the true sources of wisdom, we pray:* ◆ *For teachers, that they may earnestly encourage the minds of their students, we pray:* ◆ *For those involved in disputes, that they may look to the Holy Spirit for guidance, we pray:* ◆

Our Father . . .

Heavenly Father,
in your great wisdom
you called the Blessed Virgin Mary
to be mother of your Son, true God
    and true man.
May we, like St. Cyril of Alexandria,
use all our gifts to seek understanding
of the great mysteries of our faith.
Grant this through Christ our Lord.
    Amen.

✚ *Praise the Lord for he is good.*

✤ *Praise the Lord for he is good.*

PSALM 33 *page 409*

READING *Matthew 7:21–27*

Jesus said to his disciples: "Not everyone who says to me, 'Lord, Lord,' will enter the Kingdom of heaven, but only the one who does the will of my Father in heaven. Many will say to me on that day, 'Lord, Lord, did we not prophesy in your name? Did we not drive out demons in your name? Did we not do mighty deeds in your name?' Then I will declare to them solemnly, 'I never knew you. Depart from me, you evildoers.'

"Everyone who listens to these words of mine and acts on them will be like a wise man who built his house on rock. The rain fell, the floods came, and the winds blew and buffeted the house. But it did not collapse; it had been set solidly on rock. And everyone who listens to these words of mine but does not act on them will be like a fool who built his house on sand. The rain fell, the floods came, and the winds blew and buffeted the house. And it collapsed and was completely ruined."

REFLECTION

Acclaimed as one of the greatest bishops and theologians of the second century, St. Irenaeus was most noted for his strong and effective opposition against gnosticism: the first major Christian heresy which denied the goodness of the flesh and held that revelation was only available to an elite few. In refuting gnosticism, he argued that the Incarnation and Resurrection gave ultimate value to human flesh, and appealed to the principle of apostolic succession to show that revelation is available to everyone. Emulating St. Irenaeus, may we build our house on the rock of God's saving Word so that all will know the truth.

PRAYERS *others may be added*

Through the intercession of St. Irenaeus, we pray:

◆ Lord, graciously hear us.

That we speak the truth in the face of opposition, we pray: ◆ *That all will know the goodness of humanity, we pray:* ◆ *That we will be open to God's saving knowledge revealed in creation, we pray:* ◆

Our Father . . .

God of revelation,
you sent St. Irenaeus
to refute false teachings.
Instill in us understanding and fidelity
so that we may spread
the light of your saving message
in the darkness of heresy
    and disbelief.
Grant this through Jesus our Lord.
    Amen.

✤ *Praise the Lord for he is good.*

✚ *Their message goes out through all the earth.*

PSALM 116   *page 418*

READING   *Matthew 16:13–19*

When Jesus went into the region of Caesarea Philippi he asked his disciples, "Who do people say that the Son of Man is?" They replied, "Some say John the Baptist, others Elijah, still others Jeremiah or one of the prophets." He said to them, "But who do you say that I am?" Simon Peter said in reply, "You are the Christ, the Son of the living God." Jesus said to him in reply, "Blessed are you, Simon son of Jonah. For flesh and blood has not revealed this to you, but my heavenly Father. And so I say to you, you are Peter, and upon this rock I will build my Church, and the gates of the netherworld shall not prevail against it. I will give you the keys to the Kingdom of heaven. Whatever you bind on earth shall be bound in heaven; and whatever you loose on earth shall be loosed in heaven."

REFLECTION

The Lord works in mysterious ways. It seems almost bizarre that we have a solemnity celebrating St. Peter and St. Paul together. They were very different people. Peter, who had little formal education, was impetuous in temperament but reserved in his theology. Paul, on the other hand, was educated, shy in personality, but innovative in theology. The two were known to have argued vehemently. But through their differences and human quirks, they laid the foundations for the Church. May we, too, allow the Lord to work his mysterious ways through us.

PRAYERS   *others may be added*

In the footsteps of the apostles, we pray:

◆ Lord, graciously hear us.

Watch over our Pope and bishops, that they may wisely teach and govern your Church, we pray: ◆ Watch over missionaries, that they may effectively spread the Good News, we pray: ◆ Watch over those who debate theology, that they may struggle to know the truth in charity, we pray: ◆ Watch over the universal Church; may she hasten your kingdom, we pray: ◆

Our Father . . .

God of might,
you draw us into your kingdom in
  varied ways.
Through our different gifts, talents,
  and weaknesses,
may you work your wonders,
manifest your love, and
brighten the world with the
  knowledge of your Son.
We ask this through our Lord Jesus
  Christ, your Son,
who lives and reigns with you in the
  unity of the Holy Spirit,
one God, forever and ever. Amen.

✚ *Their message goes out through all the earth.*

✝ *Praise the Lord for he is good.*

PSALM 33 *page 409*

READING *Matthew 8:5–10, 13*

When Jesus entered Capernaum, a centurion approached him and appealed to him, saying, "Lord, my servant is lying at home paralyzed, suffering dreadfully." He said to him, "I will come and cure him." The centurion said in reply, "Lord, I am not worthy to have you enter under my roof; only say the word and my servant will be healed. For I too am a man subject to authority, with soldiers subject to me. And I say to one, 'Go,' and he goes; and to another, 'Come here,' and he comes; and to my slave, 'Do this,' and he does it." When Jesus heard this, he was amazed and said to those following him, "Amen, I say to you, in no one in Israel have I found such faith." And Jesus said to the centurion, "You may go; as you have believed, let it be done for you." And at that very hour his servant was healed.

REFLECTION

"Lord, I am not worthy. . . . only say the word and I will be healed." We recite these words every time we come to the altar of God to receive the Bread of Life and Cup of Salvation. In proclaiming these words, like the centurion, we are asking the Lord to heal our sin, reconcile our brokenness, and make our hearts pure so that we are ready to receive his Body and Blood. By becoming human, Jesus made us worthy to

sit and feast at the table of the Lord. All we must do is believe, have faith, and ask for forgiveness!

PRAYERS *others may be added*

Asking for healing, we pray:

◆ Lord, graciously hears us.

That all broken relationships will be mended, we pray: ◆ That we receive the Body and Blood of Christ with pure and faith-filled hearts, we pray: ◆ That warring nations find reconciliation, we pray: ◆ That government policies protect life, we pray: ◆

Our Father . . .

Lord of life,
you give us your Body and Blood
so that we may know redemption.
Give us the courage
to name our sin and ask
    for forgiveness
before we approach your banquet of
    everlasting joy.
We ask this through Jesus our Lord.
    Amen.

✝ *Praise the Lord for he is good.*

✝ *Praise the Lord for he is good.*

PSALM 33 *page 409*

READING *Luke 9:51, 57–62*

When the days for Jesus' being taken up were fulfilled, he resolutely determined to journey to Jerusalem, and he sent messengers ahead of him. On the way they entered a Samaritan village to prepare for his reception there, but they would not welcome him because the destination of his journey was Jerusalem.

As they were proceeding on their journey someone said to him, "I will follow you wherever you go." Jesus answered him, "Foxes have dens and birds of the sky have nests, but the Son of Man has nowhere to rest his head."

And to another he said, "Follow me." But he replied, "Lord, let me go first and bury my father." But he answered him, "Let the dead bury their dead. But you, go and proclaim the kingdom of God." And another said, "I will follow you, Lord, but first let me say farewell to my family at home." To him Jesus said, "No one who sets a hand to the plow and looks to what was left behind is fit for the kingdom of God."

REFLECTION

Today's Gospel is about resolution and determination. Jesus is so determined to get to Jerusalem that he takes the most direct route leading him through the enemy territory of Samaria. He then speaks about the single-minded characteristics of discipleship: disregard of the costs and sacrificing lesser goods. We have so much in today's world that can distract our attention and determination to follow the Lord. Let us examine our surroundings, look at even the good things in our life, and see if they are roadblocks on our way to Jerusalem, our destiny.

PRAYERS *others may be added*

With resolute hearts, we pray:

◆ Lord, graciously hear us.

That possessions and attachments may not keep us from you, we pray: ◆ *That our hearts and souls may always look to you, we pray:* ◆ *That we may always offer hospitality, we pray:* ◆ *That the Church may always follow the Lord, we pray:* ◆

Our Father . . .

Gracious God,
you sent your Son to show us the way to you.
Help us to see, know, and follow him as true disciples
so that we may enjoy the delights of your kingdom.
We ask this through our Lord Jesus Christ, your Son,
who lives and reigns with you in the unity of the Holy Spirit,
one God, forever and ever. Amen.

✝ *Praise the Lord for he is good.*

✝ *Praise the Lord for he is good.*

PSALM 33   *page 409*

READING   *Matthew 8:18–22*

When Jesus saw a crowd around him, he gave orders to cross to the other shore. A scribe approached and said to him, "Teacher, I will follow you wherever you go." Jesus answered him, "Foxes have dens and birds of the sky have nests, but the Son of Man has nowhere to rest his head." Another of his disciples said to him, "Lord, let me go first and bury my father." But Jesus answered him, "Follow me, and let the dead bury their dead."

REFLECTION

The call to discipleship demands that we follow Jesus Christ our Lord wherever he goes. Following Jesus transcends all other obligations and may even involve cutting family ties. We must cast aside all duties, responsibilities, and relationships that prevent us from being a true disciple. Jesus is not asking us to stop loving, but to love enough so that we may be free to spread his Gospel message. Let us not remain with the dead, but stand with Jesus, the life of the world, who is always calling people to see and know God's unconditional love and forgiveness.

PRAYERS   *others may be added*

Letting go of all that hinders us from following Jesus, we pray:

◆ Lord, graciously hear us.

To be love in a broken world, we pray: ◆
To be hope in a despairing world, we pray: ◆ *To be simplistic in a materialistic world, we pray:* ◆ *To be light and life in a world consumed by darkness and death, we pray:* ◆

Our Father . . .

God of life,
you call us to leave everything behind
so that we can follow your Son, Jesus.
Give us the wisdom to know
what we need on our journey to you.
We ask this through Christ our Lord.
   Amen.

✝ *Praise the Lord for he is good.*

✛ *Praise the Lord for he is good.*

PSALM 33 *page 409*

READING *John 20:24–29*

Thomas, called Didymus, one of the Twelve, was not with them when Jesus came. So the other disciples said to him, "We have seen the Lord." But Thomas said to them, "Unless I see the mark of the nails in his hands and put my finger into the nailmarks and put my hand into his side, I will not believe." Now a week later his disciple were again inside and Thomas was with them. Jesus came, although the doors were locked, and stood in their midst and said, "Peace be with you." Then he said to Thomas, "Put your finger here and see my hands, and bring your hand and put it into my side, and do not be unbelieving, but believe." Thomas answered and said to him, "My Lord and my God!" Jesus said to him, "Have you come to believe because you have seen me? Blessed are those who have not seen and have believed."

REFLECTION

Today we celebrate the unexpected. St. Thomas is said to have brought Christianity to the far reaches of Iran and India. This was quite a mission for one who, at first, refused to believe in the Resurrection. Thomas found his belief where he least expected it—in the midst of the community—and turned from disbelief to witness to the divinity of Christ. God's ways are often unexpected, and he works wonders through seemingly unlikely characters. Our God is always with us, eager to transform our disbelief.

PRAYERS *others may be added*

Through the intercession of St. Thomas, we pray:

◆ Lord, graciously hear us.

For the Christians in the far east, that they may be strengthened in their faith, we pray: ◆ *For Christian communities everywhere, that they may bring others to belief, we pray:* ◆ *For the openness to find God in the most unexpected places, we pray:* ◆ *For the grace to proclaim our God, we pray:* ◆

Our Father . . .

Loving God,
you give us the example and prayers
    of St. Thomas
to help us on our journey of belief.
Through his intercession may
    we declare
the presence and the divinity of your
    Son to all.
We ask this through Christ our Lord.
    Amen.

✛ *Praise the Lord for he is good.*

✝ *Praise the Lord for he is good.*

PSALM 33 *page 409*

READING *Matthew 8:28–34*

When Jesus came to the territory of the Gadarenes, two demoniacs who were coming from the tombs met him. They were so savage that no one could travel by that road. They cried out, "What have you to do with us, Son of God? Have you come here to torment us before the appointed time?" Some distance away a herd of many swine was feeding. The demons pleaded with him, "If you drive us out, send us into the herd of swine." And he said to them, "Go then!" They came out and entered the swine, and the whole herd rushed down the steep bank into the sea where they drowned. The swineherds ran away, and when they came to the town they reported everything, including what had happened to the demoniacs. Thereupon the whole town came out to meet Jesus, and when they saw him they begged him to leave their district.

REFLECTION

Today, as the United States celebrates the birth of its nation, it seems fitting to hear a story of Jesus casting out demons and evil. Just as the Word became flesh to rid the world of the demonic, so too did our founders sign the Declaration of Independence to dismantle the demons of oppression and inequality within society, with the goal of proclaiming the inalienable rights of all: life, liberty, and the pursuit of happiness.

Although we are very grateful to the founders of our nation, we must always remember that Jesus Christ is the true source of all freedom, rights, and equity.

PRAYERS *others may be added*

Seeking the freedom of Christ, we pray:

◆ Lord, graciously hear us.

That all nations may know your mercy, we pray: ◆ *That all nations may see your justice, we pray:* ◆ *That all nations may heed your call to equality, we pray:* ◆ *That all nations may know life in you, we pray:* ◆

Our Father . . .

God of joy,
you call us to live
your commandments freely
    and openly.
Instill in us strength of character
so that we may build a world
rooted in your reconciling love.
Grant this through Jesus our Lord.
    Amen.

✝ *Praise the Lord for he is good.*

✝ *Praise the Lord for he is good.*

PSALM 33 *page 409*

READING *Matthew 9:1–8*

After entering a boat, Jesus made the crossing, and came into his own town. And there people brought to him a paralytic lying on a stretcher. When Jesus saw their faith, he said to the paralytic, "Courage, child, your sins are forgiven." At that, some of the scribes said to themselves, "This man is blaspheming." Jesus knew what they were thinking, and said, "Why do you harbor evil thoughts? Which is easier, to say, 'Your sins are forgiven,' or to say, 'Rise and walk'? But that you may know that the Son of Man has authority on earth to forgive sins"—he then said to the paralytic, "Rise, pick up your stretcher, and go home." He rose and went home. When the crowds saw this they were struck with awe and glorified God who had given such authority to men.

REFLECTION

It is appropriate that today's Gospel is about healing and forgiveness. St. Anthony Mary Zaccaria (1502–+1539) began his adulthood as a physician and later became a priest. He eventually founded the Clerks Regular of St. Paul (the Barnabites), a religious community devoted to the liturgy, preaching, and faithful administration of the sacraments. Like St. Anthony, may we attend to the needs of the whole person as we carry on the Gospel mission of Christ.

PRAYERS *others may be added*

Glorifying God, we pray:

◆ Lord, graciously hear us.

That we may be rid of the paralysis of doubt and fear, we pray: ◆ *That we may be forgiven for the blasphemy of total self-reliance, we pray:* ◆ *That our weakened faith may be healed so that we may stand and preach your healing love, we pray:* ◆ *That we may be filled with awe of you, so that we may glory in your saving actions, we pray:* ◆

Our Father . . .

God of glory,
you fill the universe with traces of
    your majesty.
Work wonders in us through the
    power of the Holy Spirit
so that we may witness to
    the salvation
won by your Son, Jesus Christ.
Grant this in the name of Jesus, the
    Lord. Amen.

✝ *Praise the Lord for he is good.*

✝ *Praise the Lord for he is good.*

PSALM 33 page 409

READING Matthew 9:9–13

As Jesus passed by, he saw a man named Matthew sitting at the customs post. He said to him, "Follow me." And he got up and followed him. While he was at table in his house, many tax collectors and sinners came and sat with Jesus and his disciples. The Pharisees saw this and said to his disciples, "Why does your teacher eat with tax collectors and sinners?" He heard this and said, "Those who are well do not need a physician, but the sick do. Go and learn the meaning of the words, *I desire mercy, not sacrifice. I did not come to call the righteous but sinners.*"

REFLECTION

The Church esteems Saint Maria Goretti (1890–+1902) as a martyr for chastity. She was stabbed to death while resisting the sexual advances of a rapist. As she lay dying, she was not concerned with her earthly life, but rather with the soul of her perpetrator and the souls in purgatory. Her selflessness and mercy, even unto death, clearly illustrate that she knew Jesus Christ: physician for the sick, advocate of mercy, redemption for sinners.

PRAYERS *others may be added*

Through the intercession of St. Maria Goretti, we pray:

◆ Lord, graciously hear us.

For single people, that their chastity may be marked with generosity of spirit, we pray: ◆ For clergy and religious, that their vows and promises of celibacy may give witness to their devotion to Christ and his Church, we pray: ◆ For married people, that their expression of sexuality may be a sign of God's love, we pray: ◆ For our society, that chastity may become a sign of self-respect and dignity, we pray: ◆

Our Father . . .

God of mercy,
you called St. Maria Goretti
to show us the way
of fidelity, chastity, and forgiveness.
Guide and support us as we remain
chaste according to our state of life
and give witness to your
    unconditional love.
Grant this through Jesus our Lord.
    Amen.

✝ *Praise the Lord for he is good.*

✠ *Praise the Lord for he is good.*

PSALM 33 *page 409*

READING *Matthew 9:14–17*

The disciples of John approached Jesus and said, "Why do we and the Pharisees fast much, but your disciples do not fast?" Jesus answered them, "Can the wedding guests mourn as long as the bridegroom is with them? The days will come when the bridegroom is taken away from them, and then they will fast. No one patches an old cloak with a piece of unshrunken cloth, for its fullness pulls away from the cloak and the tear gets worse. People do not put new wine into old wineskins. Otherwise the skins burst, the wine spills out, and the skins are ruined. Rather, they pour new wine into fresh wineskins, and both are preserved."

REFLECTION

With Jesus everything is new, everything is different. The old ways no longer apply. In the kingdom that Jesus proclaims there is flexibility, excitement, expansion. The energy of salvation cannot be contained into stiffened old wineskins. Jesus calls us out of complacency and self-sufficiency into a grace-filled new world marked by the freedom of the Spirit and animated by the love of God. We are invited to the banquet of the Lord where we will know no hunger or thirst, where we will feast on the Lord himself.

PRAYER *others may be added*

Glorying in the newness of the kingdom, we pray:

♦ Lord, graciously hear us.

That we will know when to celebrate and when to fast, we pray: ♦ *That we will be graced with the flexibility to bend to the will of God, we pray:* ♦ *That we may be clothed in holiness, we pray:* ♦ *That we may preserve the newness of life given in Baptism, we pray:* ♦

Our Father . . .

Lord of the banquet,
you spread out a bounteous feast.
In your Son, Jesus Christ,
   you invite us
to celebrate your everlasting love
   for us
by joining with you and our brothers
   and sisters
at the table of salvation.
May we hasten to the joy of
   your presence.
We ask this through Christ our Lord.
   Amen.

✠ *Praise the Lord for he is good.*

✠ *Praise the Lord for he is good.*

PSALM 33 *page 409*

READING *Luke 10:1–9*

At that time the Lord appointed seventy-two others whom he sent ahead of him in pairs to every town and place he intended to visit. He said to them, "The harvest is abundant but the laborers are few; so ask the master of the harvest to send out laborers for his harvest. Go on your way; behold, I am sending you like lambs among wolves. Carry no money bag, no sack, no sandals; and greet no one along the way. Into whatever house you enter, first say, 'Peace to this household.' If a peaceful person lives there, your peace will rest on him; but if not, it will return to you. Stay in the same house and eat and drink what is offered to you, for the laborer deserves his payment. Do not move about from one house to another. Whatever town you enter and they welcome you, eat what is set before you, cure the sick in it and say to them, 'The kingdom of God is at hand for you.'"

REFLECTION

We are sent into God's abundant harvest as lambs preaching the Good News amidst the wolves of disbelief, doubt, and fear. Completely dependent on the Lord and trusting in the hospitality of others, we carry nothing with us but God's gift of peace. As carriers and ministers of peace, we not only bring a message, but we embody God's own personality and power. This is a grave responsibility; therefore,

we must be stewards of the kingdom, drawing attention to the one who sent us rather than to ourselves.

PRAYERS *others may be added*

Trusting in the providence of God, we pray:

♦ Lord, graciously hear us.

That we may alleviate fear and disbelief by proclaiming God's saving message, we pray: ♦ *That we may realize our total dependence on God's mercy and forgiveness, we pray:* ♦ *That we may be good stewards of God's gift of peace, we pray:* ♦

Our Father . . .

Lord of peace,
you call us to labor in the harvest
    of life
by ministering and teaching in
    your name.
May we trust in your constant care
    and support
so that we will be able to
    courageously
proclaim your saving message to all
    the ends of the earth.
We ask this through our Lord Jesus
    Christ, your Son,
who lives and reigns with you in the
    unity of the Holy Spirit,
one God, forever and ever. Amen.

✠ *Praise the Lord for he is good.*

✚ *Praise the Lord for he is good.*

PSALM 33   page 409

READING   *Matthew 9:18–26*

While Jesus was speaking, an official came forward, knelt down before him, and said, "My daughter has just died. But come, lay your hand on her, and she will live." Jesus rose and followed him, and so did his disciples. A woman suffering hemorrhages for twelve years came up behind him and touched the tassel on his cloak. She said to herself, "If only I can touch his cloak, I shall be cured." Jesus turned around and saw her, and said, "Courage, daughter! Your faith has saved you." And from that hour the woman was cured.

When Jesus arrived at the official's house and saw the flute players and the crowd who were making a commotion, he said, "Go away! The girl is not dead but sleeping." And they ridiculed him. When the crowd was put out, he came and took her by the hand, and the little girl arose. And news of this spread throughout all that land.

REFLECTION

Today we celebrate 120 martyrs of China, spanning the years 1648–1930. They represent many generations of Christians in China, always a small minority of the population. St. Augustine Zhao Rong was a diocesan priest martyred in 1815. Much of the persecution the Church has suffered in China has sprung from the notion that Christianity was an outsider's religion. In
today's Gospel, Jesus crosses the boundaries of religion and region by healing the dead girl. May we imitate these martyrs and be willing to sacrifice all for God.

PRAYERS   *others may be added*

Through the intercession of the Chinese martyrs, we pray:

◆ Lord, graciously hear us.

That the Christian faith will grow throughout the entire world, we pray: ◆
That missionaries will find new ways to overcome cultural barriers, we pray: ◆
That persecuted Christians may be strengthened by the example and prayers of the martyrs, we pray: ◆ *That the dead find rest in the Lord, we pray:* ◆

Our Father . . .

God of the martyrs,
you inspire men and women to follow
    your Son
to the cross of salvation.
May St. Augustine and
    his companions,
through their example
    and intercession,
bless the people of China and
all who seek to praise your glory.
We ask this through Christ our Lord.
    Amen.

✚ *Praise the Lord for he is good.*

Optional memorial of St. Augustine Zhao and companions   **219**

✝ *Praise the Lord for he is good.*

PSALM 33   page 409

READING   *Matthew 9:32–38*

A demoniac who could not speak was brought to Jesus, and when the demon was driven out the mute man spoke. The crowds were amazed and said, "Nothing like this has ever been seen in Israel." But the Pharisees said, "He drives out demons by the prince of demons."

Jesus went around to all the towns and villages, teaching in their synagogues, proclaiming the Gospel of the Kingdom, and curing every disease and illness. At the sight of the crowds, his heart was moved with pity for them because they were troubled and abandoned, like sheep without a shepherd. Then he said to his disciples, "The harvest is abundant but the laborers are few; so ask the master of the harvest to send out laborers for his harvest."

REFLECTION

We are all called to a particular vocation: a way of serving and loving God in the harvest of life. In order for God's face to be truly revealed in the world, we need all vocations—all ways of laboring, ministering, and loving for the Lord. While remaining faithful and steadfast in the goodness of our own vocation, the Gospel reading challenges us to pray, to invite, and to respond so that more men and women will be able to hear the Shepherd's call.

PRAYERS   *others may be added*

With open ears and hearts, we pray:

◆ Lord, graciously hear us.

That vocations to the consecrated life will increase, we pray: ◆ *That more men will heed God's invitation to enter the priesthood, we pray:* ◆ *That more people will consider serving God as lay ministers, we pray:* ◆ *That we will continue to call people to labor in the kingdom of God, we pray:* ◆

Our Father . . .

Loving Shepherd,
you call us into your harvest
to proclaim your message of hope
    and peace.
May our fervent belief and
    compassionate hearts
challenge others to take up their cross
    and follow you.
We ask this through Jesus our Lord.
    Amen.

✝ *Praise the Lord for he is good.*

✝ *Praise the Lord for he is good.*

PSALM 33 *page 409*

READING *Matthew 10:1–7*

Jesus summoned his Twelve disciples and gave them authority over unclean spirits to drive them out and to cure every disease and every illness. The names of the Twelve Apostles are these: first, Simon called Peter, and his brother Andrew; James, the son of Zebedee, and his brother John; Philip and Bartholomew, Thomas and Matthew the tax collector; James, the son of Alphaeus, and Thaddeus; Simon the Cananean, and Judas Iscariot who betrayed Jesus.

Jesus sent out these Twelve after instructing them thus, "Do not go into pagan territory or enter a Samaritan town. Go rather to the lost sheep of the house of Israel. As you go, make this proclamation: 'The Kingdom of heaven is at hand.' "

REFLECTION

Throughout the two thousand years of Christianity, many have been called to proclaim the kingdom. Few have had such far-reaching influence as St. Benedict (480– +550). Through his Rule for Monasteries and his followers, St. Benedict helped shape the history of Europe and gave us many models of sanctity. Benedict's spirituality is marked by a balanced, practical approach to life. Through a quiet, listening stance, St. Benedict teaches us that God will be encountered in the rhythms of the day and through the ordinary moments of life.

PRAYERS *others may be added*

In peace and with listening hearts, we pray:

◆ Lord, graciously hear us.

For an increase of vocations to the monastic way of life, we pray: ◆ For an appreciation of the need for balance in our lives, we pray: ◆ For a deeper spirit of prayer, we pray: ◆ For the repose of the souls of all the followers of St. Benedict who have shaped our world in so many untold ways, we pray: ◆

Our Father . . .

Loving Father,
you called St. Benedict from the
   clamor of the city
to the quiet of monastic life.
Help us to appreciate and seek out
   moments of silence
so that we may more intently listen
to your saving words uttered in the
   very midst of our lives.
We ask this through Christ our Lord.
   Amen.

✝ *Praise the Lord for he is good.*

✝ *Praise the Lord for he is good.*

PSALM 33   *page 409*

READING   *Matthew 10:7–15*

Jesus said to his Apostles: "As you go, make this proclamation: 'The Kingdom of heaven is at hand.' Cure the sick, raise the dead, cleanse the lepers, drive out demons. Without cost you have received; without cost you are to give. Do not take gold or silver or copper for your belts; no sack for the journey, or a second tunic, or sandals, or walking stick. The laborer deserves his keep. Whatever town or village you enter, look for a worthy person in it, and stay there until you leave. As you enter a house, wish it peace. If the house is worthy, let your peace come upon it; if not, let your peace return to you. Whoever will not receive you or listen to your words—go outside that house or town and shake the dust from your feet. Amen, I say to you, it will be more tolerable for the land of Sodom and Gomorrah on the day of judgment than for that town."

REFLECTION

Proclaiming God's saving message of love is not always easy, especially when it is not received or accepted. As we travel throughout life, we will enter relationships, communities, and situations receptive to God's word, but there will also be times when hearts and minds are unable to heed and hear the truth. So, what are we to do? We are told to shake the dust from our feet and move onto the next town or situation. *Let us not become discouraged when the message is rejected or despised, but remain faithful to our mission as disciples by moving onto fertile ground.*

PRAYERS   *others may be added*

Announcing the salvation of God, we pray:

◆ Lord, graciously hear us.

That we rejoice when God's word is heard and received, we pray: ◆ *That we do not become discouraged when the truth is rejected, we pray:* ◆ *That we remain faithful to our mission as disciples, we pray:* ◆ *That we leave all behind to freely proclaim the Good News of Christ, we pray:* ◆

Our Father . . .

God of strength,
you call us to remain true and faithful
to our mission as followers of your
    Son, Jesus Christ.
May we never let the darkness
of rejection and disbelief
    discourages us
from continuing on the journey
    of discipleship.
We ask this through Jesus our Lord.
    Amen.

✝ *Praise the Lord for he is good.*

✝ *Praise the Lord for he is good.*

PSALM 33 *page 409*

READING *Matthew 10:16–23*

Jesus said to his Apostles: "Behold, I am sending you like sheep in the midst of wolves; so be shrewd as serpents and simple as doves. But beware of men, for they will hand you over to courts and scourge you in their synagogues, and you will be led before governors and kings for my sake as a witness before them and the pagans. When they hand you over, do not worry about how you are to speak or what you are to say. You will be given at that moment what you are to say. For it will not be you who speak but the Spirit of your Father speaking through you. Brother will hand over brother to death, and the father his child; children will rise up against parents and have them put to death. You will be hated by all because of my name, but whoever endures to the end will be saved. When they persecute you in one town, flee to another. Amen, I say to you, you will not finish the towns of Israel before the Son of Man comes."

REFLECTION

Shrewd seems to be a perfect description of St. Henry II (972–+1024). He was holy Roman emperor for the last ten years of his life. In his early years he helped establish monasteries and cathedrals, and in his last years he supported the Pope's claim to political power over much of Italy. Today's Gospel warns us that we will face many obstacles spreading throughout the kingdom of God. St. Henry helped further establish the Church despite obstacles. May we follow the promptings of the Holy Spirit in overcoming all hardships.

PRAYERS *others may be added*

Relying on the Holy Spirit, we pray:

◆ Lord, graciously hear us.

That our Pope may lead the Church through faithful example, we pray: ◆
That our bishops may constantly sound the call to repentance, we pray: ◆
That world leaders may respect the rights of believers and work for peace, we pray: ◆
That we may be strengthened by the Holy Spirit, we pray: ◆

Our Father . . .

Creator of the universe,
you are the source of all power.
May we recognize your sovereignty
   over all creation
and give praise to you alone.
Help us in our trials, bring us to
   new life,
that we may rejoice with you forever
   in your kingdom.
Grant this through Christ our Lord.
   Amen.

✝ *Praise the Lord for he is good.*

✝ *Praise the Lord for he is good.*

PSALM 33 *page 409*

READING *Matthew 10:24–28*

Jesus said to his Apostles: "No disciple is above his teacher, no slave above his master. It is enough for the disciple that he become like his teacher, for the slave that he become like his master. If they have called the master of the house Beelzebul, how much more those of his household!

"Therefore do not be afraid of them. Nothing is concealed that will not be revealed, nor secret that will not be known. What I say to you in the darkness, speak in the light; what you hear whispered, proclaim on the housetops. And do not be afraid of those who kill the body but cannot kill the soul; rather, be afraid of the one who can destroy both soul and body in Gehenna."

REFLECTION

Bl. Kateri Tekakwitha (1656–+1680), the first Native American to be beatified, was the daughter of a Christian Algonquin and a pagan Mohawk chief. After meeting a Jesuit priest, she heard God's call to conversion: to be baptized in the faith and to receive first Holy Communion. Pledging her life and purity to God, Bl. Kateri attended Mass twice a day, fasted on Wednesdays and Saturdays, taught children, and cared for the sick. Through her devout life and acts of charity, Bl. Kateri is a model disciple—one who shouts from the rooftops what God reveals in the darkness.

PRAYERS *others may be added*

Through the intercession of Bl. Kateri Tekakwitha, we pray:

◆ Lord, graciously hear us.

For the conversion of souls, we pray: ◆ *For the pure of heart, we pray:* ◆ *For the gift of charity, we pray:* ◆ *For the well-being of Native Americans, we pray:* ◆

Our Father . . .

God of saints and sinners,
you raised your daughter Bl. Kateri
as a model of conversion, sanctity,
   and purity.
Inspired by her example,
may we live our faith with
abundant charity and joyful humility.
Grant this through Jesus our Lord.
   Amen.

✝ *Praise the Lord for he is good.*

✝ *Praise the Lord for he is good.*

PSALM 33   *page 409*

READING   *Luke 10:29b–37*

[A scholar of the law asked Jesus] "And who is my neighbor?" Jesus replied, "A man fell victim to robbers as he went down from Jerusalem to Jericho. They stripped and beat him and went off leaving him half-dead. A priest happened to be going down that road, but when he saw him, he passed by on the opposite side. Likewise a Levite came to the place, and when he saw him, he passed by on the opposite side. But a Samaritan traveler who came upon him was moved with compassion at the sight. He approached the victim, poured oil and wine over his wounds and bandaged them. Then he lifted him up on his own animal, took him to an inn, and cared for him. The next day he took out two silver coins and gave them to the innkeeper with the instruction, 'Take care of him. If you spend more than what I have given you, I shall repay you on my way back.' Which of these three, in your opinion, was neighbor to the robbers' victim?" He answered, "The one who treated him with mercy." Jesus said to him, "Go and do likewise."

REFLECTION

Today's story is timeless. The hero, the Samaritan, is all wrong according to the sensibilities of Jesus' audience. The Samaritan has the wrong race, politics, and religion. The accepted "neighbor" or hero should be a fellow Jew, not the despised Samaritan. And yet, the point of this parable is that we need to reach out to all. Everyone is our neighbor. We are to reach out to all beyond our prejudices in love and concern. The timeless message of Jesus is that we must reach out to others as the Father reaches out to us.

PRAYERS   *others may be added*

Announcing the salvation of God, we pray:

◆ Lord, graciously hear us.

That all may live lives free from prejudice and discrimination, we pray: ◆ *That health-care workers may be blessed in their work, we pray:* ◆ *That those who work in hospitality may see the Lord in all they serve, we pray:* ◆

Our Father . . .

Loving God,
you sent your Son to open our eyes
to break the barriers of pride
   and prejudice.
Send us your Holy Spirit so that we
   may see all as our neighbors
and extend your love to the
   whole world.
We ask this through our Lord Jesus
   Christ, your Son,
who lives and reigns with you in the
   unity of the Holy Spirit,
one God, forever and ever. Amen.

✝ *Praise the Lord for he is good.*

✠ *Praise the Lord for he is good.*

PSALM 33 *page 409*

READING *Matthew 10:39–42*

[Jesus said to his Apostles:] "Whoever finds his life will lose it, and whoever loses his life for my sake will find it.

"Whoever receives you receives me, and whoever receives me receives the one who sent me. Whoever receives a prophet because he is a prophet will receive a prophet's reward, and whoever receives a righteous man because he is righteous will receive a righteous man's reward. And whoever gives only a cup of cold water to one of these little ones to drink because he is a disciple—amen, I say to you, he will surely not lose his reward."

REFLECTION

On July 16, 1251, St. Simon Stock, General of the Carmelite Order, had a vision of Mary giving him a brown scapular, saying all who die wearing the scapular will be saved. We not only celebrate this apparition of Mary, but the many spiritual contributions the Carmelite family has made throughout the ages. From St. Teresa of Avila to St. John of the Cross, from St. Therese of Lisieux to St. Teresa Benedicta of the Cross (Edith Stein), our Church, our world, has been transformed by the Carmelite charism of contemplative love. Let us drink from the fountain of Elijah and ascend the heights of Carmel so that we may be clothed in the scapular of salvation.

PRAYERS *others may be added*

Celebrating the Carmelite charism, we pray:

◆ Lord, graciously hear us.

That Carmelites will remain faithful to their call of contemplation, we pray: ◆ *That all will come to know and imitate the lives and wisdom of the Carmelite saints, we pray:* ◆ *That we may rejoice in the humility and compassion of Mary, the Mother of God, we pray:* ◆ *That all may be clothed in the scapular of everlasting life, we pray:* ◆

Our Father . . .

God of peace,
you invite us to climb the mountain
    of Carmel
to see and understand your gift of
    redemptive grace.
May we look to the Carmelite family
    to learn how to
love contemplatively, sacrifice freely,
    and give abundantly.
Grant this through Jesus our Lord.
    Amen.

✠ *Praise the Lord for he is good.*

✢ *Praise the Lord for he is good.*

PSALM 33 *page 409*

READING *Matthew 11:20–24*

Jesus began to reproach the towns where most of his mighty deeds had been done, since they had not repented. "Woe to you, Chorazin! Woe to you, Bethsaida! For if the mighty deeds done in your midst had been done in Tyre and Sidon, they would long ago have repented in sackcloth and ashes. But I tell you, it will be more tolerable for Tyre and Sidon on the day of judgment than for you. And as for you, Capernaum:

Will you be exalted to heaven? / You will go down to the netherworld.

For if the mighty deeds done in your midst had been done in Sodom, it would have remained until this day. But I tell you, it will be more tolerable for the land of Sodom on the day of judgment than for you."

REFLECTION

Why did Jesus perform miracles? Many answers can be given, but today's reading suggests that the miracles of Jesus show glimpses of the kingdom. All the miracles were displays of compassion, brought wholeness, and encouraged repentance. They not only gave a view of the kingdom, but these wonders better enabled the receivers to live out the kingdom. Today, Jesus chastises those who have seen and experienced the miracles but have not accepted the kingdom of God. How have we reacted to the miracles Christ has performed in our lives?

PRAYERS *others may be added*

Pondering the mighty deeds of God, we pray:

◆ Lord, graciously hear us.

That the wonders of God's creation may be respected and protected, we pray: ◆ *That the miracles of repentance and conversion may be repeated endlessly in our world, we pray:* ◆ *That we may be ever mindful of the marvels God has done for us, we pray:* ◆ *That the dead may experience the miracle of the Resurrection, we pray:* ◆

Our Father . . .

God of power,
your kingdom breaks into our world
with every act of kindness done in
your name.
Fill us with your grace
so that we may be the miracles
others need,
and that we may see your wonderful
works in all creation.
We ask this through Christ our Lord.
Amen.

✢ *Praise the Lord for he is good.*

✚ *Praise the Lord for he is good.*

PSALM 33   *page 409*

READING   *Matthew 11:25–27*

At that time Jesus exclaimed: "I give praise to you, Father, Lord of heaven and earth, for although you have hidden these things from the wise and the learned you have revealed them to the childlike. Yes, Father, such has been your gracious will. All things have been handed over to me by my Father. No one knows the Son except the Father, and no one knows the Father except the Son and anyone to whom the Son wishes to reveal him."

REFLECTION

After fighting with the Venetian Army, contracting an incurable disease, and losing all his money gambling, St. Camillus de Lellis (1550–+1614) had a religious conversion and felt called to enter the religious life. Appalled by the state of medical care, he founded a religious community, the Order of Camillians, to care for the sick and comfort the dying. He was known for his compassion, empathy, and strong convictions. With St. John of God, St. Camillus is the patron saint of hospitals, nurses, and the sick. Following his lead, may we be childlike: always loving, giving, and believing with simplicity and without condition.

PRAYERS   *others may be added*

*Through the intercession of
St. Camillus, we pray:*

◆ Lord, graciously hear us.

For the sick and dying, we pray: ◆
For hospital administrators and nurses, we pray: ◆ *For Camillians throughout the world, we pray:* ◆ *For an increase in vocations to religious communities ministering in health care, we pray:* ◆

Our Father . . .

God of healing,
you called your servant, St. Camillus,
to found a community of men to care
for the sick and dying.
Give us hearts of compassion
so that we may give witness to your
medicinal message of new life.
We ask this through Jesus our Lord.
    Amen.

✚ *Praise the Lord for he is good.*

✝ *Praise the Lord for he is good.*

PSALM 33   page 409

READING   *Matthew 11:28–30*

Jesus said to the crowds: "Come to me, all you who labor and are burdened, and I will give you rest. Take my yoke upon you and learn from me, for I am meek and humble of heart; and you will find rest for yourselves. For my yoke is easy, and my burden light."

REFLECTION

What burdens do we carry needlessly? Are we worried about the circumstances of life over which we have no control? Are we concerned about the life choices others are making? Does the fate of the planet make us fret? Humility is letting God be God. Meekness is sharing our wisdom and letting others make up their own minds. Christ has carried the cross of salvation. He does not deny that we have legitimate burdens. But, if we follow Christ in humility and meekness, our yokes will be lighter and our rest will be complete.

PRAYERS   *others may be added*

Handing our burdens to Christ, we pray:

♦ Lord, graciously hear us.

That mental health-care professionals may use their gifts to assist those who feel overburdened, we pray: ♦ *That the Christian community may lift the burdens of the oppressed and needy, we pray:* ♦ *That we may look to Christ as our Savior, we pray:* ♦ *That all workers may receive just compensation for their labors, we pray:* ♦

Our Father . . .

Loving Redeemer,
by your cross and Resurrection
you lifted us out of the despair of sin
    and death.
Help us to know the burdens
    worth carrying
and to let go of needless anxieties
as we labor to bring your peace to
    a troubled world.
We ask this in your name. Amen.

✝ *Praise the Lord for he is good.*

✚ *Praise the Lord for he is good.*

PSALM 33 *page 409*

READING *Matthew 12:1–8*

Jesus was going through a field of grain on the sabbath. His disciples were hungry and began to pick the heads of grain and eat them. When the Pharisees saw this, they said to him, "See, your disciples are doing what is unlawful to do on the sabbath." He said to the them, "Have you not read what David did when he and his companions were hungry, how he went into the house of God and ate the bread of offering, which neither he nor his companions but only the priests could lawfully eat? Or have you not read in the law that on the sabbath the priests serving in the temple violate the sabbath and are innocent? I say to you, something greater than the temple is here. If you knew what this meant, *I desire mercy, not sacrifice,* you would not have condemned these innocent men. For the Son of Man is Lord of the sabbath."

REFLECTION

Jesus is claiming his status as authoritative interpreter of the law. Jesus isn't saying the sabbath law is a bad thing, but is critiquing those who had forgotten the spirit of the law. The laws were there to ensure that God's love for his people would not be interrupted by incessant labor, but if the law, strictly applied, is getting in the way of basic human need, then it is wrong. The law should free people to

experience God's love, not prevent them from it. Let us advocate for laws that invite the human spirit to soar to God's loving arms.

PRAYERS *others may be added*

Proclaiming the authority of Jesus Christ, we pray:

◆ Lord, graciously hear us.

That the law protects life, we pray: ◆ *That the law reverences basic human needs, we pray:* ◆ *That the law frees us to live the Gospel, we pray:* ◆ *That the law removes all barriers to experiencing God's love and forgiveness, we pray:* ◆

Our Father . . .

O God,
source of all law,
you give us rules and commands
to guide us on the path to salvation.
Instill in us a love
that invites all people to know
    and experience
your unending gifts of hope
    and peace.
Grant this through Christ our Lord.
    Amen.

✚ *Praise the Lord for he is good.*

✚ *Praise the Lord for he is good.*

PSALM 33 *page 409*

READING *Matthew 12:14–21*

The Pharisees went out and took counsel against Jesus to put him to death.

When Jesus realized this, he withdrew from that place. Many people followed him, and he cured them all, but he warned them not to make him known. This was to fulfill what had been spoken through Isaiah the prophet:

Behold, my servant whom I have chosen,/my beloved in whom I delight; / I shall place my Spirit upon him,/and he will proclaim justice to the Gentiles./ He will not contend or cry out,/nor will anyone hear his voice in the streets./ A bruised reed he will not break,/a smoldering wick he will not quench,/ until he brings justice to victory./And in his name the Gentiles will hope.

REFLECTION

St. Lawrence of Brindisi (1559–+1619) was a man clearly touched by the Holy Spirit. Becoming a Capuchin Franciscan at age 16, he was adept at languages and scriptural studies. He quickly became known as a masterful speaker. He was sent throughout Europe on preaching and diplomatic missions and was given positions of authority in his order. Through all these activities St. Lawrence often turned to prayer, finding inspiration in his devotions to the Mass, the humanity of Christ, and the Blessed Virgin Mary. May we follow St. Lawrence in turning to prayer for inspiration in our lives.

PRAYERS *others may be added*

With reverent devotion, we pray:

◆ Lord, graciously hear us.

For a renewed commitment to prayer, we pray: ◆ *For the gift of effectively speaking the word of love, we pray:* ◆ *For the courage go beyond our local surroundings to follow Christ, we pray:* ◆ *For the Franciscan family throughout the world, that they may live out their charism in joy, we pray:* ◆

Our Father . . .

God of wisdom,
you endowed St. Lawrence with
　　the ability
to spread your word.
Fill us with your Spirit
so that we may proclaim your Son
　　with devotion
to a world yearning for hope.
We ask this through Christ our Lord.
　　Amen.

✚ *Praise the Lord for he is good.*

✛ *I will bless the Lord at all times.*

PSALM 34   *page 410*

READING   *Luke 10:38–42*

Jesus entered a village where a woman whose name was Martha welcomed him. She had a sister named Mary who sat beside the Lord at his feet listening to him speak. Martha, burdened with much serving, came to him and said, "Lord, do you not care that my sister has left me by myself to do the serving? Tell her to help me." The Lord said to her in reply, "Martha, Martha, you are anxious and worried about many things. There is need of only one thing. Mary has chosen the better part and it will not be taken from her."

REFLECTION

Before we can serve others we must first make time to be with Jesus—to listen to his word. Our lives are filled with chaos, noise, and distraction; therefore, it is very difficult for us to find space and time for prayer. We are called, like Mary, to sit by our Lord, to lovingly gaze upon him, so we are able to hear and heed his message of salvation. Then, in the spirit of Martha, we will be able to extend the hospitality and love of God to all our brothers and sisters.

PRAYERS   *others may be added*

Heeding the word of God, we pray:

◆ Fill us with your compassion.

That we make more time for prayer and contemplation, we pray: ◆ *That we listen for the voice of God within our world, we pray:* ◆ *That we remove all distractions and chaos keeping us from the love of God, we pray:* ◆ *That our service to others be rooted in a personal relationship with the Lord, we pray:* ◆

Our Father . . .

Loving God,
you sent your Son, Jesus,
to speak your words of truth and life.
May we always listen with
open minds and loving hearts.
We ask this through our Lord Jesus
   Christ, your Son,
who lives and reigns with you in the
   unity of the Holy Spirit,
one God, forever and ever. Amen.

✛ *I will bless the Lord at all times.*

✚ *I will bless the Lord at all times.*

PSALM 34   page 410

READING   *Matthew 12:38–42*

Some of the scribes and Pharisees said to Jesus, "Teacher, we wish to see a sign from you." He said to them in reply, "An evil and unfaithful generation seeks a sign, but no sign will be given it except the sign of Jonah the prophet. Just as Jonah was in the belly of the whale three days and three nights, so will the Son of Man be in the heart of the earth three days and three nights. At the judgment, the men of Nineveh will arise with this generation and condemn it, because they repented at the preaching of Jonah; and there is something greater than Jonah here. At the judgment the queen of the south will arise with this generation and condemn it, because she came from the ends of the earth to hear the wisdom of Solomon; and there is something greater than Solomon here."

REFLECTION

Are we as blind as the Pharisees? Or, do we see the signs and wonders that the Lord is constantly working? Whether we are healed, fed, restored to life, or have our demons cast out, the miracles are meant to enable us to carry out the Gospel mission. St. Bridget of Sweden (1303–+1373) experienced many miraculous visions. However, she was canonized not for her visions, but for her work with the poor, founding the Brigittine order, and for her diplomatic work in Rome. May we, too, see and use the miracles in our lives to help bring about the kingdom of God.

PRAYERS   *others may be added*

To our wondrous God, we pray:

◆ Fill us with your compassion.

That those who are ill in body, mind, or soul may be healed, we pray: ◆
That those who experience physical or spiritual hungers may be fed, we pray: ◆
That those who are spiritually dead may be raised to new life, we pray: ◆
That those who are afflicted with demons of any kind, may be cleansed, we pray: ◆

Our Father . . .

Almighty God,
you are the source of all that is good
   and beautiful.
Send us the Holy Spirit, so that like
   your Son
we may work wonders,
reach out to all in love,
and help bring about your kingdom in
   our world.
We ask this through Christ our Lord.
   Amen.

✚ *I will bless the Lord at all times.*

✚ *I will bless the Lord at all times.*

PSALM 34   *page 410*

READING   *Matthew 12:46–50*

While Jesus was speaking to the crowds, his mother and his brothers appeared outside, wishing to speak with him. Someone told him, "Your mother and your brothers are standing outside, asking to speak with you." But he said in reply to the one who told him, "Who is my mother? Who are my brothers?" And stretching out his hand toward his disciples, he said, "Here are my mother and my brothers. For whoever does the will of my heavenly Father is my brother, and sister, and mother."

REFLECTION

There is a great resurgence in our world to research and discover our familial lineage: the individuals who have shared our blood and name throughout history. We long to know our family tree, our story. In today's Gospel, we are told to look beyond blood and name to see the one, true, holy family of Jesus: those who obey the will of God. Bound by belief, conviction, and the waters of Baptism, we are called to define our family by the ties of heaven, not the precepts and limitations of humanity.

PRAYERS   *others may be added*

*As one family in Jesus Christ,
we pray:*

◆ Fill us with your compassion.

To be a family of forgiveness, we pray: ◆
To be a family of hospitality, we pray: ◆
To be a family of humility, we pray: ◆
To be a family of love, we pray: ◆

Our Father . . .

God of compassion,
you call us to be one family,
proclaiming your reconciling
    message of hope.
Give us strong faith and
    unending mercy
so that we are worthy to be called
    your sons and daughters.
Grant this through Jesus our Lord.
    Amen.

✚ *I will bless the Lord at all times.*

✛ *I will bless the Lord at all times.*

PSALM 34   page 410

READING   Matthew 20:20–28

The mother of the sons of Zebedee approached Jesus with her sons and did him homage, wishing to ask him for something. He said to her, "What do you wish?" She answered him, "Command that these two sons of mine sit, one at your right and the other at your left, in your Kingdom." Jesus said in reply, "You do not know what you are asking. Can you drink the chalice that I am going to drink?" They said to him, "We can." He replied, "My chalice you will indeed drink, but to sit at my right and at my left, this is not mine to give but is for those for whom it has been prepared by my Father." When the ten heard this, they became indignant at the two brothers. But Jesus summoned them and said, "You know that the rulers of the Gentiles lord it over them, and the great ones make their authority over them felt. But it shall not be so among you. Rather, whoever wishes to be great among you shall be your servant; whoever wishes to be first among you shall be your slave. Just so, the Son of Man did not come to be served but to serve and to give his life as a ransom for many."

REFLECTION

The brothers mentioned today are St. James and St. John. Somewhat impetuous and even more prophetic, St. James and his brother are quick to say they can accept the cup of suffering. St. James, whom today we celebrate, was the first apostle to be martyred, but not before he followed Christ's instructions to be servant leader. St. James became leader of the Christian community in Jerusalem after Pentecost. In this role he lost his life for the faith. May we, too, give ourselves fully to our faith.

PRAYERS   others may be added

    With confidence in the Lord, we pray:

◆ Fill us with your compassion.

That we may be willing to give until it hurts, we pray: ◆ *That we may be as enthusiastic about following Christ as St. James and his brother, we pray:* ◆ *That we may seek to be servants to all, we pray:* ◆ *That the dead may share the glory of the kingdom with all the apostles, we pray:* ◆

Our Father . . .

Father,
you called St. James to follow
   your Son
in service to the Gospel.
By the example and prayers of
   the apostles,
may we, too, have a share in
   spreading your word,
thus bringing greater glory to
   your name.
Grant this through Christ our Lord.
   Amen.

✛ *I will bless the Lord at all times.*

✛ *I will bless the Lord at all times.*

PSALM 34 page 410

READING Matthew 13:10–13, 16–17

The disciples approached Jesus and said, "Why do you speak to the crowd in parables?" He said to them in reply, "Because knowledge of the mysteries of the Kingdom of heaven has been granted to you, but to them it has not been granted. To anyone who has more will be given and he will grow rich; from anyone who has not, even what he has will be taken away. This is why I speak to them in parables, because *they look but do not see and hear but do not listen or understand.*

"But blessed are your eyes, because they see, and your ears, because they hear. Amen, I say to you, many prophets and righteous people longed to see what you see but did not see it, and to hear what you hear but did not hear it."

REFLECTION

Neither St. Joachim nor St. Anne are mentioned in the New Testament, but there are numerous apocryphal stories about their lives. The stories speak of an elderly and childless couple visited by an angel, proclaiming that they shall conceive and bear a child who would become famous throughout the world: yet another story where God turns despair into joy by making the impossible possible! We celebrate St. Joachim and St. Anne, the parents of the Blessed Virgin Mary, because they were able to see the wonderful hand and hear the resounding voice of God working in and through their brokenness. Not only did they see and hear, but they believed!

PRAYERS others may be added

Through the intercession of St. Joachim and St. Anne, we pray:

◆ Fill us with your compassion.

That parents may be models of fervent faith in their children, we pray: ◆
That parents may model forgiveness and reconciliation to their children, we pray: ◆
That parents may model sacrifice and repentance to their children, we pray: ◆
That parents may unconditionally love and accept their children, we pray: ◆

Our Father . . .

Father of us all,
you called your servants St. Joachim
    and St. Anne
to bear witness to your saving action.
Nurtured by your unconditional love
    and acceptance,
may we glorify your redeeming name
    to all the world.
We ask this through Jesus our Lord.
    Amen.

✛ *I will bless the Lord at all times.*

✙ *I will bless the Lord at all times.*

PSALM 34 *page 410*

READING *Matthew 13:18–23*

Jesus said to his disciples: "Hear the parable of the sower. The seed sown on the path is the one who hears the word of the Kingdom without understanding it, and the Evil One comes and steals away what was sown in his heart. The seed sown on rocky ground is the one who hears the word and receives it at once with joy. But he has no root and lasts only for a time. When some tribulation or persecution comes because of the word, he immediately falls away. The seed sown among thorns is the one who hears the word, but then worldly anxiety and the lure of riches choke the word and it bears no fruit. But the seed sown on rich soil is the one who hears the word and understands it, who indeed bears fruit and yields a hundred or sixty or thirty-fold."

REFLECTION

The fact that God became man is a wondrous and miraculous mystery. Yet, we should not be surprised. Our God always works through his creation to reach out to us, to speak to us, to teach us, to love us. Every rock, every blade of grass is a manifestation of God. The Holy Spirit is at work through all of nature. We only need to activate our senses in faith to catch glimpses of our God who wants nothing more than to love us and for us to love in return.

PRAYERS *others may be added*

Trusting in our Creator, we pray:

◆ Fill us with your compassion.

For farmers and all who work in the open air, we pray: ◆ *For the preservation of our natural resources, we pray:* ◆ *For a bountiful harvest, we pray:* ◆ *For all who sow the word of God, we pray:* ◆

Our Father . . .

Lord of creation,
the earth is your handiwork
and we are your children.
Conform us to your word,
make us grow in your grace,
and bring us to your kingdom with
     your Son.
We ask this through Christ our Lord.
     Amen.

✙ *I will bless the Lord at all times.*

✜ *I will bless the Lord at all times.*

PSALM 34 *page 410*

READING *Matthew 13:24–30*

Jesus proposed a parable to the crowds. "The Kingdom of heaven may be likened to a man who sowed good seed in his field. While everyone was asleep his enemy came and sowed weeds all through the wheat, and then went off. When the crop grew and bore fruit, the weeds appeared as well. The slaves of the householder came to him and said, 'Master, did you not sow good seed in your field? Where have the weeds come from?' He answered, 'An enemy has done this.' His slaves said to him, 'Do you want us to go and pull them up?' He replied, 'No, if you pull up the weeds you might uproot the wheat along with them. Let them grow together until harvest; then at harvest time I will say to the harvesters, "First collect the weeds and tie them in bundles for burning; but gather the wheat into my barn."'"

REFLECTION

There are so many weeds growing within our world. We see weeds of intolerance, skepticism, false idols, disrespect for human life, and violence growing amid God's beautiful wheat of love, acceptance, and forgiveness. We are afraid the weeds are going to choke and smother the wheat of salvation. What are we to do? We are told not to despair or feel discouraged, for in the harvest—the final judgment, God's justice—his definite decisions will bundle the weeds for burning and gather the wheat into his heavenly care.

PRAYERS *others may be added*

Trusting in the power of God, we pray:

◆ Fill us with your compassion.

That God will transform the weed of intolerance into wheat of acceptance, we pray: ◆ That God will transform the weed of skepticism into wheat of faith, we pray: ◆ That God will transform the weed of disrespect into the wheat of reverence, we pray: ◆ That God will turn the weed of discouragement into the wheat of hope, we pray: ◆

Our Father . . .

God of the harvest,
you sent your Son, Jesus,
to redeem us from the weeds of sin
    and evil.
Give us discerning eyes and hearts
so that we may distinguish your
    good wheat
from the weeds of the enemy.
We ask this through Jesus our Lord.
    Amen.

✜ *I will bless the Lord at all times.*

✠ *I will bless the Lord at all times.*

PSALM 34 *page 410*

READING *Luke 11:9–13*

"And I tell you, ask and you will receive; seek and you will find; knock and the door will be opened to you. For everyone who asks, receives; and the one who seeks, finds; and to the one who knocks, the door will be opened. What father among you would hand his son a snake when he asks for a fish? Or hand him a scorpion when he asks for an egg? If you then, who are wicked, know how to give good gifts to your children, how much more will the Father in heaven give the Holy Spirit to those who ask him?"

REFLECTION

How do we approach prayer? Are we like the child who carefully crafts his request, worried that the wrong words will bring the wrong response? Or, do we take to heart the words of Jesus; do we have confidence in the wisdom and generosity of the Father? There are no secret formulas, no special incantations, no requirements whatsoever to approach the Father in prayer other than a sincere heart and faith in a God who lives for giving.

PRAYERS *others may be added*

With sincere hearts, we pray:

◆ Fill us with your compassion.

That our prayers of praise may be offered in humility, we pray: ◆ *That our prayers of contrition may be offered with sincerity, we pray:* ◆ *That our prayers of thanksgiving may be offered with deep appreciation for all God has done, we pray:* ◆ *That our prayers of petition may be offered for all those in need, we pray:* ◆

Our Father . . .

God of all bounty,
you give us all good things—even
    your very life.
Enlivened by the Holy Spirit and
    redeemed by your Son,
may we always approach you with
    confidence and faith.
We ask this through our Lord Jesus
    Christ, your Son,
who lives and reigns with you in the
    unity of the Holy Spirit,
one God, forever and ever. Amen.

✠ *I will bless the Lord at all times.*

✛ *I will bless the Lord at all times.*

PSALM 34   *page 410*

READING   *Matthew 13:31–35*

Jesus proposed a parable to the crowds. "The Kingdom of heaven is like a mustard seed that a person took and sowed in a field. It is the smallest of all the seeds, yet when full-grown it is the largest of plants. It becomes a large bush, and the 'birds of the sky come and dwell in its branches.'"

He spoke to them another parable. "The Kingdom of heaven is like yeast that a woman took and mixed with three measures of wheat flour until the whole batch was leavened."

All these things Jesus spoke to the crowds in parables. He spoke to them only in parables, to fulfill what had been said through the prophet:

I will open my mouth in parables, / I will announce what has lain hidden from the foundation of the world.

REFLECTION

St. Peter Chrysologus (380–+450) was well known for his ability to articulate scripture and Church teaching eloquently and with great clarity. His sermons were marked by careful preparation, human warmth, and divine fervor. He is particularly noted for his avid defense of the importance and orthodoxy of St. Leo the Great's teaching on the Incarnation. Esteemed for his positive views of humanity and the flesh, St. Peter's words were like a mustard seed and yeast, sheltering and leavening God's saving story of love, mercy, and forgiveness.

PRAYERS   *others may be added*

Through the intercession of St. Peter, we pray:

◆ Fill us with your compassion.

That we give witness to the Gospel message, we pray: ◆ *That we authentically articulate the teachings of the Church, we pray:* ◆ *That our lives are marked by divine fervor and holiness, we pray:* ◆ *That we are like yeast, leavening the hopes and dreams of the Christian community, we pray:* ◆

Our Father . . .

Father of truth,
you called your holy witness,
    St. Peter,
to preach your saving word
with great conviction
    and compassion.
May our lives be a living testimony
    and sermon,
announcing your free offer of grace
    and redemption.
We ask this through Jesus our Lord.
    Amen.

✛ *I will bless the Lord at all times.*

✠ *I will bless the Lord at all times.*

PSALM 34 *page 410*

READING *Matthew 13:36–43*

Jesus dismissed the crowds and went into the house. His disciples approached him and said, "Explain to us the parable of the weeds in the field." He said in reply, "He who sows good seed is the Son of Man, the field is the world, the good seed the children of the Kingdom. The weeds are the children of the Evil One, and the enemy who sows them is the Devil. The harvest is the end of the age, and the harvesters are angels. Just as weeds are collected and burned up with fire, so will it be at the end of the age. The Son of Man will send his angels, and they will collect out of his Kingdom all who cause others to sin and all evildoers. They will throw them into the fiery furnace, where there will be wailing and grinding of teeth. Then the righteous will shine like the sun in the Kingdom of their Father. Whoever has ears ought to hear."

REFLECTION

The parable of the weeds is about the extremes of good and evil, of heaven and hell. St. Ignatius (1491–+1556) also knew of extremes: beginning with a life of indulgence and wantonness; converting to the penitential life of a hermit; and engaging in the active apostolate by founding the Jesuits and creating the Spiritual Exercises. Both the community and the spirituality founded by St. Ignatius are marked by personal conversion and individual sanctification. May we follow the example of St. Ignatius and shine like the sun through conversion and holiness of life.

PRAYERS *others may be added*

With earnest hearts, we pray:

◆ Fill us with your compassion.

For educators, especially those in Jesuit schools, we pray: ◆ For religious who live out the Ignatian charism, we pray: ◆ For those involved in retreat ministry, especially those directing and following the Spiritual Exercises, we pray: ◆ For missionaries throughout the world, we pray: ◆

Our Father . . .

Loving Father,
you called St. Ignatius to a life
    of conversion.
Through his example
    and intercession,
may we endeavor to know more
    about you,
love you more fully,
and grow in holiness until the
    last day.
We ask this through Christ our Lord.
    Amen.

✠ *I will bless the Lord at all times.*

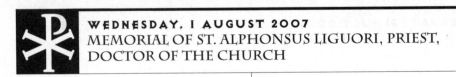
✛ *I will bless the Lord at all times.*

PSALM 34 *page 410*

READING *Matthew 13:44–46*

Jesus said to his disciples: "The Kingdom of heaven is like a treasure buried in a field, which a person finds and hides again, and out of joy goes and sells all that he has and buys that field. Again, the Kingdom of heaven is like a merchant searching for fine pearls. When he finds a pearl of great price, he goes and sells all that he has and buys it."

REFLECTION

So many of the great saints, including St. Alphonsus Liguori (1696–+1787), sold all their goods to follow the Lord. It is easy to think of this as a hardship they endured for the faith. However, as in today's parables, we see that the old goods were joyfully jettisoned for a much greater good. St. Alphonsus worked tirelessly to bring the word of God to the rural poor. He endured hardships in founding the Redemptorists, but he enthusiastically pressed on joyfully pursuing the pearl of great price. May we do the same.

PRAYERS *others may be added*

With joy and enthusiasm, we pray:

◆ Fill us with your compassion.

That we may have care and concern for the economically poor, we pray: ◆
That there may be an increase of vocations to religious life and the priesthood, we pray: ◆ *That those who preach the word of God do so in joy, we pray:* ◆
That we may attend to our moral growth, we pray: ◆

Our Father . . .

Ever-living God,
your Son has won redemption for us
      through the cross.
Through the prayers and example
      of St. Alphonsus Liguori,
may we grow in our knowledge
      of you,
help to spread the Good News,
and live in the joy of the Resurrection.
Grant this through Christ our Lord.
      Amen.

✛ *I will bless the Lord at all times.*

✝ *I will bless the Lord at all times.*

PSALM 34   page 410

READING   *Matthew 13:47–53*

Jesus said to the disciples: "The King-dom of heaven is like a net thrown into the sea, which collects fish of every kind. When it is full they haul it ashore and sit down to put what is good into buckets. What is bad they throw away. Thus it will be at the end of the age. The angels will go out and separate the wicked from the righteous and throw them into the fiery furnace, where there will be wailing and grinding of teeth."

"Do you understand all these things?" They answered, "Yes." And he replied, "Then every scribe who has been instructed in the Kingdom of heaven is like the head of a household who brings from his storeroom both the new and the old." When Jesus fin-ished these parables, he went away from there.

REFLECTION

What do we need to throw away? What keeps us from the knowledge, wisdom, and love of God? Today's Gospel passage calls us to name, identify, and discard those things that keep us from being true disci-ples of Christ. As followers of Christ, our lives need to critique and challenge a world consumed by money, power, and possessions. Let us call upon God to rid our lives and world of the glamour of sin and evil so that on the last day we will be deemed righteous and be saved from the fiery furnace.

PRAYERS   *others may be added*

Striving to be authentic disciples of Christ, we pray:

◆ Fill us with your compassion.

For a spirit of forgiveness, we pray: ◆
For a spirit of honesty, we pray: ◆
For a spirit of simplicity, we pray: ◆
For a spirit of righteousness, we pray: ◆

Our Father . . .

O God,
you are the source of all truth
    and wisdom.
May we be holy men and women
    who reject sin
and declare your wonderful works
throughout all of creation.
Grant this through Jesus our Lord.
    Amen.

✝ *I will bless the Lord at all times.*

✚ *I will bless the Lord at all times.*

PSALM 34   *page 410*

READING   *Matthew 13:54–58*

Jesus came to his native place and taught the people in their synagogue. They were astonished and said, "Where did this man get such wisdom and mighty deeds? Is he not the carpenter's son? Is not his mother named Mary and his brothers James, Joseph, Simon, and Judas? Are not his sisters all with us? Where did this man get all this?" And they took offense at him. But Jesus said to them, "A prophet is not without honor except in his native place and in his own house." And he did not work many mighty deeds there because of their lack of faith.

REFLECTION

Sometimes the most obvious answer is the hardest to see or understand. Today's Gospel story comes after a long set of miracles. Even after all those wonders, the local townspeople still would not believe that Jesus was more than just another hometown boy. They closed themselves off to Jesus and his mighty deeds. What truth is right in front of our eyes that we are ignoring? What miracles are we missing? We needn't go very far to look for the truth; the Holy Spirit always works "in our native place and in our own house."

PRAYERS   *others may be added*

With open eyes and hearts, we pray:

◆ Fill us with your compassion.

That we may be open to the goodness and gifts of everyone we meet, we pray: ◆ That we may recognize the Lord working in those closest to us, we pray: ◆ That we may strive to be the hands of Christ for those around us, we pray: ◆ That those who have died may experience the joy of the Resurrection, we pray: ◆

Our Father . . .

Father,
you sent your Son to be flesh and
    blood among us.
May we continue to look for Christ in
    our families,
our neighbors, and our co-workers,
acknowledging the power of the
    Holy Spirit
to work in all people.
We ask this through Christ our Lord.
    Amen.

✚ *I will bless the Lord at all times.*

✤ *I will bless the Lord at all times.*

PSALM 34   *page 410*

READING   *Matthew 14:3–11*

Now Herod had arrested John, bound him, and put him in prison on account of Herodias, the wife of his brother Philip, for John had said to him, "It is not lawful for you to have her." Although he wanted to kill him, he feared the people, for they regarded him as a prophet. But at a birthday celebration for Herod, the daughter of Herodias performed a dance before the guests and delighted Herod so much that he swore to give her whatever she might ask for. Prompted by her mother, she said, "Give me here on a platter the head of John the Baptist." The king was distressed, but because of his oaths and the guests who were present, he ordered that it be given, and he had John beheaded in the prison. His head was brought in on a platter and given to the girl, who took it to her mother.

REFLECTION

Priest, teacher, healer, confessor, counselor, miracle worker! Can one man be all these things and more? Yes! St. John Mary Vianney (1786–1859), better known as the Curé d'Ars, served in all of these ministerial capacities. Not only did he fulfill these roles, but he lived them with sincerity, humility, simplicity, and compassion. Selling his robes, giving his money to the poor, and refusing any form of honor, St. John is revered as a model for parish priests, a
witness for the spiritual life, and a beacon of the Catholic faith. May we, like St. John, cast aside the trappings of this earthly life so that we can serve all those in need.

PRAYERS   *others may be added*

Living the message of St. John, we pray:

◆ Fill us with your compassion.

For parish priests, that they may proclaim the Gospel message with insight and understanding, we pray: ◆ For teachers, that they may announce the wisdom and knowledge of God, we pray: ◆ For counselors, that they may speak with the empathy of God, we pray: ◆ For healers, that they may be the merciful hands of Christ, we pray: ◆

Our Father . . .

God of the saints,
you continually call men and women
to live your truth and peace
in new and meaningful ways.
Following St. John Mary Vianney,
    may we
live our vocation with courage
    and zeal.
We ask this through Christ our Lord.
    Amen.

✤ *I will bless the Lord at all times.*

✦ *I will bless the Lord at all times.*

PSALM 34 *page 410*

READING *Luke 12:16–21*

Then he [Jesus] told them a parable. "There was a rich man whose land produced a bountiful harvest. He asked himself, 'What shall I do, for I do not have space to store my harvest?' And he said, 'This is what I shall do: I shall tear down my barns and build larger ones. There I shall store all my grain and other goods and I shall say to myself, "Now as for you, you have so many good things stored up for many years, rest, eat, drink, be merry!'" But God said to him, 'You fool, this night your life will be demanded of you; and the things you have prepared, to whom will they belong?' Thus will it be for all who store up treasure for themselves but are not rich in what matters to God."

REFLECTION

Children play with no concern for the future; they always live in the present moment. Adults live all too aware of the fragility and fleetingness of life. Somewhere in between these extremes is the wisdom that life is a precious gift, not to be squandered on the pursuit of material gains but to be lived in realization that God, the giver of the gift, is to be found in every moment—past, present, and future. May we live life to the fullest in Christ.

PRAYERS *others may be added*

With grateful souls, we pray:

◆ Fill us with your compassion.

That children may be protected from untimely loss of innocence, we pray: ◆ *That adults may appreciate living in the present moment, we pray:* ◆ *That we may learn to share our resources with those in need, we pray:* ◆ *That our highest goal may be to live in Christ, we pray:* ◆

Our Father . . .

Loving God,
you surround us with those who are filled
with an appreciation of the importance of each moment.
Through their example, help us
to look for you in the present,
be thankful for your presence in the past,
and live in joyful hope of meeting you in the future.
We ask this through our Lord Jesus Christ, your Son,
who lives and reigns with you in the unity of the Holy Spirit,
one God, forever and ever. Amen.

✦ *I will bless the Lord at all times.*

✝ *This is my beloved Son, with whom I am well pleased; listen to him.*

PSALM 27   page 408

READING   Luke 9:28b–35

Jesus took Peter, John, and James and went up a mountain to pray. While he was praying his face changed in appearance and his clothing became dazzling white. And behold, two men were conversing with him, Moses and Elijah, who appeared in glory and spoke of his exodus that he was going to accomplish in Jerusalem. Peter and his companions had been overcome by sleep, but becoming fully awake, they saw his glory and the two men standing with him. As they were about to part from him, Peter said to Jesus, "Master, it is good that we are here; let us make three tents, one for you, one for Moses, and one for Elijah." But he did not know what he was saying. While he was still speaking, a cloud came and cast a shadow over them, and they became frightened when they entered the cloud. Then from the cloud came a voice that said, "This is my chosen Son; listen to him."

REFLECTION

Imagine seeing our Lord transfigured: consumed by dazzling colors, clothed in splendor, shining in brilliant glory, radiating light, and encircled by majestic songs of an exodus. As we celebrate the Transfiguration of Jesus, our Messiah, we are invited to ask what our world would look like transfigured, transformed by God's saving light. Imagine it! Envision a world where the colors of equality, the splendor of peace, the brilliance of truth, the light of hope, and the majestic songs of reconciliation are valued and esteemed. Let's create it! Let's build it! Let's tell the story of a son, God's Son, who transfigured the world by handing over his life!

PRAYERS   *others may be added*

Celebrating the Transfiguration of the Lord, we pray:

◆ Loving God, transform our world.

For an end to violence and war, we pray: ◆ For an end to racism and elitism, we pray: ◆ For an end to poverty and hunger, we pray: ◆ For an end to abortion and capitol punishment, we pray: ◆

Our Father . . .

Transfigured Christ,
you clothe humanity
in the radiating garment of salvation.
Give us eyes to see the places in
  the world
that long to hear your song
  of redemption.
We ask this in your name. Amen.

✝ *This is my beloved Son, with whom I am well pleased; listen to him.*

✛ *I will bless the Lord at all times.*

PSALM 34   *page 410*

READING   *Matthew 14:22–33*

Jesus made the disciples get into a boat and precede him to the other side of the sea, while he dismissed the crowds. After doing so, he went up on the mountain by himself to pray. When it was evening he was there alone. Meanwhile the boat, already a few miles offshore, was being tossed about by the waves, for the wind was against it. During the fourth watch of the night, he came toward them, walking on the sea. When the disciples saw him walking on the sea they were terrified. "It is a ghost," they said, and they cried out in fear. At once Jesus spoke to them, "Take courage, it is I; do not be afraid." Peter said to him in reply, "Lord, if it is you, command me to come to you on the water." He said, "Come." Peter got out of the boat and began to walk on the water toward Jesus. But when he saw how strong the wind was he became frightened; and, beginning to sink, he cried out, "Lord, save me!" Immediately Jesus stretched out his hand and caught him, and said to him, "O you of little faith, why did you doubt?" After they got into the boat, the wind died down. Those who were in the boat did him homage, saying, "Truly, you are the Son of God."

REFLECTION

Peter, the ever-impetuous apostle, today shows us the power of faith and our need to rely on the Lord to step into the unknown. The saints we celebrate today also relied on the Lord. Of these saints, St. Sixtus II (+258) became Pope just as a new round of persecutions began. His martyrdom occurred as he was addressing a congregation. Sixtus protected his people by not fleeing his executioners. By trusting in the Lord, he saved his flock and won the crown of everlasting life. Our trust in Christ, our step into the unknown, can do no less.

PRAYERS   *others may be added*

Trusting in the Lord, we pray:

◆ Fill us with your compassion.

That we may look to the Lord in the storms of our lives, we pray: ◆ *That our prayers may reflect the trust of Peter's words, "Lord, save me," we pray:* ◆ *That we may be willing to risk all in our service of each other, we pray:* ◆ *That all the saints may intercede for us, we pray:* ◆

Our Father . . .

Almighty God,
through your saints you have given us
    examples of trust.
Help our weakened spirits look to you
    for strength,
rely on you for help,
and see you as our final destiny.
We ask this through Christ our Lord.
    Amen.

✛ *I will bless the Lord at all times.*

✝ *I will bless the Lord at all times.*

PSALM 34   page 410

READING   Matthew 15:21–28

At that time Jesus withdrew to the region of Tyre and Sidon. And behold, a Canaanite woman of that district came and called out, "Have pity on me, Lord, Son of David! My daughter is tormented by a demon." But he did not say a word in answer to her. His disciples came and asked him, "Send her away, for she keeps calling out after us." He said in reply, "I was sent only to the lost sheep of the house of Israel." But the woman came and did him homage, saying, "Lord, help me." He said in reply, "It is not right to take the food of the children and throw it to the dogs." She said, "Please, Lord, for eve the dogs eat the scraps that fall from the table of their masters." Then Jesus said to her in reply, "O woman, great is your faith! Let it be done for you as you wish." And her daughter was healed from that hour.

REFLECTION

St. Dominic lived during an outbreak of Albigensianism, a heresy that regarded the physical world as evil. By espousing poverty and a humble manner, Dominic and his followers worked tirelessly at preaching the truth, even winning special papal approval for their work. May we, too, spread the Gospel truth in simplicity and humility.

PRAYERS   *others may be added*

Through the intercession of St. Dominic, we pray:

◆ Fill us with your compassion.

For the Church, that she may stand strong with the keys of the kingdom, we pray: ◆ *For an appreciation of the goodness of creation, we pray:* ◆ *For the men and women of the Dominican order, we pray:* ◆ *For the repose of the souls of the faithful departed, we pray:* ◆

Our Father . . .

God of all creation,
you manifest your glory and
    your love
through the wonders of the universe.
In St. Dominic you reminded us
    of the goodness
of the created order.
By his example and prayers,
may we respect your works
and sing your praises to all we meet.
We ask this through Christ our Lord.
    Amen.

✝ *I will bless the Lord at all times.*

✛ *I will bless the Lord at all times.*

PSALM 34   *page 410*

READING   *Matthew 16:13–19*

Jesus went into the region of Caesarea Philippi and he asked his disciples, "Who do people say that the Son of Man is?" They replied, "Some say John the Baptist, others Elijah, still others Jeremiah or one of the prophets." He said to them, "But who do you say that I am?" Simon Peter said in reply, "You are the Christ, the Son of the living God." Jesus said to him in reply, "Blessed are you, Simon son of Jonah. For flesh and blood has not revealed this to you, but my heavenly Father. And so I say to you, you are Peter, and upon this rock I will build my Church, and the gates of the netherworld shall not prevail against it. I will give you the keys to the Kingdom of heaven."

REFLECTION

After reading an autobiography of St. Teresa of Avila, St. Teresa Benedicta of the Cross (1891–+1942), also known as Edith Stein, chose to leave Judaism and converted to Catholicism. After engaging in various intellectual endeavors, St. Teresa decided to enter the Carmelite order. With growing anti-Semitism under Hitler's regime, St. Teresa began to foresee her fate: starved and stripped, standing in a gas chamber inhaling the fumes of death. Having died at Auschwitz, she is venerated for her unbelievable courage, contemplative love, intellectual aptitudes, and the way she cared for children and mothers in the concentration camp. May we never forget our sister and friend, St. Teresa, who saw her death as an act of atonement for the evil of her time!

PRAYERS   *others may be added*

Proclaiming the life and witness of St. Teresa, we pray:

◆ Fill us with your compassion.

For those exterminated in death camps, we pray: ◆ For survivors of the Holocaust, we pray: ◆ For an end to anti-Semitism, we pray: ◆ For the Carmelite order, we pray: ◆

Our Father . . .

Loving Father,
you called your servant St. Teresa
    Benedicta of the Cross
to live courageously and sacrifice
    compassionately.
Give us the strength
to stand up for what is right and good
so that the darkness of sin and death
will no longer suffocate your
    saving word.
Grant this through Jesus our Lord.
    Amen.

✛ *I will bless the Lord at all times.*

✝ *I will bless the Lord at all times.*

PSALM 34 *page 410*

READING *John 12:24–26*

Jesus said to his disciples: "Amen, amen, I say to you, unless a grain of wheat falls to the ground and dies, it remains just a grain of wheat; but if it dies, it produces much fruit. Whoever loves his life loses it, and whoever hates his life in this world will preserve it for eternal life. Whoever serves me must follow me, and where I am, there also will my servant be. The Father will honor whoever serves me."

REFLECTION

During the persecutions of Valerian, St. Lawrence (+258), a deacon to Pope Sixtus II, was martyred: roasted alive on a gridiron. Right before his death, St. Lawrence, unwilling to surrender the Church's riches to the Roman prefect, distributed the Church's possessions to the poor and proclaimed that they, the poor, were the Church's greatest treasure. Included in the First Eucharistic Prayer and the Church's martyrology, St. Lawrence is a model of sacrificial love: a grain of wheat that died so God's fruit, God's word, would flourish and abound.

PRAYERS *others may be added*

Through the intercession of St. Lawrence, we pray:

◆ Fill us with your compassion.

That we are willing to sacrifice our life for the Gospel, we pray: ◆ *That we lift up the martyrs as models and witnesses to the spiritual life, we pray:* ◆ *That those facing persecution and death because of their faith will be comforted by God's healing hand, we pray:* ◆ *That the poor will have their fill and know the riches of the kingdom, we pray:* ◆

Our Father . . .

God of the martyrs,
you called St. Lawrence
to sacrifice his life for your
    saving peace.
May we proclaim your light and hope
    in a world
that crucifies your redeeming truth.
Grant this through Jesus our Lord.
    Amen.

✝ *I will bless the Lord at all times.*

✚ *I will bless the Lord at all times.*

PSALM 34 *page 410*

READING *Matthew 17:14–20*

A man came up to Jesus, knelt down before him, and said, "Lord, have pity on my son, who is a lunatic and suffers severely; often he falls into fire, and often into water. I brought him to your disciples, but they could not cure him." Jesus said in reply, "O faithless and perverse generation, how long will I be with you? How long will I endure you? Bring the boy here to me." Jesus rebuked him and the demon came out of him, and from that hour the boy was cured. Then the disciples approached Jesus in private and said, "Why could we not drive it out?" He said to them, "Because of your little faith. Amen, I say to you, if you have faith the size of a mustard seed, you will say to this mountain, 'Move from here to there,' and it will move. Nothing will be impossible for you."

REFLECTION

With faith the size of a mustard seed and under the influence of her close spiritual companion, St. Francis of Assisi, St. Clare of Assisi (1193–+1253) renounced all of her possessions and took the habit of a nun so she could live the Gospel with great fervor and simplicity. As foundress of the Poor Clares—a religious community marked by poverty and austerity, and sustained entirely by alms—St. Clare and her sisters lived a penitential life rooted in the providential action of God. St. Clare truly models faith, a faith which can move mountains and overcome impossibility.

PRAYERS *others may be added*

Seeking faith the size of a mustard seed, we pray:

◆ Fill us with your compassion.

For Poor Clares throughout the world, we pray: ◆ *For the Franciscan charism, we pray:* ◆ *For the founding of new religious communities, we pray:* ◆ *For the poor in our midst, we pray:* ◆

Our Father . . .

God of simplicity,
you raised up your daughter,
St. Clare,
as a beacon of light in a
disbelieving world.
Enkindle in us a spirit of humility
and obedience.
We ask this through Jesus our Lord.
Amen.

✚ *I will bless the Lord at all times.*

✚ *I will bless the Lord at all times.*

PSALM 34 *page 410*

READING *Luke 12:32–37a*

Jesus said to his disciples: "Do not be afraid any longer, little flock, for your Father is pleased to give you the kingdom. Sell your belongings and give alms. Provide money bags for yourselves that do not wear out, an inexhaustible treasure in heaven that no thief can reach nor moth destroy. For where your treasure is, there also will your heart be.

"Gird your loins and light your lamps and be like servants who await their master's return from a wedding, ready to open immediately when he comes and knocks. Blessed are those servants whom the master finds vigilant on his arrival."

REFLECTION

Where does our treasure lie? Do we find meaning and strength in worldly possessions, earthly power, and human prestige? Or, does the hope of the Gospel, the power of the cross, and the promise of heaven enflame our hearts and give purpose to our existence? We must delve deep into our souls to answer these questions with honesty and sincerity so we can gird our loins, light our lamps, and be like servants, ready and waiting for the coming of the Son of Man. Let us be vigilant, placing our treasure in heaven, so we will know the glory of eternal life.

PRAYERS *others may be added*

Awaiting the Son of Man, we pray:

◆ Fill us with your compassion.

That we renounce the promises of this world to gain the riches of heaven, we pray: ◆ *That we live vigilant, holy lives, we pray:* ◆ *That our world is governed by the virtues of God, we pray:* ◆ *That the Church calls all people to place their hope in the story of salvation, we pray:* ◆

Our Father . . .

O God,
you are the one, true treasure
    of all life.
Following in the footsteps of your
    Son, Jesus,
may we preach the fortune of
    everlasting peace.
We ask this through our Lord Jesus
    Christ, your Son,
who lives and reigns with you in the
    unity of the Holy Spirit,
one God, forever and ever. Amen.

✚ *I will bless the Lord at all times.*

✜ *I will bless the Lord at all times.*

PSALM 34   *page 410*

READING   *Matthew 17:22–27*

As Jesus and his disciples were gathering in Galilee, Jesus said to them, "The Son of Man is to be handed over to men, and they will kill him, and he will be raised on the third day." And they were overwhelmed with grief.

When they came to Capernaum, the collectors of the temple tax approached Peter and said, "Does not your teacher pay the temple tax?" "Yes," he said. When he came into the house, before he had time to speak, Jesus asked him, "What is your opinion, Simon? From whom do the kings of the earth take tolls or census tax? From their subjects or from foreigners?" When he said, "From foreigners," Jesus said to him, "Then the subjects are exempt. But that we may not offend them, go to the sea, drop in a hook, and take the first fish that comes up. Open its mouth and you will find a coin worth twice the temple tax. Give that to them for me and for you."

REFLECTION

From the time of Jesus to the present day, Christians have struggled with civil governments. St. Pontian (+235) and St. Hippolytus (+236) lived through a regime change that brought new persecutions to the Church. At this time, these two men were disputing theology and politics. The persecutions led to their imprisonment together and eventually martyrdom. The government that captured and killed them was also the cause of their reconciliation. Today's puzzling parable reminds us of another saying of Jesus: we must be as sly as foxes when dealing with the powers of this world. While respect for government is appropriate, we must never mistake the differences between God and country.*

PRAYERS   *others may be added*

   With true devotion, we pray:

◆ Fill us with your compassion.

For our Holy Father, we pray: ◆
For all priests and bishops, we pray: ◆
For all government officials, we pray: ◆
For Christians suffering persecution,
we pray: ◆

Our Father . . .

Father,
you called St. Pontian and
   St. Hippolytus
to reconcile their differences and
   be joined
in their witness to the faith.
Inspire us to seek the truth,
reconcile with one another,
and lead us to your kingdom forever.
We ask this through Christ our Lord.
   Amen.

✜ *I will bless the Lord at all times.*

✝ *I will bless the Lord at all times.*

PSALM 34 *page 410*

READING *Matthew 18:1–5, 10, 12–14*

The disciples approached Jesus and said, "Who is the greatest in the Kingdom of heaven?" He called a child over, placed it in their midst, and said, "Amen, I say to you, unless you turn and become like children, you will not enter the Kingdom of heaven. Whoever becomes humble like this child is the greatest in the Kingdom of heaven. And whoever receives one child such as this in my name receives me.

"See that you do not despise one of these little ones, for I say to you that their angels in heaven always look upon the face of my heavenly Father. What is your opinion? If a man has a hundred sheep and one of them goes astray, will he not leave the ninety-nine in the hills and go in search of the stray? And if he finds it, amen, I say to you, he rejoices more over it than over the ninety-nine that did not stray. In just the same way, it is not the will of your heavenly Father that one of these little ones be lost."

REFLECTION

Not unlike Jewish society in the time of Jesus, our world is enamored by status and position. We idolize praise, recognition, personal agendas, the corporate world, and wealth. Jesus tells us that these things are not of heaven. We are to become like children in ancient times who had no legal rights, were totally dependent on their parents, and received everything as gift. Let us realize that status and position are not part of the promise of salvation, and become child-like, realizing that all is gift!

PRAYERS *others may be added*

Seeking to become humble like a child, we pray:

◆ Fill us with your compassion.

To renounce power and prestige, we pray: ◆ *To sacrifice personal agendas and gain, we pray:* ◆ *To announce God's promise of salvation, we pray:* ◆ *To realize that all is gift, we pray:* ◆

Our Father . . .

Jesus, our Messiah,
you call us to have
the humility, simplicity, and
   dependence of a child.
Plant your word in our hearts
so that we can stand in awe
at the gift of redemption.
Grant this through Christ our Lord.
   Amen.

✝ *I will bless the Lord at all times.*

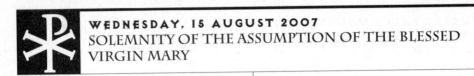

✦ *Here I am, Lord; I come to do your will.*

PSALM 40   *page 411*

READING   *Luke 11:27–28*

While Jesus was speaking, a woman from the crowd called out and said to him, "Blessed is the womb that carried you and the breasts at which you nursed." He replied, "Rather, blessed are those who hear the word of God and observe it."

REFLECTION

Mary is the image of the Church; she is what we are meant to be. At the same time, she is our consolation; by the fulfillment of God's promises to her, she strengthens our hope in God's promises to us. Pope Pius XII proclaimed the Assumption a dogma of the Church as a message to a world that had just experienced World War II. This dogma flies in the face of a world given to destruction of life and desecration of the human body. Today and always, may Mary help us hear God's word and keep it in bodies sanctified for God's work.

PRAYERS   *others may be added*

Trusting in God's word, we pray:

◆ Fill us with your compassion.

That we may avoid all sin and corruption, we pray: ◆ *That we may work for a world that respects the human body, we pray:* ◆ *That we may bear the word of God to all we meet, we pray:* ◆ *That those who have died will be united with the Blessed Virgin Mary to Christ in the kingdom of heaven, we pray:* ◆

Our Father . . .

Almighty God,
the Blessed Virgin Mary was assumed
    into heaven,
and now shares in your Son's glory in
    body and soul.
Through her intercession, may the
    weak be strengthened,
the sorrowing be comforted, sinners
    be pardoned, and
may all be reunited in your kingdom
    with the saints forever.
We ask this through our Lord Jesus
    Christ, your Son,
who lives and reigns with you and the
    Holy Spirit,
one God, forever and ever. Amen.

✦ *Here I am, Lord; I come to do your will.*

✝ *I will bless the Lord at all times.*

PSALM 34 *page 410*

READING *Matthew 18:21—27*

Peter approached Jesus and asked him, "Lord, if my brother sins against me, how often must I forgive him? As many as seven times?" Jesus answered, "I say to you, not seven times but seventy-seven times. That is why the Kingdom of heaven may be likened to a king who decided to settle accounts with his servants. When he began the accounting, a debtor was brought before him who owed him a huge amount. Since he had no way of paying it back, his master ordered him to be sold, along with his wife, his children, and all his property, in payment of the debt. At that, the servant fell down, did him homage, and said, 'Be patient with me, and I will pay you back in full.' Moved with compassion the master of that servant let him go and forgave him the loan."

REFLECTION

The master goes beyond what has been requested and forgives the debt rather than just giving more time for repayment. We, too, have been forgiven the debt of our sin, a debt we could never hope to repay. We are tempted to think in terms of justice: I deserve this reward, or, he deserves that punishment. But God does not work that way. He is more than just; he is generous, merciful, compassionate. God tries to teach us that the only way out of hopelessness is to give mercy generously, to go beyond simple justice.

PRAYERS *others may be added*

With generous hearts, we pray:

◆ Fill us with your compassion.

That we may offer forgiveness without counting the cost, we pray: ◆ That we may learn to love those who are most difficult to forgive, we pray: ◆ That the nations of the world will follow Gospel principles in their dealings with each other, we pray: ◆ That justice may always be tempered with mercy, we pray: ◆

Our Father . . .

Loving Father,
you spared no generosity in forgiving
  our sins.
Through the death and Resurrection
  of your Son,
may we learn the meaning of mercy
and practice it every day of our lives.
We ask this through Christ our Lord.
  Amen.

✝ *I will bless the Lord at all times.*

✝ *I will bless the Lord at all times.*

PSALM 34   *page 410*

READING   *Matthew 19:3–6*

Some Pharisees approached Jesus, and tested him, saying, "Is it lawful for a man to divorce his wife for any cause whatever?" He said in reply, "Have you not read that from the beginning the Creator *made them male and female* and said, *For this reason a man shall leave his father and mother and be joined to his wife, and the two shall become one flesh?* So they are no longer two, but one flesh. Therefore, what God has joined together, man must not separate."

REFLECTION   *Gaudium et spes, 48*

Firmly established by the Lord, the unity of marriage will radiate from the equal personal dignity of wife and husband, a dignity acknowledged by mutual and total love. The constant fulfillment of the duties of this Christian vocation demands notable virtue. For this reason, strengthened by grace for holiness of life, the couple will painstakingly cultivate and pray for steadiness of love, large heartedness and the spirit of sacrifice.

PRAYERS   *others may be added*

In love and fidelity of spirit, we pray:

◆ Fill us with your compassion.

For married couples, that they may work together with a giving spirit to live out their commitment to one another, we pray: ◆ *For religious celibates, that their lives may be marked by generosity and love, we pray:* ◆ *For divorced people, that they may find comfort and love in the Christian community, we pray:* ◆ *For those seeking their path in life, that they may make choices guided by the Holy Spirit, we pray:* ◆

Our Father . . .

God,
your love transforms us from
   lowly creatures
to the stature of spouse for your Son.
May the dignity you have given us
inspire us to spend our lives in service
   to others
and in praise of you.
Grant this through Christ our Lord.
   Amen.

✝ *I will bless the Lord at all times.*

✠ *I will bless the Lord at all times.*

PSALM 34 *page 410*

READING *Matthew 19:13–15*

Children were brought to Jesus that he might lay his hands on them and pray. The disciples rebuked them, but Jesus said, "Let the children come to me, and do not prevent them; for the Kingdom of heaven belongs to such as these." After he placed his hands on them, he went away.

REFLECTION

Under the direction and influence of St. Francis de Sales, St. Jane de Chantal (1572–+1641) founded a non-conventional religious community, the Congregation of the Visitation of the Virgin Mary, for women who were prevented from entering the enclosed religious orders for reasons of health. Modeled on Mary's visit to Elizabeth, the Congregation would be marked by humility, meekness, and its merciful service to the poor and sick. Having been married and a mother prior to founding the community, St. Jane was noted for her wisdom, understanding, and nurturing care. May we, like St. Jane, have confidence in God, have the courage to do his will, and seek holiness of life.

PRAYERS *others may be added*

Through the intercession of St. Jane, we pray:

◆ Fill us with your compassion.

For the mission of the Visitation Sisters, we pray: ◆ *For the ministry of the Oblates of St. Francis de Sales, we pray:* ◆ *For the gift of spiritual friendship and companionship, we pray:* ◆ *For the poor and sick, we pray:* ◆

Our Father . . .

God of new life,
you called St. Jane de Chantal
to found a humble and meek
    community of women
to serve the poor and sick.
Give us innovative spirits so that we
    can create
places where all are welcome and can
    find a home.
We ask this through Jesus our Lord.
    Amen.

✠ *I will bless the Lord at all times.*

✝ *Come with joy into the presence of the Lord.*

PSALM 100   *page 417*

READING   *Luke 12:49–53*

Jesus said to his disciples: "I have come to set the earth on fire, and how I wish it were already blazing! There is a baptism with which I must be baptized, and how great is my anguish until it is accomplished! Do you think that I have come to establish peace on the earth? No, I tell you, but rather division. From now on a household of five will be divided, three against two and two against three; a father will be divided against his son and a son against his father, a mother against her daughter and a daughter against her mother, a mother-in-law against her daughter-in-law and a daughter-in-law against her mother-in-law."

REFLECTION

Fire's ability to refine, purify, and transform makes it a reliable icon of God's presence. But just as some encounters with fire are unwelcome, so too do some reject the presence of God. The division Jesus brings is the great divide between those who are comforted by and welcome God's presence and those who reject it. If we expect Jesus to bring a worldly peace— one where all differences are sacrificed for a false harmony—we are mistaken. Our Baptism, like that of Jesus, is the call to sacrifice and reject all that refuses to be purified by God's burning love.

PRAYERS   *others may be added*

With souls afire with love, we pray:

◆ Lord of life, hear us.

That families may be united in love and faith, we pray: ◆ *That Church leaders may be on fire with the message of Christ, we pray:* ◆ *That world leaders may work for a true and lasting peace, we pray:* ◆ *That all the sick may be comforted by their faith and assisted by their communities, we pray:* ◆

Our Father . . .

Loving Father,
you send the Holy Spirit to enflame
   our hearts
with devotion to you.
May the love we share in Christ Jesus
burn out the desire for sin
and purify us so that we may share in
   your kingdom forever.
We ask this through our Lord Jesus
   Christ, your Son,
who lives and reigns with you in the
   unity of the Holy Spirit,
one God, forever and ever. Amen.

✝ *Come with joy into the presence of the Lord.*

✠ *Come with joy into the presence of the Lord.*

PSALM 100 *page 417*

READING *Matthew 19:16–22*

A young man approached Jesus and said, "Teacher, what good must I do to gain eternal life?" He answered him, "Why do you ask me about the good? There is only One who is good. If you wish to enter into life, keep the commandments." He asked him, "Which ones?" And Jesus replied, *"You shall not kill; you shall not commit adultery; you shall not steal; you shall not bear false witness; honor your father and your mother; and you shall love your neighbor as yourself."* The young man said to him, "All of these I have observed. What do I still lack?" Jesus said to him, "If you wish to be perfect, go, sell what you have and give to the poor, and you will have treasure in heaven. Then come, follow me." When the young man heard this statement, he went away sad, for he had many possessions.

REFLECTION

Jesus didn't ask everyone he met to sell all they owned. When he did, it was for a specific purpose. He didn't want possessions to slow the disciples down during their urgent mission to spread the Good News. Here, for this rich young man, it was probably because Jesus sensed that his possessions had become his idols, his demons. In a sense, this man's possessions had come to possess him. Possessions aren't bad
unless they possess us. What is holding us back, what possesses us?

PRAYERS *others may be added*

Through the intercession of St. Bernard, we pray:

◆ Lord of life, hear us.

That we give up whatever holds us back from serving God, we pray: ◆ *That we give time to prayer and silence in our lives, we pray:* ◆ *That there be an increase in vocations to the religious life, we pray:* ◆ *That all those who work as negotiators for peace may look to St. Bernard as their model, we pray:* ◆

Our Father . . .

Bountiful God,
you fill the world with an abundance
   of your gifts.
Help us to be open to the Holy Spirit
   and the workings of grace
that we, like Saint Bernard, may be
   catalysts for change in the world.
We ask this through Christ our Lord.
   Amen.

✠ *Come with joy into the presence of the Lord.*

✠ *Come with joy into the presence of the Lord.*

PSALM 100   *page 417*

READING   *Matthew 19:23–26*

Jesus said to his disciples: "Amen, I say to you, it will be hard for one who is rich to enter the Kingdom of heaven. Again I say to you, it is easier for a camel to pass through the eye of a needle than for one who is rich to enter the Kingdom of God." When the disciples heard this, they were greatly astonished and said, "Who then can be saved?" Jesus looked at them and said, "For men this is impossible, but for God all things are possible."

REFLECTION

St. Pius X (1835–+1914) was a man of strong beliefs and deeply held convictions. Born into a poor family in northern Italy, he rose through the ranks of Church service, garnering a reputation for humility, simplicity of life, and fierce devotion to the papacy. He is perhaps best remembered for encouraging frequent Communion and lowering the age for first Communion. St. Pius X was known to have been uncomfortable with the rich trappings of his office to such an extent that he asked for the simplest of tombs. May we share this saint's love of simplicity and join him in the kingdom of heaven.

PRAYERS   *others may be added*

With humility and devotion, we pray:

◆ Lord of life, hear us.

That our Pope may be protected from harm and kept safe in your service, we pray: ◆ *That all Church leaders may be preserved from error, we pray:* ◆ *That your people may be nourished with the Bread of Life, we pray:* ◆ *That all may be insured to receive their basic human needs, we pray:* ◆

Our Father . . .

King of heaven,
you give us leadership in the
    successors of Peter.
Through the example and intercession
    of St. Pius X,
may we lead lives of simplicity,
    humility,
and devotion to your presence in the
    Blessed Sacrament,
so that all will know your
    saving power.
We ask this in your name. Amen.

✠ *Come with joy into the presence of the Lord.*

✛ *Come with joy into the presence of the Lord.*

PSALM 100   *page 417*

READING   *Matthew 20:1, 6–8a, 9–16*

Jesus told his disciples this parable: "The Kingdom of heaven is like a landowner who went out at dawn to hire laborers for his vineyard. After agreeing with them for the usual daily wage, he sent them into his vineyard. Going out about five o'clock, he found others standing around, and said to them, 'Why do you stand here idle all day?' They answered, 'Because no one has hired us.' He said to them, 'You too go into my vineyard.' When it was evening the owner of the vineyard said to his foreman, 'Summon the laborers and give them their pay. . . . When those who had started about five o'clock came, each received the usual daily wage. So when the first came, they thought that they would receive more, but each of them also got the usual wage. And on receiving it they grumbled against the landowner, saying, 'These last ones worked only one hour, and you have made them equal to us, who bore the day's burden and the heat.' He said to one of them in reply, 'My friend, I am not cheating you. Did you not agree with me for the usual daily wage? Take what is yours and go. What if I wish to give this last one the same as you? Or am I not free to do as I wish with my own money? Are you envious because I am generous?' Thus, the last will be first, and the first will be last."

REFLECTION

Today we celebrate Mary's crowning as Queen of Heaven. From early Christian times Mary has been venerated and praised as queen of the angels and saints. We see in the Blessed Virgin most clearly what we are meant to be and where we are called to go. Whether we heed the call of the Lord at the first hour or at the last hour, our God is generous to those who accept his word and keep it.

PRAYERS   *others may be added*

    Answering God's call, we pray:

◆ Lord of life, hear us.

That Mary will bear in her heart the prayers we place before Christ, we pray: ◆ *That world leaders may encourage nonviolence, we pray:* ◆ *That all will attend to the ministry of prayer, we pray:* ◆ *That the faithful departed may be raised and join Mary, their Queen, in the heavenly kingdom, we pray:* ◆

Our Father . . .

Lord of the universe,
you honored the Blessed Virgin Mary,
making her a diadem in your crown.
May Mary, the crowning glory
    of humanity,
inspire us to greater acts of love,
pray for our needs,
and welcome us home on the last day.
We ask this through Christ our Lord.
    Amen.

✛ *Come with joy into the presence of the Lord.*

✢ *Come with joy into the presence of the Lord.*

PSALM 100 page 417

READING Matthew 22:1–9

Jesus again in reply spoke to the chief priests and the elders of the people in parables saying, "The Kingdom of heaven may be likened to a king who gave a wedding feast for his son. He dispatched his servants to summon the invited guests to the feast, but they refused to come. A second time he sent other servants, saying, 'Tell those invited: "Behold, I have prepared my banquet, my calves and fattened cattle are killed, and everything is ready; come to the feast." ' Some ignored the invitation and went away, one to his farm, another to his business. The rest laid hold of his servants, mistreated them, and killed them. The king was enraged and sent his troops, destroyed those murderers, and burned their city. Then the king said to his servants, 'The feast is ready, but those who were invited were not worthy to come. Go out, therefore, into the main roads and invite to the feast whomever you find.'"

REFLECTION

Today's parable recounts how God's chosen people wouldn't accept the salvation offered by Christ, so others were given the offer. Now the invitation is ours. St. Rose (1586–+1617) accepted Christ's call wholeheartedly both in the form of personal penitential practices and in service to destitute children and sick, elderly people. Known
for her beauty as well as her work among the poor, this Third Order Dominican became the first canonized saint of the Americas in 1671. We may not all have Rose's physical beauty, but we can definitely develop her spiritual beauty to be fit for the wedding feast.

PRAYERS others may be added

Through the intercession of St. Rose of Lima, we pray:

◆ Lord of life, hear us.

That the people of Latin America may find special blessings on this day, we pray: ◆
That those who work with the sick and the destitute may find encouragement in Christ and his Church, we pray: ◆
That we may develop a penitential spirit, we pray: ◆

Our Father . . .

Almighty God,
you called St. Rose of Lima to
   a life of service to the poor.
May her example and
   prayers enkindle
a love of service, simplicity,
   and humility
in all people
so that we may be worthy guests
   at your feast.
We ask this through Christ our Lord.
   Amen.

✢ *Come with joy into the presence of the Lord.*

✤ *Come with joy into the presence of the Lord.*

PSALM 100 page 417

READING John 1:45–51

Philip found Nathanael and told him, "We have found the one about whom Moses wrote in the law, and also the prophets, Jesus son of Joseph, from Nazareth." But Nathanael said to him, "Can anything good come from Nazareth?" Philip said to him, "Come and see." Jesus saw Nathanael coming toward him and said of him, "Here is a true child of Israel. There is no duplicity in him." Nathanael said to him, "How do you know me?" Jesus answered and said to him, "Before Philip called you, I saw you under the fig tree." Nathanael answered him, "Rabbi, you are the Son of God; you are the King of Israel." Jesus answered and said to him, "Do you believe because I told you that I saw you under the fig tree? You will see greater things than this." And he said to him, "Amen, amen, I say to you, you will see heaven opened and the angels of God ascending and descending on the Son of Man."

REFLECTION

What a promise! To see heaven and earth connected; to see the great divide between God and creation crossed is the promise given to Nathanael, also known as Bartholomew. This promise is also given to us. Our life in Christ is the fulfillment of that promise. At every Eucharist we participate in the Father's heavenly banquet; in every loving act of service we are one with Christ Jesus; and in every moment we spend in prayer the Holy Spirit is at work within us. How joyous to share in the promises made to the apostles!

PRAYERS *others may be added*

With apostolic zeal, we pray:

◆ Lord of life, hear us.

For the Church, in union with the apostles, that she may worthily proclaim the Gospel promises, we pray: ◆ *For each local church, that the faithful with their bishop may be visible signs of the kingdom to come, we pray:* ◆ *For the spread of the Gospel, that we may encourage and support missionaries, we pray:* ◆ *For the dead, that they may enjoy the company of St. Bartholomew in heaven, we pray:* ◆

Our Father . . .

God of salvation,
in Christ you have given the Church
   your firm foundation.
May the Gospel preached by
   St. Bartholomew
root us firmly in Christ,
through whom we have been
   redeemed
and brought into your presence.
Grant this in the name of Jesus the
   Lord. Amen.

✤ *Come with joy into the presence of the Lord.*

✝ *Come with joy into the presence of the Lord.*

PSALM 100   *page 417*

READING   *Matthew 23:1–12*

Jesus spoke to the crowds and to his disciples, saying, "The scribes and the Pharisees have taken their seat on the chair of Moses. Therefore, do and observe all things whatsoever they tell you, but do not follow their example. For they preach but they do not practice. They tie up heavy burdens hard to carry and lay them on people's shoulders, but they will not lift a finger to move them. All their works are performed to be seen. They widen their phylacteries and lengthen their tassels. They love places of honor at banquets, seats of honor in synagogues, greetings in marketplaces, and the salutation 'Rabbi.' As for you, do not be called 'Rabbi.' You have but one teacher, and you are all brothers. Call no one on earth your father; you have but one Father in heaven. Do not be called 'Master'; you have but one master, the Christ. The greatest among you must be your servant. Whoever exalts himself will be humbled; but whoever humbles himself will be exalted."

REFLECTION   *St. Louis*

Be kindhearted to the poor, the unfortunate and the afflicted. Give them as much help and consolation as you can. Thank God for all the benefits he has bestowed upon you, that you may be worthy to receive greater.

PRAYERS   *others may be added*

With single-hearted sincerity, we pray:

◆ Lord of life, hear us.

That all followers of Christ may preach by heartfelt actions, we pray: ◆ *That we may work to lessen the burdens of humanity, we pray:* ◆ *That we may avoid having our works of charity seen by others, we pray:* ◆ *That we may seek last place and leave honors to others, we pray:* ◆

Our Father . . .

Loving Father,
you are the Master of the universe
and Lord of all creation.
You called St. Louis to rule
   with sincerity.
Through his prayers and example,
   may we be single-hearted
in following your Son so that we may
   be united
in your kingdom forever.
We ask through Christ our Lord.
   Amen.

✝ *Come with joy into the presence of the Lord.*

✠ *Come with joy into the presence of the Lord.*

PSALM 100 *page 417*

READING *Luke 13:24–27, 29–30*

[Jesus said] "Strive to enter through the narrow gate, for many, I tell you, will attempt to enter but will not be strong enough. After the master of the house has arisen and locked the door, then will you stand outside knocking and saying, 'Lord, open the door for us.' He will say to you in reply, 'I do not know where you are from.' And you will say, 'We ate and drank in your company and you taught in our streets.' Then he will say to you, 'I do not know where you are from. Depart from me, all you evildoers!' And people will come from the east and the west and from the north and the south and will recline at table in the kingdom of God. For behold, some are last who will be first, and some are first who will be last."

REFLECTION

It is so easy to be smug. Perhaps we're really trying to convince ourselves that all is well. Or, perhaps we have low self-esteem and need to see others fail in order for us to feel important. Whatever the reason, today Jesus warns us against smugness. He tells us that some "insiders" will be left out of the kingdom and some "outsiders" will be included. That judgment is up to the Lord. We need to try to enter through the narrow gate of other-centeredness and leave the rest to God.

PRAYERS *others may be added*

With humility, we pray:

◆ Lord of life, hear us.

For those who feel excluded from the table of life, that they may hear the invitation of Christ, we pray: ◆ For those who have much to share, that they may extend their blessings to others, we pray: ◆ For those we have personally excluded, that we may seek their pardon, we pray: ◆ For those who have barred us from their presence, that we may offer them our forgiveness and prayers, we pray: ◆

Our Father . . .

Father,
you sent your Son as our
    personal invitation
to your feast.
May we heed his call with sincerity
    of heart.
We ask this through our Lord Jesus
    Christ, your Son,
who lives and reigns with you in the
    unity of the Holy Spirit,
one God, forever and ever. Amen.

✠ *Come with joy into the presence of the Lord.*

✝ *Come with joy into the presence of the Lord.*

PSALM 100 *page 417*

READING *Matthew 23:13–17*

Jesus said to the crowds and to his disciples: "Woe to you, scribes and Pharisees, you hypocrites. You lock the Kingdom of heaven before men. You do not enter yourselves, nor do you allow entrance to those trying to enter.

"Woe to you, scribes and Pharisees, you hypocrites. You traverse sea and land to make one convert, and when that happens you make him a child of Gehenna twice as much as yourselves.

"Woe to you, blind guides, who say, 'If one swears by the temple, it means nothing, but if one swears by the gold of the temple, one is obligated.' Blind fools, which is greater, the gold, or the temple that made the gold sacred?"

REFLECTION

Jesus saves his severest criticisms for religious hypocrites and gives the highest praise to the single-hearted. St. Monica (332–+387), the mother of St. Augustine, was a single-hearted woman. Having an abusive husband, a meddling mother-in-law, and a dissolute son, St. Monica spent her life praying, fasting, and keeping vigil for their Christian conversion. Her persistence was rewarded, seeing them all convert. May we, too, persevere in our efforts to cooperate with grace.

PRAYERS *others may be added*

Trusting in God's providence, we pray:

◆ Lord of life, hear us.

That Church leaders may reflect the simplicity and honesty of Christ, we pray: ◆ *That God's sustaining love may support those recovering from addictions, we pray:* ◆ *That we may join parents in prayer for the conversion of their children, we pray:* ◆ *That Christian wives and mothers may show the faith of St. Monica, we pray:* ◆

Our Father . . .

Loving Father,
you gave St. Monica the faith
    and persistence
to see the conversion of her son,
    St. Augustine.
Send us your Holy Spirit so that we
may persevere in prayer and faith
and one day be united with you
    in glory.
Grant this through Christ our Lord.
    Amen.

✝ *Come with joy into the presence of the Lord.*

✛   *Come with joy into the presence of the Lord.*

PSALM 100 · page 417

READING · Matthew 23:23-26

Jesus said: "Woe to you, scribes and Pharisees, you hypocrites. You pay tithes of mint and dill and cummin, and have neglected the weightier things of the law: judgment and mercy and fidelity. But these you should have done, without neglecting the others. Blind guides, who strain out the gnat and swallow the camel!

"Woe to you, scribes and Pharisees, you hypocrites. You cleanse the outside of cup and dish, but inside they are full of plunder and self-indulgence. Blind Pharisee, cleanse first the inside of the cup, so that the outside also may be clean."

REFLECTION · St. Augustine

O eternal truth, true love and beloved eternity. You are my God. To you do I sigh day and night. When I first came to know you, you drew me to yourself so that I might see that there were things for me to see, but that I overcame the weakness of my vision, sending forth most strongly the beams of your light, and I trembled at once with love and dread. I learned that I was in a region unlike yours and far distant from you, and I thought I heard your voice from on high: "I am the food of grown men; grow then, and you will feed on me. Nor will you change me into yourself like bodily food, but you will be changed into me."

PRAYERS · others may be added

With the desire for pure hearts, we pray:

◆   Lord of life, hear us.

That all may appreciate the workings of grace in their lives, we pray: ◆ *That we may respect people of all faiths, we pray:* ◆ *That we may strive for purity of heart and action, we pray:* ◆ *That we may yearn for total conversion, we pray:* ◆

Our Father . . .

God of all,
you are the source of all goodness
    and grace.
Fill us with your Holy Spirit,
that we may turn completely
to the Gospel and follow your Son
to Resurrection glory.
We ask this through Christ our Lord.
    Amen.

✛   *Come with joy into the presence of the Lord.*

+ *Come with joy into the presence of the Lord.*

PSALM 100   *page 417*

READING   *Mark 6:21b–22, 24–29*

Herod, on his birthday, gave a banquet for his courtiers, his military officers, and the leading men of Galilee. Herodias' own daughter came in and performed a dance that delighted Herod and his guests. The king said to the girl, "Ask of me whatever you wish and I will grant it to you." She went out and said to her mother, "What shall I ask for?" She replied, "The head of John the Baptist." The girl hurried back to the king's presence and made her request, "I want you to give me at once on a platter the head of John the Baptist." The king was deeply distressed, but because of his oaths and the guests he did not wish to break his word to her. So he promptly dispatched an executioner with orders to bring back his head. He went off and beheaded him in the prison. He brought in the head on a platter and gave it to the girl. The girl in turn gave it to her mother. When his disciples heard about it, they came and took his body and laid it in a tomb.

REFLECTION

John the Baptist was a man unafraid to speak the truth, to cry out when he saw evil regardless of the cost. Today we see the cost of the truth, the cost of discipleship, the cost of love as the Church continues to suffer persecution for upholding the truth. This story is not a tragedy for John, but it is a triumph. He knew that true life, true love, is giving of oneself. On this day we celebrate the Forerunner's total gift of self. We know this total giving of self leads to life everlasting. Let us follow, let us truly live.

PRAYERS   *others may be added*

Through the intercession of St. John the Baptist, we pray:

◆ Lord of life, hear us.

For the Church, that we take up our share in the prophetic ministry of Christ, we pray: ◆ *For Church leaders, that they may have the fortitude to speak out against evil, we pray:* ◆ *For those who suffer violence for the sake of the Gospel, that they remain firm in faith, we pray:* ◆ *For civic leaders, that they may live and work with high ethical standards, we pray:* ◆

Our Father . . .

Father,
you sent your Son to show us that
by giving our lives we gain life.
Inspired by St. John the Baptist,
may we give ourselves to the truth of
   the Gospel.
We ask this through Christ our Lord.
   Amen.

+ *Come with joy into the presence of the Lord.*

✝ *Come with joy into the presence of the Lord.*

PSALM 100   *page 417*

READING   *Matthew 24:42–51*

Jesus said to his disciples: "Stay awake! For you do not know on which day your Lord will come. Be sure of this: if the master of the house had known the hour of night when the thief was coming, he would have stayed awake and not let his house be broken into. So too, you also must be prepared, for at an hour you do not expect, the Son of Man will come.

"Who, then, is the faithful and prudent servant, whom the master has put in charge of his household to distribute to them their food at the proper time? Blessed is that servant whom his master on his arrival finds doing so. Amen, I say to you, he will put him in charge of all his property. But if that wicked servant says to himself, 'My master is long delayed,' and begins to beat his fellow servants, and eat and drink with drunkards, the servant's master will come on an unexpected day and at an unknown hour and will punish him severely and assign him a place with the hypocrites, where there will be wailing and grinding of teeth."

REFLECTION   *St. Ephrem*

To prevent his disciples from asking the time of his coming, Christ said: About that hour no one knows, neither the angels nor the Son. It is not for you to know times or moments. *He has kept those things hidden so that we may keep watch, each of us thinking that he will come in our own day. If he had revealed the time of his coming, his coming would have lost its savior: it would no longer be an object of yearning for the nations and the age in which it will be revealed. He promised that he would come but did not say when he would come, and so all generations and ages await him eagerly.*

PRAYERS   *others may be added*

With vigilant hearts, we pray:

◆ Lord of life, hear us.

That you may help us to be awake to the possibilities for love, we pray: ◆ *That you may help us be alert to the needs of others, we pray:* ◆ *That you may help us to be conscious of your call, we pray:* ◆ *That you may help us to be prepared for our last hour, we pray:* ◆

Our Father . . .

Loving God,
you give us the freedom to choose
   our way.
Inspired by the Holy Spirit,
may we follow your Son's Gospel
   way of life
so that we may rejoice with you
at the finish of our last hour.
We ask this in the name of Jesus the
   Lord. Amen.

✝ *Come with joy into the presence of the Lord.*

✛   *Come with joy into the presence of the Lord.*

PSALM 100   *page 417*

READING   *Matthew 25:1–13*

Jesus told his disciples this parable: "The Kingdom of heaven will be like ten virgins who took their lamps and went out to meet the bridegroom. Five of them were foolish and five were wise. The foolish ones, when taking their lamps, brought no oil with them, but the wise brought flasks of oil with their lamps. Since the bridegroom was long delayed, they all became drowsy and fell asleep. At midnight, there was a cry, 'Behold, the bridegroom! Come out to meet him!' Then all those virgins got up and trimmed their lamps. The foolish ones said to the wise, 'Give us some of your oil, for our lamps are going out.' But the wise ones replied, 'No, for there may not be enough for us and you. Go instead to the merchants and buy some for yourselves.' While they went off to buy it, the bridegroom came and those who were ready went into the wedding feast with him. Then the door was locked. Afterwards the other virgins came and said, 'Lord, Lord, open the door for us!' But he said in reply, 'Amen, I say to you, I do not know you.' Therefore, stay awake, for you know neither the day nor the hour."

REFLECTION

The virgins without oil were not evil, just foolish. However, in their foolishness they ignored the special favor that had been bestowed on them. As Christians we have been given the greatest gift at our Baptism: the life of God within us. Are we being foolish? It is very easy to slip into habits of poor behavior or excuse improper ways under the pretext of personal freedom or experimentation. How easily the sleepy nod off; how easily the foolish become lax. Be alert, be wise, be prepared.

PRAYERS   *others may be added*

With lamps burning, we pray:

◆   Lord of life, hear us.

That our faith may burn brightly through frequent participation in the sacraments, we pray: ◆ That our spirits may fight off the sleepiness of sin and ignorance through prayer and study, we pray: ◆ That our Church may be a beacon of light for a darkened world through steadfast following of the way of Christ, we pray: ◆

Our Father . . .

God of light,
you showed us your burning love
    for us
through the sacrifice of your Son.
May our spirits burn with desire to
    demonstrate our gratitude
and spread the Good News of your
    kingdom.
We ask this through Christ our Lord.
    Amen.

✛   *Come with joy into the presence of the Lord.*

✝ *Come with joy into the presence of the Lord.*

PSALM 100   page 417

READING   Matthew 25:14–19

Jesus told his disciples this parable: "A man going on a journey called in his servants and entrusted his possessions to them. To one he gave five talents; to another, two; to a third, one—to each according to his ability. Then he went away. Immediately the one who received five talents went and traded with them, and made another five. Likewise, the one who received two made another two. But the man who received one went off and dug a hole in the ground and buried his master's money. After a long time the master of those servants came back and settled accounts with them."

REFLECTION

At the close of this familiar parable, the master rewards those who used their talents and took away the talent from the one who merely guarded his. So many things go to waste if they are not used: muscles wither away, cars get rusty, printers dry up, etc. Our personal talents, our gifts, and most importantly our love all wither and dry up if they go unused. Love is given to be given away. Love only remains alive as long as it remains active. Give your love away and watch it grow.

PRAYERS   *others may be added*

Alive with love, we pray:

♦ Lord of life, hear us.

For the grace to use our gifts fully, we pray: ♦ *For the ability to appreciate the aptitudes of others, we pray:* ♦ *For those who work to develop the talents of others, we pray:* ♦ *For those who believe they have no special abilities, we pray:* ♦

Our Father . . .

Ever-loving God,
through the Holy Spirit
you have showered the world with
   a flood of gifts.
Your Son has gathered us into
   the Church.
Through our talents, help us
to be a steady flow of your love to a
   parched world.
We ask this through Christ our Lord.
   Amen.

✝ *Come with joy into the presence of the Lord.*

✦ *Come with joy into the presence of the Lord.*

PSALM 100 *page 417*

READING *Luke 14:1,7–11*

On a sabbath Jesus went to dine at the home of one of the leading Pharisees, and the people there were observing him carefully.

He told a parable to those who had been invited, noticing how they were choosing the places of honor at the table. "When you are invited by someone to a wedding banquet, do not recline at table in the place of honor. A more distinguished guest than you may have been invited by him, and the host who invited both of you may approach you and say, 'Give your place to this man,' and then you would proceed with embarrassment to take the lowest place. Rather, when you are invited, go and take the lowest place so that when the host comes to you he may say, 'My friend, move up to a higher position.' Then you will enjoy the esteem of your companions at the table. For every one who exalts himself will be humbled, but the one who humbles himself will be exalted."

REFLECTION

In today's Gospel Jesus teaches by his actions as well as his words. Jesus accepted an invitation to dine with people who were, at best, skeptical of him. Even enemies can't be won over if we won't meet and open ourselves to them. This openness to the other is what Jesus speaks about today. Humility is being open to the possibility that another opinion is wiser, that another person deserves the limelight, that someone else needs to be heard. If we accept the invitation to be humble, we will gain the highest honor of all.

PRAYERS *others may be added*

With heads and hearts bowed, we pray:

◆ Lord of life, hear us.

That we may look for the importance in others rather than ourselves, we pray: ◆ *That nations may display an openness to peace and harmony, we pray:* ◆ *That we may concern ourselves about those not invited to society's table, we pray:* ◆ *That the faithful departed may be raised to eternal life, we pray:* ◆

Our Father . . .

Almighty God,
you deserve all praise and honor,
for in our brokenness you gave us
    your Son
to rescue us from sin.
May we never forget your majesty
    and power.
We ask this through our Lord Jesus
    Christ, your Son,
who lives and reigns with you in the
    unity of the Holy Spirit,
one God, forever and ever. Amen.

✦ *Come with joy into the presence of the Lord.*

✚ *Come with joy into the presence of the Lord.*

PSALM 100   *page 417*

READING   *Matthew 6:31–34**

Jesus said to his disciples: "Do not worry and say, 'What are we to eat?' or 'What are we to drink?' or 'What are we to wear?' All these things the pagans seek. Your heavenly Father knows that you need them all. But seek first the Kingdom of God and his righteousness, and all these things will be given you besides. Do not worry about tomorrow; tomorrow will take care of itself. Sufficient for a day is its own evil."

REFLECTION   *Pope John Paul II*

From the beginning of my Pontificate, my thoughts, prayers and actions were motivated by one desire: to witness that Christ, the Good Shepherd, is present and active in his Church. He is constantly searching for every stray sheep, to lead it back to the sheepfold, to bind up its wounds; he tends the sheep that are weak and sickly and protects those that are strong. This is why, from the very first day, I have never ceased to urge people: "Do not be afraid to welcome Christ and accept his power!" Today I forcefully repeat: "Open, indeed, open wide the doors to Christ!" Let him guide you! Trust in his love!

PRAYERS   *others may be added*

Through the intercession of St. Gregory the Great, we pray:

◆ Lord of life, hear us.

For the Pope, that he may follow the example of St. Gregory, we pray: ◆ *For all who administer pastoral care, that they may remember they are the hands of Christ, we pray:* ◆ *For musicians, that their music may uplift our spirits, we pray:* ◆ *For the unemployed and under-employed, that they may find work that sustains and fosters their human dignity, we pray:* ◆

Our Father . . .

O God of great bounty,
your care extends to everything that
   has being.
We look to you in our need,
relying on the word of your Son.
Give dignity to our labors and
   bless us.
We ask this through Christ our Lord.
   Amen.

✚ *Come with joy into the presence of the Lord.*

---

*Today's reading is from the Mass for the Blessing of Human Labor.

✦ *Come with joy into the presence of the Lord.*

PSALM 100 *page 417*

READING *Luke 4:31–37*

Jesus went down to Capernaum, a town of Galilee. He taught them on the sabbath, and they were astonished at his teaching because he spoke with authority. In the synagogue there was a man with the spirit of an unclean demon, and he cried out in a loud voice, "What have you to do with us, Jesus of Nazareth? Have you come to destroy us? I know who you are—the Holy One of God!" Jesus rebuked him and said, "Be quiet! Come out of him!" Then the demon threw the man down in front of them and came out of him without doing him any harm. They were all amazed and said to one another, "What is there about his word? For with authority and power he commands the unclean spirits, and they come out." And news of him spread everywhere in the surrounding region.

REFLECTION

Jesus rid this man of his demons. All were amazed, but most did not know what to make of it. Their wonderment did not lead to belief. The same can happen to us. All of us have experienced the wonders of our God. Our attention has been grabbed for the moment—unfortunately, often the amazement fades and we go on as usual. We are faced with choices every day. Let us make the most of the opportunities given to us by God. Believe!

PRAYERS *others may be added*

Believing in the wonders of God, we pray:

◆ Lord of life, hear us.

That the Church may offer her people sustenance in word and sacrament, we pray: ◆ *That all believers may be united in faith and belief, we pray:* ◆ *That vocations to the priesthood and religious life may flourish, we pray:* ◆ *That we may recognize the Lord in our everyday life, we pray:* ◆

Our Father . . .

Eternal God,
all creatures look to you for life
    and goodness.
Lead us by your wonderful works
to a greater belief and a deeper faith
so that we may lead lives that amaze
    the world
with your glory.
Grant this through Christ our Lord.
    Amen.

✦ *Come with joy into the presence of the Lord.*

✦ *Come with joy into the presence of the Lord.*

PSALM 100 *page 417*

READING *Luke 4:38–44*

After Jesus left the synagogue, he entered the house of Simon. Simon's mother-in-law was afflicted with a severe fever, and they interceded with him about her. He stood over her, rebuked the fever, and it left her. She got up immediately and waited on them. At sunset, all who had people sick with various diseases brought them to him. He laid his hands on each of them and cured them. And demons also came out from many, shouting, "You are the Son of God." But he rebuked them and did not allow them to speak because they knew that he was the Christ.

At daybreak, Jesus left and went to a deserted place. The crowds went looking for him, and when they came to him, they tried to prevent him from leaving them. But he said to them, "To the other towns also I must proclaim the good news of the Kingdom of God, because for this purpose I have been sent." And he was preaching in the synagogues of Judea.

REFLECTION

After Jesus healed Peter's mother-in-law, the amazed crowds at Capernaum tried to keep him from leaving, just as his enemies tried to restrain him at other places. From his childhood experience in the temple to the meeting with Mary Magdalene in the garden of the Resurrection, people tried to hold on to Jesus and keep him from moving about. Today, our Savior shows us that love must not be held back. Our love must be kept alive by constantly being shared, by moving with the freedom of the Spirit.

PRAYERS *others may be added*

Inspired by the Holy Spirit, we pray:

◆ Lord of life, hear us.

That the sick may find comfort and healing in their faith, we pray: ◆
That health-care and hospice workers may be strengthened in their work by our support and prayers, we pray: ◆ *That we may delight in the freedom of the Holy Spirit, we pray:* ◆ *That the dead might rejoice with the Lord this day, we pray:* ◆

Our Father . . .

O God,
your presence pervades all time
   and space.
In the few moments we exist
   in eternity,
you reach out to us in love.
Help us to spread that love
   ever farther
so that all may know of your
   saving grace.
We ask this through Christ our Lord.
   Amen.

✦ *Come with joy into the presence of the Lord.*

✛ *Come with joy into the presence of the Lord.*

PSALM 100   *page 417*

READING   *Luke 5:4–11*

After he [Jesus] had finished speaking, he said to Simon, "Put out into deep water and lower your nets for a catch." Simon said in reply, "Master, we have worked hard all night and have caught nothing, but at your command I will lower the nets." When they had done this, they caught a great number of fish and their nets were tearing. They signaled to their partners in the other boat to come to help them. They came and filled both boats so that the boats were in danger of sinking. When Simon Peter saw this, he fell at the knees of Jesus and said, "Depart from me, Lord, for I am a sinful man." For astonishment at the catch of fish they had made seized him and all those with him, and likewise James and John, the sons of Zebedee, who were partners of Simon. Jesus said to Simon, "Do not be afraid; from now on you will be catching men." When they brought their boats to the shore, they left everything and followed him.

REFLECTION

Peter, astonished by Jesus, thinks that he must stay away from the Lord. It is a common reaction when we realize our sinfulness or our feebleness; we can't imagine anyone wanting to be with us. But that is precisely why the Son of God came among us: to dispel our fears, to strengthen us, to save us from the paralysis and isolation of sin. We are not alone. Christ has come. He and the Father have sent the Holy Spirit. And, through the power of the Spirit we will catch others in the net of God's love.

PRAYERS   *others may be added*

Marveling at God's works, we pray:

◆ Lord of life, hear us.

For the Church, that we may walk in the unity of the Holy Spirit, we pray: ◆ *For those who are frightened, that the Consoler may work through us to lift their spirits, we pray:* ◆ *For the nations of the world, that they may flourish in peace and justice, we pray:* ◆ *For those who are lost, that they may be caught in the net of God's love, we pray:* ◆

Our Father . . .

Giver of all good gifts,
you have gathered us into your
    loving care.
Inspire us by your wonders to cast
    our nets of concern
and bring a lost world to knowledge
    of your salvation.
We ask this through Christ our Lord.
    Amen.

✛ *Come with joy into the presence of the Lord.*

✚ *Come with joy into the presence of the Lord.*

PSALM 100   page 417

READING   *Luke 5:33–39*

The scribes and Pharisees said to Jesus, "The disciples of John the Baptist fast often and offer prayers, and the disciples of the Pharisees do the same; but yours eat and drink." Jesus answered them, "Can you make the wedding guests fast while the bridegroom is with them? But the days will come, and when the bridegroom is taken away from them, then they will fast in those days." And he also told them a parable. "No one tears a piece from a new cloak to patch an old one. Otherwise, he will tear the new and the piece from it will not match the old cloak. Likewise, no one pours new wine into old wineskins. Otherwise, the new wine will burst the skins, and it will be spilled, and the skins will be ruined. Rather, new wine must be poured into fresh wineskins. And no one who has been drinking old wine desires new, for he says, 'The old is good.' "

REFLECTION

Typically, each new generation challenges the status quo in some way. Usually the older generations defend their way of doing things. This results in a dynamic tension that leads to new developments in society. In today's Gospel Jesus challenges us to look at our way of life. The challenge is to be open to new ways the Holy Spirit will work in our lives, new opportunities for love, new people giving us new ideas. The Spirit blows where it will; let's not miss it.

PRAYERS   *others may be added*

Open to the Holy Spirit, we pray:

◆ Lord of life, hear us.

That the old wineskins of stagnancy and complacency may be discarded from our lives, we pray: ◆ *That we may patch up our differences with the love of Christ, we pray:* ◆ *That we may freely eat of the Bread of Life and drink from the Cup of Salvation, we pray:* ◆ *That the dead may partake of the heavenly wedding feast, we pray:* ◆

Our Father . . .

Heavenly Father,
you hear the prayers of the needy
and fill the hungry with good things.
In our need, help us to be open to the
    challenges of the Gospel
and bring us together on the last day.
We ask this through Christ our Lord.
    Amen.

✚ *Come with joy into the presence of the Lord.*

✦ *Come with joy into the presence of the Lord.*

PSALM 100   *page 417*

READING   *Matthew 1:18–23*

This is how the birth of Jesus Christ came about. When his mother Mary was betrothed to Joseph, but before they lived together, she was found with child through the Holy Spirit. Joseph her husband, since he was a righteous man, yet unwilling to expose her to shame, decided to divorce her quietly. Such was his intention when, behold, the angel of the Lord appeared to him in a dream and said, "Joseph, son of David, do not be afraid to take Mary your wife into your home. For it is through the Holy Spirit that this child has been conceived in her. She will bear a son and you are to name him Jesus, because he will save his people from their sins." All this took place to fulfill what the Lord had said through the prophet:

Behold, the virgin shall be with child and bear a son, and they shall name him Emmanuel,

which means "God is with us."

REFLECTION   *St. Andrew of Crete*

This is the highest, all-embracing benefit that Christ has bestowed upon us. This is the revelation of the mystery, this is the emptying out of the divine nature, the union of God and man, and the deification of the manhood that was assumed. This radiant and manifest coming of God to men most certainly needed a joyful prelude to introduce the great gift of salvation to us. The present festival, the birth of the Mother of God, is the prelude, while the final act is the foreordained union of the Word with flesh. Today the Virgin is born, tended and formed, and prepared for her role as Mother of God, who is the universal King of the ages.

PRAYERS   *others may be added*

Trusting in God's Word, we pray:

◆ Lord of life, hear us.

That we may respond wholeheartedly to God's call like the Blessed Virgin Mary, we pray: ◆ *That we may use all our gifts to point to the goodness of God, we pray:* ◆ *That we may spend our life in service to others, we pray:* ◆ *That we may bring the message of the angels to all we meet, we pray:* ◆

Our Father . . .

Lord God,
today the Virgin Mary was born of the house of David.
Through her, salvation was born to a world lost in sin;
may we be inspired by her devotion, assisted by her prayers,
and brought by her into your presence at our final hour.
We ask this through Christ our Lord. Amen.

✦ *Come with joy into the presence of the Lord.*

✝ *Come with joy into the presence of the Lord.*

PSALM 100   *page 417*

READING   *Luke 14:25–33*

Great crowds were traveling with Jesus, and he turned and addressed them, "If anyone comes to me without hating his father and mother, wife and children, brothers and sisters, and even his own life, he cannot be my disciple. Whoever does not carry his own cross and come after me cannot be my disciple. Which of you wishing to construct a tower does not first sit down and calculate the cost to see if there is enough for its completion? Otherwise, after laying the foundation and finding himself unable to finish the work the onlookers should laugh at him and say, 'This one began to build but did not have the resources to finish.' Or what king marching into battle would not first sit down and decide whether with ten thousand troops he can successfully oppose another king advancing upon him with twenty thousand troops? But if not, while he is still far away, he will send a delegation to ask for peace terms. In the same way, anyone of you who does not renounce all his possessions cannot be my disciple."

REFLECTION

Jesus is not one given to soft-pedaling his message. That is especially true as he speaks of the cost of discipleship. There are no halfway measures; following Jesus is an all-consuming vocation. Half hearted disciples are the worst kind; their lives give one message and their words give another. These are the hypocrites that Jesus warns against. We are invited to be aware of the cost of full discipleship, the cross, and become true disciples of Christ.

PRAYERS   *others may be added*

With eyes wide open, we pray:

◆ Lord of life, hear us.

For Church leaders, that their actions and words may be sincere, we pray: ◆ *For Christians everywhere, that we may truly be the Body of Christ in the world, we pray:* ◆ *For an end to hostilities among all people, we pray:* ◆ *For those who suffer for the faith, that their lives may inspire us, we pray:* ◆

Our Father . . .

Loving God,
help us to express our faith
    in sincerity
and be true disciples of your Son,
    our Lord Jesus Christ,
who lives and reigns with you in the
    unity of the Holy Spirit,
one God, forever and ever. Amen.

✝ *Come with joy into the presence of the Lord.*

✦ Come with joy into the presence of the Lord.

PSALM 100   *page 417*

READING   *Luke 6:6-11*

On a certain sabbath Jesus went into the synagogue and taught, and there was a man there whose right hand was withered. The scribes and the Pharisees watched him closely to see if he would cure on the sabbath so that they might discover a reason to accuse him. But he realized their intentions and said to the man with the withered hand, "Come up and stand before us." And he rose and stood there. Then Jesus said to them, "I ask you, is it lawful to do good on the sabbath rather than to do evil, to save life rather than to destroy it?" Looking around at them all, he then said to him, "Stretch out your hand." He did so and his hand was restored. But they became enraged and discussed together what they might do to Jesus.

REFLECTION

If we look closely at the question Jesus poses to the Pharisees, he implies that not to do the good thing is to do evil. At a time when we need "good Samaritan" laws to protect those who would selflessly help others, it may seem harsh to say that we have a positive responsibility to do the good. However, this is the radically new vision of humanity that Jesus preaches. Jesus wants to cure our withering souls; all we have to do is stretch out our hearts.

PRAYERS   *others may be added*

Reaching out in love, we pray:

◆ Lord of life, hear us.

That we may stretch out our hands to those who are separated from family and homeland, we pray: ◆ *That artists and artisans may give glory to God in their labors, we pray:* ◆ *That we may reach out to those who grieve, we pray:* ◆ *That all may be united with Christ on the last day, we pray:* ◆

Our Father . . .

Loving God of all creation,
the works of your hand sing
    your praises.
Your Son showed us the way
    to salvation
and won for us a place in
    your kingdom.
Help us to fulfill our destiny and be
    the glory
of your creation.
We ask this through Christ our Lord.
    Amen.

✦ Come with joy into the presence of the Lord.

✚ *Come with joy into the presence of the Lord.*

PSALM 100   *page 417*

READING   *Luke 6:12–19*

Jesus departed to the mountain to pray, and he spent the night in prayer to God. When day came, he called his disciples to himself, and from them he chose Twelve, whom he also named Apostles: Simon, whom he named Peter, and his brother Andrew, James, John, Philip, Bartholomew, Matthew, Thomas, James the son of Alphaeus, Simon who was called a Zealot, and Judas the son of James, and Judas Iscariot, who became a traitor.

And he came down with them and stood on a stretch of level ground. A great crowd of his disciples and a large number of the people from all Judea and Jerusalem and the coastal region of Tyre and Sidon came to hear him and to be healed of their diseases; and even those who were tormented by unclean spirits were cured. Everyone in the crowd sought to touch him because power came forth from him and healed them all.

REFLECTION

Most of us have had the experience of staying up the better part of the night, mulling over some aspect of our life — sometimes it's worry, sometimes it's weighing options, sometimes it's searching for the right answer. Jesus devoted a whole night to prayer in anticipation of naming the Twelve. The invitation, the call that we

have received, has been given the same deliberation by God. Each of us has a very special place in God's providence. May we find our place with the apostles.

PRAYER   *others may be added*

Taking our place among the called, we pray:

◆ Lord of life, hear us.

For bishops, the successors of the apostles, we pray: ◆ For teachers and professors, we pray: ◆ For students and seekers, we pray: ◆ For health-care workers, we pray: ◆

Our Father . . .

Lord,
you have called us each by name.
Comfort us with your loving embrace
so that we may follow your will
and spread your Good News
in a world distracted by sin.
We ask this through Christ our Lord.
   Amen.

✚ *Come with joy into the presence of the Lord.*

✠ *Here I am, Lord, I come to do your will.*

PSALM 40   *page 411*

READING   *Luke 6:20–26*

Raising his eyes toward his disciples Jesus said:

"Blessed are you who are poor,/for the Kingdom of God is yours./Blessed are you who are now hungry,/for you will be satisfied./Blessed are you who are now weeping,/for you will laugh./ Blessed are you when people hate you,/ and when they exclude and insult you,/ and denounce your name as evil/on account of the Son of Man.

"Rejoice and leap for joy on that day! Behold, your reward will be great in heaven. For their ancestors treated the prophets in the same way./But woe to you who are rich,/for you have received your consolation./But woe to you who are filled now,/for you will be hungry./Woe to you who laugh now,/for you will grieve and weep./ Woe to you when all speak well of you,/for their ancestors treated the false prophets in this way."

REFLECTION

It is fitting that we hear the Beatitudes on the same day we celebrate the Blessed Virgin Mary. The Beatitudes are the ideals of the Gospel, and Mary is the ideal Christian. Today's celebration was instituted as a reminder to always turn to God in prayer, through the intercession of Mary, for all our needs. This memorial of Mary's name has its origin in 1683

when the army defending Vienna against Saracen invaders invoked the name of Mary in their prayers and attributed their victory to Mary. May we invoke the intercession of Mary for all our needs.

PRAYERS   *others may be added*

Calling on the name of Mary, we pray:

◆ Lord of life, hear us.

That hostilities among nations may cease, we pray: ◆ *That we may turn to God in prayer for all our needs, we pray:* ◆ *That we may look to Mary as a sign of discipleship, we pray:* ◆ *That all Christians may be concerned for the less fortunate, we pray:* ◆

Our Father . . .

God of all creation,
you formed the stars above and the
    sea below.
The Blessed Virgin Mary is the
    crowning glory of creation;
may we call upon her name in our
    hour of need
and be assured of your constant love.
Grant this through Christ our Lord.
    Amen.

✠ *Here I am, Lord, I come to do your will.*

✠ *Come with joy into the presence of the Lord.*

PSALM 100   *page 417*

READING   *Luke 6:27–35*

Jesus said to his disciples: "To you who hear I say, love your enemies, do good to those who hate you, bless those who curse you, pray for those who mistreat you. To the person who strikes you on one cheek, offer the other one as well, and from the person who takes your cloak, do not withhold even your tunic. Give to everyone who asks of you, and from the one who takes what is yours do not demand it back. Do to others as you would have them do to you. For if you love those who love you, what credit is that to you? Even sinners love those who love them. And if you do good to those who do good to you, what credit is that to you? Even sinners do the same. But rather, love your enemies and do good to them, and lend expecting nothing back; then your reward will be great and you will be children of the Most High, for he himself is kind to the ungrateful and the wicked. Be merciful, just as also your Father is merciful."

REFLECTION

St. John Chrysostom (347–+407) was well acquainted with ill treatment. He rose quickly through the Church hierarchy due to his compelling preaching and holiness of life. When he became patriarch of Constantinople he instituted a number of reforms for the clergy and religious.

For these reforms he was twice exiled by his fellow clerics. Each time he returned he followed the admonitions of today's Gospel; he kept giving to his people; he loved his enemies; and he did not condemn those who maligned him. Through St. John Chrysostom's intercession, may we be generous and forgiving to those who wrong us.

PRAYERS   *others may be added*

Knowing our neediness, we pray:

◆ Lord of life, hear us.

That the bishops of the world may be leaders modeled on St. John Chrysostom, we pray: ◆ That the people of God may be nourished by gifted preachers, we pray: ◆ That the Holy Spirit may be present in the quest for Christian unity, we pray: ◆

Our Father . . .

Father,
you gave your people St. John
    Chrysostom
as a gifted minister of your word
    and sacrament.
Through our participation in
    the Eucharist,
may we, too, face adversity with
    grace and joy.
We ask this through Christ our Lord.
    Amen.

✠ *Come with joy into the presence of the Lord.*

✝ *Come with joy into the presence of the Lord.*

PSALM 100   *page 417*

READING   *John 3:13–17*

Jesus said to Nicodemus: "No one has gone up to heaven except the one who has come down from heaven, the Son of Man. And just as Moses lifted up the serpent in the desert, so must the Son of Man be lifted up, so that everyone who believes in him may have eternal life."

For God so loved the world that he gave his only Son, so that everyone who believes in him might not perish but might have eternal life. For God did not send his Son into the world to condemn the world, but that the world might be saved through him.

REFLECTION

Today we celebrate the central symbol of Christianity, the cross, an instrument of torture and cruel death. But for us it is the instrument of salvation. Lifted up on the cross, Christ broke the power of death and sin, showed us the Father's love, and we became adopted sons and daughters of God. The cross is not just a symbol but a way of life. We each have our share in this mystery. Our willingness to embrace the cross, to give of ourselves totally, marks us as true followers of Christ.

PRAYERS   *others may be added*

Gazing upon the cross of salvation, we pray:

◆ Lord of life, hear us.

By your cross, save us from the darkness of sin, we pray: ◆ *By your cross you emptied yourself; may we be humble, we pray:* ◆ *By your cross you obeyed the Father; may we willingly accept our trials, we pray:* ◆ *By your cross you were lifted up; may the faithful departed be lifted into your kingdom, we pray:* ◆

Our Father . . .

Merciful Father,
your Son, Jesus Christ,
revealed to us your love
by his saving death upon the cross.
Marked by the cross at Baptism,
    may we live sacrificial lives and one day
share in the Resurrection.
Grant this through Christ our Lord.
    Amen.

✝ *Come with joy into the presence of the Lord.*

✝ *Come with joy into the presence of the Lord.*

PSALM 40   *page 411*

READING   *John 19:25–27*

Standing by the cross of Jesus were his mother and his mother's sister, Mary the wife of Clopas, and Mary Magdalene. When Jesus saw his mother and the disciple there whom he loved he said to his mother, "Woman, behold, your son." Then he said to the disciple, "Behold, your mother." And from that hour the disciple took her into his home.

REFLECTION

Today's memorial, formerly known as the Seven Sorrows of Mary, occurs after the feast of the Holy Cross and on the octave day of the Nativity of Mary. It is a memorial that not only remembers the heartbreaking scene of Mary at the foot of the cross and the other sorrows that the she endured in life, but the sorrows that she shares from her throne of glory in heaven. Our sorrows are her sorrows. As our mother, she grieves for each pain we endure. She stands at the foot of our crosses; and as she held her son's lifeless body, she, too, holds us. We have in Mary a great intercessor, a companion in crisis, and a caring mother who cradles our pain.

PRAYERS   *others may be added*

With Mary, our mother, at our side, we pray:

◆ Lord of life, hear us.

For those who are in sorrow, that they may receive comfort from the prayers of the Blessed Virgin Mary, we pray: ◆
For mothers enduring hardships, that they may be encouraged by the example of the Mother of God, we pray: ◆ *For all believers, that we might be one in Christ through prayer with Mary, the Mother of the Church, we pray:* ◆

Our Father . . .

At the cross her station keeping,
Stood the mournful Mother weeping,
    Close to Jesus to the last.

Through her heart, his sorrow sharing,
All his bitter anguish bearing,
    Now at length the sword had
        passed. . . .
Christ, when you shall call me hence,
Be your Mother my defense,
    Be your cross my victory.

While my body here decays,
May my soul your goodness praise,
    Safe in heaven eternally.
Amen. (Alleluia.)

✝ *Come with joy into the presence of the Lord.*

✛ *We praise you, O Lord, for all your works are wonderful.*

PSALM 33 *page 409*

READING *Luke 15:1–7*

Tax collectors and sinners were all drawing near to listen to Jesus, but the Pharisees and scribes began to complain, saying, "This man welcomes sinners and eats with them." So to them he addressed this parable. "What man among you having a hundred sheep and losing one of them would not leave the ninety-nine in the desert and go after the lost one until he finds it? And when he does find it, he sets it on his shoulders with great joy and, upon his arrival home, he calls together his friends and neighbors and says to them, 'Rejoice with me because I have found my lost sheep.' I tell you, in just the same way there will be more joy in heaven over one sinner who repents than over ninety-nine righteous people who have no need of repentance."

REFLECTION

Today's parable encapsulates the essence of Jesus' teaching about the Father. Our God is one who actively seeks us. We do not have to be pristine, totally without sin, in order to approach him; in fact, he proactively searches out the grimiest souls in order to cleanse them and bring them to himself. So often we are lost in a world of consumerism, apathy, and self-absorption. Today, Jesus tells us that our God is calling to us; let's go home with him.

PRAYERS *others may be added*

Reaching out to the Lord, we pray:

◆ God, our help, hear us.

That those who are lost in sin may know that the Lord has come to save them, we pray: ◆ *That those who wish us harm may be converted to love by our example, we pray:* ◆ *That the faithful departed may rest in the loving arms of the Lord, we pray:* ◆

Our Father . . .

Father in heaven,
you sent your Son, the
    Good Shepherd,
to seek out and rescue all who
    are lost.
May we be his partners in this
    saving task
by reaching out to all those in need.
We ask this through our Lord Jesus
    Christ, your Son,
who lives and reigns with you in the
    unity of the Holy Spirit,
one God, forever and ever. Amen.

✛ *We praise you, O Lord, for all your works are wonderful.*

✦ *We praise you, O Lord, for all your works are wonderful.*

PSALM 33 *page 409*

READING *Luke 7:1–10*

When Jesus had finished all his words to the people, he entered Capernaum. A centurion there had a slave who was ill and about to die, and he was valuable to him. When he heard about Jesus, he sent elders of the Jews to him, asking him to come and save the life of his slave. They approached Jesus and strongly urged him to come, saying, "He deserves to have you do this for him, for he loves our nation and he built the synagogue for us." And Jesus went with them, but when he was only a short distance from the house, the centurion sent friends to tell him, "Lord, do not trouble yourself, for I am not worthy to have you enter under my roof. Therefore, I did not consider myself worthy to come to you; but say the word and let my servant be healed. For I too am a person subject to authority, with soldiers subject to me. And I say to one, 'Go,' and he goes; and to another, 'Come here,' and he comes; and to my slave, 'Do this,' and he does it." When Jesus heard this he was amazed at him and, turning, said to the crowd following him, "I tell you, not even in Israel have I found such faith." When the messengers returned to the house, they found the slave in good health.

REFLECTION

Here is a true reversal of fortunes, at least as the world would see it. A Roman conqueror humbles himself before a subject, and a devout Jew praises the faith of a Gentile. So often we are caught in stereotypes, in little worlds of our own construct. The Gospel challenges us to expand our views, our worlds, our hearts. The message of Jesus is that the Father's creation is much larger than we imagine; God's love is infinitely greater than we expect. Let's allow ourselves to be amazed at the wonders in the world of God's creation.

PRAYERS *others may be added*

Through the intercession of St. Robert, we pray:

◆ God, our help, hear us.

For an end to all prejudice, we pray: ◆
For those we have hurt by our narrow-mindedness, we pray: ◆

Our Father . . .

Mighty God,
you created the vast universe.
May we heed the words of your Son
and allow our small hearts and minds
    to be opened
so that we may go out to the
    whole world
and spread your Good News.
We ask this through Christ our Lord.
    Amen.

✦ *We praise you, O Lord, for all your works are wonderful.*

Optional memorial of St. Robert Bellarmine

✣ *We praise you, O Lord, for all your works are wonderful.*

PSALM 33   *page 409*

READING   *Luke 7:11–17*

Jesus journeyed to a city called Nain, and his disciples and a large crowd accompanied him. As he drew near to the gate of the city, a man who had died was being carried out, the only son of his mother, and she was a widow. A large crowd from the city was with her. When the Lord saw her, he was moved with pity for her and said to her, "Do not weep." He stepped forward and touched the coffin; at this the bearers halted, and he said, "Young man, I tell you, arise!" The dead man sat up and began to speak, and Jesus gave him to his mother. Fear seized them all, and they glorified God, exclaiming, "A great prophet has arisen in our midst," and "God has visited his people." This report about him spread through the whole of Judea and in all the surrounding region.

REFLECTION

Anyone who has buried a child or has seen it happen knows the extreme emotions felt by those in today's Gospel. Jesus is clearly touched; he performs this miracle without first looking for faith. Perhaps he is moved by the coming parallel with his own mother. In any case, here we see how our God reaches out to us in our deepest times of need. We are not alone; we have a tender-hearted God who wants to help us, to raise us up, if only we let him.

PRAYERS   *others may be added*

Glorifying the Lord, we pray:

◆ God, our help, hear us.

That all those who are grieving may be comforted by their faith and their fellow Christians, we pray: ◆ *That parents may be strengthened in their special role, we pray:* ◆ *That children may love and respect their parents, we pray:* ◆ *That the dying may find their way in the Lord, we pray:* ◆

Our Father . . .

Lord of life,
you animate creation by the power
    of the Holy Spirit.
Bring our cold and hardened hearts
    a new vibrancy
so that we may joyfully report your
    great deeds
to a world asleep in the grip of sin.
Grant this through Christ our Lord.
    Amen.

✣ *We praise you, O Lord, for all your works are wonderful.*

✦ *We praise you, O Lord, for all your works are wonderful.*

PSALM 33   *page 409*

READING   *Luke 7:31–35*

Jesus said to the crowds: "To what shall I compare the people of this generation? What are they like? They are like children who sit in the marketplace and call to one another,

'We played the flute for you, but you did not dance./We sang a dirge, but you did not weep.'

For John the Baptist came neither eating food nor drinking wine, and you said, 'He is possessed by a demon.' The Son of Man came eating and drinking and you said, 'Look, he is a glutton and a drunkard, a friend of tax collectors and sinners.' But wisdom is vindicated by all her children."

REFLECTION

The world of advertising tries its best to make us very fickle creatures. What is "in" this season is "out" the next. Styles are developed for different age groups, so that what is "chic" for one group is completely unfashionable for another. The goal is to get us to buy more and more. This is not the way of the Gospel. The disciple is truly satisfied living for others. Love is never out of style.

PRAYERS   *others may be added*

For the steadfastness of the martyrs, we pray:

◆ God, our help, hear us.

For the dampening of a consumerist mentality, we pray: ◆ *For grace to be present in our relationships with God, self, and neighbor, we pray:* ◆ *For the joy of simple Gospel living, we pray:* ◆ *For those who suffer at the hands of society's wastefulness, we pray:* ◆

Our Father . . .

Loving God,
with your masterful creation
you have surrounded us with
   physical beauty.
Help us to see and love the splendor
that comes from being in right
   relationship
with you and each other,
so that our example may shine
with all your saints.
We ask this through Christ our Lord.
   Amen.

✦ *We praise you, O Lord, for all your works are wonderful.*

Optional memorial of St. Januarius

✝ *We praise you, O Lord, for all your works are wonderful.*

PSALM 33   *page 409*

READING   *Luke 7:44–50*

[Jesus said,] "Do you see this woman? When I entered your house, you did not give me water for my feet, but she has bathed them with her tears and wiped them with her hair. You did not give me a kiss, but she has not ceased kissing my feet since the time I entered. You did not anoint my head with oil, but she anointed my feet with oint-ment. So I tell you, her many sins have been forgiven; hence, she has shown great love. But the one to whom little is forgiven, loves little." He said to her, "Your sins are forgiven." The others at table said to themselves, "Who is this who even forgives sins?" But he said to the woman, "Your faith has saved you; go in peace."

REFLECTION

In today's Gospel the Pharisee host was scandalized that Jesus allowed an unknown woman to touch him. The touch of an unknown person could transmit ritual uncleanness. Perhaps the host didn't greet Jesus with a kiss because he was afraid of becoming unclean from Jesus. What irony! Fear and ignorance kept this person from really accepting Jesus in his life. Today we celebrate the mid-nineteenth century saints of Korea. Fear and ignorance brought persecutions and martyrdom upon them. Do we live in fear or do we stand firm in the faith like the Korean martyrs?

PRAYERS   *others may be added*

Through the intercession of the Korean martyrs, we pray:

◆ God, our help, hear us.

That the Church in Korea and all of Asia may flourish, we pray: ◆ *That fear and ignorance may be replaced with steadfast faith, we pray:* ◆ *That forgiveness may be a defining feature of every Christian, we pray:* ◆ *That peace may reign on earth, we pray:* ◆

Our Father . . .

Father,
it is your desire that all should
    be saved.
Your Son endured his Passion and
    death to liberate us
from the fear and ignorance of sin.
Through the intercession of the
    martyrs, may our lives
be beacons of faith in your
    loving care.
We ask this through Christ our Lord.
    Amen.

✝ *We praise you, O Lord, for all your works are wonderful.*

✙ *We praise you, O Lord, for all your works are wonderful.*

PSALM 33   *page 409*

READING   *Matthew 9:9–13*

As Jesus passed by, he saw a man named Matthew sitting at the customs post. He said to him, "Follow me." And he got up and followed him. While he was at table in his house, many tax collectors and sinners came and sat with Jesus and his disciples. The Pharisees saw this and said to his disciples, "Why does your teacher eat with tax collectors and sinners?" He heard this and said, "Those who are well do not need a physician, but the sick do. Go and learn the meaning of the words, *I desire mercy, not sacrifice.* I did not come to call the righteous but sinners."

REFLECTION

We can only imagine the party that Matthew must have given. As tax collector at the border, he was hated by Jews and Gentiles alike. With two simple words, Jesus, the wonder worker, changed all that. What a party. What a cast of characters. What a celebration! And, as always, party spoilers were standing out on the fringe. Those in the party were reveling in the mercy and goodness of God. Those outside were standing in judgment. We, too, have been called, have been shown the mercy of God. May we spend our life celebrating our call by telling others of the one who works wonders in our lives.

PRAYERS   *others may be added*

Celebrating the wonders of God, we pray:

◆ God, our help, hear us.

That all bishops, successors of the apostles, may preach the mercy of God, we pray: ◆ *That public officials may use their positions for the betterment of society, we pray:* ◆ *That we may have special concern for the outcasts of the world, we pray:* ◆ *That we may tell everyone of the wonders of the Lord, we pray:* ◆

Our Father . . .

Almighty God,
your Son sought out sinners
    and outcasts.
In our neediness may we never
    neglect
to look to you for our support
and reach out to those most in need
    of your saving word.
Grant this through Christ our Lord.
    Amen.

✙ *We praise you, O Lord, for all your works are wonderful.*

✝ *We praise you, O Lord, for all your*
works are wonderful.

PSALM 33   page 409

READING   Luke 8:4b–10

[Jesus spoke in a parable:] "A sower went out to sow his seed. And as he sowed, some seed fell on the path and was trampled, and the birds of the sky ate it up. Some seed fell on rocky ground, and when it grew, it withered for lack of moisture. Some seed fell among thorns, and the thorns grew with it and choked it. And some seed fell on good soil, and when it grew, it produced fruit a hundredfold." After saying this, he called out, "Whoever has ears to hear ought to hear."

Then his disciples asked him what the meaning of this parable might be. He answered, "Knowledge of the mysteries of the Kingdom of God has been granted to you; but to the rest, they are made known through parables so that *they may look but not see, and hear but not understand.*

REFLECTION

God doesn't take out billboards. Jesus didn't have a catchy jingle to help remember him by. And, as much as we try to adapt evangelization methods to our day and age, all the professional public relations people cannot overcome the truth of the words of Jesus today: one must have an ear willing to hear the message. The parables were not meant to confuse people; they were meant to be a gentle wake-up call. The Lord does not force the Good

News upon us. He quietly invites us by word and deed. We are asked to do the same.

PRAYERS   *others may be added*

Trusting in the Lord, we pray:

◆ God, our help, hear us.

For those who preach the word of God through artful stories, we pray: ◆ *For lay catechists, that they may see the fruits of the seeds they planted, we pray:* ◆ *For quiet times in our lives, that we might hear the gentle words of our Lord, we pray:* ◆ *For a bountiful harvest, we pray:* ◆

Our Father . . .

God of all nations,
you sent your Son as your Word-
    made-flesh.
Having heard your gentle whispers,
may the seed of our Baptism produce
lives that enflesh your Gospel for all
    to see.
We ask this through Christ our Lord.
    Amen.

✝ *We praise you, O Lord, for all your*
works are wonderful.

✛ *We praise you, O Lord, for all your works are wonderful.*

PSALM 33   *page 409*

READING   *Luke 16:10-13*

Jesus said to his disciples: "The person who is trustworthy in very small matters is also trustworthy in great ones; and the person who is dishonest in very small matters is also dishonest in great ones. If, therefore, you are not trustworthy with dishonest wealth, who will trust you with true wealth? If you are not trustworthy with what belongs to another, who will give you what is yours? No servant can serve two masters. He will either hate one and love the other, or be devoted to one and despise the other. You cannot serve both God and mammon."

REFLECTION   *Pope John Paul II*

In this life, conversion is a goal which is never fully attained: on the path which the disciple is called to follow in the footsteps of Jesus, conversion is a lifelong task. While we are in this world, our intention to repent is always exposed to temptations. Since "no one can serve two masters" (Matthew 6:24), the change of mentality (metanoia) means striving to assimilate the values of the Gospel, which contradict the dominant tendencies of the world. Hence, there is a need to renew constantly "the encounter with the living Jesus Christ," since this . . . is the way "which leads us to continuing conversion."

PRAYERS   *others may be added*

Looking to the Lord, we pray:

◆ God, our help, hear us.

That our Pope may continue to be energized by the Holy Spirit in his work, we pray: ◆ *That civic leaders may promote the social good, we pray:* ◆ *That Christians may renew and invigorate their determination to serve the Lord, we pray:* ◆

Our Father . . .

God,
you are single-hearted in your love
    for us.
May we look to your Son's devotion
    to you,
and, enflamed by the Holy Spirit,
may we share that love
with a world caught up in
    other pursuits.
We ask this through our Lord Jesus
    Christ, your Son,
who lives and reigns with you in the
    unity of the Holy Spirit,
one God, forever and ever. Amen.

✛ *We praise you, O Lord, for all your works are wonderful.*

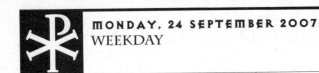

MONDAY, 24 SEPTEMBER 2007
WEEKDAY

✚ *We praise you, O Lord, for all your works are wonderful.*

PSALM 33 *page 409*

READING *Luke 8:16-18*

Jesus said to the crowd: "No one who lights a lamp conceals it with a vessel or sets it under a bed; rather, he places it on a lampstand so that those who enter may see the light. For there is nothing hidden that will not become visible, and nothing secret that will not be known and come to light. Take care, then, how you hear. To anyone who has, more will be given, and from the one who has not, even what he seems to have will be taken away."

REFLECTION

It's usually easy to see when someone is in love. There is an exuberance, a bounce in the step, a look in the eyes that is unmistakable, especially in the presence of the loved one. Jesus came to deliver a love message from the Father. We are loved more than anyone can imagine. Our God is hopelessly in love with us. God knows our darkest secrets and still he loves us. That's a message to shout from the rooftops. That's a reason to celebrate!

PRAYERS *others may be added*

With hearts afire, we pray:

◆ God, our help, hear us.

For those who bring the light of hope to those suffering with depression, we pray: ◆ *For those who ignite the spirits of the apathetic, we pray:* ◆ *For those who elevate the lowly and downtrodden of the world, we pray:* ◆ *For those who show us by their exuberance how to celebrate the love of God, we pray:* ◆

Our Father . . .

God,
your love is everlasting,
your forgiveness is complete.
Shine your life-giving light on
    us always,
and may we be beacons of
    radiant love,
burning brightly in a world darkened
by apathy and indifference.
We ask this through Christ our Lord.
    Amen.

✚ *We praise you, O Lord, for all your works are wonderful.*

296

✦ *We praise you, O Lord, for all your works are wonderful.*

PSALM 33 *page 409*

READING *Luke 8:19-21*

The mother of Jesus and his brothers came to him but were unable to join him because of the crowd. He was told, "Your mother and your brothers are standing outside and they wish to see you." He said to them in reply, "My mother and my brothers are those who hear the word of God and act on it."

REFLECTION *Gaudium et spes, 24*

God, Who has fatherly concern for everyone, has willed that all men should constitute one family and treat one another in a spirit of brotherhood. For having been created in the image of God, Who "from one man has created the whole human race and made them live all over the face of the earth" (Acts 17:26), all men are called to one and the same goal, namely God Himself.

PRAYERS *others may be added*

With the word of God in our hearts, we pray:

✦ God, our help, hear us.

That families will center their lives on the Gospel, we pray: ✦ *That orphans, widows, and widowers may find comfort and nurturing in the Christian community, we pray:* ✦ *That those separated from family and homeland may find companionship with the people of God, we pray:* ✦ *That life at every stage may be respected and sanctified, we pray:* ✦

Our Father . . .

God of perfect peace,
you have sent the Holy Spirit among us
to animate your Church as the Body
     of Christ.
May we find harmony, unity,
     and fulfillment
as your adopted family
and know each other as brothers and
     sisters in the Lord,
through whom we pray. Amen.

✦ *We praise you, O Lord, for all your works are wonderful.*

✦ *We praise you, O Lord, for all your works are wonderful.*

PSALM 33
page 409

READING
Luke 9:1–6

Jesus summoned the Twelve and gave them power and authority over all demons and to cure diseases, and he sent them to proclaim the Kingdom of God and to heal the sick. He said to them, "Take nothing for the journey, neither walking stick, nor sack, nor food, nor money, and let no one take a second tunic. Whatever house you enter, stay there and leave from there. And as for those who do not welcome you, when you leave that town, shake the dust from your feet in testimony against them." Then they set out and went from village to village proclaiming the good news and curing diseases everywhere.

REFLECTION

The ability to heal someone is truly a gift. Anyone who has endured illness will agree that to receive relief from suffering is miraculous. St. Cosmas and St. Damian (+287) were twin brothers who became physicians and Christians. It is said that they accepted no money for their services. They healed freely, thus revealing a spirit of true Christian generosity. This generosity showed them to be Christians and they were martyred. We, too, have been sent to reveal ourselves as Christians by bringing the miracle of healing to those in need.

PRAYER
others may be added

Addressing the Great Physician, we pray:

◆ God, our help, hear us.

That we may offer forgiveness as healing balm to sorrowing hearts, we pray: ◆ *That we may lend a listening ear as soothing ointment to the troubled, we pray:* ◆ *That we may feed a malnourished soul with words of encouragement, we pray:* ◆ *That we may mend broken spirits by opening our hearts and homes to the outcast, we pray:* ◆

Our Father . . .

Father,
you are sovereign ruler of all that is.
You saw our brokenness, had pity,
and sent your Son to bring us salvation.
Through the intercession of
    St. Cosmas and St. Damian,
may we learn your healing ways
and bring your word as medicine to
    an ailing world
We ask this through Christ our Lord.
    Amen.

✦ *We praise you, O Lord, for all your works are wonderful.*

✝ *We praise you, O Lord, for all your works are wonderful.*

PSALM 33   page 409

READING   *Luke 9:7–9*

Herod the tetrarch heard about all that was happening, and he was greatly perplexed because some were saying, "John has been raised from the dead"; others were saying, "Elijah has appeared"; still others, "One of the ancient prophets has arisen." But Herod said, "John I beheaded. Who then is this about whom I hear such things?" And he kept trying to see him.

REFLECTION

For some people, like Herod, religion is a matter of curiosity or a hobby. But for true Christians, like St. Vincent de Paul (1581–+1660), religion is their life's passion. St. Vincent spent his entire life bringing the Gospel to the sick and poor through preaching, works of mercy, and the founding of the Vincentians. Among his friends were St. Frances de Sales, Cardinal Bérulle, and St. Louise de Marillac, with whom he cofounded the Daughters of Charity and in whom he found a spiritual soul mate. With religion as St. Vincent's passion, unlike Herod, he didn't have to try to see Jesus; he saw him in every face he met.

PRAYERS   *others may be added*

In the spirit of service, we pray:

◆ God, our help, hear us.

For those who dedicate their lives to service of the sick and poor, we pray: ◆
For those who teach us how to be passionate about God, we pray: ◆
For those religious who follow the Vincentian charism, we pray: ◆ *For those who, like St. Vincent de Paul, give care and compassion to the sick, poor, and homebound, we pray:* ◆

Our Father . . .

God our Father,
you blessed St. Vincent de Paul
with an apostolic zeal for those most
   in need of care.
Through his intercession,
may we be filled with a desire to see
   the face of Christ
in whom we meet and spread the light
   of faith
in a society darkened by faithlessness.
We ask this in the name of Jesus the
   Lord. Amen.

✝ *We praise you, O Lord, for all your works are wonderful.*

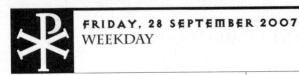

✝ *We praise you, O Lord, for all your works are wonderful.*

PSALM 33 *page 409*

READING *Luke 9:18–22*

Once when Jesus was praying in solitude, and the disciples were with him, he asked them, "Who do the crowds say that I am?" They said in reply, "John the Baptist; others, Elijah; still others, 'One of the ancient prophets has arisen.'" Then he said to them, "But who do you say that I am?" Peter said in reply, "The Christ of God." He rebuked them and directed them not to tell this to anyone. He said, "The Son of Man must suffer greatly and be rejected by the elders, the chief priests, and the scribes, and be killed and on the third day be raised."

REFLECTION

Today's two saints come from different lands and different times, but both had the same answer for the question Jesus raises. Both St. Wenceslaus (907–+927) of Bohemia and St. Lawrence (1600–+1637) of the Philippines answered with their lives that Jesus is the Christ of God, the one who has come to set us free from sin and death. Wencelaus was a political leader in eastern Europe at a time when Christianity was new to that part of the world. Lawrence was a Filipino refugee in Japan when persecutions of Christians were rampant. Both were killed for their answer to Jesus. Today the question is the same: Who do we say that Jesus is? The challenge is to back up our answer with our lives.

PRAYERS *others may be added*

Looking to the witness of the martyrs, we pray:

◆ God, our help, hear us.

That political leaders may look to the Gospel for inspiration, we pray: ◆ That refugees may find shelter and relief among the Christian community, we pray: ◆ That the victims of natural and man-made disasters may be comforted by their faith and our actions, we pray: ◆ That those who suffer for the faith may be strengthened by the prayers of the martyrs, we pray: ◆

Our Father . . .

All-powerful, ever-living God,
you are a tower of strength.
As you gave the martyrs the fortitude
to suffer death for Christ,
give us the strength to live as faithful
    witnesses to you.
Grant this through Christ our Lord.
    Amen.

✝ *We praise you, O Lord, for all your works are wonderful.*

✠ *We praise you, O Lord, for all your works are wonderful.*

PSALM 33   page 409

READING   *John 1:47–51*

Jesus saw Nathanael coming toward him and said of him, "Here is a true child of Israel. There is no duplicity in him." Nathanael said to him, "How do you know me?" Jesus answered and said to him, "Before Philip called you, I saw you under the fig tree." Nathanael answered him, "Rabbi, you are the Son of God; you are the King of Israel." Jesus answered and said to him, "Do you believe because I told you that I saw you under the fig tree? You will see greater things than this." And he said to him, "Amen, amen, I say to you, you will see heaven opened and the angels of God ascending and descending on the Son of Man."

REFLECTION

Angels are always doing something. They are spirits created to do God's bidding. The archangels have tasks of the utmost importance. Their names reveal their mission: Michael means "who is like God"; Gabriel means "the strength of God"; and Raphael means "God's remedy." Thus Michael appears when God's supremacy is asserted; Gabriel brings God's strongest messages; and Raphael brought healing to Tobit. The kingdom of God is not just a state of mind; it is action, the action of love. Belief without action is not belief at all. Like the archangels, we are called to work

for the kingdom. Our name is Christian; may we always bring Christ to others.

PRAYERS   *others may be added*

Entrusting our prayers to the angels, we pray:

◆ God, our help, hear us.

Through the intercession of St. Michael, that the Church may be protected from evil, we pray: ◆ Through the intercession of St. Gabriel, that the Church may announce powerful tidings of God's love, we pray: ◆ Through the intercession of St. Raphael, that the Church may continue the healing mission of salvation, we pray: ◆ Through the intercession of Mary, Queen of Angels, that the dead may be welcomed to the kingdom by the choirs of angels, we pray: ◆

Our Father . . .

God our Father,
the angels and archangels attend to you and do your will.
May we look to their example, listen to your voice,
and heed your call;
and may the heavenly host keep us safe from all harm.
We ask this through Christ our Lord. Amen.

✠ *We praise you, O Lord, for all your works are wonderful.*

✠ *We praise you, O Lord, for all your works are wonderful.*

PSALM 33 *page 409*

READING *Luke 16:19–26*

Jesus said to the Pharisees: "There was a rich man who dressed in purple garments and fine linen and dined sumptuously each day. And lying at his door was a poor man named Lazarus, covered with sores, who would gladly have eaten his fill of the scraps that fell from the rich man's table. Dogs even used to come and lick his sores. When the poor man died, he was carried away by angels to the bosom of Abraham. The rich man also died and was buried, and from the netherworld, where he was in torment, he raised his eyes and saw Abraham far off and Lazarus at his side. And he cried out, 'Father Abraham, have pity on me. Send Lazarus to dip the tip of his finger in water and cool my tongue, for I am suffering torment in these flames.' Abraham replied, 'My child, remember that you received what was good during your lifetime while Lazarus likewise received what was bad; but now he is comforted here, whereas you are tormented. Moreover, between us and you a great chasm is established to prevent anyone from crossing who might wish to go from our side to yours or from your side to ours.'"

REFLECTION

This Gospel, like the London Underground, says, "please mind the gap." Our God is a God of connections. As Creator, all creation depends on him for being. The Son told us he is the vine and we are the branches. The Spirit unites us as the Body of Christ. Any gaps that exist are of our own making. The gap between the poor and the rich, between the hungry and the satisfied, between the suffering and those who experience pleasure, between the damned and the saved—they are all of human making. Salvation is offered to all; only those who refuse it are damned. The gaps are created by us, but our God has built a bridge; let's follow his lead.

PRAYERS *others may be added*

United in care for one another, we pray:

◆ God, our help, hear us.

For the poor and hungry, we pray: ◆ *For the outcasts, we pray:* ◆ *For those who cause division, we pray:* ◆ *For our enemies, we pray:* ◆

Our Father . . .

God of all creation,
you unite all that is under your
loving care.
Grant us the grace to avoid division
and work toward a world bonded in
your Spirit.
We ask this through Christ our Lord.
Amen.

✠ *We praise you, O Lord, for all your works are wonderful.*

✦ *May your love be upon us, O Lord,*
as we place all our hope in you.

PSALM 33   page 409

READING   *Luke 9:46–50*

An argument arose among the disciples about which of them was the greatest. Jesus realized the intention of their hearts and took a child and placed it by his side and said to them, "Whoever receives this child in my name receives me, and whoever receives me receives the one who sent me. For the one who is least among all of you is the one who is the greatest."

Then John said in reply, "Master, we saw someone casting out demons in your name and we tried to prevent him because he does not follow in our company." Jesus said to him, "Do not prevent him, for whoever is not against you is for you."

REFLECTION

The story of a young woman, an image of a simple soul, the beauty of a delicate flower, a quiet beacon who changed the Church: St. Thérèse (1873–1897), a Carmelite nun, was known for her innate ability to make the ordinary and mundane extraordinary and holy. She was able to turn everyday tasks of washing dishes or tending to the garden into moments of contemplation and grace. Living during a time when people were enamored by ecstatic and visionary experiences, St. Thérèse opened the door to a practical spirituality, a "little way," where all could find a home. Following in her footsteps, let us never seek to be the greatest, but always seek to be the least—the one who transforms the heart by living every day with great humility and zeal.*

PRAYERS   *others may be added*

Living the message of St. Thérèse, we pray:

◆ God, our help, hear us.

That Christians live simply and humbly, we pray: ◆ *That more men and women consider vocations to the Carmelite way of life, we pray:* ◆ *That Carmelites throughout the world proclaim their rich spiritual tradition in word and deed, we pray:* ◆ *That the saints of Carmel challenge all to drink from the fountain of salvation, we pray:* ◆

Our Father . . .

God of humility, you called your little flower, St. Thérèse,
to live the spiritual life
with the meekness and simplicity
of a child.
Instill in us the strength to seek you
in the most ordinary and
unexpected places.
We ask this in the name of Jesus our Lord. Amen.

✦ *May your love be upon us, O Lord,*
as we place all our hope in you.

✠ *May your love be upon us, O Lord,*
as we place all our hope in you.

PSALM 33   *page 409*

READING   *Matthew 18:1–5, 10*

The disciples approached Jesus and said, "Who is the greatest in the Kingdom of heaven?" He called a child over, placed it in their midst, and said, "Amen, I say to you, unless you turn and become like children, you will not enter the Kingdom of heaven. Whoever humbles himself like this child is the greatest in the Kingdom of heaven. And whoever receives one child such as this in my name receives me.

"See that you do not despise one of these little ones, for I say to you that their angels in heaven always look upon the face of my heavenly Father."

REFLECTION

We live during a time when people are enamored by angels. When we walk into stores, we find angel paraphernalia, from statues to lapel pins, coffee mugs to bumper stickers, and books to movies. When turning on the television we find shows and stories revolving around angel sightings and miracles. As we celebrate the memorial of the Guardian Angels, we are reminded that we are continually surrounded by God's holy heralds—heralds who protect the lowly and little ones. May we look beyond our stores and televisions to see God's magnificent action through the angelic voices and mighty arms of our guardian angels—the ones who shield us from the terror of the night.

PRAYERS   *others may be added*

Seeking the protection of our guardian angels, we pray:

◆ God, our help, hear us.

To hear the merciful whisper of the Holy Spirit, we pray: ◆ *To live the truth of Christ, we pray:* ◆ *To recognize the saving action of God, we pray:* ◆ *To call upon our guardian angels in times of difficulty, we pray:* ◆

Our Father . . .

God of heaven,
you send guardian angels into
    our lives
to shelter us from the sinful ways
    of humanity.
May we herald your saving message
throughout the land.
Grant this through Christ our Lord.
    Amen.

✠ *May your love be upon us, O Lord,*
as we place all our hope in you.

✝ *We praise you, O Lord, for all your works are wonderful.*

PSALM 33 *page 409*

READING *Luke 9:57–62*

As Jesus and his disciples were proceeding on their journey, someone said to him, "I will follow you wherever you go." Jesus answered him, "Foxes have dens and birds of the sky have nests, but the Son of Man has nowhere to rest his head." And to another he said, "Follow me." But he replied, "Lord, let me go first and bury my father." But he answered him, "Let the dead bury their dead. But you, go and proclaim the Kingdom of God." And another said, "I will follow you, Lord, but first let me say farewell to my family at home." Jesus answered him, "No one who sets a hand to the plow and looks to what was left behind is fit for the Kingdom of God."

REFLECTION

Jesus is dead serious about his mission and the demands on his disciples. He is on the road to glory, but that path is directly through suffering. There is no mincing of words, no lack of honesty. And, nothing takes precedence over this mission. The Gospel message is that simple. The way to love and wholeness hurts; and there is no other way to happiness and fulfillment. We are invited. We are more than welcome. It is the only way to life. Are we ready? Will we go?

PRAYERS *others may be added*

Trusting in the Lord, we pray:

◆ God, our help, hear us.

That Christians will renew their commitment to follow the Lord, we pray: ◆ That more people listen and answer the call to priesthood and religious life, we pray: ◆ That individuals assisting those considering vocations in the Church may be filled with the Holy Spirit, we pray: ◆ That the Lord will reward the dead who have faithfully traveled the road of discipleship, we pray: ◆

Our Father . . .

God of salvation,
we rely on your help to show us the
way to glory.
Strengthen us on our way,
enlighten those discerning their call,
and bring us all to our heavenly
homeland.
Grant this through Christ our Lord.
Amen.

✝ *We praise you, O Lord, for all your works are wonderful.*

✤ *I will praise your name for ever, my king and my God.*

PSALM 33 *page 409*

READING *Luke 10:1–11*

Jesus appointed seventy-two other disciples whom he sent ahead of him in pairs to every town and place he intended to visit. He said to them, "The harvest is abundant but the laborers are few; so ask the master of the harvest to send out laborers for his harvest. Go on your way; behold, I am sending you like lambs among wolves. Carry no money bag, no sack, no sandals; and greet no one along the way. Into whatever house you enter, first say, 'Peace to this household.' If a peaceful person lives there, your peace will rest on him; but if not, it will return to you. Stay in the same house and eat and drink what is offered to you, for the laborer deserves his payment. Do not move about from one house to another. Whatever town you enter and they welcome you, eat what is set before you, cure the sick in it and say to them, 'The Kingdom of God is at hand for you.'"

REFLECTION

St. Francis (1181–+1226) is one who took the words of today's Gospel to heart. After living life with abandon during his youth, Francis had a conversion experience that put him on the road to discipleship described by Jesus. He developed a love for joyful poverty which enabled him and, later, his followers to depend wholly on God for

their needs. As founder of the Franciscans, Francis has become a role model for countless men and women, both lay and religious. May we imitate the joyful simplicity of this holy man and greet everyone with peace.

PRAYERS *others may be added*

Through the intercession of St. Francis, we pray:

◆ God, our help, hear us.

For Church leaders, we pray: ◆
For peace among nations, we pray: ◆
For those who minister to the poor and the sick, we pray: ◆ *For those who work to protect the environment, we pray:* ◆

Our Father . . .

God of creation,
your presence infuses heaven
     and earth.
Through the prayers and example
     of St. Francis,
may we strive to live peacefully
     and simply,
reach out to those in need,
and share the love of Christ.
We ask this through Christ our Lord.
     Amen.

✤ *I will praise your name for ever, my king and my God.*

✦ *We praise you, O Lord, for all your works are wonderful.*

PSALM 33   page 409

READING   Luke 10:13–16

Jesus said to them, "Woe to you, Chorazin! Woe to you, Bethsaida! For if the mighty deeds done in your midst had been done in Tyre and Sidon, they would long ago have repented, sitting in sackcloth and ashes. But it will be more tolerable for Tyre and Sidon at the judgment than for you. And as for you, Capernaum, 'Will you be exalted to heaven? You will go down to the netherworld.' Whoever listens to you listens to me. Whoever rejects you rejects me. And whoever rejects me rejects the one who sent me."

REFLECTION

The urgency of the message of Jesus reflected the political scene of the time. As an occupied people, they were playing with fire, trying to go the way of revenge and violence. Disaster came when, after an uprising in 70 AD, the Romans destroyed the temple and most of Jerusalem. The Gospel message is no less urgent now. With our ability to inflict violence on one another across the globe at a moment's notice, we need to heed the call to peace, love, and other-centeredness. In our daily relationships, too, violence of words as well as action must be rejected.

PRAYERS   others may be added

Accepting the Gospel message, we pray:

◆ God, our help, hear us.

That Church leaders may be energetic in preaching the Gospel, we pray: ◆
That world leaders may pursue the path of peace, we pray: ◆ *That all Christians may understand the importance of following the word of God, we pray:* ◆
That all victims of violence may forgive their persecutors, we pray: ◆

Our Father . . .

God of justice,
you are full of mercy and love.
We are the victims of our own refusal
    to follow your Son;
save us from our sinful ways,
and send the Holy Spirit to guide us
on the path of virtue and
    righteousness.
We ask this through Christ our Lord.
    Amen.

✦ *We praise you, O Lord, for all your works are wonderful.*

✢ *We praise you, O Lord, for all your*
   works are wonderful.

PSALM 33   *page 409*

READING   *Luke 10:17–22*
The seventy-two disciples returned
rejoicing and said to Jesus, "Lord,
even the demons are subject to us
because of your name." Jesus said, "I
have observed Satan fall like lightning
from the sky. Behold, I have given you
the power 'to tread upon serpents' and
scorpions and upon the full force of
the enemy and nothing will harm you.
Nevertheless, do not rejoice because
the spirits are subject to you, but rejoice
because your names are written in
heaven." At that very moment he
rejoiced in the Holy Spirit and said, "I
give you praise, Father, Lord of heaven
and earth, for although you have hidden these things from the wise and the
learned you have revealed them to the
childlike. Yes, Father, such has been
your gracious will. All things have
been handed over to me by my Father.
No one knows who the Son is except
the Father, and who the Father is
except the Son and anyone to whom
the Son wishes to reveal him."

REFLECTION
The power of God is amazing indeed!
Today we celebrate two holy people who
accomplished deeds that can only be
attributed to the grace of God. Despite the
fact that she was considered too sickly for
religious life, Bl. Marie-Rose (1811–+1849)
founded the Sisters of the Most Holy

Names of Jesus and Mary, a community
dedicated to teaching the poor. St. Bruno
(1032–1101) founded the Carthusian order
while being required by Pope Urban II to
help with Church matters. May we be as
open to the workings of God in our own
lives as were these two holy people.

PRAYERS   *others may be added*
   Relying on the grace of God, we pray:

◆ God, our help, hear us.

That Church leaders may be open to the
promptings of the Holy Spirit, we pray: ◆
That world leaders may look to the
holy ones for counsel, we pray: ◆
That cloistered religious may continue
to model a prayerful solitude to a busy
world, we pray: ◆ *That men and women*
may continue to heed the call to religious
life, we pray: ◆

Our Father . . .

Loving Father,
your call extends to the lively and the
   quiet alike.
Send us your Holy Spirit to help
   us discern
the path to holiness that best suits us
   and your will.
May we always be inspired and
   helped by your saints.
Grant this through Christ our Lord.
   Amen.

✢ *We praise you, O Lord, for all your*
   works are wonderful.

✝ *We praise you, O Lord, for all your works are wonderful.*

PSALM 33   page 409

READING   *Luke 17:5-10*

The apostles said to the Lord, "Increase our faith." The Lord replied, "If you have faith the size of a mustard seed, you would say to this mulberry tree, 'Be uprooted and planted in the sea,' and it would obey you. "Who among you would say to your servant who has just come in from plowing or tending sheep in the field, 'Come here immediately and take your place at table'? Would he not rather say to him, 'Prepare something for me to eat. Put on your apron and wait on me while I eat and drink. You may eat and drink when I am finished'? Is he grateful to that servant because he did what was commanded? So should it be with you. When you have done all you have been commanded, say, 'We are unprofitable servants; we have done what we were obliged to do.'"

REFLECTION

In a capitalist society, today's Gospel may seem strange. We are tempted to object to being called unprofitable servants if we do our job. We expect compensation for all we do, and the higher the compensation, the better. There is nothing wrong with receiving a just wage. However, the life of faith does not work the same way as economics does. Our faith is a gift, salvation is a gift, our very life is a gift. We cannot earn anything from God. Our acts of service should be acts of gratitude for all God has given us.

PRAYERS   *others may be added*

With faith and gratitude, we pray:

◆ God, our help, hear us.

For those who care for our basic needs, we pray: ◆ *For migrant workers, we pray:* ◆ *For volunteer workers, we pray:* ◆ *For hospitality workers, we pray:* ◆

Our Father . . .

Almighty God,
you are the giver of all good gifts.
Through your generosity and love,
we have been offered salvation by
    your Son.
May we always act as
    worthy disciples
and show our gratitude.
We ask this through our Lord Jesus
    Christ, your Son,
who lives and reigns with you in the
    unity of the Holy Spirit,
one God, forever and ever. Amen.

✝ *We praise you, O Lord, for all your works are wonderful.*

✠ *We praise you, O Lord, for all your works are wonderful.*

PSALM 33   page 409

READING   Luke 10:29a–37

[A scholar of the law said to Jesus,] "And who is my neighbor?" Jesus replied, "A man fell victim to robbers as he went down from Jerusalem to Jericho. They stripped and beat him and went off leaving him half-dead. A priest happened to be going down that road, but when he saw him, he passed by on the opposite side. Likewise a Levite came to the place, and when he saw him, he passed by on the opposite side. But a Samaritan traveler who came upon him was moved with compassion at the sight. He approached the victim, poured oil and wine over his wounds and bandaged them. Then he lifted him up on his own animal, took him to an inn, and cared for him. The next day he took out two silver coins and gave them to the innkeeper with the instruction, 'Take care of him. If you spend more than what I have given you, I shall repay you on my way back.' Which of these three, in your opinion, was neighbor to the robbers' victim?" He answered, "The one who treated him with mercy." Jesus said to him, "Go and do likewise."

REFLECTION

Whom do I hate? Hate is a strong word, so maybe I prefer the phrase, dislike consistently, or some other euphemism. We may or may not be aware of our own prejudices, resentments, or loathing. However, whatever my answer may be, it is also the answer to the question, who is my neighbor? The story of the good Samaritan simply shows us that there is good in everyone, especially in those whom we least expect it. We are challenged to drop the hate, look for their good, and go do likewise.

PRAYERS   others may be added

Looking to the Master, we pray:

◆ God, our help, hear us.

For those who wish us harm, we pray: ◆ *For those we find difficult to love, we pray:* ◆ *For people who go unnoticed (or who fade into the crowd), we pray:* ◆ *For the grace to see all as neighbors worthy of our care, we pray:* ◆

Our Father . . .

Lord, God of all goodness,
you have created all peoples in your
    image and likeness.
Help us to see your imprint on every
    person we meet,
and guide us to give them the care,
    respect, and love
offered to us by your Son.
We ask this through Christ our Lord.
    Amen.

✠ *We praise you, O Lord, for all your works are wonderful.*

✝ *We praise you, O Lord, for all your works are wonderful.*

PSALM 33   page 409

READING   *Luke 10:38–42*

Jesus entered a village where a woman whose name was Martha welcomed him. She had a sister named Mary who sat beside the Lord at his feet listening to him speak. Martha, burdened with much serving, came to him and said, "Lord, do you not care that my sister has left me by myself to do the serving? Tell her to help me." The Lord said to her in reply, "Martha, Martha, you are anxious and worried about many things. There is need of only one thing. Mary has chosen the better part and it will not be taken from her."

REFLECTION

Both of today's saints were aware of the message of Jesus in this Gospel passage. Both St. Denis (+258) and St. John Leonardi (1542–+1609) were people of action. St. Denis was the first bishop and evangelizer of Paris, and St. John founded the Clerks Regular of the Mother of God, a community committed to the reform of priestly life. Both of these men knew that all their actions had to be based on listening to the word of God. May we, too, listen to God's word in our lives.

PRAYERS   *others may be added*

Attending to the word of God, we pray:

◆ God, our help, hear us.

That bishops may be led by the same zeal that inspired St. Denis, we pray: ◆
That the nations may be open to the Holy Spirit's promptings, we pray: ◆
That our service may be based in love and rooted in God's word, we pray: ◆
That catechists may be inspired by the wisdom of St. John, we pray: ◆

Our Father . . .

Almighty God,
your glory fills all your works,
and your love surpasses all
    understanding.
Help us to listen to the promptings of
    your Holy Spirit
as we hear your word and celebrate
    your sacraments.
We ask this through Christ our Lord.
    Amen.

✝ *We praise you, O Lord, for all your works are wonderful.*

✦ *We praise you, O Lord, for all your works are wonderful.*

PSALM 33 *page 409*

READING *Luke 11:1–4*

Jesus was praying in a certain place, and when he had finished, one of his disciples said to him, "Lord, teach us to pray just as John taught his disciples." He said to them, "When you pray, say:

Father, hallowed be your name,/ your Kingdom come./Give us each day our daily bread/and forgive us our sins/for we ourselves forgive everyone in debt to us,/and do not subject us to the final test."

REFLECTION

No relationship can last, never mind flourish, without communication. The disciples realized this when they asked Jesus to teach them to pray. They wanted to know how best to communicate with the Father. Jesus taught that there was a new relationship with the Father, and that called for a new way of addressing him. So often words fail us at important moments. That is why these words of Jesus are so important. This is how we should speak to the Father; this is how we should grow in our relationship with the Father.

PRAYERS *others may be added*

In love, we pray:

◆ God, our help, hear us.

That we may grow in our appreciation of prayer, we pray: ◆ *That we may allow times of quiet to be a part of our regular daily routine, we pray:* ◆ *That we may model the devotion of the saints in our prayers, we pray:* ◆ *That we may be inspired by the Holy Spirit to pray as we ought, we pray:* ◆

Our Father . . .

Heavenly Father,
your paternal care for us is
    without measure.
Your Son taught us to look to you
    in praise
and in our need.
We approach you with confidence as
    we face our daily needs,
and we ask that you continue to
    nurture our faith.
We ask this through Christ our Lord.
    Amen.

✦ *We praise you, O Lord, for all your works are wonderful.*

✛ *We praise you, O Lord, for all your works are wonderful.*

PSALM 33   *page 409*

READING   *Luke 11:5–13*

Jesus said to his disciples: "Suppose one of you has a friend to whom he goes at midnight and says, 'Friend, lend me three loaves of bread, for a friend of mine has arrived at my house from a journey and I have nothing to offer him,' and he says in reply from within, 'Do not bother me; the door has already been locked and my children and I are already in bed. I cannot get up to give you anything.' I tell you, if he does not get up to give him the loaves because of their friendship, he will get up to give him whatever he needs because of his persistence.

"And I tell you, ask and you will receive; seek and you will find; knock and the door will be opened to you. For everyone who asks, receives; and the one who seeks, finds; and to the one who knocks, the door will be opened. What father among you would hand his son a snake when he asks for a fish? Or hand him a scorpion when he asks for an egg? If you then, who are wicked, know how to give good gifts to your children, how much more will the Father in heaven give the Holy Spirit to those who ask him?"

REFLECTION

So often we are tempted to think of God as stingy, harsh, or cruel. The pure and simple truth about our God is that he lives for giving: not the giving of things like Santa Claus, but the giving of a parent, the giving that gives of one's self. St. Luke specifically mentions the giving of the Holy Spirit in today's Gospel. God has given to us his very self, and he wants this gift to continue and flourish! All we need do is ask.

PRAYERS   *others may be added*

Looking to God for assistance, we pray:

◆ God, our help, hear us.

That parents may follow the Father's example of generosity, we pray: ◆ That those in need may find the Father's bounty in the Christian community, we pray: ◆ That liberality may be found in the followers of Christ, we pray: ◆ That the dead may be received in the open arm of the Father, we pray: ◆

Our Father . . .

Loving God,
we thrive in your garden.
Water us with your life-saving
 sacraments
so that we may bring the good news
 of your love
to those withering in sin.
Grant this through Christ our Lord.
 Amen.

✛ *We praise you, O Lord, for all your works are wonderful.*

✠ *We praise you, O Lord, for all your*
works are wonderful.

PSALM 33   *page 409*

READING   *Luke 11:15–20*

When Jesus had driven out a demon,
some of the crowd said: "By the power
of Beelzebul, the prince of demons, he
drives out demons." Others, to test
him, asked him for a sign from heaven.
But he knew their thoughts and said to
them, "Every kingdom divided against
itself will be laid waste and house will
fall against house. And if Satan is
divided against himself, how will his
kingdom stand? For you say that it is
by Beelzebul that I drive out demons.
If I, then, drive out demons by
Beelzebul, by whom do your own people drive them out? Therefore they will
be your judges. But if it is by the finger of God that I drive out demons,
then the Kingdom of God has come
upon you. When a strong man fully
armed guards his palace, his possessions are safe. But when one stronger
than he attacks and overcomes him,
he takes away the armor on which
he relied and distributes the spoils.
Whoever is not with me is against me,
and whoever does not gather with me
scatters."

REFLECTION

Jesus is passionate about his message. He
comes to bring life, literally. He comes
from the Father, who is life. He battles the
evil one, who is death. When it comes to
life and death, there are no halfway mea-
sures. One is either dead or alive; there is
no in between. Any being that doesn't
work at sustaining life is dying. Jesus is
not just zealous about an ideology; he is
the lone physician in a dying world. He
has given us salvation; thus, healing the
world from all sin and raising us to eter-
nal life.

PRAYERS   *others may be added*

  Standing with the Lord, we pray:

◆ God, our help, hear us.

That warring nations will opt for peace,
we pray: ◆ *That hostilities and tensions*
may cease among the followers of
Christ, we pray: ◆ *That we may be fully*
committed to the Gospel, we pray: ◆
That the sick may be comforted by their
faith in the Lord of life, we pray: ◆

Our Father . . .

Lord God,
you teach us that to follow your Son
is the essence of life.
Fill us with grace and the Holy Spirit,
that we may walk the way of life
and be united with you forever.
We ask this through Christ our Lord.
  Amen.

✠ *We praise you, O Lord, for all your*
works are wonderful.

✤ *We praise you, O Lord, for all your works are wonderful.*

PSALM 33 *page 409*

READING *Luke 11:27-28*

While Jesus was speaking, a woman from the crowd called out and said to him, "Blessed is the womb that carried you and the breasts at which you nursed." He replied, "Rather, blessed are those who hear the word of God and observe it."

REFLECTION

Mary is known by many different titles and portrayed in a multitude of images. The most significant title was given to her by the Council of Ephesus in 431: Mother of God (in Greek, Theotokos*). The literal translation is "God Bearer." The significance of this title and the point Jesus makes in today's Gospel is that more important than the blood ties between this mother and son is the fact that Mary brought God into the world. She received the Word and brought it forth for all of us. As Christians living after Christ's Ascension, we are called to embody, to bear the Word of God into the world. We are asked to continue the vocation of Mary; we are asked to deliver Christ here today.*

PRAYERS *others may be added*

Through the intercession of the Mother of God, we pray:

◆ God, our help, hear us.

For those who continue Mary's ministry of prayer, we pray: ◆ *For those who spread the Gospel through the arts, we pray:* ◆ *For priests, deacons, and Extraordinary Ministers of Holy Communion who bring the Eucharist to the faithful, we pray:* ◆ *For those who are waiting to be freed by Christ's saving love, we pray:* ◆

Our Father . . .

Father,
you chose the Blessed Virgin Mary
to be the mother of your Son.
Through her prayers,
may we continue to bear Christ in
    the world
and one day dwell in your
    glorious kingdom
with Mary and all the angels
    and saints.
We ask this through Christ our Lord.
    Amen.

✤ *We praise you, O Lord, for all your works are wonderful.*

✠ *Lord, you have the words of*
everlasting life.

PSALM 19 page 405

READING *Luke 17:11–19*

As Jesus continued his journey to Jerusalem, he traveled through Samaria and Galilee. As he was entering a village, ten lepers met him. They stood at a distance from him and raised their voices, saying, "Jesus, Master! Have pity on us!" And when he saw them, he said, "Go show yourselves to the priests." As they were going they were cleansed. And one of them, realizing he had been healed, returned, glorifying God in a loud voice; and he fell at the feet of Jesus and thanked him. He was a Samaritan. Jesus said in reply, "Ten were cleansed, were they not? Where are the other nine? Has none but this foreigner returned to give thanks to God?" Then he said to him, "Stand up and go; your faith has saved you."

REFLECTION

One of the worst feelings a person can have is to feel like an outsider, an outcast, rejected. Whether one is left out of playground games, barred from employment, shunned by certain social circles, or simply rejected by strangers, the feeling is terrible. In the time of Jesus, the status of outsider was imposed by law on lepers. Jesus rescued these men. Only one was grateful. We, too, have been rescued by the Lord. Are we grateful?

PRAYERS *others may be added*

With grateful hearts, we pray:

◆ God, receive our prayer.

For those who are outcasts in today's society, that they may be welcomed in the Church, we pray: ◆ *For those we have caused to feel like outsiders, that we may reach out to them, we pray:* ◆ *For health-care workers, that we may grasp the importance of their mission, we pray:* ◆ *For lawmakers, that they may work for laws that are inclusive and respectful of the dignity of human life, we pray:* ◆

Our Father . . .

Lord God,
your glory shines through every facet
   of creation.
Help us to mend the divisions caused
   by sin and fear,
and bring us together as one
   grateful family.
We ask this through our Lord Jesus
   Christ, your Son,
who lives and reigns with you in the
   unity of the Holy Spirit,
one God, forever and ever. Amen.

✠ *Lord, you have the words of*
everlasting life.

✚ *Lord, you have the words of everlasting life.*

PSALM 19 page 405

READING Luke 11:29–32

While still more people gathered in the crowd, Jesus said to them, "This generation is an evil generation; it seeks a sign, but no sign will be given it, except the sign of Jonah. Just as Jonah became a sign to the Ninevites, so will the Son of Man be to this generation. At the judgment the queen of the south will rise with the men of this generation and she will condemn them, because she came from the ends of the earth to hear the wisdom of Solomon, and there is something greater than Solomon here. At the judgment the men of Nineveh will arise with this generation and condemn it, because at the preaching of Jonah they repented, and there is something greater than Jonah here."

REFLECTION

So often we feel bereft of signs of God in our lives. Usually that happens because we are not looking in the right places for God. St. Teresa (1515–+1582) was one who didn't look specifically for signs of God, but yet found them anyway. St. Teresa, one of the Church's foremost mystics and exponents on the signs of God, found within her mystical experiences the strength to found a more rigorous form of Carmelite life. May we be strengthened in our Christian life by the signs of God's love always surrounding us.

PRAYERS *others may be added*

Surrounded by God's love, we pray:

◆ God, receive our prayer.

That the Church may always search the signs of the times for the work of the Holy Spirit, we pray: ◆ *That the civic leaders may be attentive to the needs of the people they serve, we pray:* ◆ *That the Carmelite family may be blessed with new and worthy members, we pray:* ◆ *That all Christians may grow in appreciation of the signs of God's love, we pray:* ◆

Our Father . . .

God of hope,
you touch our world in countless ways
with signs of your tender concern.
Through the prayers and example
   of St. Teresa,
may we be attentive to your actions in
   our lives
and be encouraged to do your
   wondrous works.
We ask this through Christ our Lord.
   Amen.

✚ *Lord, you have the words of everlasting life.*

✝ *Lord, you have the words of everlasting life.*

PSALM 19   *page 405*

READING   *Luke 11:37–41*

After Jesus had spoken, a Pharisee invited him to dine at his home. He entered and reclined at table to eat. The Pharisee was amazed to see that he did not observe the prescribed washing before the meal. The Lord said to him, "Oh you Pharisees! Although you cleanse the outside of the cup and the dish, inside you are filled with plunder and evil. You fools! Did not the maker of the outside also make the inside? But as to what is within, give alms, and behold, everything will be clean for you."

REFLECTION

Both of today's saints cherished interior values rather than outward appearances. St. Hedwig (1174–+1243), a married noblewoman, used her vast wealth to found monasteries and hospitals for the poor. St. Margaret Mary Alacoque (1674–+1690), through messages received in visions of the Sacred Heart, helped spread this now-popular devotion. Both saints help us to understand that our inner values must be reflected in our outward religious practices and that our God values giving, tender hearts.

PRAYERS   *others may be added*

In sincerity of heart, we pray:

◆ God, receive our prayer.

That the Church may always strive for the inner values esteemed by Christ, we pray: ◆ *That popular devotions may lead us to true worship of our loving God, we pray:* ◆ *That we may be generous in our almsgiving, we pray:* ◆ *That the faithful departed may rest in peace, we pray:* ◆

Our Father . . .

God of tender mercies,
you sent your Son out of love
to free us from the grip of death
    and selfishness.
Fill our hearts with generosity
    and thankfulness,
so that we may sincerely proclaim
the message of salvation.
We ask this through Christ our Lord.
    Amen.

✝ *Lord, you have the words of everlasting life.*

✝ *Lord, you have the words of everlasting life.*

PSALM 19 — page 405

READING — *Luke 11:42–46*

The Lord said: "Woe to you Pharisees! You pay tithes of mint and of rue and of every garden herb, but you pay no attention to judgment and to love for God. These you should have done, without overlooking the others. Woe to you Pharisees! You love the seat of honor in synagogues and greetings in marketplaces. Woe to you! You are like unseen graves over which people unknowingly walk."

Then one of the scholars of the law said to him in reply, "Teacher, by saying this you are insulting us too." And he said, "Woe also to you scholars of the law! You impose on people burdens hard to carry, but you yourselves do not lift one finger to touch them."

REFLECTION — *St. Ignatius*

No earthly pleasures, no kingdoms of this world can benefit me in any way. I prefer death in Christ Jesus to power over the farthest limits of the earth. He who died in place of us is the one object of my quest. He who rose for our sakes is my one desire.

PRAYERS — *others may be added*

With steadfast conviction, we pray:

◆ God, receive our prayer.

For our bishops, successors to the apostles, that they may stand bravely for their beliefs, we pray: ◆ *For Christians facing persecution throughout the world, that they may be inspired to remain strong, we pray:* ◆ *For those who persecute the Church, that they may be converted by the love of Christ, we pray:* ◆ *For those killed in service of the Gospel, that they may rejoice in the heavenly banquet, we pray:* ◆

Our Father . . .

God of the martyrs,
your strength helps holy men
    and women
throughout time give witness to
    your love.
Through the prayers and example of
    your martyr St. Ignatius,
may we, too, stand for the values
    of salvation
and proclaim the victory of
    your kingdom.
Grant this through Christ our Lord.
    Amen.

✝ *Lord, you have the words of everlasting life.*

✤ *Lord, you have the words of everlasting life.*

PSALM 19   page 405

READING   *Luke 10:1–9*

The Lord Jesus appointed seventy-two disciples whom he sent ahead of him in pairs to every town and place he intended to visit. He said to them, "The harvest is abundant but the laborers are few; so ask the master of the harvest to send out laborers for his harvest. Go on your way; behold, I am sending you like lambs among wolves. Carry no money bag, no sack, no sandals; and greet no one along the way. Into whatever house you enter, first say, 'Peace to this household.' If a peaceful person lives there, your peace will rest on him; but if not, it will return to you. Stay in the same house and eat and drink what is offered to you, for the laborer deserves payment. Do not move about from one house to another. Whatever town you enter and they welcome you, eat what is set before you, cure the sick in it and say to them, 'The Kingdom of God is at hand for you.'"

REFLECTION

St. Luke (first century), author of Acts and the third Gospel, was a laborer for the harvest of Christ. He is thought to have journeyed with Paul, being mentioned as the "beloved physician." Luke's writing's emphasize the human nature of Christ and the workings of the Holy Spirit. We, too, are called and sent to proclaim salvation and the kingdom of love.

PRAYERS   *others may be added*

Proclaiming salvation, we pray:

◆ God, receive our prayer.

That Church leaders may continue evangelizing in the spirit of St. Luke, we pray: ◆ *That our lives may be marked with compassion for the poor and downtrodden, we pray:* ◆ *That the dignity of all humanity may be honored, we pray:* ◆ *That we may recognize the workings of the Holy Spirit in our daily lives, we pray:* ◆

Our Father . . .

God of wisdom,
you inspired St. Luke to write works proclaiming
the wonders of your Son and
    his Church.
May we imitate the example of your
    evangelists and
sing the praises of your works to all
    we meet.
We ask this through Christ our Lord.
    Amen.

✤ *Lord, you have the words of everlasting life.*

✝ *Lord, you have the words of everlasting life.*

PSALM 19 page 405

READING Luke 12:1–7

At that time: So many people were crowding together that they were trampling one another underfoot. Jesus began to speak, first to his disciples, "Beware of the leaven—that is, the hypocrisy—of the Pharisees.

"There is nothing concealed that will not be revealed, nor secret that will not be known. Therefore whatever you have said in the darkness will be heard in the light, and what you have whispered behind closed doors will be proclaimed on the housetops. I tell you, my friends, do not be afraid of those who kill the body but after that can do no more. I shall show you whom to fear. Be afraid of the one who after killing has the power to cast into Gehenna; yes, I tell you, be afraid of that one. Are not five sparrows sold for two small coins? Yet not one of them has escaped the notice of God. Even the hairs of your head have all been counted. Do not be afraid. You are worth more than many sparrows."

REFLECTION St. John de Brébeuf

Jesus, my Lord and Savior, what can I give you in return for all the favors you have first conferred on me? I will take from your hand the cup of your sufferings and call on your name. I vow before your eternal Father and the Holy Spirit, before your most holy Mother and her most chaste spouse, before the angels, apostles and martyrs, before my blessed fathers Saint Ignatius and Saint Francis Xavier—in truth I vow to you, Jesus my Savior, that as far as I have the strength I will never fail to accept the grace of martyrdom, if some day you in your infinite mercy should offer it to me, your most unworthy servant.

PRAYERS others may be added

With faith in the living God, we pray:

◆ God, receive our prayer.

For missionaries throughout the world, that they may be filled with courage and perseverance, we pray: ◆ *For native peoples, that their heritage may be respected, we pray:* ◆ *For North Americans, that they may live out the salvation won by Christ Jesus, we pray:* ◆ *For the repose of the souls of the faithful departed, we pray:* ◆

Our Father . . .

God of all nations,
you created diverse peoples
to love, serve, and praise you.
May we learn to respect our
    differences,
appreciate our gifts,
and revel in the salvation offered to
    us all.
Grant this through Christ our Lord.
    Amen.

✝ *Lord, you have the words of everlasting life.*

✠ *Lord, you have the words of everlasting life.*

PSALM 19 *page 405*

READING *Luke 12:8–12*

Jesus said to his disciples: "I tell you, everyone who acknowledges me before others the Son of Man will acknowledge before the angels of God. But whoever denies me before others will be denied before the angels of God.

"Everyone who speaks a word against the Son of Man will be forgiven, but the one who blasphemes against the Holy Spirit will not be forgiven. When they take you before synagogues and before rulers and authorities, do not worry about how or what your defense will be or about what you are to say. For the Holy Spirit will teach you at that moment what you should say."

REFLECTION

St. Paul of the Cross (1694–+1775) was a man who was not afraid to acknowledge Christ. After a vision, he founded the Congregation of the Passion, a community dedicated to preaching the Passion of Christ. Because of the success of their preaching methods (involving active participation of the laity in devotions) and their ministry to lapsed Catholics, the Passionists quickly became popular and in high demand. May we follow their example of forgiving hearts, combined with a thorough understanding of the role of suffering in salvation.

PRAYERS *others may be added*

Through the intercession of St. Paul of the Cross, we pray:

◆ God, receive our prayer.

That Church leaders may approach their ministry with forgiving hearts, we pray: ◆ That lay people strive for active participation in all aspects of their spiritual life, we pray: ◆ That the Passionists be blessed with many worthy members, we pray: ◆ That lapsed Catholics find a welcoming home in the Church, we pray: ◆

Our Father . . .

Forgiving Father,
your Son endured the Passion for
   our salvation.
May we strive to alleviate
   unnecessary suffering in the world,
offer solace to those in need,
and work for the salvation of all.
We ask this through Christ our Lord.
   Amen.

✠ *Lord, you have the words of everlasting life.*

✣ *Lord, you have the words of everlasting life.*

PSALM 19 *page 405*

READING *Luke 18:1–8*

Jesus told his disciples a parable about the necessity for them to pray always without becoming weary. He said, "There was a judge in a certain town who neither feared God nor respected any human being. And a widow in that town used to come to him and say, 'Render a just decision for me against my adversary.' For a long time the judge was unwilling, but eventually he thought, 'While it is true that I neither fear God nor respect any human being, because this widow keeps bothering me I shall deliver a just decision for her lest she finally come and strike me.'" The Lord said, "Pay attention to what the dishonest judge says. Will not God then secure the rights of his chosen ones who call out to him day and night? Will he be slow to answer them? I tell you, he will see to it that justice is done for them speedily. But when the Son of Man comes, will he find faith on earth?"

REFLECTION

In today's world there are so many things competing for our attention: job, home, family, entertainment, investments, working out, and the list goes on. The widow in today's Gospel shows amazing persistence and focus on God. Faith is focusing on the promises of God with the expectation that they will be fulfilled. Jesus asks us and invites us to aim our focus, our faith, on God. God is faithful; we just need to pay attention.

PRAYERS *others may be added*

With faithful persistence, we pray:

◆ God, receive our prayer.

For the grace to remain focused on the Lord through all life's distractions, we pray: ◆ *For those who have experienced injustice, we pray:* ◆ *For orphans, widows, and widowers, that they may find comfort, we pray:* ◆ *For the victims of natural disasters, we pray:* ◆

Our Father . . .

Father,
your care extends to all of creation.
Help us to look to you as our support
   and guide
in all that we do, say, and believe,
so that we may serve as reminders to
   all around us
that you are the God of salvation.
We ask this through our Lord Jesus
   Christ, your Son,
who lives and reigns with you in the
   unity of the Holy Spirit,
one God, forever and ever. Amen.

✣ *Lord, you have the words of everlasting life.*

✝ *Lord, you have the words of everlasting life.*

PSALM 19   *page 405*

READING   *Luke 12:13–21*

Someone in the crowd said to Jesus, "Teacher, tell my brother to share the inheritance with me." He replied to him, "Friend, who appointed me as your judge and arbitrator?" Then he said to the crowd, "Take care to guard against all greed, for though one may be rich, one's life does not consist of possessions."

Then he told them a parable. "There was a rich man whose land produced a bountiful harvest. He asked himself, 'What shall I do, for I do not have space to store my harvest?' And he said, 'This is what I shall do: I shall tear down my barns and build larger ones. There I shall store all my grain and other goods and I shall say to myself, "Now as for you, you have so many good things stored up for many years, rest, eat, drink, be merry!" ' But God said to him, 'You fool, this night your life will be demanded of you; and the things you have prepared, to whom will they belong?' Thus will it be for the one who stores up treasure for himself but is not rich in what matters to God."

REFLECTION   *St. John of the Cross*

We must then dig deeply in Christ. He is like a rich mine with many pockets containing treasures: however deep we dig, we will never find their end or their limit. Indeed, in every pocket new seams of fresh riches are discovered on all sides.

For this reason the apostle Paul said of Christ, "In him are hidden all the treasures of the wisdom and knowledge of God." The soul cannot enter into these treasures, nor attain them, unless it first crosses into and enters the thicket of suffering, enduring interior and exterior labors, and unless it first receives from God very many blessings in the intellect and in the senses, and has undergone long spiritual training.

PRAYERS   *others may be added*

Guarding against greed, we pray:

◆ God, receive our prayer.

That Church leaders will live the simplicity of the Gospel they preach, we pray: ◆ That civic leaders will work for a just distribution of goods and resources, we pray: ◆ That we may work for and store up the treasures of God, we pray: ◆ That all may safeguard the environment for future use, we pray: ◆

Our Father . . .

Almighty God,
your love for us exceeds
all we could ask for.
Forgive us our greed for the things
    that perish,
teach us the value of your grace,
and lead us home to you where our
    true treasure lies.
We ask this through Christ our Lord.
    Amen.

✝ *Lord, you have the words of everlasting life.*

✠ *Lord, you have the words of everlasting life.*

PSALM 19 page 405

READING Luke 12:35–38

Jesus said to his disciples: "Gird your loins and light your lamps and be like servants who await their master's return from a wedding, ready to open immediately when he comes and knocks. Blessed are those servants whom the master finds vigilant on his arrival. Amen, I say to you, he will gird himself, have them recline at table, and proceed to wait on them. And should he come in the second or third watch and find them prepared in this way, blessed are those servants."

REFLECTION

St. John of Capistrano (1386– +1456) was always ready to be of service to the Church. He became a Franciscan after receiving a vision of St. Francis of Assisi. St. John was a successful teacher and popular preacher. Pope Callistus II sent him throughout Europe on many missions to preach against heresies. He was a tireless reformer of his own community, insisting that change must begin with himself. May we be filled with the same zeal for service that marked St. John.

PRAYERS *others may be added*

With zeal for the Lord, we pray:

◆ God, receive our prayer.

That those who preach may be inspired by the Holy Spirit, we pray: ◆ That those who minister to the poor and downtrodden may be humble in spirit, we pray: ◆ That those with hopeless spirits may be lifted with God's loving embrace, we pray: ◆ That all Christians may zealously spread the Gospel, we pray: ◆

Our Father . . .

God of life,
you send the Holy Spirit to bring life
    and vigor to your Church.
Through the prayers and example of
    St. John of Capistrano,
may we be filled with zeal for your
    service and
one day be joined together in our
    heavenly homeland.
We ask this through Christ our Lord.
    Amen.

✠ *Lord, you have the words of everlasting life.*

✝ *Lord, you have the words of everlasting life.*

PSALM 19   *page 405*

READING   *Luke 12:39–43, 48*

Jesus said to his disciples: "Be sure of this: if the master of the house had known the hour when the thief was coming, he would not have let his house be broken into. You also must be prepared, for at an hour you do not expect, the Son of Man will come."

Then Peter said, "Lord, is this parable meant for us or for everyone?" And the Lord replied, "Who, then, is the faithful and prudent steward whom the master will put in charge of his servants to distribute the food allowance at the proper time? Blessed is that servant whom his master on arrival finds doing so. Much will be required of the person entrusted with much, and still more will be demanded of the person entrusted with more."

REFLECTION

St. Anthony Mary Claret (1807–+1870) was a man of great fortitude and drive. A Spanish diocesan priest, he founded the Missionary Sons of the Immaculate Heart of Mary (the Claretians). During his life he founded libraries, published many theological works, and was appointed Archbishop of Santiago, Cuba. Later, he resigned this position and was appointed chaplain to the queen of Spain. Throughout his life at court, he continued many penitential practices and used his influence to launch and support institutions of the liberal arts.

Much was entrusted to St. Anthony and he persevered in faith. May we, too, persevere in proclaiming salvation.

PRAYERS   *others may be added*

Through the intercession of St. Anthony Mary Claret, we pray:

◆ God, receive our prayer.

For bishops and religious superiors, that they may be inspired by St. Anthony, we pray: ◆ *For diocesan clergy, that they may have zeal for God's work, we pray:* ◆ *For the Claretians, that they may have an increase in worthy vocations, we pray:* ◆ *For the peoples of Cuba and Spain, that they may experience a renewal of faith, we pray:* ◆

Our Father . . .

Loving God,
you give us worthy shepherds
to guide and inspire us.
May we follow your precepts of
    charity and service
entrusted to us by your Son
and give you glory forever in your
    kingdom.
We ask this through Christ our Lord.
    Amen.

✝ *Lord, you have the words of everlasting life.*

✝ *Lord, you have the words of everlasting life.*

PSALM 19   *page 405*

READING   *Luke 12:49–53*

Jesus said to his disciples: "I have come to set the earth on fire, and how I wish it were already blazing! There is a baptism with which I must be baptized, and how great is my anguish until it is accomplished! Do you think that I have come to establish peace on the earth? No, I tell you, but rather division. From now on a household of five will be divided, three against two and two against three; a father will be divided against his son and a son against his father, a mother against her daughter and a daughter against her mother, a mother-in-law against her daughter-in-law and a daughter-in-law against her mother-in-law."

REFLECTION

There are many comforting words in the Gospels. Our God is a God of love and mercy. This passage may seem to show a different side of Christ, but actually we see the same love and concern. Just as a parent sternly warns a child of the dangers of crossing the street or touching a hot stove, here Christ gives a warning that those closest to us may try to keep us from wholeheartedly following the Gospel. Keeping peace in the family is no excuse for ignoring the Lord. Let's keep our hearts ablaze with the love of God—no matter what.

PRAYERS   *others may be added*

Looking to the true light, we pray:

◆ God, receive our prayer.

That family unity may inspire us to follow the Gospel, we pray: ◆ *That all Christians may be filled with a passionate devotion to their path of discipleship, we pray:* ◆ *That the harvest may be bountiful, we pray:* ◆ *That all who preach may not be afraid to challenge themselves as well as the People of God, we pray:* ◆

Our Father . . .

God of hosts,
the angels do your bidding,
and nature follows the course you
    have laid out for her.
May we look to your will,
follow it with loving obedience,
and gather the nations into your
    loving embrace.
Grant this through Christ our Lord.
    Amen.

✝ *Lord, you have the words of everlasting life.*

✝ *Lord, you have the words of everlasting life.*

PSALM 19   *page 405*

READING   *Luke 12:54–59*

Jesus said to the crowds, "When you see a cloud rising in the west you say immediately that it is going to rain—and so it does; and when you notice that the wind is blowing from the south you say that it is going to be hot—and so it is. You hypocrites! You know how to interpret the appearance of the earth and the sky; why do you not know how to interpret the present time?

"Why do you not judge for yourselves what is right? If you are to go with your opponent before a magistrate, make an effort to settle the matter on the way; otherwise your opponent will turn you over to the judge, and the judge hand you over to the constable, and the constable throw you into prison. I say to you, you will not be released until you have paid the last penny."

REFLECTION

We live in the information age. We have more facts, figures, and data available to us now than at any other time. Every day there are new tools to help us find and manage this information. Many of us pride ourselves on knowing the smallest details of certain areas: business, investing, sports, etc. Today our Lord asks us to use the same kind of energy, know-how, and enthusiasm to look after our souls. We are here for a short time; we also need to be concerned about eternity.

PRAYERS   *others may be added*

Turning to the Just Judge, we pray:

◆ God, receive our prayer.

For the grace of right judgment, especially at crucial moments, we pray: ◆ *For the virtue of patience, especially when we are attacked, we pray:* ◆ *For the gift of hope, especially when faced with dilemmas, we pray:* ◆ *For the quality of enthusiasm, especially when we are tired, we pray:* ◆

Our Father . . .

Lord God,
guide us as you guide creation
in accord with your love.
May we see what you want us
    to treasure
and ignore the allure of
    passing riches,
so that we may be united with you in
    the kingdom.
We ask this through Christ our Lord.
    Amen.

✝ *Lord, you have the words of everlasting life.*

✚ *Lord, you have the words of everlasting life.*

PSALM 19 *page 405*

READING *Luke 13:1–9*

Some people told Jesus about the Galileans whose blood Pilate had mingled with the blood of their sacrifices. He said to them in reply, "Do you think that because these Galileans suffered in this way they were greater sinners than all other Galileans? By no means! But I tell you, if you do not repent, you will all perish as they did! Or those eighteen people who were killed when the tower at Siloam fell on them— do you think they were more guilty than everyone else who lived in Jerusalem? By no means! But I tell you, if you do not repent, you will all perish as they did!"

And he told them this parable: "There once was a person who had a fig tree planted in his orchard, and when he came in search of fruit on it but found none, he said to the gardener, 'For three years now I have come in search of fruit on this fig tree but have found none. So cut it down. Why should it exhaust the soil?' He said to him in reply, 'Sir, leave it for this year also, and I shall cultivate the ground around it and fertilize it; it may bear fruit in the future. If not you can cut it down.' "

REFLECTION

In business, the question is, what's the bottom line; did we make a profit? In science, the question is, does the experiment prove the hypothesis? In faith, the question is, does your belief bear good fruit; are you more Christ-like? Jesus brings us the Good News that he is the gardener come to fertilize and cultivate us. But, there is a day of reckoning; we must bear the fruits of faith, which are acts of love and selflessness. Are we ready for the harvest?

PRAYERS *others may be added*

In faith, we pray:

◆ God, receive our prayer.

That our faith may blossom into acts of mercy and love, we pray: ◆ That our hope may encourage others, we pray: ◆ That our love may grow like a watered garden, we pray: ◆ That our suffering may be redemptive, we pray: ◆

Our Father . . .

Lord,
you have planted us
amid a world of uncertainty.
May we grow and bear the fruit of
saving acts of love.
We ask this through Christ our Lord.
    Amen.

✚ *Lord, you have the words of everlasting life.*

✠ *Lord, you have the words of*
   everlasting life.

PSALM 19   *page 405*

READING   *Luke 18:9–14*

Jesus addressed this parable to those
who were convinced of their own righteousness and despised everyone else.
"Two people went up to the temple
area to pray; one was a Pharisee and
the other was a tax collector. The
Pharisee took up his position and
spoke this prayer to himself, 'O God,
I thank you that I am not like the
rest of humanity—greedy, dishonest,
adulterous—or even like this tax collector. I fast twice a week, and I pay
tithes on my whole income.' But the
tax collector stood off at a distance and
would not even raise his eyes to
heaven but beat his breast and prayed,
'O God, be merciful to me a sinner.' I
tell you, the latter went home justified,
not the former; for whoever exalts
himself will be humbled, and the one
who humbles himself will be exalted."

REFLECTION

Humility is truth; or more correctly, humil-
ity is admitting the truth of who I am,
especially in relation to God. In today's
Gospel the tax collector acknowledges
himself as a sinner and asks for forgive-
ness. He offers no excuses and he knows
that only God can forgive his sins. He is
humble. The Pharisee accurately recounts
his religious practices, but he seems to
think he has accomplished all this on his
own. Worse, he judges the tax collector. All

our goodness is a gift from God. All for-
giveness is a gift from God. Knowing this
is true humility.

PRAYERS   *others may be added*

   In humility, we pray:

◆ God, receive our prayer.

That ordained ministers and all the
faithful may grow in humility and holiness,
we pray: ◆ *That we may be mindful*
of the wonders you work for and through
us, we pray: ◆ *That all Christians may*
readily ask for forgiveness, we pray: ◆
That the dead may be exalted in your
kingdom, we pray: ◆

Our Father . . .

Father,
you shed light on our true selves
and illumine our way to the kingdom.
Give us eyes to see your glory and
     our lowliness,
and may we acknowledge our debt to
     you in all things.
We ask this through our Lord Jesus
     Christ, your Son,
who lives and reigns with you in the
     unity of the Holy Spirit,
one God, forever and ever. Amen.

✠ *Lord, you have the words of*
   everlasting life.

✠ *Lord, you have the words of everlasting life.*

PSALM 19   *page 405*

READING   *Luke 13:10–17*

Jesus was teaching in a synagogue on the sabbath. And a woman was there who for eighteen years had been crippled by a spirit; she was bent over, completely incapable of standing erect. When Jesus saw her, he called to her and said, "Woman, you are set free of your infirmity." He laid his hands on her, and she at once stood up straight and glorified God. But the leader of the synagogue, indignant that Jesus had cured on the sabbath, said to the crowd in reply, "There are six days when work should be done. Come on those days to be cured, not on the sabbath day." The Lord said to him in reply, "Hypocrites! Does not each one of you on the sabbath untie his ox or his ass from the manger and lead it out for watering? This daughter of Abraham, whom Satan has bound for eighteen years now, ought she not to have been set free on the sabbath day from this bondage?" When he said this, all his adversaries were humiliated; and the whole crowd rejoiced at all the splendid deeds done by him.

REFLECTION

The devil is in the details. The crippled woman in today's Gospel was bent over, unable to stand erect. When someone is bent over, she or he looks at herself or himself all the time. One who stands erect
looks at others and can look up to God. This healing on the sabbath was justified in that it allowed the woman to do what the Sabbath was created for—worship of God and focusing on others. Christianity is other focused. Jesus has come to help us stand erect and look out at all that surrounds us.*

PRAYERS   *others may be added*

Standing upright, we pray:

◆ God, receive our prayer.

That Christians may look out for the needs of those around them, we pray: ◆
That the sick may be relieved of their ills so that they may actively work to further the Gospel, we pray: ◆ *That health-care workers continue their saving work inspired by the Lord, we pray:* ◆ *That we may keep the Lord's Day holy in spirit and action, we pray:* ◆

Our Father . . .

God of power,
you endowed humanity with
    the dignity
of your likeness and image.
Send us the Holy Spirit to inspire
    us to
maintain a posture worthy of
    your creation
so that we may accomplish your will.
We ask this through Christ our Lord.
    Amen.

✠ *Lord, you have the words of everlasting life.*

✛ *Lord, you have the words of everlasting life.*

PSALM 19 *page 405*

READING *Luke 13:18–21*

Jesus said, "What is the Kingdom of God like? To what can I compare it? It is like a mustard seed that a man took and planted in the garden. When it was fully grown, it became a large bush and *the birds of the sky dwelt in its branches.*"

Again he said, "To what shall I compare the Kingdom of God? It is like yeast that a woman took and mixed in with three measures of wheat flour until the whole batch of dough was leavened."

REFLECTION *Ann M. Garrido*

The kingdom of God, Jesus said, is like a mustard seed—"the smallest seed of all." If you have ever held one of these tiny seeds on the tip of your finger, you must know what he means. Unlike their American counterparts, mustard seeds from the land of Palestine are no larger than a fleck of pepper. And yet, they grow to such a size that the "birds of the sky" come to build nests in their branches. How could this be? How could something this small carry such energy and power within it?

PRAYERS *others may be added*

Awed at the power of love, we pray:

◆ God, receive our prayer.

That all will find a home in the sheltering branches of the Church, we pray: ◆ *That our tiny acts of kindness may sprout into endless living vines of love, we pray:* ◆ *That our faith may act as a leaven of righteousness in today's society, we pray:* ◆ *That all may have unwavering confidence in the promises of God, we pray:* ◆

Our Father . . .

Lord God,
you are the sower and we are
the seeds;
all the good that we do and
accomplish
is inspired by the Holy Spirit.
Fill us with confidence and fervor
so that we may continue to spread
your kingdom
one loving act at a time.
Grant this in the name of Jesus the
Lord. Amen.

✛ *Lord, you have the words of everlasting life.*

✝ *Lord, you have the words of everlasting life.*

PSALM 19   page 405

READING   Luke 13:22–30

Jesus passed through towns and villages, teaching as he went and making his way to Jerusalem. Someone asked him, "Lord, will only a few people be saved?" He answered them, "Strive to enter through the narrow gate, for many, I tell you, will attempt to enter but will not be strong enough. After the master of the house has arisen and locked the door, then will you stand outside knocking and saying, 'Lord, open the door for us.' He will say to you in reply, 'I do not know where you are from.' And you will say, 'We ate and drank in your company and you taught in our streets.' Then he will say to you, 'I do not know where you are from. Depart from me, all you evil-doers!' And there will be wailing and grinding of teeth when you see Abraham, Isaac, and Jacob and all the prophets in the Kingdom of God and you yourselves cast out. And people will come from the east and the west and from the north and the south and will recline at table in the Kingdom of God. For behold, some are last who will be first, and some are first who will be last."

REFLECTION

"Strive!" Today's Gospel message is simple enough, but has enormous implications. No one will enter the kingdom by mistake, by randomly strolling in. Strive; work at it; put muscle into your efforts. We have all received the invitation, we are all welcome. However, we must make the decision to follow Christ and accept the help of the Holy Spirit. We are not alone; we have all the help we need, but we must strive to enter through the narrow gate. Today and always, let us strive!

PRAYERS   *others may be added*

Striving, we pray:

◆ God, receive our prayer.

For the growth of the Church, we pray: ◆ For a greater participation in the sacraments, we pray: ◆ For a heightened sense of vigor in our lives of faith, we pray: ◆ For the salvation of the dead, we pray: ◆

Our Father . . .

Almighty Father,
you call us through your Son
and empower us with your grace.
Assist us in our efforts to cooperate
with the Holy Spirit,
and bring us home to you on the
    last day.
We ask this through Christ our Lord.
    Amen.

✝ *Lord, you have the words of everlasting life.*

✠ *Lord, this is the people that longs to see your face.*

PSALM 27   *page 408*

READING   *Matthew 5:1–12a*

When Jesus saw the crowds, he went up the mountain, and after he had sat down, his disciples came to him. He began to teach them, saying:

"Blessed are the poor in spirit,/for theirs is the Kingdom of heaven./ Blessed are they who mourn,/for they will be comforted./Blessed are the meek,/for they will inherit the land./ Blessed are they who hunger and thirst for righteousness,/for they will be satisfied./Blessed are the merciful,/for they will be shown mercy./Blessed are the clean of heart,/for they will see God./Blessed are the peacemakers,/ for they will be called children of God./ Blessed are they who are persecuted for the sake of righteousness,/for theirs is the Kingdom of heaven./Blessed are you when they insult you and persecute you/and utter every kind of evil against you falsely because of me./ Rejoice and be glad, for your reward will be great in heaven."

REFLECTION

Today, on the solemnity of All Saints, we celebrate with those who have gone before us in holiness. Those who stand before the throne of God intercede for us, serving as a "cloud of witnesses" to Christ's love, pointing to the redemption that we too will one day share. May these martyrs and virgins, aesthetics and missionaries, married

and single, clergy, religious and lay, all holy men and women, pray for us as we continue our journey to Christ.

PRAYERS   *others may be added*

United in Christ, we pray:

◆ Saints of God, pray for us.

May the Pope, clergy, religious, and the laity live lives of holiness, we pray: ◆
That we may understand and live the true spirit of the Gospel, we pray: ◆
That we may look to the example of the countless souls who have gone before us and persevere to our last day, we pray: ◆
That the world may be transformed by the saintly lives of Christians, we pray: ◆

Our Father . . .

Lord God,
you grant the gift of holiness to all who will accept it.
Inspire us by the example and prayers
    of your saints
to live the Gospel in our daily lives.
We ask this through our Lord Jesus
    Christ, your Son,
who lives and reigns with you in the
    unity of the Holy Spirit,
one God, forever and ever. Amen.

✠ *Lord, this is the people that longs to see your face.*

✝ *I believe that I shall see the good things of the Lord in the land of the living.*

PSALM 27 *page 408*

READING *John 6:37–40*

Jesus said to the crowds: "Everything that the Father gives me will come to me, and I will not reject anyone who comes to me, because I came down from heaven not to do my own will but the will of the one who sent me. And this is the will of the one who sent me, that I should not lose anything of what he gave me, but that I should raise it on the last day. For this is the will of my Father, that everyone who sees the Son and believes in him may have eternal life, and I shall raise him on the last day."

REFLECTION *St. Ambrose*

We see that death is gain, life is loss. Paul says: For me life is Christ, and death a gain. *What does* Christ *mean but to die in the body, and receive the breath of life? Let us then die with Christ, to live with Christ. We should have a daily familiarity with death, a daily desire for death. By this kind of detachment our soul must learn to free itself from the desires of the body. It must soar above earthly lusts to a place where they cannot come near, to hold it fast. It must take on the likeness of death, to avoid the punishment of death. The law of our fallen nature is at war with the law of our reason and subjects the law of reason to the law of error. What is the remedy? Who will set me free me from this* dead body? The grace of God, through Jesus Christ our Lord.

PRAYERS *others may be added*

Remembering the mercy of God, we pray:

◆ Lord, hear our prayer.

That all of God's children may receive is gift of life through his consolation and love, we pray: ◆ *That we may be granted forgiveness, through God's mercy and kindness, we pray:* ◆ *That all who have died may receive eternal light and joy, we pray:* ◆

Our Father . . .

Lord God,
hope of humanity,
all the faithful departed look to you
as their final joy.
Be merciful to us sinners
and help us to remain faithful,
so that we, along with all the souls
   in purgatory
may see your glory.
We ask this through Christ our Lord.
   Amen.

✝ *I believe that I shall see the good things of the Lord in the land of the living.*

✢ *Lord, you have the words of everlasting life.*

PSALM 19   page 405

READING   Luke 14:1,7–11

On a sabbath Jesus went to dine at the home of one of the leading Pharisees, and the people there were observing him carefully.

He told a parable to those who had been invited, noticing how they were choosing the places of honor at the table. "When you are invited by someone to a wedding banquet, do not recline at table in the place of honor. A more distinguished guest than you may have been invited by him, and the host who invited both of you may approach you and say, 'Give your place to this man.' and then you would proceed with embarrassment to take the lowest place. Rather, when you are invited, go and take the lowest place so that when the host comes to you he may say, 'My friend, move up to a higher position.' Then you will enjoy the esteem of your companions at the table. For everyone who exalts himself will be humbled, but the one who humbles himself will be exalted."

REFLECTION

Today we honor St. Martin de Porres, a Dominican lay brother of mixed race. His fellow religious held him in high esteem because of his care of the poor and his other works of mercy. But Martin remained humble, even using negative words to describe himself. No one can foster good relations of any kind if he or she thinks too highly of himself or herself. It is only humble people, like St. Martin de Porres, who can truly bring the justice and mercy of God to this world.

PRAYERS   others may be added

Through the intercession of St. Martin de Porres, we pray:

◆ Lord, hear our prayer.

For racial harmony, we pray: ◆
For increased concern and care for the world's poor, we pray: ◆ *For those who perform works of mercy, we pray:* ◆
For humbleness of heart and action, we pray: ◆

Our Father . . .

Loving God,
you exalted the humble
Martin de Porres
by granting him a place in
your kingdom.
Assist us to follow his example of
    service and humility
so that we, too, may one day share in
    your kingdom.
We ask this through Christ our Lord.
    Amen.

✢ *Lord, you have the words of everlasting life.*

✝ *Lord, you have the words of everlasting life.*

PSALM 19 *page 405*

READING *Luke 19:1-10*

At that time, Jesus came to Jericho and intended to pass through the town. Now a man there named Zacchaeus, who was a chief tax collector and also a wealthy man, was seeking to see who Jesus was; but he could not see him because of the crowd, for he was short in stature. So he ran ahead and climbed a sycamore tree in order to see Jesus, who was about to pass that way. When he reached the place, Jesus looked up and said, "Zacchaeus, come down quickly, for today I must stay at your house." And he came down quickly and received him with joy. When they all saw this, they began to grumble, saying, "He has gone to stay at the house of a sinner." But Zacchaeus stood there and said to the Lord, "Behold, half of my possessions, Lord, I shall give to the poor, and if I have extorted anything from anyone I shall repay it four times over." And Jesus said to him, "Today salvation has come to this house because this man too is a descendant of Abraham. For the Son of Man has come to seek and to save what was lost."

REFLECTION

Jesus and Zacchaeus seem to be trying to outdo each other in generosity. Zacchaeus offers the better part of his fortune to the poor, and Jesus offers salvation to a public sinner. Our God cannot be outdone in generosity. There is no need to try; we are too short to stand up to God. However, we are invited to give hospitality to all who cross our paths and to emulate the profound giving nature of our God.

PRAYERS *others may be added*

With giving hearts, we pray:

◆ Lord, hear our prayer.

That we may strive to overcome the obstacles preventing us from following the Lord Jesus, we pray: ◆ *That Christians may be known by their generosity of heart, we pray:* ◆ *That we may be willing to offer the love of God to all we meet, we pray:* ◆ *That we may recognize our need for the salvation offered by God, we pray:* ◆

Our Father . . .

Almighty God,
you shower us with your
    bountiful grace
and fill us with your love.
May we accept your gifts in humility
and work to help all realize the
    wonders of salvation.
We ask this through our Lord Jesus
    Christ, your Son,
who lives and reigns with you in the
    unity of the Holy Spirit,
one God, forever and ever. Amen.

✝ *Lord, you have the words of everlasting life.*

✚ *Lord, you have the words of everlasting life.*

PSALM 19   page 405

READING   Luke 14:12–14

On a sabbath Jesus went to dine at the home of one of the leading Pharisees. He said to the host who invited him, "When you hold a lunch or a dinner, do not invite your friends or your brothers or sisters or your relatives or your wealthy neighbors, in case they may invite you back and you have repayment. Rather, when you hold a banquet, invite the poor, the crippled, the lame, the blind; blessed indeed will you be because of their inability to repay you. For you will be repaid at the resurrection of the righteous."

REFLECTION

There is a piece of common wisdom, which says that often it is the oppressed who become the oppressors. Victims often resort to victimizing others. This vengeful reaction is counter to the way of the Gospel. Jesus invites us to follow his lead and reverse the vicious cycle of sin. We have been invited to the Lord's Eucharistic table; we who were sinners have been saved from our sinful ways. We who have experienced the hospitality and forgiveness of God are asked in return to offer our bounty to those in need.

PRAYERS   others may be added

Reaching out to those in need, we pray:

◆ Lord, hear our prayer.

That our participation in the sacraments may lead us to greater concern for those who are in need, we pray: ◆ *That we may satisfy our inner hungers by sharing in God's word, we pray:* ◆ *That we may be shown support in our efforts to embody the meaning of the Gospel, we pray:* ◆ *That the dead may be brought into the fulfillment of the eternal banquet, we pray:* ◆

Our Father . . .

God of glory,
you give us a glimpse of your
    heavenly banquet
in the Eucharistic celebration.
May we be inspired by your generous
    gift of salvation
to lift up the downtrodden,
to heal the wounded,
and to feed the hungry.
We ask this through Christ our Lord.
    Amen.

✚ *Lord, you have the words of everlasting life.*

✤ *Lord, you have the words of everlasting life.*

PSALM 19   page 405

READING   Luke 14:15–24

One of those at table with Jesus said to him, "Blessed is the one who will dine in the Kingdom of God." He replied to him, "A man gave a great dinner to which he invited many. When the time for the dinner came, he dispatched his servant to say to those invited, 'Come, everything is now ready.' But one by one, they all began to excuse themselves. The first said to him, 'I have purchased a field and must go to examine it; I ask you, consider me excused.' And another said, 'I have purchased five yoke of oxen and am on my way to evaluate them; I ask you, consider me excused.' And another said, 'I have just married a woman, and therefore I cannot come.' The servant went and reported this to his master. Then the master of the house in a rage commanded his servant, 'Go out quickly into the streets and alleys of the town and bring in here the poor and the crippled, the blind and the lame.' The servant reported, 'Sir, your orders have been carried out and still there is room.' The master then ordered the servant, 'Go out to the highways and hedgerows and make people come in that my home may be filled. For, I tell you, none of those men who were invited will taste my dinner.' "

REFLECTION

We have each received the greatest invitation that could ever be offered: salvation. So very often we offer excuses not to accept this gift, but excuses as lame as those offered in today's Gospel: I can't go to church because I have shopping to do; I can't volunteer my time because I have gardening to do; I can't help out the homeless because I'll be late for my luncheon appointment. It doesn't make sense. We have been called, we have been invited, we have begged. Let us go and dine in the kingdom of God.

PRAYERS   others may be added

Accepting the Lord's invitation, we pray:

◆ Lord, hear our prayer.

For the poor and needy, we pray: ◆
For the sick and elderly, we pray: ◆
For peace in our homes, we pray: ◆
For the acceptance of God's call, we pray: ◆

Our Father . . .

Lord,
you are the joy of all who know you.
Help us to hear your word, answer your call,
and share your love,
so that all may rejoice in your presence.
Grant this through Christ our Lord. Amen.

✤ *Lord, you have the words of everlasting life.*

✝ *Lord, you have the words of everlasting life.*

PSALM 19   page 405

READING   Luke 14:25–33

Great crowds were traveling with Jesus, and he turned and addressed them, "If anyone comes to me without hating his father and mother, wife and children, brothers and sisters, and even his own life, he cannot be my disciple. Whoever does not carry his own cross and come after me cannot be my disciple. Which of you wishing to construct a tower does not first sit down and calculate the cost to see if there is enough for its completion? Otherwise, after laying the foundation and finding himself unable to finish the work the onlookers should laugh at him and say, 'This one began to build but did not have the resources to finish.' Or what king marching into battle would not first sit down and decide whether with ten thousand troops he can successfully oppose another king advancing upon him with twenty thousand troops? But if not, while he is still far away, he will send a delegation to ask for peace terms. In the same way, everyone of you who does not renounce all his possessions cannot be my disciple."

REFLECTION

Today, Jesus invites us to take up our cross and follow him. Each of us needs to answer the following questions: Am I ready to give what it takes to be a true follower of Christ? Am I ready to bear the weight of the burden it may bring? Have I laid the proper foundation for my life? Have I spent time in prayer? Have I read scripture? Have I studied my faith? Am I ready to accept the strength offered to me through grace? Will I accept my cross? With the help of God we can overcome any obstacle.

PRAYERS   others may be added

Looking to the Lord, we pray:

◆ Lord, hear our prayer.

That Church leaders may stay true to their calling, we pray: ◆ *That civic leaders may work for the common good, we pray:* ◆ *That Christians may remain steady on the path of discipleship, we pray:* ◆ *That the faithful departed may share in the Resurrection, we pray:* ◆

Our Father . . .

God of wisdom,
you sent your Son to bring us
    everlasting love.
Through the working of the
    Holy Spirit,
may we accept the grace you offer us
and be present in the world as faithful
    followers of the Gospel.
We ask this through Christ our Lord.
    Amen.

✝ *Lord, you have the words of everlasting life.*

✠ *Lord, you have the words of everlasting life.*

PSALM 19 *page 405*

READING *Luke 15:1–10*

The tax collectors and sinners were all drawing near to listen to Jesus, but the Pharisees and scribes began to complain, saying, "This man welcomes sinners and eats with them." So Jesus addressed this parable to them. "What man among you having a hundred sheep and losing one of them would not leave the ninety-nine in the desert and go after the lost one until he finds it? And when he does find it, he sets it on his shoulders with great joy and, upon his arrival home, he calls together his friends and neighbors and says to them, 'Rejoice with me because I have found my lost sheep.' I tell you, in just the same way there will be more joy in heaven over one sinner who repents than over ninety-nine righteous people who have no need of repentance.

"Or what woman having ten coins and losing one would not light a lamp and sweep the house, searching carefully until she finds it? And when she does find it, she calls together her friends and neighbors and says to them, 'Rejoice with me because I have found the coin that I lost.' In just the same way, I tell you, there will be rejoicing among the angels of God over one sinner who repents."

REFLECTION

The people Jesus associated with, his actions, and sayings all caused people to wonder what he was up to. Jesus often did the unexpected. He did these things to bring his message into focus and to accomplish his task. There is no greater act than revealing the love of the Father to the world. As followers of Christ, we too are charged with the same responsibility. We need to ask ourselves if our associations, our actions, and our words truly give witness to the Father's love.

PRAYERS *others may be added*

With conviction, we pray:

◆ Lord, hear our prayer.

For those who are lost, we pray: ◆
For the needy and destitute, we pray: ◆
For the gift of repentance, we pray: ◆
For the grace to be faithful followers of Christ, we pray: ◆

Our Father . . .

Almighty God,
our hope and our strength,
without you we falter.
Help us to follow Christ
and to live according to your will.
We ask this through Christ our Lord.

✠ *Lord, you have the words of everlasting life.*

✚ *Lord, you have the words of*
everlasting life.

PSALM 19 *page 405*

READING *John 2:13–22*

Since the Passover of the Jews was near, Jesus went up to Jerusalem. He found in the temple area those who sold oxen, sheep, and doves, as well as the money-changers seated there. He made a whip out of cords and drove them all out of the temple area, with the sheep and oxen, and spilled the coins of the money-changers and overturned their tables, and to those who sold doves he said, "Take these out of here, and stop making my Father's house a marketplace." His disciples recalled the words of Scripture, *Zeal for your house will consume me.* At this the Jews answered and said to him, "What sign can you show us for doing this?" Jesus answered and said to them, "Destroy this temple and in three days I will raise it up." The Jews said, "This temple has been under construction for forty-six years, and you will raise it up in three days?" But he was speaking about the temple of his Body. Therefore, when he was raised from the dead, his disciples remembered that he had said this, and they came to believe the Scripture and the word Jesus had spoken.

REFLECTION

Today we celebrate the dedication of the cathedral church of Rome. It is considered the ecumenical Mother Church of all *Catholic churches throughout the world. But let us not make the same mistake as the Jewish officials in today's Gospel. More important than the physical structure of our worship space is the fact that we are a living temple, a living church; we are part of the risen body of Christ. Let us not sully that body with actions that will need to be cleansed by the wrath of Christ.*

PRAYERS *others may be added*

As the Church of Christ, we pray:

◆ Lord, hear our prayer.

For purity of heart, we pray: ◆
For sincerity, we pray: ◆ *For zealous faith, we pray:* ◆ *For reverence of the Lord and his people, we pray:* ◆

Our Father . . .

God,
how wonderful is your
dwelling place.
May we be found worthy
to be the building stones of
your temple of glory
in a world darkened by sin.
We ask this through Christ our Lord.
Amen.

✚ *Lord, you have the words of*
everlasting life.

✦ *Lord, you have the words of everlasting life.*

PSALM 19   page 405

READING   Luke 16:9–15

Jesus said to his disciples: "I tell you, make friends for yourselves with dishonest wealth, so that when it fails, you will be welcomed into eternal dwellings. The person who is trustworthy in very small matters is also trustworthy in great ones; and the person who is dishonest in very small matters is also dishonest in great ones. If, therefore, you are not trustworthy with dishonest wealth, who will trust you with true wealth? If you are not trustworthy with what belongs to another, who will give you what is yours? No servant can serve two masters. He will either hate one and love the other, or be devoted to one and despise the other. You cannot serve God and mammon."

The Pharisees who loved money, heard all these things and sneered at him. And he said to them, "You justify yourselves in the sight of others, but God knows your hearts; for what is of human esteem is an abomination in the sight of God."

REFLECTION

St. Leo (+461) is one of two popes known as "the Great." His greatness was apparent in many areas. In the political arena, he confronted Attila the Hun and persuaded him not to destroy Rome. In Church matters, he convincingly stated and defended
the notion that the Pope was the successor of St. Peter. And, theologically, he strongly defended the belief that Christ was both fully human and fully divine. This servant of the servants of God served only one master and left for us a worthy example.

PRAYERS   *others may be added*

Through the intercession of St. Leo the Great, we pray:

◆ Lord, hear our prayer.

That our Pope and all the bishops may be inspired by the example of St. Leo, we pray: ◆ *That political leaders will avert strife and discord, we pray:* ◆ *That theologians and religious educators may protect the truth of Christ, we pray:* ◆ *That Christians may serve Christ as the one master, we pray:* ◆

Our Father . . .

O God,
you bless your Church with leaders
worthy to serve you alone.
May we strive to serve all
with the same spirit that animated
St. Leo the Great and one day
    be joined
in your kingdom forever.
We ask this through Christ our Lord.
    Amen.

✦ *Lord, you have the words of everlasting life.*

✦ *I will bless the Lord at all times.*

PSALM 34 *page 410*

READING *Luke 20:27, 34–38*

Some Sadducees, those who deny that there is a resurrection, came forward.

Jesus said to them, "The children of this age marry and remarry; but those who are deemed worthy to attain to the coming age and to the resurrection of the dead neither marry nor are given in marriage. They can no longer die, for they are like angels; and they are the children of God because they are the ones who will rise. That the dead will rise even Moses made known in the passage about the bush, when he called out 'Lord,' the God of Abraham, the God of Isaac, and the God of Jacob; and he is not God of the dead, but of the living, for to him all are alive."

REFLECTION *St. Bernard*

He has given his angels charge over you to guard you in all your ways. Let them thank the Lord for his mercy; his wonderful works are for the children of men. Let them give thanks and say among the nations, the Lord has done great things for them. O Lord, what is man that you have made yourself known to him, or why do you incline your heart to him? And you do incline your heart to him; you show him your care and your concern. Finally, you send your only Son and the grace of your Spirit, and promise him a vision of your countenance. And so, that nothing in heaven should be wanting in your concern for us, you send those blessed spirits to serve us, assigning them as our guardians and our teachers.

PRAYERS *others may be added*

With faith in our God, we pray:

◆ Lord, we trust in you.

That widows and widowers may be solaced in their grief, we pray: ◆ *That orphans and refugees may be given care and shelter, we pray:* ◆ *That the angels and saints may protect us always, we pray,* ◆ *That the faithful departed may find rest in God, we pray:* ◆

Our Father . . .

Loving God,
you have granted us eternal life
    through your Son.
May we proclaim your salvation to
    the whole world,
that all might believe
and share in your heavenly
kingdom forever,
singing your praise in the company of
    all the angels and saints.
We ask this through our Lord Jesus
    Christ, your Son,
who lives and reigns with you in the
    unity of the Holy Spirit,
one God, forever and ever. Amen.

✦ *I will bless the Lord at all times.*

✠ *I will bless the Lord at all times.*

PSALM 34 *page 410*

READING *Luke 17:1–6*

Jesus said to his disciples, "Things that cause sin will inevitably occur, but woe to the one through whom they occur. It would be better for him if a millstone were put around his neck and he be thrown into the sea than for him to cause one of these little ones to sin. Be on your guard! If your brother sins, rebuke him; and if he repents, forgive him. And if he wrongs you seven times in one day and returns to you seven times saying, 'I am sorry,' you should forgive him."

And the Apostles said to the Lord, "Increase our faith." The Lord replied, "If you have faith the size of a mustard seed, you would say to this mulberry tree, 'Be uprooted and planted in the sea,' and it would obey you."

REFLECTION

St. Josaphat (1580–+1623) was a man who worked tirelessly for the healing of the divisions between Eastern and Western Christianity. As a Ukrainian, Josaphat was part of the Eastern or Byzantine tradition. He became a monk, was ordained a priest, and ultimately became an archbishop. St. Josaphat instituted many reforms, and in doing so also made some enemies. He was martyred for his attempts to bring the Ukrainian Church in union with Rome. May St. Josaphat's example of reconciliation inspire us to follow the Gospel in ardent faith.

PRAYERS *others may be added*

Through the intercession of St. Josaphat, we pray:

◆ Lord, we trust in you.

That Christians of the East and the West may pray for and work toward unity, we pray: ◆ *That all may grow in knowledge and appreciation of the many expressions of the faith, we pray:* ◆ *That the Church may be a living witness of forgiveness and faithfulness, we pray:* ◆

Our Father . . .

O God,
you are the source of all unity.
Through the prayers and example of
    St. Josaphat,
may the Church work tirelessly to end
    the divisions
that mar the unity Christ gives to
    the world.
In his name, we pray. Amen.

✠ *I will bless the Lord at all times.*

✠ *I will bless the Lord at all times.*

PSALM 34 *page 410*

READING *Luke 17:7–10*

Jesus said to the Apostles: "Who among you would say to your servant who has just come in from plowing or tending sheep in the field, 'Come here immediately and take your place at table'? Would he not rather say to him, 'Prepare something for me to eat. Put on your apron and wait on me while I eat and drink. You may eat and drink when I am finished'? Is he grateful to that servant because he did what was commanded? So should it be with you. When you have done all you have been commanded, say, 'We are unprofitable servants; we have done what we were obliged to do.' "

REFLECTION

Mother Cabrini (1850–+1917), born in Italy, was the first United States citizen canonized to be a saint. Having founded the Missionary Sisters of the Sacred Heart, she was specifically asked by Pope Leo XIII to start a mission to the Italian immigrants in the United States. Arriving in New York in 1889, Mother Cabrini founded a substantial number of hospitals and orphanages throughout the United States before her death. She traveled and worked tirelessly for the poor. St. Frances Xavier Cabrini gives us a fine example of obedience to the will of God, an obedience that does not expect high praise.

PRAYERS *others may be added*

Looking to the Sacred Heart of Jesus, we pray:

◆ Lord, we trust in you.

That the missionary efforts of the Church may bring hope to all, we pray: ◆
That our care for the homeless and refugees may be inspired by love, we pray: ◆ *That those who care for the ill and dying may give witness to the healing touch of Christ, we pray:* ◆
That all immigrants may find hospitality in their new homelands, we pray: ◆

Our Father . . .

God of all nations,
you are present in all lands
and at all times.
Through the intercession of
    St. Frances Cabrini,
may all the downcast of the
    world find
loving hearts to care for them
and be led to their heavenly
    homeland.
We ask this through Christ our Lord.
    Amen.

✠ *I will bless the Lord at all times.*

✛ *I will bless the Lord at all times.*

PSALM 34 *page 410*

READING *Luke 17:11–19*

As Jesus continued his journey to Jerusalem, he traveled through Samaria and Galilee. As he was entering a village, ten lepers met him. They stood at a distance from him and raised their voice, saying, "Jesus, Master! Have pity on us!" And when he saw them, he said, "Go show yourselves to the priests." As they were going they were cleansed. And one of them, realizing he had been healed, returned, glorifying God in a loud voice; and he fell at the feet of Jesus and thanked him. He was a Samaritan. Jesus said in reply, "Ten were cleansed, were they not? Where are the other nine? Has none but this foreigner returned to give thanks to God?" Then he said to him, "Stand up and go; your faith has saved you."

REFLECTION *St. Clement*

Beloved, how blessed and wonderful are God's gifts! There is life everlasting, joy in righteousness, truth in freedom, faith, confidence, and self-control in holiness. And these are the gifts that we can comprehend; what of all the others that are being prepared for those who look to him. Only the Creator, the Father of the ages, the all-holy, knows their grandeur and their loveliness. And so we should strive to be found among those who wait for him so that we may share in these promised gifts. And how is this to be, beloved brothers? It will come about if by our faith our minds remain fixed on God; if we aim at what is pleasing and acceptable to him, if we accomplish what is in harmony with his faultless will and follow the path of truth, rejecting all injustice, viciousness, covetousness, quarrels, malice and deceit.

PRAYERS *others may be added*

With thankful hearts, we pray:

◆ Lord, we trust in you.

For eyes opened to the gifts we have received, we pray: ◆ *For mouths filled with thanks and praise to God, we pray:* ◆ *For souls filled with faith, we pray:* ◆ *For lives that proclaim the wonders of our God, we pray:* ◆

Our Father . . .

God of all creation,
the universe is only a small sign of
    your creative power.
As you surround us with the wonders
    of your might,
may we be filled with a sense of
    marvel and awe
and exude boundless faith in your
    endless love.
We ask this through Christ our Lord.
    Amen.

✛ *I will bless the Lord at all times.*

✦ *I will bless the Lord at all times.*

PSALM 34 *page 410*

READING *Luke 17:20–25*

Asked by the Pharisees when the Kingdom of God would come, Jesus said in reply, "The coming of the Kingdom of God cannot be observed, and no one will announce, 'Look, here it is,' or, 'There it is.' For behold, the Kingdom of God is among you."

Then he said to his disciples, "The days will come when you will long to see one of the days of the Son of Man, but you will not see it. There will be those who will say to you, 'Look, there he is,' or 'Look, here he is.' Do not go off, do not run in pursuit. For just as lightning flashes and lights up the sky from one side to the other, so will the Son of Man be in his day. But first he must suffer greatly and be rejected by this generation."

REFLECTION

St. Albert the Great (1200–+1280) was a Dominican as was his student St. Thomas Aquinas. While perhaps lesser known than his famous student, whom he outlived, St. Albert was no less a genius and great theologian. His reputation for wisdom and holiness was widely recognized in his time; his contemporaries giving him the name, "the Great." It is in people such as St. Albert and St. Thomas that the coming of the kingdom can be seen. May we, too, be harbingers of the Son of Man.

PRAYERS *others may be added*

Proclaiming God's kingdom, we pray:

◆ Lord, we trust in you.

That people of learning will put their knowledge to God's work, we pray: ◆
That doctors and scientists may respect God's gift of life, we pray: ◆
That teachers may be devoted to the growth of their students, we pray: ◆
That theologians will foster loving unity in the Church, we pray: ◆

Our Father . . .

Lord God,
you are the source and summit of
    all knowledge.
In the midst of our faltering and
    floundering,
send the Holy Spirit to inspire us and
    guide our way
so that we may always be signs of
    your kingdom
in the midst of our world.
Grant this through Christ our Lord.
    Amen.

✦ *I will bless the Lord at all times.*

✦ *I will bless the Lord at all times.*

PSALM 34   page 410

READING   Luke 17:26–37

Jesus said to his disciples: "As it was in the days of Noah, so it will be in the days of the Son of Man; they were eating and drinking, marrying and giving in marriage up to the day that Noah entered the ark, and the flood came and destroyed them all. Similarly, as it was in the days of Lot: they were eating, drinking, buying, selling, planting, building; on the day when Lot left Sodom, fire and brimstone rained from the sky to destroy them all. So it will be on the day the Son of Man is revealed. On that day, someone who is on the housetop and whose belongings are in the house must not go down to get them, and likewise one in the field must not return to what was left behind. Remember the wife of Lot. Whoever seeks to preserve his life will lose it, but whoever loses it will save it. I tell you, on that night there will be two people in one bed; one will be taken, the other left. And there will be two women grinding meal together; one will be taken, the other left." They said to him in reply, "Where, Lord?" He said to them, "Where the body is, there also the vultures will gather."

REFLECTION

Today's saints, Margaret of Scotland (1046–+1093) and Gertrude (1256–+1302), lived centuries apart. One was a queen and one was a Benedictine nun.

These two very different women shared a concern for the kingdom over their personal comfort. They gave up the usual occupations of women to labor for the Lord. St. Margaret provided care for the sick and the poor, while St. Gertrude devoted her life to God as a contemplative nun, having mystical experiences and spreading devotion to the Sacred Heart. Through their examples and prayers, may we always be attentive to the Lord's work.

PRAYERS   others may be added

Seeking the Lord, we pray:

◆ Lord, we trust in you.

For those who care for the sick and poor, we pray: ◆ *For those who offer hospitality to strangers, we pray:* ◆ *For those who teach us to pray, we pray:* ◆ *For those who give witness to holiness, we pray:* ◆

Our Father . . .

O God,
your glory exceeds all we
can imagine.
May your saints inspire us to work
   ceaselessly
for the coming of your kingdom.
We ask this through Christ our Lord.
   Amen.

✦ *I will bless the Lord at all times.*

✛ *I will bless the Lord at all times.*

PSALM 34   page 410

READING   Luke 18:1–8

Jesus told his disciples a parable about the necessity for them to pray always without becoming weary. He said, "There was a judge in a certain town who neither feared God nor respected any human being. And a widow in that town used to come to him and say, 'Render a just decision for me against my adversary.' For a long time the judge was unwilling, but eventually he thought, 'While it is true that I neither fear God nor respect any human being, because this widow keeps bothering me I shall deliver a just decision for her lest she finally come and strike me.'" The Lord said, "Pay attention to what the dishonest judge says. Will not God then secure the rights of his chosen ones who call out to him day and night? Will he be slow to answer them? I tell you, he will see to it that justice is done for them speedily. But when the Son of Man comes, will he find faith on earth?"

REFLECTION

St. Elizabeth of Hungary (1207–+1231) is patron saint of charities. While queen of Hungary, Elizabeth devoted herself to a life of prayer and almsgiving, to the point of establishing a hospital for the poor in her own palace. After her husband's early death, she became a third-order Franciscan and continued her work with the poor. She was canonized only four years after her early death (at age 24). She was a witness to the presence of Christ in the poor she so deeply loved. May we, too, be unrelenting advocates for those in need.

PRAYERS   others may be added

*Through the intercession of
St. Elizabeth of Hungary, we pray:*

◆ Lord, we trust in you.

For world leaders, that they may have deep concern for the underprivileged, we pray: ◆ *For lay men and women, that they may devote themselves to prayer and minister to the needy, we pray:* ◆
For those who mourn, we pray: ◆
For third-order Franciscans, we pray: ◆

Our Father . . .

God of all nations,
you called St. Elizabeth of Hungary
to work for the poor and the sick.
May we be inspired by her example
and led by her prayers to reach out to
     those in need.
We ask this through Christ our Lord.
     Amen.

✛ *I will bless the Lord at all times.*

✚ *I will bless the Lord at all times.*

PSALM 34   *page 410*

READING   *Luke 21:10–19*

He [Jesus] said to them, "Nation will rise against nation, and kingdom against kingdom. There will be powerful earthquakes, famines, and plagues from place to place; and awesome sights and mighty signs will come from the sky.

"Before all this happens, however, they will seize and persecute you, they will hand you over to the synagogues and to prisons, and they will have you led before kings and governors because of my name. It will lead to your giving testimony. Remember, you are not to prepare your defense beforehand, for I myself shall give you a wisdom in speaking that all your adversaries will be powerless to resist or refute. You will even be handed over by parents, brothers, relatives, and friends, and they will put some of you to death. You will be hated by all because of my name, but not a hair on your head will be destroyed. By your perseverance you will secure your lives."

REFLECTION   *Aelred R. Rosser*

There is a subtle form of presumption that afflicts many Christians. They seem to be motivated by the conviction that if they work hard, do the right thing, and avoid the bad thing, then their lives (and the world situation) should "every day, in every way, get better and better." Where this presumption originates is hard to determine, for there are no guarantees or time frames in God's promise to renew the face of the earth. It will happen, but the question of "when" remains unanswered. Times of apparent growth and peace can suddenly be followed by cataclysmic upheaval and disorder. Tragedy is all the more tragic when it strikes at a time of prosperity and apparent predictability.

PRAYERS   *others may be added*

In faith, we pray:

◆ Lord, we trust in you.

For those suffering from the effects of natural disasters, we pray: ◆ *For those afflicted by religious or political persecutions, we pray:* ◆ *For those abandoned by family and friends, we pray:* ◆ *For those caught up in the strife of war, we pray:* ◆

Our Father . . .

Almighty God,
you rule over the universe
with mercy and love.
May we acknowledge your might
and proclaim your goodness as we
    await the day
when all creation glorifies your name.
We ask this through our Lord Jesus
    Christ, your Son,
who lives and reigns with you in the
    unity of the Holy Spirit,
one God, forever and ever. Amen.

✚ *I will bless the Lord at all times.*

MONDAY, 19 NOVEMBER 2007
WEEKDAY

✙ *I will bless the Lord at all times.*

PSALM 34 *page 410*

READING *Luke 18:35–43*

As Jesus approached Jericho a blind man was sitting by the roadside begging, and hearing a crowd going by, he inquired what was happening. They told him, "Jesus of Nazareth is passing by." He shouted, "Jesus, Son of David, have pity on me!" The people walking in front rebuked him, telling him to be silent, but he kept calling out all the more, "Son of David, have pity on me!" Then Jesus stopped and ordered that he be brought to him; and when he came near, Jesus asked him, "What do you want me to do for you?" He replied, "Lord, please let me see." Jesus told him, "Have sight; your faith has saved you." He immediately received his sight and followed him, giving glory to God. When they saw this, all the people gave praise to God.

REFLECTION

"What do you want me to do for you?" How would I answer that question?

It would have been so easy for the blind man to ask for money or food, but he went out on a limb and asked for healing. He took the blind leap of faith. We are invited to do the same. How do I need to be healed? Christ is waiting to work his miracles on us; we only need say the word. We only have to ask and we will be healed.

PRAYERS *others may be added*

Asking for God's help, we pray:

◆ Lord, we trust in you.

That preachers of the Gospel may bring the healing word of God to the world, we pray: ◆ *That we may have the faith to approach God in confidence, we pray:* ◆ *That people of faith will ignore discouragement and scorn, we pray:* ◆ *That the dead may give praise to God in heaven, we pray:* ◆

Our Father . . .

Lord of might,
you hold the power of healing in your
    merciful hands.
We are afflicted with illnesses of
    every kind,
separated from your unfailing love.
May we be strengthened
so that we may ask for your help
and be healed of all that ails and
    inflicts us.
We ask this through Christ our Lord.
    Amen.

✙ *I will bless the Lord at all times.*

✙ *I will bless the Lord at all times.*

PSALM 34   page 410

READING   Luke 19:1–10

At that time Jesus came to Jericho and intended to pass through the town. Now a man there named Zacchaeus, who was a chief tax collector and also a wealthy man, was seeking to see who Jesus was; but he could not see him because of the crowd, for he was short in stature. So he ran ahead and climbed a sycamore tree in order to see Jesus, who was about to pass that way. When he reached the place, Jesus looked up and said, "Zacchaeus, come down quickly, for today I must stay at your house." And he came down quickly and received him with joy. When they saw this, they began to grumble, saying, "He has gone to stay at the house of a sinner." But Zacchaeus stood there and said to the Lord, "Behold, half of my possessions, Lord, I shall give to the poor, and if I have extorted anything from anyone I shall repay it four times over." And Jesus said to him, "Today salvation has come to this house because this man too is a descendant of Abraham. For the Son of Man has come to seek and to save what was lost."

REFLECTION

Today's Gospel is about losing things. Zacchaeus loses his dignity by climbing the tree, and, later, he loses much of his wealth by giving it away for atonement. Jesus loses the respect of some when he goes to the house of a sinner. But, ironically, Jesus says he comes to save what was lost. In fact, Jesus saves what is truly worth saving: our souls. Jesus will lose not only his dignity but his life on a tree of the cross. However, that loss occurs to save all of humanity. What must we lose to save what is important?

PRAYERS   others may be added

    Seeking Christ, we pray:

◆ Lord, we trust in you.

That we may be willing to climb to new heights in service of others, we pray: ◆ *That we may seek out the company of those in need, we pray:* ◆ *That we may search for those who have lost their way, we pray:* ◆

Our Father . . .

Loving God,
you sent us your Son to find us when
    we were lost.
By our willingness to climb to new
    heights of faith,
may we be blessed with the ability to
    seek out
the lost souls of our time
and bring all into your loving
    embrace.
Grant this through Christ our Lord.
    Amen.

✙ *I will bless the Lord at all times.*

✦ *I will bless the Lord at all times.*

PSALM 40   *page 411*

READING   *Matthew 12:46–50*

While Jesus was speaking to the crowds, his mother and his brothers appearing outside, wishing to speak with him. Someone told him, "Your mother and your brothers are standing outside, asking to speak with you." But he said in reply to the one who told him, "Who is my mother? Who are my brothers?" And stretching out his hand toward his disciples, he said, "Here are my mother and my brothers. For whoever does the will of my heavenly Father is my brother, and sister, and mother."

REFLECTION   *St. Augustine*

Stretching out his hand over his disciples, the Lord Christ declared: Here are my mother and my brothers, anyone who does the will of my Father who sent me is my brother and my sister and my mother. I urge you to ponder these words. Did the Virgin Mary, who believed by faith and conceived by faith, who was the chosen one from whom our Savior was born among men, who was created by Christ before Christ was created in her—did she not do the will of the Father? Indeed the blessed Mary certainly did the Father's will, and so it was for her a greater thing to have been Christ's disciple than to have been his mother, and she was more blessed in her discipleship than in her motherhood. Hers was the happiness of first bearing in her womb him whom she would obey as her master.

PRAYERS   *others may be added*

Placing ourselves in Mary's care,
we pray:

◆ Lord, we trust in you.

For the preservation of the innocence of children, we pray: ◆ For those entrusted with the care of children, we pray: ◆ For the stability of family life, we pray: ◆ For increased devotion and prayer, we pray: ◆

Our Father . . .

God,
you granted many blessings to the
    Blessed Virgin Mary.
Through her prayers and example,
may we be inspired to lead lives
    of holiness
and one day be reunited with you in
    the heavenly banquet.
We ask this through Christ our Lord.
    Amen.

✦ *I will bless the Lord at all times.*

✝ *I will bless the Lord at all times.*

PSALM 34   *page 410*

READING   *Luke 19:41–44*

As Jesus drew near Jerusalem, he saw the city and wept over it, saying, "If this day you only knew what makes for peace—but now it is hidden from your eyes. For the days are coming upon you when your enemies will raise a palisade against you; they will encircle you and hem you in on all sides. They will smash you to the ground and your children within you, and they will not leave one stone upon another within you because you did not recognize the time of your visitation."

REFLECTION

Today's somber Gospel stands in stark contrast with the United States celebration of Thanksgiving, but yet fits the natural cycle of life occurring during this time of the year. Jesus cries for the destruction of Jerusalem. In the northern hemisphere, crops are harvested; fields are cleared and left barren for the coming winter. Whoever has not prepared for the coming frosts of winter will not survive. But for those who have recognized the time, there is reason for celebration and thanks. As the coming cold chills and freezes our land, it is fitting to turn to St. Cecilia, the patron of music, and to pray for the gift of a song in our heart to give thanks and praise for all the blessings of our compassionate Lord.

PRAYERS   *others may be added*

With grateful hearts, we pray:

◆ Lord, we trust in you.

That world leaders will work tirelessly for peace on earth, we pray: ◆
That nations blessed with an abundance of goods will share their resources with those less fortunate, we pray: ◆
That people of faith will recognize the signs of the times and prepare for the coming of the Lord, we pray: ◆
That musicians and artists will use their talents to glorify God, we pray: ◆

Our Father . . .

Loving Father,
you bless us with many gifts
    and graces;
you fill our world with signs of
    your love.
May our hearts be filled with songs
    of thanks
and our lips proclaim your
    saving works,
so that all may glorify you.
We ask this through Christ our Lord.
    Amen.

✝ *I will bless the Lord at all times.*

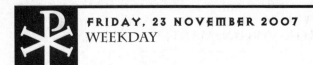
✝ *I will bless the Lord at all times.*

PSALM 34 *page 410*

READING *Luke 19:45–48*

Jesus entered the temple area and proceeded to drive out those who were selling things, saying to them, "It is written, *My house shall be a house of prayer, but you have made it a den of thieves.*" And every day he was teaching in the temple area. The chief priests, the scribes, and the leaders of the people, meanwhile, were seeking to put him to death, but they could find no way to accomplish their purpose because all the people were hanging on his words.

REFLECTION

All three of today's saints worked to build the new temple of Christ, the Church. St. Clement (+101), one of the earliest popes, left us his letter to the people of Corinth, which serves as an example of early Church leadership. St. Columban (543–+615), an Irish missionary monk, preached the Gospel throughout Burgundy, Austria, and northern Italy. And, Bl. Miguel (1891–+1927) was executed in Mexico simply for being a priest. These three people, and countless others, have followed Christ in cleansing the temple, in building up the Church. The question remains for us: Will we make the Lord's house a house of prayer or a den of thieves?

PRAYERS *others may be added*

Looking to the example of the saints, we pray:

◆ Lord, we trust in you.

That our Pope and bishops may lead the Church in holiness, we pray: ◆
That missionaries may bring the inspiring word of God to all peoples and lands, we pray: ◆ *That Christians enduring persecution for their faith may be strengthened and sustained, we pray:* ◆
That we may be faithful to our call as Christians, we pray: ◆

Our Father . . .

Lord God,
throughout time you have given us
upstanding men and women to inspire
  our faith.
May we rely on the prayers of these
  holy people
and bring your love to our
  darkened world.
We ask this in the name of Jesus the
  Lord. Amen.

✝ *I will bless the Lord at all times.*

✝ *I will bless the Lord at all times.*

PSALM 34 page 410

READING Luke 20:27–40

Some Sadducees, those who deny that there is a resurrection, came forward and put this question to Jesus, saying, "Teacher, Moses wrote for us, *If someone's brother dies leaving a wife but no child, his brother must take the wife and raise up descendants for his brother.* Now there were seven brothers; the first married a woman but died childless. Then the second and the third married her, and likewise all the seven died childless. Finally the woman also died. Now at the resurrection whose wife will that woman be? For all seven had been married to her." Jesus said to them, "The children of this age marry and remarry; but those who are deemed worthy to attain to the coming age and to the resurrection of the dead neither marry nor are given in marriage. They can no longer die, for they are like angels; and they are the children of God because they are the ones who will rise. That the dead will rise even Moses made known in the passage about the bush, when he called 'Lord' the God of Abraham, the God of Isaac, and the God of Jacob; and he is not God of the dead, but of the living, for to him all are alive." Some of the scribes said in reply, "Teacher, you have answered well." And they no longer dared to ask him anything.

REFLECTION

While he leaves no doubt about his belief, Jesus will not be trapped into giving a physical description of the resurrection. What life after death will be like is not as important as the fact that there is a resurrection. Jesus is a prophet of hope. With hope, we believe in more than what meets the eye. With hope, we know that what awaits us is better than we can imagine. Hope is what sustains the martyrs of every age. May we be filled with the same hope that inspired St. Andrew Dung-Lac (+ 1839) as he faced death in his native Vietnam.

PRAYERS *others may be added*

Through the intercession of the martyrs, we pray:

◆ Lord, we trust in you.

For the sick and the dying, we pray: ◆
For those who are hopeless, we pray: ◆
For widows and orphans, we pray: ◆
For all the dead, we pray: ◆

Our Father . . .

God of life,
we look to you for all that we need.
May our faith in your Son
give us strength to live the Gospel
and be granted eternal life.
We ask this through Christ our Lord.
   Amen.

✝ *I will bless the Lord at all times.*

✛ *The Lord is king; he is robed*
in majesty.

PSALM 47   *page 412*

READING   *Luke 23:35–43*

The rulers sneered at Jesus and said, "He saved others, let him save himself if he is the chosen one, the Christ of God." Even the soldiers jeered at him. As they approached to offer him wine they called out, "If you are King of the Jews, save yourself." Above him there was an inscription that read, "This is the King of the Jews."

Now one of the criminals hanging there reviled Jesus, saying, "Are you not the Christ? Save yourself and us." The other, however, rebuking him, said in reply, "Have you no fear of God, for you are subject to the same condemnation? And indeed, we have been condemned justly, for the sentence we received corresponds to our crimes, but this man has done nothing criminal." Then he said, "Jesus, remember me when you come into your kingdom." He replied to him, "Amen, I say to you, today you will be with me in Paradise."

REFLECTION

We have a king and he is a crucified king. His throne is the cross, his courtiers are his executioners, and his ministers are criminals. Instead of adulation there is mockery; in place of finery there is nakedness. Yet, in this scene is contained a power far greater than anything in the universe. It is the power of love; the power of life and death. Jesus reaches out to us across the millennia from his unlikely throne to promise us paradise. The Church crowns the liturgical year with this celebration of the dominion of Christ over all. Let us sing praise to our God and king.

PRAYERS   *others may be added*

We call out to our shepherd:

◆ Lord our King, we trust in you.

That the Good Shepherd may gather all nations into the pasture of plenty, we pray: ◆ That the Prince of Peace may banish all weapons of war, we pray: ◆ That our Savior may heal the sick, seek out the lost, and guide all on the way, we pray: ◆ That the firstborn of the dead may lead all those who have died to life everlasting, we pray: ◆

Our Father . . .

Lord God,
you crowned your Son with the glory
      of resurrection.
Your decrees of forgiveness are
      written on
the flesh of Jesus the Lord.
May we always submit to your power
      and love.
We ask this through our Lord Jesus
      Christ, your Son,
who lives and reigns with you in the
      unity of the Holy Spirit,
one God, forever and ever. Amen.

✛ *The Lord is king; he is robed*
in majesty.

✠ *I will bless the Lord at all times.*

PSALM 34 *page 410*

READING *Luke 21:1–4*

When Jesus looked up he saw some wealthy people putting their offerings into the treasury and he noticed a poor widow putting in two small coins. He said, "I tell you truly, this poor widow put in more than all the rest; for those others have all made offerings from their surplus wealth, but she, from her poverty, has offered her whole livelihood."

REFLECTION

There is no compromising with God. We are asked to give our all and to give it unconditionally. The widow gave her all and was immortalized for all time by the words of Jesus. Each of us will be asked for those last two coins; these may be time, patience, an open heart and mind, or simply a life well lived. Without a doubt, when we least expect it, perhaps when no one is looking, we will be asked for our gift. Will you give it?

PRAYERS *others may be added*

Offering ourselves to God, we pray:

◆ Lord, we trust in you.

That all clergy and religious may give freely of their lives, we pray: ◆ *That all God's people may stand ready to be of service to anyone in need, we pray:* ◆ *That the poor may humbly show the world simplicity of life, we pray:* ◆ *That the rich may live for others and not for gain of wealth, we pray:* ◆

Our Father . . .

God of love,
you search the hearts of all
    your creatures.
Purify our intentions,
inspire our actions,
open our imaginations,
that all that we do glorifies your name
and leads all to your kingdom.
We ask this through Christ our Lord.
    Amen.

✠ *I will bless the Lord at all times.*

✝ *I will bless the Lord at all times.*

PSALM 34 — *page 410*

READING — *Luke 21:5–11*

While some people were speaking about how the temple was adorned with costly stones and votive offerings, Jesus said, "All that you see here--the days will come when there will not be left a stone upon another stone that will not be thrown down."

Then they asked him, "Teacher, when will this happen? And what sign will there be when all these things are about to happen?" He answered, "See that you not be deceived, for many will come in my name, saying, 'I am he,' and 'The time has come.' Do not follow them! When you hear of wars and insurrections, do not be terrified; for such things must happen first, but it will not immediately be the end." Then he said to them, "Nation will rise against nation, and kingdom against kingdom. There will be powerful earthquakes, famines, and plagues from place to place; and awesome sights and mighty signs will come from the sky."

REFLECTION

The followers of Jesus repeatedly try to find out when the end of time will come, when the final judgment will occur. However, each time they ask, Jesus does not give the answer they want to hear. Instead, they are told to be ready. Jesus does spend a good deal of energy alluding that many things will happen to discourage, distract, and even confuse. But, the consistent answer is to be ready; don't put off what is needed to prepare for our final hour. The Lord will come again!

PRAYERS — *others may be added*

Ready for the Lord's coming, we pray:

◆ Lord, we trust in you.

For our Pope and all Church leaders, that they may be guided by the Holy Spirit, we pray: ◆ *For world leaders, that they may work for peace among nations, we pray:* ◆ *For those who are suffering from natural disasters, we pray:* ◆ *For our faithful departed, that they may be given eternal life, we pray:* ◆

Our Father . . .

Lord God,
you are the source of all that is good.
We ask for forgiveness for our sins.
Relying on your mercy and grace,
we pray for the hastening of your
   coming kingdom
so we may rejoice in heaven
   with you.
We ask this through Christ our Lord.
   Amen.

✝ *I will bless the Lord at all times.*

✝ *I will bless the Lord at all times.*

PSALM 34   *page 410*

READING   *Luke 21:12–19*

Jesus said to the crowd: "They will seize and persecute you, they will hand you over to the synagogues and to prisons, and they will have you led before kings and governors because of my name. It will lead to your giving testimony. Remember, you are not to prepare your defense beforehand, for I myself shall give you a wisdom in speaking that all your adversaries will be powerless to resist or refute. You will even be handed over by parents, brothers, relatives, and friends, and they will put some of you to death. You will be hated by all because of my name, but not a hair on your head will be destroyed. By your perseverance you will secure your lives."

REFLECTION

This is a Gospel full of promises, comforting promises. Although Jesus asserts that his followers will encounter difficulties, he emphasizes that we will receive the help that we need to overcome these difficulties. It is prudent to commit the promises of Jesus to memory in preparation for troubling times. Jesus is our comfort, our shelter, and our hope. He will protect us through all our trials.

PRAYERS   *others may be added*

Keeping the promises of Christ in mind, we pray:

◆ Lord, we trust in you.

That those who are persecuted for their faith may be supported by our prayers, we pray: ◆ *That individuals undergoing personal difficulties may find the Church a place of solace, we pray:* ◆ *That families struggling with financial and emotional burdens may find the strength of Christ, we pray:* ◆ *That we may do our best to reach out to those in need, we pray:* ◆

Our Father . . .

Father,
you sent your Son to the world to reveal your love for us.
In turn, your Son has promised us the aid of the Holy Spirit.
May your love sustain, guide, and inspire us,
so that we may build your kingdom here on earth.
We ask this through Christ our Lord. Amen.

✝ *I will bless the Lord at all times.*

✝ *I will bless the Lord at all times.*

PSALM 34 *page 410*

READING *Luke 21:20–28*

Jesus said to his disciples: "When you see Jerusalem surrounded by armies, know that its desolation is at hand. Then those in Judea must flee to the mountains. Let those within the city escape from it, and let those in the countryside not enter the city, for these days are the time of punishment when all the Scriptures are fulfilled. Woe to pregnant women and nursing mothers in those days, for a terrible calamity will come upon the earth and a wrathful judgment upon this people. They will fall by the edge of the sword and be taken as captives to all the Gentiles; and Jerusalem will be trampled underfoot by the Gentiles until the times of the Gentiles are fulfilled.

"There will be signs in the sun, the moon, and the stars, and on earth nations will be in dismay, perplexed by the roaring of the sea and the waves. People will die of fright in anticipation of what is coming upon the world, for the powers of the heavens will be shaken. And then they will see the Son of Man coming in a cloud with power and great glory. But when these signs begin to happen, stand erect and raise your heads because your redemption is at hand."

REFLECTION

Jesus wants to bolster our courage in the face of disaster. The Gospel is a message of hope, not despair—the ultimate victory of love, not death. It is the news that our God deeply loves us and will not let his creation suffer. In the face of hardship, suffering, or privation we can stand tall because we have been redeemed by our Lord.

PRAYERS *others may be added*

Standing with our God, we pray:

◆ Lord, we trust in you.

For the clergy, religious, and laity, we pray: ◆ *For civic leaders, we pray:* ◆ *For artists and artisans, we pray:* ◆ *For prophets, we pray:* ◆

Our Father . . .

God,
all of creation gives you praise.
May our lives, filled with hope
    inspired by the Gospel,
be examples to others.
Grant this through Christ our Lord.
    Amen.

✝ *I will bless the Lord at all times.*

✝ *I will bless the Lord at all times.*

PSALM 34 *page 410*

READING *Matthew 4:18–22*

As Jesus was walking by the Sea of Galilee, he saw two brothers, Simon who is called Peter, and his brother Andrew, casting a net into the sea; they were fishermen. He said to them, "Come after me, and I will make you fishers of men." At once they left their nets and followed him. He walked along from there and saw two other brothers, James, the son of Zebedee, and his brother John. They were in a boat, with their father Zebedee, mending their nets. He called them, and immediately they left their boat and their father and followed him.

REFLECTION

St. Andrew received a personal invitation from Jesus to follow him. We are told he responded "at once." We do not have the benefit of seeing Jesus face to face, yet God is present. We encounter him through his presence in word and sacrament — most especially in the Eucharist, in those who minister in his name, and those gathered in worship. But we have the ability to rely upon two thousand years of tradition, the examples of those before us, the wonders worked in the name of Jesus, and the persistence of firm belief. With all these benefits shouldn't we too respond "at once" to our call?

PRAYERS *others may be added*

Hearing the voice of Christ, we pray:

◆ Lord, we trust in you.

That more men and women will respond to the invitation of Christ to serve the Church, we pray: ◆ *That family members will be examples of faith to one another, we pray:* ◆ *That Christians will study with interest the deeds of the holy ones who have preceded us, we pray:* ◆ *That the faithful departed will rest in the eternal embrace of God, we pray:* ◆

Our Father . . .

Almighty God,
you sent the apostles
to lay the early foundations of
   the Church.
May their prayers and examples
   help us
to bring the Gospel to all we meet
so that we may one day be united in
   faith and praise
in your kingdom.
We ask this through Christ our Lord.
   Amen.

✝ *I will bless the Lord at all times.*

✠ *I will bless the Lord at all times.*

PSALM 34 *page 410*

READING *Luke 21:34–36*

Jesus said to his disciples: "Beware that your hearts do not become drowsy from carousing and drunkenness and the anxieties of daily life, and that day catch you by surprise like a trap. For that day will assault everyone who lives on the face of the earth. Be vigilant at all times and pray that you have the strength to escape the tribulations that are imminent and to stand before the Son of Man."

REFLECTION

On this last day of the Church year, the Gospel tells us to be ready for the coming of the Lord. Tomorrow begins the great season of Advent when we liturgically prepare for the coming of the Lord, and our own last day. But even before that, we must always be prepared to meet Christ in every person we encounter and in every circumstance of life. We prepare ourselves to grow in the love of God on earth so that we may be ever more ready to enter his heavenly paradise.

PRAYERS *others may be added*

Waiting to encounter Christ, we pray:

◆ Lord, we trust in you.

That all bishops and priests will be men of prayer, we pray: ◆ *That religious men and women will be strong examples of vigilance before the Lord, we pray:* ◆ *That all peoples will embrace lives of prayer and devotion, we pray:* ◆

Our Father . . .

Lord God,
you are worthy of all honor and praise.
May all your creatures join together
   in prayer
to proclaim your majesty
and acknowledge your dominion
   over all,
that one day we may rejoice at your
   heavenly banquet.
Grant this through Christ our Lord.
   Amen.

✠ *I will bless the Lord at all times.*

✠ *Lord, show us your mercy and love.*

PSALM 25 *page 407*

READING *Matthew 24:42–44*

[Jesus said,] "Therefore, stay awake! For you do not know on which day your Lord will come. Be sure of this: if the master of the house had known the hour of night when the thief was coming, he would have stayed awake and not let his house be broken into. So too, you also must be prepared, for at an hour you do not expect, the Son of Man will come."

REFLECTION

As the new Church year begins, Jesus tells his disciples to be prepared. What does that mean? It means avoid complacency; it means avoid boxing in our expectations of God; it means look in different places to meet the Lord; it means be open to all. We are not receiving a dire warning today; we are being notified that anything is possible with God. So, keep your eyes and heart open; our God is near.

PRAYERS *others may be added*

Confident in God, we pray:

◆ Light of the nations, hear us.

That we may be filled with eagerness to do God's work, we pray: ◆ That we may always be open to the surprising ways of God, we pray: ◆ That we may be optimistic for the coming of the Lord, we pray: ◆

Our Father . . .

O God,
you are larger than our expectations
and grander than our imaginations.
Open our small minds,
and help us to look in every heart to
    find your love,
that we may work for your kingdom
while we wait for your coming
    in glory.
We ask this through our Lord Jesus
    Christ, your Son,
who lives and reigns with you in the
    unity of the Holy Spirit,
one God, forever and ever. Amen.

✠ *Lord, show us your mercy and love.*

✛ *Lord, show us your mercy and love.*

PSALM 25   *page 407*

READING   *Matthew 8:5-11*

When Jesus entered Capernaum, a centurion approached him and appealed to him, saying, "Lord, my servant is lying at home paralyzed, suffering dreadfully." He said to him, "I will come and cure him." The centurion said in reply, "Lord, I am not worthy to have you enter under my roof; only say the word and my servant will be healed. For I too am a man subject to authority, with soldiers subject to me. And I say to one, 'Go,' and he goes; and to another, 'Come here,' and he comes; and to my slave, 'Do this,' and he does it." When Jesus heard this, he was amazed and said to those following him, "Amen, I say to you, in no one in Israel have I found such faith. I say to you, many will come from the east and the west, and will recline with Abraham, Isaac, and Jacob at the banquet in the Kingdom of heaven."

REFLECTION

Nothing that happens in this Gospel should be expected: A soldier caring so much about his slave; a Roman asking a Jew for help; a Jew helping a Roman; deep faith from a pagan. And yet, the Gospel means for us to look in different places and people for the inspiration we need to accomplish the work of the Lord. Faith abounds around us. God works his wonders, as he will. We need not be surprised; we need to be awake!

PRAYERS   *others may be added*

Looking for God's wonders, we pray:

◆ Light of the nations, hear us.

For immigrants and foreigners, that they may be welcomed in new homelands and new areas, we pray: ◆ *For health-care workers, that they may show concern for all in need, we pray:* ◆ *For members of the armed services, that they may promote the cause of peace, we pray:* ◆ *For all missionaries, that they may spread the Gospel of the Lord, we pray:* ◆

Our Father . . .

Lord of all nations,
you created us to be the works of
    your hands.
Help us to delight in our differences,
appreciate our commonalities, and
work together in harmony for your
    greater glory.
We ask this through Christ our Lord.
    Amen.

✛ *Lord, show us your mercy and love.*

✝ *Lord, show us your mercy and love.*

PSALM 25   *page 407*

READING   *Luke 10:21-24*

Jesus rejoiced in the Holy Spirit and said, "I give you praise, Father, Lord of heaven and earth, for although you have hidden these things from the wise and the learned you have revealed them to the childlike. Yes, Father, such has been your gracious will. All things have been handed over to me by my Father. No one knows who the Son is except the Father, and who the Father is except the Son and anyone to whom the Son wishes to reveal him."

Turning to the disciples in private he said, "Blessed are the eyes that see what you see. For I say to you, many prophets and kings desired to see what you see, but did not see it, and to hear what you hear, but did not hear it."

REFLECTION   *St. John Damascene*

By the blessing of the Holy Spirit, you prepared my creation and my existence, not because man willed it or flesh desired it, but by your ineffable grace. The birth you prepared for me was such that it surpassed the laws of our nature. You sent me forth into the light by adopting me as your son and you enrolled me among the children of your holy and spotless Church.

PRAYERS   *others may be added*

With open hearts, we pray:

◆ Light of the nations, hear us.

That we may discover the hidden presence of Christ in our lives, we pray: ◆ For the courage to be Christ for others, we pray: ◆ For the protection of the innocence of children, we pray: ◆ For the spirit of joy to fill us all during this Advent season, we pray: ◆

Our Father . . .

Blessed are you,
Lord of all creation,
for you have given us the gift
    of yourself,
in your Son, Christ Jesus.
Give us the grace to see him in all
    we know
and in all we do.
In his name we pray. Amen.

✝ *Lord, show us your mercy and love.*

WEDNESDAY, 5 DECEMBER 2007
ADVENT WEEKDAY

✦ *Lord, show us your mercy and love.*

PSALM 25 page 407

READING *Matthew 15:32–37*

Jesus summoned his disciples and said, "My heart is moved with pity for the crowd, for they have been with me now for three days and have nothing to eat. I do not want to send them away hungry, for fear they may collapse on the way." The disciples said to him, "Where could we ever get enough bread in this deserted place to satisfy such a crowd?" Jesus said to them, "How many loaves do you have?" "Seven," they replied, "and a few fish." He ordered the crowd to sit down on the ground. Then he took the seven loaves and the fish, gave thanks, broke the loaves, and gave them to the disciples, who in turn gave them to the crowds. They all ate and were satisfied. They picked up the fragments left over—seven baskets full.

REFLECTION

Like the crowd in today's Gospel, we wait. We have been given the gift of God's love in the Bread of Life and Cup of Salvation, yet we still wait. We wait for his return in glory when all will be one. Advent reminds us of this call—the call to "wait in joyful hope for the coming of our Savior." Jesus Christ lived, died, and rose from death, but he will come again! And so we cry, "Maranatha, Lord"—come in glory.

PRAYERS *others may be added*

Longing for the Bread of Heaven, we pray:

◆ Light of the nations, hear us.

For those who are hungry, that they may be filled with God's love, we pray: ◆ *For those who are lonely, that they may be brought into the presence of God, we pray:* ◆ *For those who long, that they may wait in joyful hope for Christ's return, we pray:* ◆

Our Father . . .

Bread of Life,
You feed us and give us salvation
    and peace.
May we be like the crowd in
    today's Gospel,
always waiting,
hungering to feast on your presence.
We ask this through Jesus Christ our
    Lord. Amen.

✦ *Lord, show us your mercy and love.*

✛ *Lord, show us your mercy and love.*

PSALM 25   *page 407*

READING   *Matthew 7:21, 24–27*

Jesus said to his disciples: "Not every-one who says to me, 'Lord, Lord,' will enter the Kingdom of heaven, but only the one who does the will of my Father in heaven.

"Everyone who listens to these words of mine and acts on them will be like a wise man who built his house on rock. The rain fell, the floods came, and the winds blew and buffeted the house. But it did not collapse; it had been set solidly on rock. And everyone who listens to these words of mine but does not act on them will be like a fool who built his house on sand. The rain fell, the floods came, and the winds blew and buffeted the house. And it collapsed and was completely ruined."

REFLECTION

Today the Church celebrates the optional memorial of St. Nicholas. Known as the protector of the innocent, legend tells us that Nicholas, a fourth-century bishop of Myra, prevented an impoverished father from selling his daughters into prostitution in order to make ends meet. Throwing three bags of gold into the man's window, Nicholas was able to provide them safety. Nicholas is a sign of the goodness of God—a goodness with which we strive to model as we wait for his return in glory.

PRAYERS   *others may be added*

Trusting in God's word, we pray:

◆ Light of the nations, hear us.

For those who protect the innocent, we pray: ◆ For those who provide assistance to the less fortunate, we pray: ◆ For those who pray for a world imbued with peace and love, we pray: ◆ For the coming of our Lord, Jesus Christ in glory, we pray: ◆

Our Father . . .

Lord of heaven,
you are our hope and salvation.
Fill us with your wisdom,
love, and understanding,
so that we may give comfort,
hope, and peace
to those who walk in darkness.
We ask this through Christ our Lord.
    Amen.

✛ *Lord, show us your mercy and love.*

✚ *Lord, show us your mercy and love.*

PSALM 25   *page 407*

READING   *Matthew 9:27-31*

As Jesus passed by, two blind men followed him, crying out, "Son of David, have pity on us!" When he entered the house, the blind men approached him and Jesus said to them, "Do you believe that I can do this?" "Yes, Lord," they said to him. Then he touched their eyes and said, "Let it be done for you according to your faith." And their eyes were opened. Jesus warned them sternly, "See that no one knows about this." But they went out and spread word of him through all that land.

REFLECTION

God is always present. Yet, it is often that we are blind to his presence, failing to recognize him in our daily lives. In today's Gospel, it is the faith of the blind men that enabled them to see the saving power of God. Let us be filled with this faith. Let us open our eyes to the presence of God dwelling among us.

PRAYERS   *others may be added*

Through the intercession of St. Ambrose, we pray:

◆ Light of the nations, hear us.

For the spiritual, mental, and physical healing of all our dear ones, we pray: ◆ For the selfless use of power by world leaders, we pray: ◆ For those in the healing professions, we pray: ◆ For the elimination of all our personal demons, we pray: ◆

Our Father . . .

God of power,
O Great Physician,
there is no wound you cannot heal.
Cleanse our spirits, mend our bodies,
and raise us to new life.
Renewed in you, may we spread the
    justice of Christ,
who lives and reigns with you in the
    unity of the Holy Spirit,
one God, forever and ever. Amen.

✚ *Lord, show us your mercy and love.*

✜ *Sing to the Lord a new song for he has done marvelous deeds.*

PSALM 98   *Page 416*

READING   *Luke 1:30–35, 38*

The angel said to her, "Do not be afraid, Mary, for you have found favor with God. Behold, you will conceive in your womb and bear a son, and you shall name him Jesus. He will be great and will be called Son of the Most High, and the Lord God will give him the throne of David his father, and he will rule over the house of Jacob forever, and of his Kingdom there will be no end." But Mary said to the angel, "How can this be, since I have no relations with a man?" And the angel said to her in reply, "The Holy Spirit will come upon you, and the power of the Most High will overshadow you. Therefore the child to be born will be called holy, the Son of God." Mary said, "Behold, I am the handmaid of the Lord. May it be done to me according to your word." Then the angel departed from her.

REFLECTION

For the solemnity of the Immaculate Conception of the Blessed Virgin Mary, we hear an account of one woman's courage to say "yes" to God's infinite plan of salvation. This "yes" profoundly changed the history of humanity. Mary's openness to trust in God is a tapestry illuminating God's saving hand at work in unexpected places. Following in her footsteps, we are called during this sacred season to say "yes" *to God's plan being conceived in and through us.*

PRAYERS   *others may be added*

Seeking the courage to say "yes" to God, we pray:

◆ Light of the nations, hear us.

That laypeople answer God's call to bring the Gospel message to the workplace, we pray: ◆ *That religious answer God's call to be open to transformation and renewal, we pray:* ◆ *That priests answer God's call to preach God's will, we pray:* ◆ *That Church leaders answer God's call to seek justice for all, we pray:* ◆

Our Father . . .

God of the lowly,
you chose Mary
to bear the Light,
which no darkness can overcome.
Following Mary's example,
may we always have the courage
   to say,
"May it be done to me according to
   your word."
We ask this through our Lord, Jesus
   Christ, your Son,
who lives and reigns with you in the
   unity of the Holy Spirit,
one God, forever and ever. Amen.

✜ *Sing to the Lord a new song for he has done marvelous deeds.*

✝ *Lord, show us your mercy and love.*

PSALM 25 page 407

READING *Matthew 3:1–3*

John the Baptist appeared, preaching in the desert of Judea and saying, "Repent, for the kingdom of heaven is at hand!" It was of him that the prophet Isaiah had spoken when he said: *A voice of one crying out in the desert, / Prepare the way of the Lord, / make straight his paths.*

REFLECTION

We live with anticipation for the fulfillment of God's kingdom. John the Baptist cries, "Prepare the way of the Lord, make straight his paths!" If we truly prepare, we must embrace Christ-filled lives of repentance, integrity, and humility. Gone are the days of self-fulfillment and self-assurance. We must look beyond ourselves to the one who is greater. It is only here that we will know the salvation of God.

PRAYERS *others may be added*

Waiting for the kingdom, we pray:

◆ Light of the nations, hear us.

To be a repentant people, we pray: ◆
To be a forgiving people, we pray: ◆
To be a listening people, we pray: ◆
To be an Advent people, we pray: ◆

Our Father . . .

God of salvation,
you called the prophets
to announce the coming of
    your kingdom.
May we be like John and Isaiah,
proclaiming your truth in a world
longing to hear your voice and see
    your face.
We ask this through our Lord, Jesus
    Christ, your Son,
who lives and reigns with you in the
    unity of the Holy Spirit,
one God, forever and ever. Amen.

✝ *Lord, show us your mercy and love.*

✠ *Lord, show us your mercy and love.*

PSALM 25 *page 407*

READING *Luke 5:17–26*

One day as Jesus was teaching, Pharisees and teachers of the law, who had come from every village of Galilee and Judea and Jerusalem, were sitting there, and the power of the Lord was with him for healing. And some men brought on a stretcher a man who was paralyzed; they were trying to bring him in and set him in his presence. But not finding a way to bring him in because of the crowd, they went up on the roof and lowered him on the stretcher through the tiles into the middle in front of Jesus. When Jesus saw their faith, he said, "As for you, your sins are forgiven."

Then the scribes and Pharisees began to ask themselves, "Who is this who speaks blasphemies? Who but God alone can forgive sins?" Jesus knew their thoughts and said to them in reply, "What are you thinking in your hearts? Which is easier, to say, 'Your sins are forgiven,' or to say, 'Rise and walk'? But that you may know that the Son of Man has authority on earth to forgive sins"—he said to the one who was paralyzed, "I say to you, rise, pick up your stretcher, and go home."

He stood up immediately before them, picked up what he had been lying on, and went home, glorifying God. Then astonishment seized them all and they glorified God, and, struck with awe, they said, "We have seen incredible things today."

REFLECTION

The greatest ministry of the Church is that of reconciliation. Today, Jesus tells us that there is no greater debilitation than sin. Before we can effect real change in this world, we must first be reconciled with one another. When we do this we will be astonished by the incredible things we see.

PRAYERS *others may be added*

Glorifying God, we pray:

◆ Light of the nations, hear us.

That we may be filled with eagerness to do the work of God, we pray: ◆ *That we may be open to the surprising ways of God, we pray:* ◆ *That all people may promote a spirit of reconciliation, we pray:* ◆ *That we may break open the roofs of disbelief, we pray:* ◆

Our Father . . .

Loving Father,
you offer forgiveness to all who sin.
Dispel our disbelief,
carry us with your healing hands,
and raise us to new life by
    your mercy.
We ask this through Christ our Lord.
    Amen.

✠ *Lord, show us your mercy and love.*

✦ *Lord, show us your mercy and love.*

PSALM 25 *page 407*

READING *Matthew 18:12-14*

Jesus said to his disciples: "What is your opinion? If a man has a hundred sheep and one of them goes astray, will he not leave the ninety-nine in the hills and go in search of the stray? And if he finds it, amen, I say to you, he rejoices more over it than over the ninety-nine that did not stray. In just the same way, it is not the will of your heavenly Father that one of these little ones be lost."

REFLECTION *St. Gregory the Great*

Beloved . . . let us set out for these pastures where we shall keep joyful festival with so many of our fellow citizens. May the thought of their happiness urge us on! Let us stir up our hearts, rekindle our faith, and long eagerly for what heaven has in store for us. To love thus is to be already on our way. No matter what obstacles we encounter, we must not allow them to turn us aside from the joy of that heavenly feast. Anyone who is determined to reach his destination is not deterred by the roughness of the road that leads to it. Nor must we allow the charm of success to seduce us, or we shall be like a foolish traveler who is so distracted by the pleasant meadows through which he is passing that he forgets where he is going.

PRAYERS *others may be added*

Rejoicing in forgiveness, we pray:

◆ Light of the nations, hear us.

That Church leaders may be shepherds of God's truth, we pray: ◆ *That nations may base peace on forgiveness and mutual trust, we pray:* ◆ *That we may give to those in need, we pray:* ◆ *That the dead may receive the Lord's forgiveness and live in eternal peace, we pray:* ◆

Our Father . . .

Lord of compassion,
may your grace bring hope
to a world darkened by despair,
and reconcile all in need of
    your mercy.
We ask this through Christ our Lord.
    Amen.

✦ *Lord, show us your mercy and love.*

✦ *Sing to the Lord a new song for he
has done marvelous deeds.*

PSALM 40 *page 411*

READING *Luke 1:39–47*

Mary set out and traveled to the hill
country in haste to a town of Judah,
where she entered the house of
Zechariah and greeted Elizabeth.
When Elizabeth heard Mary's greeting, the infant leaped in her womb, and
Elizabeth, filled with the Holy Spirit,
cried out in a loud voice and said,
"Most blessed are you among women,
and blessed is the fruit of your womb.
And how does this happen to me, that
the mother of my Lord should come to
me? For at the moment the sound of
your greeting reached my ears, the
infant in my womb leaped for joy.
Blessed are you who believed that
what was spoken to you by the Lord
would be fulfilled." And Mary said:

"My soul proclaims the greatness of
the Lord;/my spirit rejoices in God my
savior."

REFLECTION *Our Lady of Guadalupe*

*"I ardently wish and greatly desire that
they build my temple for me here, where I
will reveal, I will make known, and I will
give to people all my love, my compassion,
my aid and my protection, for I am your
compassionate mother. . . ."*

PRAYERS *others may be added*

*Proclaiming the greatness of our Lord
and Savior, we pray:*

◆ Light of the nations, hear us.

*For those struggling with infertility,
that God's presence may surround
them in their time of trial, we pray:* ◆
*For expectant couples, that they may
embrace the gift of life with joy, we pray:* ◆
*For all nations, governments, and
peoples, that they may protect the dignity
of human life from the moment of
conception until natural death, we pray:* ◆
*For those who have died, that they
may be brought into the fulfillment of
eternal life, we pray:* ◆

Our Father . . .

God of life,
you have revealed yourself
in many ways and many faces.
May we like Mary,
poor and humble,
be willing to become a womb
for your word of life.
We ask this in the name of Jesus our
Lord. Amen.

✦ *Sing to the Lord a new song for he
has done marvelous deeds.*

✠   *Lord, show us your mercy and love.*

PSALM 25   *Page 407*

READING   *Matthew 11: 11–15*

Jesus said to the crowds: "Amen, I say to you, among those born of women there has been none greater than John the Baptist; yet the least in the Kingdom of heaven is greater than he. From the days of John the Baptist until now, the Kingdom of heaven suffers violence, and the violent are taking it by force. All the prophets and the law prophesied up to the time of John. And if you are willing to accept it, he is Elijah, the one who is to come. Whoever has ears ought to hear."

REFLECTION

Today we celebrate an early martyr whose fame has spread throughout Christendom. There is little known about this virgin and martyr, other than her heroic faith. However, the fact that her name means "light" lends particular importance to her commemoration during Advent. Like contemplatives at vigil in the early morning hours, we await the light of the Second Coming of Christ. As we prepare for his coming in glory, may we ask for the prayers of St. Lucy, patroness of the blind, that our eyes may be opened to the grace of God through Christ, the Light of the world.

PRAYERS   *others may be added*

Waiting for Christ, we pray:

◆ Light of the nations, hear us.

For those waiting for deliverance from persecution, we pray: ◆ *For those struggling with blindness of spirit or body, we pray:* ◆ *For those who work to bring the Light of Christ to those in darkness, we pray:* ◆ *For the victims of physical and emotional abuse, we pray:* ◆

Our Father . . .

Father of Light,
you have granted us the vision of
    your love
in your Son, Jesus Christ.
Help us to carry the candle of faith
to the darkest corners of the world,
and may we one day share in
    your glory.
Grant this through Christ our Lord.
    Amen.

✠   *Lord, show us your mercy and love.*

✛ *Lord, show us your mercy and love.*

PSALM 25   *page 407*

READING   *Matthew 11:16–19*

Jesus said to the crowds: "To what shall I compare this generation? It is like children who sit in marketplaces and call to one another, 'We played the flute for you, but you did not dance, we sang a dirge but you did not mourn.' For John came neither eating nor drinking, and they said, 'He is possessed by a demon.' The Son of Man came eating and drinking and they said, 'Look, he is a glutton and a drunkard, a friend of tax collectors and sinners.' But wisdom is vindicated by her works."

REFLECTION   *St. John of the Cross*

O my soul, created to enjoy such exquisite gifts, what are you doing, where is your life going? How wretched is the blindness of Adam's children, if indeed we are blind to such a brilliant light and deaf to so insistent a voice.

PRAYERS   *others may be added*

Through the intercession of St. John of the Cross, we pray:

◆ Light of the nations, hear us.

That the Church may seek only to serve in the name of the Lord, we pray: ◆ *That all nations of the earth, forsaking violence and vengeance, may greet one another as brothers and sisters, we pray:* ◆ *That Christians may hasten to the aid of those who are in any anguish, we pray:* ◆ *That all who have gone to their rest may receive the blessedness promised to those who believe, we pray:* ◆

Our Father . . .

Lord our God,
already in our midst,
and yet to come,
your presence delights us even now
as we long for your peace.
Winnow from our lives the chaff of
    selfishness and sin.
Sow in us a harvest
of gentleness and generosity,
for we rejoice in you,
even as you exult and sing for joy
    over us.
Grant this through Christ our Lord.
    Amen.

✛ *Lord, show us your mercy and love.*

377

✦ *Lord, show us your mercy and love.*

PSALM 25 *page 407*

READING *Matthew 17:9a, 10–13*

As they were coming down from the mountain, the disciples asked Jesus, "Why do the scribes say that Elijah must come first?" He said in reply, "Elijah will indeed come and restore all things; but I tell you that Elijah has already come, and they did not recognize him but did to him whatever they pleased. So also will the Son of Man suffer at their hands." Then the disciples understood that he was speaking to them of John the Baptist.

REFLECTION

In today's Gospel, Jesus is proclaiming to the people that they have failed to recognize the one announcing God's reign, John the Baptist. And, just as they were unable to see and hear the message of John the Baptist, so too Jesus asserts that they will not know the Promised One when he comes. Not only will they not know him, but their inability to identify him will lead to much suffering and pain. We must prepare our hearts and be vigilant so we can recognize the Son of Man when he comes.

PRAYERS *others may be added*

Hoping to recognize the Son of Man when he comes, we pray:

◆ Light of the nations, hear us.

That we may be a people of awareness, we pray: ◆ *That we may be a people of peace, we pray:* ◆ *That we may be a people of justice, we pray:* ◆ *That we may be a people of prophetic hope, we pray:* ◆

Our Father . . .

God of justice,
you gave us John the Baptist,
the prophetic announcer
of your coming kingdom.
May we be ready for your word and
    kingdom
to be born anew as an inner flame
within our hearts,
burning away the darkness of hatred,
    pain, and suffering.
We ask this in the name of Jesus our
    Lord. Amen.

✦ *Lord, show us your mercy and love.*

✝ *Rejoice, Jerusalem, let your joy overflow; your Savior will come to you, alleluia.*

PSALM 25 *page 407*

READING *Matthew 11:2–6*

When John the Baptist heard in prison of the works of the Christ, he sent his disciples to Jesus with this question, "Are you the one who is to come, or should we look for another?" Jesus said to them in reply, "Go and tell John what you hear and see: the blind regain their sight, the lame walk, lepers are cleansed, the deaf hear, the dead are raised, and the poor have the good news proclaimed to them. And blessed is the one who takes no offense at me."

REFLECTION

As we reach the midpoint of our Advent journey looking to the fulfillment of the Lord's promises, we are presented with a vision of the kingdom as embodied by Jesus. There are healings, the dead are raised, and forgiveness is offered to sinners. This is the kingdom we await, the kingdom we preach, the kingdom we work to bring about. However, just as John the Baptist heard this news in prison, we too must wait patiently for the coming of the kingdom. Meanwhile, we rejoice for the Lord is near!

PRAYERS *others may be added*

With joy and hope, we pray:

◆ Light of the nations, hear us.

That sorrow and sighing may flee the earth, as songs of gladness announce the welcomed return of peace, we pray: ◆ *That those weakened by life's burdens may find hope in the care they receive from others, we pray:* ◆ *That the dead may be brought to eternal life, we pray:* ◆

Our Father . . .

Loving Creator,
you unfold a magnificent and
    ever-changing pattern
in your wondrous universe.
Help us to take the time
to appreciate the infinite manifestations
    of your love
and fill us with joy as we wait for
the fulfillment of your promises.
We ask this through our Lord Jesus
    Christ, your Son,
who lives and reigns with you and the
    Holy Spirit,
one God, forever and ever. Amen.

✝ *Rejoice, Jerusalem, let your joy overflow; your Savior will come to you, alleluia.*

✝ *Wisdom, O holy Word of God, come and show your people the way to salvation.*

PSALM 25   *page 407*

READING   *Matthew 1:1, 17*

The book of the genealogy of Jesus Christ, the son of David, the son of Abraham.

Thus the total number of generations from Abraham to David is fourteen generations; from David to the Babylonian exile, fourteen generations; from the Babylonian exile to the Christ, fourteen generations.

REFLECTION

Today's Gospel provides the genealogy, the human ancestry, of Jesus Christ. He is situated within the history of his people. The list of his ancestors contains the flawed as well as the famous. But with the beginning of the O Antiphons today, we also acknowledge the divine origins of the Christ. Today we acclaim the wisdom of our God. It is the wise hand of God that offers us guidance. May we have the grace to accept this offer of God's help.

PRAYERS   *others may be added*

Trusting in your tender care, we pray:

◆ Come, O Wisdom, show us the way.

That we may learn to share all that we have, we pray: ◆ *That Church leaders may always point to the Lord, we pray:* ◆ *That we may preach the Good News in our daily lives, we pray:* ◆ *That we may always live in the joy of the Word of God, we pray:* ◆

Our Father . . .

Loving Father,
you sent your Son, the Word
    made flesh,
to free us from sin.
Lead us in your wisdom to embody
    your Son,
who lives and reigns with you in the
    unity of the Holy Spirit,
one God, forever and ever. Amen.

✝ *Wisdom, O holy Word of God, come and show your people the way to salvation.*

✠ *O sacred Lord of ancient Israel,*
come, stretch out your mighty hand
to set us free.

PSALM 25 *page 407*

READING *Matthew 1:18–25*

This is how the birth of Jesus Christ came about. When his mother Mary was betrothed to Joseph, but before they lived together, she was found with child through the Holy Spirit. Joseph her husband, since he was a righteous man, yet unwilling to expose her to shame, decided to divorce her quietly. Such was his intention when, behold, the angel of the Lord appeared to him in a dream and said, "Joseph, son of David, do not be afraid to take Mary your wife into your home. For it is through the Holy Spirit that this child has been conceived in her. She will bear a son and you are to name him Jesus, because he will save his people from their sins." All this took place to fulfill what the Lord had said through the prophet:

Behold, the virgin shall be with child and bear a son, / and they shall name him Emmanuel,

which means "God is with us." When Joseph awoke, he did as the angel of the Lord had commanded him and took his wife into his home. He had no relations with her until she bore a son, and he named him Jesus.

REFLECTION

Like Joseph, the Lord of Israel calls to us, speaking challenging, but consoling words of hope and peace. We often do not want to hear God's calling because it may disrupt our plans or take us to foreign lands. As Christians, we are called to find the Light, illuminating and beckoning us to become part of God's infinite story of compassion.

PRAYERS *others may be added*

Opening our hearts for the just one, we pray:

◆ O Sacred Lord, break down the walls of injustice.

That the hungry may feast on your banquet of life, we pray: ◆ *That the homeless may be sheltered in the warmth of your love, we pray:* ◆ *That the weak may be protected by your arm of strength, we pray:* ◆ *That the despairing may find consolation in your word of hope, we pray:* ◆

Our Father . . .

Lord of Israel,
you are love beyond all measure,
challenging us to become
    an instrument
in your symphony of salvation.
Give us the courage
to sing of your coming
with harmonious sounds of hope
    and justice.
Grant this through Jesus Christ our
    Lord. Amen.

✠ *O sacred Lord of ancient Israel,*
come, stretch out your mighty hand
to set us free.

✦ *O Flower of Jesse's stem, come,*
let nothing keep you from coming to
our aid.

PSALM 25   *page 407*

READING   *Luke 1:14–17*

"And you will have joy and gladness, and many will rejoice at his birth, for he will be great in the sight of the Lord. He will drink neither wine nor strong drink. He will be filled with the Holy Spirit even from his mother's womb, and he will turn many of the children of Israel to the Lord their God. He will go before him in the spirit and power of Elijah to turn the hearts of fathers toward children and the disobedient to the understanding of the righteous, to prepare a people fit for the Lord."

REFLECTION   *Suzanne M. Lewis*

The centerpiece of God's counsel, his loving design, has been to make creatures in his own image, filled with his breath and aided by the Holy Spirit, who would freely cooperate with this plan for fulfillment. When the time came, he gave us himself, in the person of Jesus Christ, in order to allure us.

PRAYERS   *others may be added*

Open to your generosity, we pray:

◆ Come, O Flower of Jesse's stem.

That we may be open to your wondrous ways, we pray: ◆ *That we may bring wonder to all we meet, we pray:* ◆ *That we may speak freely the word of God, we pray:* ◆ *That we may blossom into your image, we pray:* ◆

Our Father . . .

Loving God,
you bring forth the fruitfulness
    of grace.
Kings are silent in your presence,
and the nations bow down before you.
Send us your gift of salvation
in the coming of your Son,
    Jesus Christ,
who lives and reigns with you in the
    unity of the Holy Spirit,
one God, forever and ever. Amen.

✦ *O Flower of Jesse's stem, come,*
let nothing keep you from coming to
our aid.

✦ *O Key of David, come, break down the prison walls of death for those who dwell in darkness and the shadow of death; and lead your captive people into freedom.*

PSALM 25   *page 407*

READING   *Luke 1:26–32*

In the sixth month, the angel Gabriel was sent from God to a town of Galilee called Nazareth, to a virgin betrothed to a man named Joseph, of the house of David, and the virgin's name was Mary. And coming to her, he said, "Hail, full of grace! The Lord is with you." But she was greatly troubled at what was said and pondered what sort of greeting this might be. Then the angel said to her, "Do not be afraid, Mary, for you have found favor with God. Behold, you will conceive in your womb and bear a son, and you shall name him Jesus. He will be great and will be called Son of the Most High . . . ."

REFLECTION

Today's Gospel illustrates that Advent is a time and season of miracles—for all that seems impossible is made possible through the all-inclusive and all-powerful love of God. We, like the Virgin Mary, are sacred vessels though which God transforms impossibility into promising artistic expressions of reconciliation, liberation, and hope. Advent challenges us to move beyond skepticism and unbelief in order to see the many miracles God works through and around us. Everything and anything is possible with our God!

PRAYERS   *others may be added*

Becoming aware of the miracles around us, we pray:

◆ O Key of David, lead your captive people into freedom.

That women who experience unplanned pregnancies may see the possibility of life, we pray: ◆ *That women who cannot conceive children may see the possibility of life, we pray:* ◆ *That the sick may see the possibility of life, we pray:* ◆ *That the dying and grieving may see the possibility of life, we pray:* ◆

Our Father . . .

O Key of David,
you called Mary
to envision the many possibilities
of your love.
May we be like them,
able to see a world
touched by your saving hand.
We ask this in the name of Jesus.
    Amen.

✦ *O Key of David, come, break down the prison walls of death for those who dwell in darkness and the shadow of death; and lead your captive people into freedom.*

✚ *O Radiant Dawn, come, shine on those who dwell in darkness and the shadow of death.*

PSALM 25   *page 407*

READING   *Luke 1:39–45*

Mary set out in those days and traveled to the hill country in haste to a town of Judah, where she entered the house of Zechariah and greeted Elizabeth. When Elizabeth heard Mary's greeting, the infant leaped in her womb, and Elizabeth, filled with the Holy Spirit, cried out in a loud voice and said, "Most blessed are you among women, and blessed is the fruit of your womb. And how does this happen to me, that the mother of my Lord should come to me? For at the moment the sound of your greeting reached my ears, the infant in my womb leaped for joy. Blessed are you who believed that what was spoken to you by the Lord would be fulfilled."

REFLECTION

Today's recounting of the visitation inspires us with Mary's tender outreach to her pregnant cousin, Elizabeth. Mary undertakes this arduous journey while she, too, is pregnant. Earlier in this season we heard that some burdens are light when they are inspired by a higher purpose. Here Mary celebrates the end of her cousin's infertility; she helps Elizabeth enjoy a new dawn in life. We all have a share of darkness in our life, but with the help of others we can look forward to new dawn.

PRAYERS   *others may be added*

Looking to your eternal light, we pray:

◆ Come, O Radiant Dawn.

For those who visit the sick and dying, we pray: ◆ For those who reach out in spite of their own troubles, we pray: ◆ For expectant mothers, we pray: ◆ For those who are living in darkness, we pray: ◆

Our Father . . .

Dear Lord,
let me always rejoice in you.
Let me be amazed by joy,
and help me always to remember
to ask, again and again,
why this joy should be mine. Amen.

✚ *O Radiant Dawn, come, shine on those who dwell in darkness and the shadow of death.*

✦ *O King of all the nations, the only joy of every human heart, come and save the creature you fashioned from the dust.*

PSALM 25   Page 407

READING   Luke 1:46–55

Mary said:

"My soul proclaims the greatness of the Lord;/my spirit rejoices in God my savior,/for he has looked upon his lowly servant./From this day all generations will call me blessed:/the Almighty has done great things for me,/and holy is his Name./He has mercy on those who fear him/in every generation./He has shown the strength of his arm,/and has scattered the proud in their conceit./He has cast down the mighty from their thrones/and has lifted up the lowly./He has filled the hungry with good things,/and the rich he has sent away empty./He has come to the help of his servant Israel/for he remembered his promise/of mercy,/the promise he made to our fathers,/to Abraham and his children for ever."

REFLECTION   Suzanne M. Lewis

Your mercy is always there, always available, always outlasting the interval between my first breath and my last. I know that your mercy will enfold my children, and my children's children, with a strength and finality I can never possess. And so I offer myself up entirely to your mercy; please let it carry my prayer for peace into every generation.

PRAYERS   *others may be added*

Preparing our hearts for the merciful Word of God, we pray:

◆ O Keystone, encircle us with your compassion.

For an end to hatred, we pray: ◆ For an end to violence, we pray: ◆ For an end to hunger, we pray: ◆ For an end to over consumption, we pray: ◆

Our Father . . .

King of all the nations,
you raised up a lowly virgin
to bear witness to the Word,
which no noise can silence.
Sustain us in our call, like Mary,
to become bearers of your
    liberating Word
so that all generations
will know your mercy.
Grant this through Jesus Christ our
    Lord. Amen.

✦ *O King of all the nations, the only joy of every human heart, come and save the creature you fashioned from the dust.*

✦ *O Emmanuel, desire of the nations,*
come and set us free.

PSALM 25   *page 407*

READING   *Matthew 1:18–24*

This is how the birth of Jesus Christ came about. When his mother Mary was betrothed to Joseph, but before they lived together, she was found with child through the Holy Spirit. Joseph her husband, since he was a righteous man, yet unwilling to expose her to shame, decided to divorce her quietly. Such was his intention when, behold, the angel of the Lord appeared to him in a dream and said, "Joseph, son of David, do not be afraid to take Mary your wife into your home. For it is through the Holy Spirit that this child has been conceived in her. She will bear a son and you are to name him Jesus, because he will save his people from their sins." All this took place to fulfill what the Lord had said through the prophet: *Behold, the virgin shall conceive and bear a son,/and they shall name him Emmanuel,/*which means "God is with us." When Joseph awoke, he did as the angel of the Lord had commanded him and took his wife into his home.

REFLECTION

What's in a name? On one level it is merely a label, but it can also be a reflection of identity. Naming his child John, a name never used by his family, Zechariah signaled that his son was to be someone special. Likewise, the angel called Mary's
child Emmanuel, meaning "God is with us." Names and words have profound power. As we approach the great feast of Christmas, may we be aware of the power invested in the movement of our lips.

PRAYERS   *others may be added*

With thankful hearts, we pray:

◆ O Emmanuel, come and set us free.

That we may be made worthy of the name Christian, we pray: ◆ *That we may be made aware of the power of our words, we pray:* ◆ *That we may rejoice at your saving works, we pray:* ◆ *That we may be ready for your arrival, we pray:* ◆

Our Father . . .

God of our ancestors,
from all eternity you show yourself
worthy of your name, Emmanuel.
Come to us, O desire of the nations,
and fill us with your love and mercy
so that we will be able to celebrate
    the coming of your Son, our Lord
    Jesus Christ,
who live and reigns with you in the
    unity of the Holy Spirit,
one God forever and ever. Amen.

✦ *O Emmanuel, desire of the nations,*
come and set us free.

✝ *Lord, show us your mercy and love.*

PSALM 25 — Page 407

READING — *Luke 1:67–79*

Zechariah his father, filled with the Holy Spirit, prophesied, saying:

"Blessed be the Lord, the God of Israel;/for he has come to his people and set them free./He has raised up for us a mighty Savior,/born of the house of his servant David./Through his prophets he promised of old/that he would save us from our enemies,/from the hands of all who hate us./He promised to show mercy to our fathers/and to remember his holy covenant./This was the oath he swore to our father Abraham:/to set us free from the hand of our enemies,/free to worship him without fear,/holy and righteous in his sight all the days of our life./You, my child, shall be called the prophet of the Most High,/for you will go before the Lord to prepare his way,/to give his people knowledge of salvation/by the forgiveness of their sins./In the tender compassion of our God/the dawn from on high shall break upon us,/to shine on those who dwell in darkness and the shadow of death,/and to guide our feet into the way of peace."

REFLECTION

We have spent this Advent season preparing our hearts, setting our tables, and adorning our homes for the arrival of the divine guest. We look forward to tomorrow when we will leap, like the infant in Elizabeth's womb, with joy and sing out, "The Great and Holy One is among us." Let us rejoice, for the Light has overcome the darknesss, guiding all to the humble stable of life.

PRAYERS — *others may be added*

Preparing our lives for Christmas joy, we pray:

◆ Come, Emmanuel, fill us with your peace.

For all who travel this holiday season, that they may arrive safely to and from their destinations, we pray: ◆ *For all poor children who will not receive presents this holiday season, that they may be clothed in God's gift of eternal life, we pray:* ◆ *For all who have no food at their table this holiday season, that they may feast on the Bread of Life, we pray:* ◆

Our Father . . .

Emmanuel, God with us,
help us to make a world
where all will have a voice
and place at the table of life.
May we be renewed by your coming
and heed your calling
to build a more just world
so that no one will go hungry, be
lonely, or
be deprived of the promise of
Christmas.
Grant this through our Lord Jesus
Christ, your Son,
who lives and reigns with you in the
unity of the Holy Spirit,
one God, forever and ever. Amen.

✝ *Lord, show us your mercy and love.*

✝ *A little child is born for us today; little and yet called the mighty God, Alleluia!*

PSALM 98 page 416

READING Luke 2:1, 4–7

In those days a decree went out from Caesar Augustus that the whole world should be enrolled. So all went to be enrolled, each to his own town. And Joseph too went up from Galilee from the town of Nazareth to Judea, to the city of David that is called Bethlehem, because he was of the house and family of David, to be enrolled with Mary, his betrothed, who was with child. While they were there, the time came for her to have her child, and she gave birth to her firstborn son. She wrapped him in swaddling clothes and laid him in a manger, because there was no room for them in the inn.

REFLECTION

The Christmas story is filled with contrasts. We hear about the great Roman emperor, Augustus, and also lowly Joseph, the carpenter; we hear about humble people living in fields and stables and also about angels from heaven. Salvation is needed by all, from the most prestigious to the humblest. Today's great message is that no one should be afraid; salvation is offered to all. That tiny baby in the manger is the mighty God who brings peace, joy, and love to all.

PRAYERS others may be added

Looking to the Christ child, we pray:

◆ May your light surround us.

For the powerful, that they may be humble like a child, we pray: ◆ *For the lowly, that they may be filled with joy and hope, we pray:* ◆ *For all of us, that we may be filled with the Good News of great joy, we pray:* ◆ *For peace to all on earth, we pray:* ◆

Our Father . . .

Lord our God,
you break through the darkness of our
    sin and ignorance
and fill us with the light of Christ,
    your Son.
On this great feast of your love,
renew in us the desire to spread
your peace, hope, and love to the
    whole world.
We ask this through our Lord Jesus
    Christ, your Son,
who lives and reigns with you in the
    unity of the Holy Spirit,
one God, forever and ever. Amen.

✝ *A little child is born for us today; little and yet called the mighty God, Alleluia!*

✝ *Come, you nations, and adore the Lord. A great light has come upon the earth. Alleluia!*

PSALM 98   page 416

READING   *Matthew 10:17–22*

Jesus said to his disciples: "Beware of men, for they will hand you over to courts and scourge you in their synagogues, and you will be led before governors and kings for my sake as a witness before them and the pagans. When they hand you over, do not worry about how you are to speak or what you are to say. You will be given at that moment what you are to say. For it will not be you who speak but the Spirit of your Father speaking through you. Brother will hand over brother to death, and the father his child; children will rise up against parents and have them put to death. You will be hated by all because of my name, but whoever endures to the end will be saved."

REFLECTION   *St. Fulgentius of Ruspe*

And so the love that brought Christ from heaven to earth raised Stephen from earth to heaven; shown first in the king, it later shone forth in his soldier. His love of God kept him from yielding to the ferocious mob; his love for his neighbor made him pray for those who were stoning him. Love inspired him to reprove those who erred, to make them amend; love led him to pray for those who stoned him, to save them from punishment.

PRAYERS   *others may be added*

Proclaiming the glorious birth of Christ, we pray:

◆ May your light surround us.

For those struggling with addictions, that they may experience courage and healing, we pray: ◆ For those experiencing persecution for the sake of the Gospel, that they may find hope in their pain, we pray: ◆ For those serving the poor, that they may experience the richness of the kingdom, we pray: ◆ For all those bound by material possessions, that they may be released, we pray: ◆

Our Father . . .

God of freedom,
you gave St. Stephen
the inner strength to sacrifice his life
as a witness to your reconciling love.
May we also give our lives
to Christ this Christmas season
and live in the warmth of his light.
We ask this in the name of Jesus our
     Lord. Amen.

✝ *Come, you nations, and adore the Lord. A great light has come upon the earth. Alleluia!*

✦ *Come, you nations, and adore the Lord. A great light has come upon the earth. Alleluia!*

PSALM 98 *page 416*

READING *John 20:1a, 2–8*

On the first day of the week, Mary Magdalene ran and went to Simon Peter and to the other disciple whom Jesus loved, and told them, "They have taken the Lord from the tomb, and we do not know where they put him." So Peter and the other disciple went out and came to the tomb. They both ran, but the other disciple ran faster than Peter and arrived at the tomb first; he bent down and saw the burial cloths there, but did not go in. When Simon Peter arrived after him, he went into the tomb and saw the burial cloths there, and the cloth that had covered his head, not with the burial cloths but rolled up in a separate place. Then the other disciple also went in, the one who had arrived at the tomb first, and he saw and believed.

REFLECTION *St. Augustine*

Consider what is said to you: Love God. If you say to me: Show me whom I am to love, what shall I say if not what Saint John says: No one has ever seen God! But in case you should think that you are completely cut off from the sight of God, he says: God is love and he who remains in love remains in God. Love your neighbor, then, and see within yourself the power by which you love your neighbor; there you will see God, as far as you are able.

PRAYERS *others may be added*

Through the intercession of St. John the evangelist, we pray:

◆ May your light surround us.

John witnessed the Transfiguration; that we may always recognize the glory of the Lord, we pray: ◆ *John stood at the foot of the cross; that we may remain steady in times of trouble, we pray:* ◆ *John saw the discarded burial cloths; that we may believe in the impossible, we pray:* ◆ *John took Mary into his care; that we may safeguard innocence, we pray:* ◆

Our Father . . .
Loving God,
you sent John the evangelist
to instruct us about the divinity and
love of Christ.
Give us the same strength of
character, tender spirit, and
zealous heart to spread the love of
your Son.
We ask this through Jesus Christ our
Lord. Amen.

✦ *Come, you nations, and adore the Lord. A great light has come upon the earth. Alleluia!*

✝ *Come, you nations, and adore the Lord. A great light has come upon the earth. Alleluia!*

PSALM 98   *page 416*

READING   *Matthew 2:13–16*

When the magi had departed, behold, the angel of the Lord appeared to Joseph in a dream and said, "Rise, take the child and his mother, flee to Egypt, and stay there until I tell you. Herod is going to search for the child to destroy him." Joseph rose and took the child and his mother by night and departed for Egypt. He stayed there until the death of Herod, that what the Lord had said through the prophet might be fulfilled, *Out of Egypt I called my son.*

When Herod realized that he had been deceived by the magi, he became furious. He ordered the massacre of all the boys in Bethlehem and its vicinity two years old and under, in accordance with the time he had ascertained from the magi.

REFLECTION

During this time of holiday celebration, it seems rather odd to hear a story of the vengeful Herod who orders death to squelch the truth and light that came in a tiny child lying in a manger. For fear his plan might not come to fruition, he orders the massacre of baby boys to ensure the death of the Light who came to burn away the darkness. We are called, like Joseph, to protect, to run, and to accompany the Word so that the Herods of the world may not destroy what God created.

PRAYERS   *others may be added*

Crying out with joy and gladness, we pray:

◆ May your light surround us.

That we reverence all life from conception to death, we pray: ◆ *That we give witness to the Word of life, we pray:* ◆ *That we nurture faith in children, we pray:* ◆ *That we live Christmas joy throughout the entire year, we pray:* ◆

Our Father . . .

God, flame of hope,
you called Joseph
to carry the Word of God to safety.
Empower us to be a Christmas womb
in which faith, love, and hope
can be birthed anew and
pave the way to peace.
Grant this in the name of Jesus our
    Lord. Amen.

✝ *Come, you nations, and adore the Lord. A great light has come upon the earth. Alleluia!*

✝ *Come, you nations, and adore the Lord. A great light has come upon the earth. Alleluia!*

PSALM 98 — page 416

READING — Luke 2:25–35

Now there was a man in Jerusalem whose name was Simeon. This man was righteous and devout, awaiting the consolation of Israel, and the Holy Spirit was upon him. It had been revealed to him by the Holy Spirit that he should not see death before he had seen the Christ of the Lord. He came in the Spirit into the temple; and when the parents brought in the child Jesus to perform the custom of the law in regard to him, he took him into his arms and blessed God, saying:

"Lord, now you let your servant go in peace;/your word has been fulfilled:/my own eyes have seen the salvation/which you prepared in the sight of every people,/a light to reveal you to the nations/and the glory of your people Israel."

The child's father and mother were amazed at what was said about him; and Simeon blessed them and said to Mary his mother, "Behold, this child is destined for the fall and rise of many in Israel, and to be a sign that will be contradicted (and you yourself a sword will pierce) so that the thoughts of many hearts may be revealed."

REFLECTION

Lord, your word has been fulfilled. We are now at peace, conscious of your wondrous glory that fills all of creation. Our eyes have been opened to your salvation, and we are ever amazed in your sight. Guide us, Lord. Guide us with your Light.

PRAYERS — *others may be added*

Relying on God's promises, we pray:

◆ May your light surround us.

That Church leaders may fulfill the promises they make to the Church, we pray: ◆ *That family members may fulfill the promises they make to one another, we pray:* ◆ *That we may cradle the gifts we have been given, we pray:* ◆ *That we may have the courage to reveal the Lord's light to the world, we pray:* ◆

Our Father . . .

God of the prophets,
you revealed your promises in
    various ways.
Help us to recognize the fulfillment
    of your promises,
and lead us to proclaim your
    Christmas glory.
Grant this through Christ our Lord.
    Amen.

✝ *Come, you nations, and adore the Lord. A great light has come upon the earth. Alleluia!*

✠ *Come, you nations, and adore the Lord. A great light has come upon the earth. Alleluia!*

PSALM 98 *page 416*

READING *Matthew 2:13–15*

When the magi had departed, behold, the angel of the Lord appeared to Joseph in a dream and said, "Rise, take the child and his mother; flee to Egypt, and stay there until I tell you. Herod is going to search for the child to destroy him." Joseph rose and took the child and his mother by night and departed from Egypt. He stayed there until the death of Herod, that what the Lord had said through the prophet might be fulfilled, *Out of Egypt I called my son.*

REFLECTION

Today's feast highlights for us that God continues to reveal himself in the everyday circumstances of our lives. For most of us, the ordinary includes some form of family. It is within this intimate circle that God is present. It is here that we will grow in wisdom and grace. It is here we learn to keep things in our hearts until God grants us understanding.

PRAYERS *others may be added*

Trusting in the gentleness of God, we pray:

◆ May your light surround us.

That all families may be forgiving and patient, we pray: ◆ *That we recognize the wisdom of the young, we pray:* ◆ *That the young strive to be obedient, we pray:* ◆ *That we find God in the ordinary, we pray:* ◆

Our Father . . .

O Trinity of unity,
your very being models the love
    of family.
Help us to embrace that love
and bring Christmas joy to the hearts
    of all.
We ask this through our Lord, Jesus
    Christ, your Son,
who lives and reigns with you in the
    unity of the Holy Spirit,
one God, forever and ever. Amen.

✠ *Come, you nations, and adore the Lord. A great light has come upon the earth. Alleluia!*

✦ *Come, you nations, and adore the Lord. A great light has come upon the earth. Alleluia!*

PSALM 98   *page 416*

READING   *John 1:1–5, 14, 16–18*

In the beginning was the Word, / and the Word was with God, / and the Word was God. / He was in the beginning with God. / All things came to be through him, / and without him nothing came to be. / What came to be through him was life, / and this life was the light of the human race; / the light shines in the darkness, / and the darkness has not overcome it.

And the Word became flesh / and made his dwelling among us, / and we saw his glory, / the glory as of the Father's only-begotten Son, / full of grace and truth.

From his fullness we have all received, grace in place of grace, because while the law was given through Moses, grace and truth came through Jesus Christ. No one has ever seen God. The only-begotten Son, God, who is at the Father's side, has revealed him.

REFLECTION

Jesus is our path to the Father, our light to the Father, our word about the Father. Not only is Jesus our way to the Father, but he offers us power, grace, adoption, and love beyond measure. By God's own will we have received the greatest gift possible: our entry to the heart of God. We will face troubles and struggles, but nothing will ever overcome the goodness of our God who has come to dwell among us.

PRAYERS   *others may be added*

Glorying in our adoption, we pray:

◆ May your light surround us.

For the Church throughout the world, that our worship and praise may give glory to God, we pray: ◆ *For peoples of every race and nation, that the celebration of the birth of the Prince of Peace may encourage a new birth of righteousness and justice, we pray:* ◆ *For family and friends near and far, for the hospitalized and homebound, that the good news of Christmas may bring joy and peace, we pray:* ◆

Our Father . . .

Lord our God,
you break through the darkness of our
   sin and ignorance
and fill us with the light of Christ,
   your Son.
On this great feast of your love,
renew in us the desire to spread
your peace, hope, and love to the
   whole world.
We ask this through Christ our Lord.
   Amen.

✦ *Come, you nations, and adore the Lord. A great light has come upon the earth. Alleluia!*

SOURCES

All Gospel excerpts used in this work are taken from the *Lectionary for Mass for Use in the Dioceses of the United States of America, second typical edition, Volume 1* copyright © 1970, 1986, 1992, 1998, 2001 Confraternity of Christian Doctrine, Washington, D.C. All rights reserved. No part of this work may be reproduced or transmitted in any form or by any means, electronic or mechanical, including photocopying, recording, or by any information storage retrieval system, without permission in writing from the copyright owner.

Psalms (portions or entirely) 19B, 22, 25, 27, 33, 34, 40, 47, 66, 85, 91, 98, 100, 116, 118, 130, and 145 from *The Grail* copyright © 1963, *The Grail,* England, GIA Publications, Inc., exclusive North American agent, 7404 S. Mason Ave., Chicago, IL 60638, www.giamusic.com, 800-442-1358. All rights reserved. Used by permission.

Opening and closing verses: The English translation of the Psalm Responses are from the *Lectionary for Mass,* © 1997, 1981, 1969, International Committee on English in the Liturgy, Inc.; The English translation of the O Antiphons, © 1974, International Committee on English in the Liturgy, Inc.; The English Translation of the *Roman Missal,* © 1973, International Committee on English in the Liturgy, Inc. All rights reserved.

11 December 2006: From a treatise on John by St. Augustine, bishop. The English translation of *The Liturgy of the Hours* © 1974 International Committee on English in the Liturgy, Inc. All rights reserved.

16 December 2006: From *An Advent Sourcebook* (Chicago: LTP, 1988), p. 57.

18 December 2005: From *At Home with the Word 2005* (Chicago: LTP, 2004), p. 23.

20 December 2006: From *At Home with the Word 2005* (Chicago: LTP, 2004), p. 23.

21 December 2006: From *Living in Joyful Hope* (Chicago: LTP, 2005), p. 34.

23 December 2006: From *Living in Joyful Hope* (Chicago: LTP, 2004), p. 62.

28 December 2006: From *Living in Joyful Hope* (Chicago: LTP, 2005), p. 106.

31 December 2006: An excerpt from Pope John Paul II's homily during the Mass at Uhuru Park, Kenya, September 19, 1995. Available from http://www.catholic-forum.com/saints/pope0264ep.htm.

24 January 2007: Closing Prayer from the English translation of the Opening Prayers from *The Roman Missal* © 1973, International Committee on English in the Liturgy.

27 January 2007: Closing Prayer from the English translation of the Opening Prayers from *The Roman Missal* © 1973, International Committee on English in the Liturgy.

27 May 2007: The poetic English translation of the Pentecost sequence is taken from the *Roman Missal* approved by the National Conference of Catholic Bishops of the United States © 1964 by the National Catholic Welfare Conference, Inc. All rights reserved.

17 August 2007: *Gaudium et spes,* 48, available from http://www.vatican.va/archive/hist_councils/ii_vatican_council/documents/vat-ii_cons_19651207_gaudium-et-spes_en.html.

25 August 2007: From a spiritual testament to his son by St. Louis. The English translation of *The Liturgy of the Hours* © 1974 International Committee on English in the Liturgy, Inc. All rights reserved.

28 August 2007: From the *Confessions of Saint Augustine,* bishop. The English translation of *The Liturgy of the Hours* © 1974 International Committee on English in the Liturgy, Inc. All rights reserved.

30 August 2007: From a commentary on the Diatessaron by St. Ephrem, deacon. The English translation of *The Liturgy of the Hours* © 1974 International Committee on English in the Liturgy, Inc. All rights reserved.

3 September 2007: *Homily at the Mass of the 25th Anniversary of the Pontificate of Pope John Paul II,* 16 October 2003, available from http://www.vatican.va/holy_father/john_paul_ii/homilies/2003/documents/hf_jp-ii_hom_20031016_xxv-pontificate_en.html.

8 September 2007: From a discourse by St. Andrew of Crete, bishop. The English translation of *The Liturgy of the Hours*

15 September 2007: The poetic English translation of the sequence for the memorial of Our Lady of Sorrows is taken from the *Roman Missal* approved by the National Conference of Catholic Bishops of the United States

23 September 2007: Post Synodal Apostolic Exhortation Ecclesia in America of the Holy Father John Paul II, available from http://www.usccb.org/pope/popemesseng.htm.

25 September 2007: *Gaudium et spes:* Available from http://www.vatican.va/archive/hist_councils/ii_vatican_council/documents/lvat-ii_cons_19651207_gaudium-et-spes_en.html.

17 October 2007: From a letter to the Romans by St. Ignatius, bishop and martyr. The English translation of *The Liturgy of the Hours*

19 October 2007: From the spiritual diaries by St. John de Brébeuf, priest and martyr. The English translation of *The Liturgy of the Hours*

22 October 2007: From a spiritual canticle by St. John of the Cross. The English translation of The Liturgy of the Hours

30 October 2007: From *Mustard Seed Preaching* (Chicago: LTP, 2004), p. xii.

2 November 2007: From a book on the death of his brother Satyrus by St. Ambrose, bishop. The English translation of *The Liturgy of the Hours*

8 November 2007: Closing Prayer from the English translation of the Opening Prayers from *The Roman Missal*

11 November 2007: From a sermon by St. Bernard, abbot. The English translation of *The Liturgy of the Hours*

14 November 2007: From a letter to the Corinthians by St. Clement, pope. The English translation of *The Liturgy of the Hours*

18 November 2007: From *Workbook for Lectors 2004, Year C* (Chicago: LTP, 2003), p. 288.

21 November 2007: From a sermon by St. Augustine, bishop. The English translation of *The Liturgy of the Hours*

4 December 2007: From *The Statement of Faith* by St. John Damascene [Damascus], priest. The English translation of *The Liturgy of the Hours*

11 December 2007: From a homily on the Gospels by St. Gregory the Great, pope. The English translation of *The Liturgy of the Hours*

12 December 2007: Words of Our Lady of Guadalupe to St. Juan Diego at Tepeyac.

13 December 2007: Prayer of the Faithful adapted from *Prayers for Sundays and Seasons, Year C* (Chicago: LTP, 1997), p. 8.

14 December 2007: From *A Spiritual Canticle* by St. John of the Cross, priest. The English translation of the *Liturgy of the Hours*

SCRIPTURE INDEX

The following list represents the scriptural citations from the *Lectionary for Mass* used in *Daily Prayer 2007*. In some cases, excerpts of scripture were used; however, *the complete citation* is noted below. These readings are the Gospels proclaimed in the daily Mass. In some cases, the Lectionary provides various options. The readings in *Daily Prayer 2007* have been selected from among those options. What is listed below are only those readings that were used in this resource. For a complete listing of the readings and options, consult LTP's *A Simple Guide to the Daily Mass Readings*.

1st Sunday of Advent •
Luke 21:25–28, 34–36

Monday • *Matthew 8:5–11*

Tuesday • *Luke 10:21–24*

Wednesday • *Matthew 15:29–37*

Thursday • *Matthew 7:21, 24–27*

Friday, Immaculate Conception •
Luke 1:26–38

Saturday • *Matthew 9:35—10:1, 5a, 6–8*

2nd Sunday of Advent • *Luke 3:1–6*

Monday • *Luke 5:17–26*

Tuesday, Our Lady of Guadalupe •
Luke 1:39–47

Wednesday • *Matthew 11:28–30*

Thursday • *Matthew 11:11–15*

Friday • *Matthew 11:16–19*

Saturday • *Matthew 17:9a, 10–13*

3rd Sunday of Advent • *Luke 3:10–18*

Monday • *Matthew 1:18–25*

Tuesday • *Luke 1:5–25*

Wednesday • *Luke 1:26–38*

Thursday • *Luke 1:39–45*

Friday • *Luke 1:46–56*

Saturday • *Luke 1:57–66*

4th Sunday of Advent • *Luke 1:39–45*

Monday, Nativity of the Lord
(Mass at Midnight) • *Luke 2:1–14*

Tuesday, St. Stephen • *Matthew 10:17–22*

Wednesday, St. John • *John 20:1a, 2–8*

Thursday, Holy Innocents • *Matthew 2:13–18*

Friday, 5th Day in the Octave • *Luke 2:22–35*

Saturday, 6th Day in the Octave •
Luke 2:36–40

Holy Family of Jesus, Mary, and Joseph •
Luke 2:41–52

Monday • Mary, Mother of God •
Luke 2:16–21

Tuesday • *John 1:19–28*

Wednesday • *John 1:29–34*

Thursday • *John 1:35–42*

Friday • *John 1:43–51*

Saturday • *Mark 1:7–1*

Epiphany of the Lord • *Matthew 2:1–12*

Monday, Baptism of the Lord •
Luke 3:15–16, 21–22

Tuesday, First Week in O.T.• *Mark 1:21–28*

Wednesday • *Mark 1:29–39*

Thursday • *Mark 1:40–45*

Friday • *Mark 2:1–12*

Saturday • *Mark 2:13–17*

2nd Sunday of O.T. • *John 2:1–11*

Monday • *Mark 2:18–22*

Tuesday • *Mark 2:23–28*

Wednesday • *Mark 3:1–6*

Thursday • *Mark 3:7–12*

Friday • *Mark 3:13–19*

Saturday • *Mark 3:20–21*

3rd Sunday of O.T. • *Luke 1:1–4; 4: 14–21*

Monday • *Mark 3:22–30*

Tuesday • *Mark 3:31–35*

Wednesday • *Mark 4:1–20*

Thursday, Conversion of St. Paul •
Mark 16:15–18

Friday • *Mark 4:26–34*

Saturday • *Mark 4:35–41*

4th Sunday of O.T. • *Luke 4:21–30*

Monday • *Mark 5:1–20*

Tuesday • *Mark 5:21–43*

Wednesday • *Mark 6:1–6*

Thursday • *Mark 6:7–13*

Friday, Presentation •
   Luke 2:22–40 or 2:22–32

Saturday • *Mark 6:30–34*

5th Sunday of O.T. • *Luke 5:1–11*

Monday • *Mark 6:53–56*

Tuesday • *Mark 7:1–13*

Wednesday • *Mark 7:14–23*

Thursday • *Mark 7:24–30*

Friday • *Mark 7:31–37*

Saturday • *Mark 8:1–10*

6th Sunday of O.T. • *Luke 6:17, 20–26*

Monday • *Mark 8:11–13*

Tuesday • *Mark 8:14–21*

Wednesday • *Mark 8:22–26*

Thursday • *Mark 8:27–33*

Friday • *Mark 8:34—9:1*

Saturday • *Mark 9:2–13*

7th Sunday of O.T. • *Luke 6:27–38*

Monday • *Mark 9:14–29*

Tuesday • *Mark 9:30–37*

Wednesday, Ash Wednesday •
   Matthew 6:1–6, 16–18

Thursday, Chair of St. Peter •
   Matthew 16:13–19

Friday • *Matthew 9:14–15*

Saturday • *Luke 5:27–32*

1st Sunday of Lent • *Luke 4:1–13*

Monday • *Matthew 25:31–46*

Tuesday • *Matthew 6:7–15*

Wednesday • *Luke 11:29–32*

Thursday • *Matthew 7:7–12*

Friday • *Matthew 5:20–26*

Saturday • *Matthew 5:43–48*

2nd Sunday of Lent • *Luke 9:28b–36*

Monday • *Luke 6:36–38*

Tuesday • *Matthew 23:1–12*

Wednesday • *Mathew 20:17–28*

Thursday • *Luke 16:19–31*

Friday • *Matthew 21:33–43, 45–46*

Saturday • *Luke 15:1–3, 11–32*

3rd Sunday of Lent • *Luke 13:1–9*

Monday • *Luke 4:24–30*

Tuesday • *Matthew 18:21–35*

Wednesday • *Matthew 5:17–19*

Thursday • *Luke 11:14–23*

Friday • *Mark 12:28–34*

Saturday • *Luke 18:9–14*

4th Sunday of Lent • *Luke 15:1–3, 11–32*

Monday, St. Joseph •
   Matthew 1:16, 18–21, 24a

Tuesday • *John 5:1–16*

Wednesday • *John 5:17–30*

Thursday • *John 5:31–47*

Friday • *John 7:1–2, 10, 25–30*

Saturday • *John 7:40–53*

5th Sunday of Lent • *John 8:1–11*

Monday, Annunciation • *Luke 1:26–38*

Tuesday • *John 8:21–30*

Wednesday • *John 8:31–42*

Thursday • *John 8:51–59*

Friday • *John 10:31–42*

Saturday • *John 11:45–56*

Palm Sunday, (Procession with Palms) •
   Luke 19:28–40

Monday, Holy Week • *John 12:1–11*

Tuesday, Holy Week • *John 13:21–33, 36–38*

Wednesday, Holy Week • *Matthew 26:14–25*

Holy Thursday (Mass of the Lord's Supper) •
   John 13:1–15

Good Friday • *John 18:1—19:42*

Holy Saturday • *Luke 23:50–56*

Easter Sunday • *John 20:1–9*

Monday, Octave • *Matthew 28:8–15*

Tuesday, Octave • *John 20:11–18*

Wednesday, Octave • *Luke 24:13–35*

Thursday, Octave • *Luke 24:35–48*

Friday, Octave • *John 21:1–14*

Saturday, Octave • *Mark 16:9–15*

2nd Sunday of Easter/Divine Mercy •
  John 20:19–31

Monday • *John 3:1–8*

Tuesday • *John 3:7b–15*

Wednesday • *John 3:16–21*

Thursday • *John 3:31–36*

Friday • *John 6:1–15*

Saturday • *John 6:16–21*

3rd Sunday of Easter •
  John 21:1–19 or 21:1–14

Monday • *John 6:22–29*

Tuesday • *John 6:30–35*

Wednesday, St. Mark • *Mark 16:15–20*

Thursday • *John 6:44–51*

Friday • *John 6:52–59*

Saturday • *John 6:60–69*

4th Sunday of Easter • *John 10:27–30*

Monday • *John 10:1–10*

Tuesday • *John 10:22–30*

Wednesday • *John 12:44–50*

Thursday, St. Philip and St. James •
  John 14:6–14

Friday • *John 14:1–6*

Saturday • *John 14:7–14*

5th Sunday of Easter •
  John 13:31–33a, 34–35

Monday • *John 14:21–26*

Tuesday • *John 14:27–31a*

Wednesday • *John 15:1–8*

Thursday • *John 15:9–11*

Friday • *John 15:12–17*

Saturday • *John 15:18–21*

6th Sunday of Easter • *John 14:23–29*

Monday, St. Matthias • *John 15:9–17*

Tuesday • *John 16:5–11*

Wednesday • *John 16:12–15*

Thursday, Ascension • *Luke 24:46–53*

Friday • *John 16:20–23*

Saturday • *John 16:23b–28*

7th Sunday of Easter • *John 17:20–26*

Monday • *John 16:29–33*

Tuesday • *John 17:1–11a*

Wednesday • *John 17:11b–19*

Thursday • *John 17:20–26*

Friday • *John 21:15–19*

Saturday • *John 21:20–25*

Pentecost • *John 20:19–23*

Monday • *Mark 10:17–27*

Tuesday • *Mark 10:28–31*

Wednesday • *Mark 10:32–45*

Thursday, Visitation • *Luke 1:39–56*

Friday • *Mark 11:11–26*

Saturday • *Mark 11:27–33*

Most Holy Trinity • *John 16:12–15*

Monday, 9th Week in O.T. • *Mark 12:1–12*

Tuesday • *Mark 12:13–17*

Wednesday • *Mark 12:18–27*

Thursday • *Mark 12:28–34*

Friday • *Mark 12:35–37*

Saturday • *Mark 12:38–44*

Most Holy Body and Blood of Christ •
  Luke 9:11b–17

Monday, 10th Week in O.T. • *Matthew 10:7–13*

Tuesday • *Matthew 5:13–16*

Wednesday • *Matthew 5:17–19*

Thursday • *Matthew 5:20–26*

Friday, Most Sacred Heart • *Luke 15:3–7*

Saturday, Immaculate Heart • *Luke 2:41–51*

11th Sunday of O.T. •
  Luke 7:36—8:3 or 7:36–50

Monday • *Matthew 5:38–42*

Tuesday • *Matthew 5:43–48*

Wednesday • *Matthew 6:1–6, 16–18*

Thursday • *Matthew 6:7–15*

Friday • *Matthew 6:19–23*

Saturday • *Matthew 6:24–34*

Nativity of St. John the Baptist •
Luke 1:57–66, 80

Monday, 12th Week in O.T. • *Matthew 7:1–5*

Tuesday • *Matthew 7:6, 12–14*

Wednesday • *Matthew 7:15–20*

Thursday • *Matthew 7:21–29*

Friday, St. Peter and St. Paul •
Matthew 16:13–19

Saturday • *Matthew 8:5–17*

13th Sunday of O.T. • *Luke 9:51–62*

Monday • *Matthew 8:18–22*

Tuesday, St. Thomas • *John 20:24–29*

Wednesday • *Matthew 8:28–34*

Thursday • *Matthew 9:1–8*

Friday • *Matthew 9:9–13*

Saturday • *Matthew 9:14–17*

14th Sunday of O.T. •
Luke 10:1–12, 17–20 or 10:1–9

Monday • *Matthew 9:18–26*

Tuesday • *Matthew 9:32–38*

Wednesday • *Matthew 10:1–7*

Thursday • *Matthew 10:7–15*

Friday • *Matthew 10:16–23*

Saturday • *Matthew 10:24–33*

15th Sunday of O.T. • *Luke 10:25–37*

Monday • *Matthew 10:34—11:1*

Tuesday • *Matthew 11:20–24*

Wednesday • *Matthew 11:25–27*

Thursday • *Matthew 11:28–30*

Friday • *Matthew 12:1–8*

Saturday • *Matthew 12:14–21*

16th Sunday of O.T. • *Luke 10:38–42*

Monday • *Matthew 12:38–42*

Tuesday • *Matthew 12:46–50*

Wednesday, St. James • *Matthew 20:20–28*

Thursday • *Matthew 13:10–17*

Friday • *Matthew 13:18–23*

Saturday • *Matthew 13:24–30*

17th Sunday of O.T. • *Luke 11:1–13*

Monday • *Matthew 13:31–35*

Tuesday • *Matthew 13:36–43*

Wednesday • *Matthew 13:44–46*

Thursday • *Matthew 13:47–53*

Friday • *Matthew 13:54–58*

Saturday • *Matthew 14:1–12*

18th Sunday of O.T. • *Luke 12:13–21*

Monday, Transfiguration • *Luke 9:28b–36*

Tuesday • *Matthew 14:22–36 or
15:1–2, 10–14*

Wednesday • *Matthew 15:21–28*

Thursday • *Matthew 16:13–23*

Friday • *John 12:24–26*

Saturday • *Matthew 17:14–20*

19th Sunday of O.T. • *Luke 12:32–48 or
12:35–40*

Monday • *Matthew 17:22–27*

Tuesday • *Matthew 18:1–5, 10, 12–14*

Wednesday, Assumption (Vigil Mass) •
Luke 11:27–28

Thursday • *Matthew 18:21—19:1*

Friday • *Matthew 19:3–12*

Saturday • *Matthew 19:13–15*

20th Sunday of O.T. • *Luke 12:49–53*

Monday • *Matthew 19:16–22*

Tuesday • *Matthew 19:23–30*

Wednesday • *Matthew 20:1–16*

Thursday • *Matthew 22:1–14*

Friday, St. Bartholomew • *John 1:45–51*

Saturday • *Matthew 23: 1–12*

21st Sunday of O.T. • *Luke 13:22–30*

Monday • *Matthew 23:13–22*

Tuesday • *Matthew 23:34–26*

Wednesday • *Mark 6:17–29*

Thursday • *Matthew 24:42–51*

Friday • *Matthew 25:1–13*

Saturday • *Matthew 25:14–30*

22nd Sunday of O.T. • *Luke 14:1, 7–14*

Monday • *Matthew 6:31–34*

Tuesday • *Luke 4:31–37*

Wednesday • *Luke 4:38–44*

Thursday • *Luke 5:1–11*

Friday • *Luke 5:33–39*

Saturday, Nativity of Mary •
Matthew 1:1–16, 18–23 or 1:18–23

23rd Sunday of O.T. • *Luke 14:25–33*

Monday • *Luke 6:6–11*

Tuesday • *Luke 6:12–19*

Wednesday • *Luke 6:20–26*

Thursday • *Luke 6:27–38*

Friday, Holy Cross • *John 3:13–17*

Saturday • *John 19:25–27*

24th Sunday of O.T. • *Luke 15:1–32 or
15:1–10*

Monday • *Luke 7:1–10*

Tuesday • *Luke 7:11–17*

Wednesday • *Luke 7:31–35*

Thursday • *Luke 7:36–50*

Friday, St. Matthew • *Matthew 9:9–13*

Saturday • *Luke 8:4–15*

25th Sunday of O.T. • *Luke 16:1–13 or
16:10–13*

Monday • *Luke 8:16–18*

Tuesday • *Luke 8:19–21*

Wednesday • *Luke 9:1–6*

Thursday • *Luke 9:7–9*

Friday • *Luke 9:18–22*

Saturday • *John 1:47–51*

26th Sunday of O.T. • *Luke 16:19–31*

Monday • *Luke 9:46–50*

Tuesday • *Matthew 18:1–5, 10*

Wednesday • *Luke 9:57–62*

Thursday • *Luke 10:1–12*

Friday • *Luke 10:13–16*

Saturday • *Luke 10:17–24*

27th Sunday of O.T. • *Luke 17:5–10*

Monday • *Luke 10:25–37*

Tuesday • *Luke 10:38–42*

Wednesday • *Luke 11:1–4*

Thursday • *Luke 11:5–13*

Friday • *Luke 11:15–26*

Saturday • *Luke 11:27–28*

28th Sunday of O.T. • *Luke 17:11–19*

Monday • *Luke 11:29–32*

Tuesday • *Luke 11:37–41*

Wednesday • *Luke 11:42–46*

Thursday, St. Luke • *Luke 10:1–9*

Friday • *Luke 12:1–7*

Saturday • *Luke 12:8–12*

29th Sunday of O.T. • *Luke 18:1–8*

Monday • *Luke 12:13–21*

Tuesday • *Luke 12:35–38*

Wednesday • *Luke 12:39–48*

Thursday • *Luke 12:49–53*

Friday • *Luke 12:54–59*

Saturday • *Luke 13:1–9*

30th Sunday of O.T. • *Luke 18:9–14*

Monday • *Luke 13:10–17*

Tuesday • *Luke 13:18–21*

Wednesday • *Luke 13:22–30*

Thursday, All Saints • *Matthew 5:1–12a*

Friday, All Souls • *John 6:37–40*

Saturday • *Luke 14:1, 7–11*

31st Sunday of O.T. • *Luke 19:1–10*

Monday • *Luke 14:12–14*

Tuesday • *Luke 14:15–24*

Wednesday • *Luke 14:25–33*

Thursday • *Luke 15:1–10*

Friday, Lateran Basilica • *John 2:13–22*

Saturday • *Luke 16:9–15*

32nd Sunday of O.T. • *Luke 20:27–38 or
20:27, 34–38*

Monday • *Luke 17:1–6*

Tuesday • *Luke 17:7–10*

Wednesday • *Luke 17:11–19*

Thursday • *Luke 17:20–25*

Friday • *Luke 17:26–37*

Saturday • *Luke 18:1–8*

33rd Sunday of O.T. • *Luke 21:5–19*

Monday • *Luke 18:35–43*

Tuesday • *Luke 19:1–10*

Wednesday, Presentation of Mary •
   Luke 19:11–28

Thursday • *Luke 17:11–19*

Friday • *Luke 19:45–48*

Saturday • *Luke 20:27–40*

Christ the King • *Luke 23:35–43*

Monday • *Luke 21:1–4*

Tuesday • *Luke 21:5 –11*

Wednesday • *Luke 21:12–19*

Thursday • *Luke 21:20–28*

Friday • *Matthew 4:18–22*

Saturday • *Luke 21:34–36*

1st Sunday of Advent • *Matthew 24:37–44*

Monday • *Mathew 8:5–11*

Tuesday • *Luke 10:21–24*

Wednesday • *Matthew 15:29–37*

Thursday • *Matthew 7:21, 24–27*

Friday • *Matthew 9:27–31*

Saturday, Immaculate Conception •
   Luke 1:26–38

2nd Sunday of Advent• *Matthew 3:1–12*

Monday • *Luke 5:17–26*

Tuesday • *Matthew 18:12–14*

Wednesday, Our Lady of Guadalupe •
   Luke 1:39–47

Thursday • *Matthew 11:11–15*

Friday • *Matthew 11:16–19*

Saturday • *Matthew 17:9a, 10–13*

3rd Sunday of Advent • *Matthew 11:2–11*

Monday • *Matthew 1:1–17*

Tuesday • *Matthew 1:18–25*

Wednesday • *Luke 1:5–25*

Thursday • *Luke 1:26–38*

Friday • *Luke 1:39–45*

Saturday • *Luke 1:46–56*

4th Sunday of Advent • *Matthew 1:18–24*

Monday • *Luke 1:67–79*

Tuesday, Nativity of the Lord (Midnight Mass) •
   Luke 2:1–14

Wednesday, St. Stephen • *Matthew 10:17–22*

Thursday, St. John • *John 20:1a, 2–8*

Friday, Holy Innocents • *Matthew 2:13–18*

Saturday, 5th Day in Octave • *Luke 2:22–35*

Holy Family of Jesus, Mary, and Joseph •
   Matthew 2:13–15, 19–23

Monday, 7th Day in Octave • *John 1:1–18*

PSALM 19B

The law of the Lord is perfect,
it revives the soul.
The rule of the Lord is to be trusted,
it gives wisdom to the simple.

The precepts of the Lord are right,
they gladden the heart.
The command of the Lord is clear,
it gives light to the eyes.

The fear of the Lord is holy,
abiding for ever.
The decrees of the Lord are truth
and all of them just.

They are more to be desired than gold,
than the purest gold,
and sweeter are they than honey,
than honey from the comb.

So in them your servant finds instruction;
great reward is in their keeping.
But who can detect all his errors?

From hidden faults acquit me.
From presumption restrain your servant
and let it not rule me.
Then shall I be blameless,
clean from grave sin.

May the spoken words of my mouth,
the thoughts of my heart,
with favor in your sight, O Lord,
my rescuer, my rock!

PSALM 22:8-9, 17, 18-19, 20, 23-24

All who see me deride me.
They curl their lips, they toss their heads.
"He trusted in the Lord, let him save him;
let him release him if this is his friend."

Many dogs have surrounded me,
a band of the wicked beset me.
They tear holes in my hands and feet
and lay me in the dust of death.

I can count every one of my bones.
These people stare at me and gloat;
they divide my clothing among them.
They cast lots for my robe.

O Lord, do not leave me alone,
my strength, make haste to help me!

I will tell of your name to my brethren
and praise you where they are assembled.
"You who fear the Lord, give him praise;
all sons of Jacob, give him glory.
Revere him, Israel's sons.

PSALM 25:1-3, 4-5, 7C, 6, 7, 8-9, 10-11

To you, O Lord, I lift up my soul.
I trust you, let me not be disappointed;
do not let my enemies triumph.
Those who hope in you shall not be disappointed,
but only those who wantonly break faith.

Lord, make me know your ways.
Lord, teach me your paths.
Make me walk in your truth, and teach me:
for you are God my savior.

In you I hope all day long
because of your goodness, O Lord.
Remember your mercy, Lord,
and the love you have shown from of old.
Do not remember the sins of my youth.
In your love remember me.

The Lord is good and upright.
He shows the path to those who stray,
he guides the humble in the right path;
he teaches his way to the poor.

His ways are faithfulness and love
for those who keep his covenant and law.
Lord, for the sake of your name
forgive my guilt; for it is great.

PSALM 27

The Lord is my light and my help;
who shall I fear?
The Lord is the stronghold of my life;
before whom shall I shrink?

When evil-doers draw near
to devour my flesh,
it is they, my enemies and foes,
who stumble and fall.

Though an army encamp against me
my heart would not fear.
Though war break out against me
even then would I trust.

There is one thing I ask of the Lord,
for this I long,
to live in the house of the Lord,
all the days of my life,
to savor the sweetness of the Lord,
to behold his temple.

For there he keeps me safe in his tent
in the day of evil.
He hides me in the shelter of his tent,
on a rock he sets me safe.

And now my head shall be raised
above my foes who surround me
and I shall offer within his tent
a sacrifice of joy.

PSALM 33:4–5, 18–19, 20, 22

For the word of the Lord is faithful
and all his works to be trusted.
The Lord loves justice and right
and fills the earth with his love.

The Lord looks on those who revere him,
on those who hope in his love,
to rescue their souls from death,
to keep them alive in famine.

Our soul is waiting for the Lord.
The Lord is our help and our shield.

May your love be upon us, O Lord,
as we place all our hope in you.

PSALM 34:2–15

I will bless the Lord at all times,
his praise always on my lips;
in the Lord my soul shall make its boast.
The humble shall hear and be glad.

Glorify the Lord with me.
Together let us praise his name.
I sought the Lord and he answered me;
from all my terrors he set me free.

Look towards him and be radiant;
let your faces not be abashed.
This poor man called; the Lord heard him
and rescued him from all his distress.

The angel of the Lord is encamped
around those who revere him, to rescue them.
Taste and see that the Lord is good.
He is happy who seeks refuge in him.

Revere the Lord, you his saints.
They lack nothing, those who revere him.
Strong lions suffer want and go hungry
but those who seek the Lord lack no blessing.

Come, children, and hear me
that I may teach you the fear of the Lord.
Who is he who longs for life
and many days, to enjoy his prosperity?

Then keep your tongue from evil
and your lips from speaking deceit.
Turn aside from evil and do good;
seek and strive after peace.

PSALM 40:2, 4, 7-8, 8-9, 10

I waited for the Lord
and he stopped down to me;
he heard my cry.

He put a new song into my mouth,
praise of our God.

You do not ask for sacrifice and offerings,
but an open ear.
You do not ask for holocaust and victim.
Instead, here am I.

In the scroll of the book it stands written
that I should do your will.
My God, I delight in your law
in the depth of my heart.

Your justice I have proclaimed
in the great assembly.
My lips I have not sealed;
you know it, O Lord.

PSALM 47

All peoples, clap your hands,
cry to God with shouts of joy!
For the Lord, the Most High, we must fear,
great king over all the earth.

He subdues peoples under us
and nations under our feet.
Our inheritance, our glory, is from him,
given to Jacob out of love.

God goes up with shouts of joy;
the Lord goes up with trumpet blast.
Sing praise for God sing praise,
sing praise to our king, sing praise.

God is king of all the earth.
Sing praise with all your skill.
God is kind over the nations;
God reigns on his holy throne.

The princes of the peoples are assembled
with the people of Abraham's God.
The rulers of the earth belong to God,
to God who reigns over all.

PSALM 66

Cry out with joy to God all the earth,
O sing to the glory of his name.
O render him glorious praise.
Say to God: "How tremendous your deeds!

Because of the greatness of your strength
your enemies cringe before you.
Before you all the earth shall bow;
shall sing to you, sing to your name!"

Come and see the works of God,
tremendous his deeds among men.
He turned the sea into dry land,
they passed through the river dry-shod.

Let our joy then be in him;
he rules for ever by his might.
His eyes keep watch over the nations:
let rebels not rise against him.

O peoples, bless our God,
let the voice of his praise resound,
of the God who gave life to our souls
and kept our feet from stumbling.

For you, O God, have tested us,
you have tried us as silver is tried:
you led us, God, into the snare;
you laid a heavy burden on our backs.

You let men ride over our heads;
we went through the fire and through water
but then you brought us relief.

PSALM 85

O Lord, you once favored your land
and revived the fortunes of Jacob,
you forgave the guilt of your people
and covered all their sins.
You averted all your rage,
you calmed the heat of your anger.

Revive us now, God, our helper!
Put an end to your grievance against us.
Will you be angry with us for ever,
will your anger never cease?

Will you not restore again our life
that your people may rejoice in you?
Let us see, O Lord, your mercy
and give us your saving help.

I will hear what the Lord God has to say,
a voice that speaks of peace,
peace for his people and his friends
and those who turn to him in their hearts.
His help is near for those who fear him
and his glory will dwell in our land.

Mercy and faithfulness have met;
justice and peace have embraced.
Faithfulness shall spring from the earth
and justice look down from heaven.

The Lord will make us prosper
and our earth shall yield its fruit.
Justice shall march before him
and peace shall follow his steps.

PSALM 91:1–2, 10–11, 12–13, 14, 16

He who dwells in the shelter of the Most High
and abides in the shade of the Almighty
says to the Lord: "My refuge,
my stronghold, my God in whom I trust!"

Upon you no evil shall fall,
no plague approach where you dwell.
For you has he commanded his angels,
to keep you in all your ways.

They shall bear you upon their hands
lest you strike your foot against a stone.
On the lion and the viper you will tread
and trample the young lion and the dragon.

Since he clings to me in love, I will free him;
protect him for he knows my name.
With length of life I will content him;
I shall let him see my saving power.

PSALM 98

Sing a new song to the Lord
for he has worked wonders.
His right hand and his holy arm
have brought salvation.

The Lord has made known his salvation;
has shown his justice to the nations.
He has remembered his truth and love
for the house of Israel.

All the ends of the earth have seen
the salvation of our God.
Shout to the Lord all the earth,
ring out your joy.

Sing psalms to the Lord with the harp,
with the sound of music.
With trumpets and the sound of the horn
acclaim the King, the Lord.

Let the sea and all within it thunder;
the world, and all its peoples.
Let the rivers clap their hands
and the hills ring out their joy.

Rejoice at the presence of the Lord,
for he comes to rule the earth.
He will rule the world with justice
and the peoples with fairness.

PSALM 100

Cry out with joy to the Lord, all the earth.
Serve the Lord with gladness.
Come before him, singing for joy.

Know that he, the Lord, is God.
He made us, we belong to him,
we are his people, the sheep of his flock.

Go within his gates, giving thanks.
Enter his courts with songs of praise.
Give thanks to him and bless his name.

Indeed, how good is the Lord,
eternal his merciful love.
He is faithful from age to age.

PSALM 116:10-19

I trusted, even when I said:
"I am sorely afflicted,"
and when I said in my alarm:
"No man can be trusted."

How can I repay the Lord
for his goodness to me?
The cup of salvation I will raise;
I will call on the Lord's name.

My vows to the Lord I will fulfill
before all his people.
O precious in the eyes of the Lord
is the death of his faithful.

Your servant, Lord, your servant am I;
you have loosened my bonds.
A thanksgiving sacrifice I make:
I will call on the Lord's name.

My vows to the Lord I will fulfill
before all his people,
in the courts of the house of the Lord,
in your midst, O Jerusalem.

PSALM 118:1, 2, 16–17, 22–24

Give thanks to the Lord for he is good,
for his love endures for ever.

Let the sons of Israel say:
"His love endures for ever."

The Lord's right hand has triumphed;
his right hand raised me.
The Lord's right hand has triumphed;
I shall not die, I shall live
and recount his deeds.

The stone which the builders rejected
has become the corner stone.
This is the work of the Lord,
a marvel in our eyes.
This day was made by the Lord;
we rejoice and are glad.

PSALM 130

Out of the depths I cry to you, O Lord,
Lord, hear my voice!
O let your ears be attentive
to the voice of my pleading.

If you, O Lord, should mark our guilt,
Lord, who would survive?
But with you is found forgiveness:
for this we revere you.

My soul is waiting for the Lord,
I count on his word.
My soul is longing for the Lord
more than watchman count on daybreak
and Israel on the Lord.

Because with the Lord there is mercy
and fullness of redemption,
Israel indeed he will redeem
from all its iniquity.

PSALM 145

I will give you glory, O God my King,
I will bless your name for ever.

I will bless you day after day
and praise your name for ever.
The Lord is great, highly to be praised,
his greatness cannot be measured.

Age to age shall proclaim your works,
shall declare your mighty deeds,
shall speak of your splendor and glory,
tell the tale of your wonderful works.

They will speak of your terrible deeds,
recount your greatness and might.
They shall recall your abundant goodness;
age to age shall ring out your justice.

The Lord is kind and full of compassion,
slow to anger, abounding in love.
How good is the Lord to all,
compassionate to all his creatures.

Small Prayer Books from Liturgy Training Publications

These small, lovely prayer books offer prayers for daily use or for special situations. They include

Catholic Prayers

Come, Holy Spirit!

Prayers for Midday

Prayers of Those Who Mourn

Prayers for Later Years

Rites of the Sick

Prayers with the Dying

Prayers of Those Who Make Music

Prayers for Catechists

Prayers for the Dedication of a Church

Prayers during the Night

Prayers in Times of Crisis

Prayers out of the Depths

Other Resources from Liturgy Training Publications

Prayer Resources

Sounding the Silence

Author John Skinner provides an invitation to experience God in the prayerful moments of silent meditation. *Sounding the Silence* guides our prayer so that we can escape the chaos and distractions that life sometimes gives us and just sit, in "silence," with God. Inspired by the Carthusian tradition of silent prayer, Skinner offers simple models of praying that are both inviting and safe, proving that anyone can pray and that no prayer is the same. It provides weekly readings based on a simple half hour of stillness and threaded together to provide a year-long exploration of silence. The book can be used individually or by Catholic and ecumenical prayer groups, RCIA team members, worship team members, and parish or diocesan staff members.

An Everyday Book of Hours

William Storey, compiler of some of the best-loved prayer books of our time, has selected the most beautiful elements from the full Liturgy of the Hours and from other sources to create a simpler book for Morning and Evening Prayer. Intended for individuals and groups who want to taste the venerable tradition of using scripture to offer praise, thanksgiving, and intercession at dawn and sunset, this book provides a four-week cycle of prayer.

At Home with the Word

An annual book that contains the Sunday Mass readings for the current year, with materials for reflection, prayer, and action. Available in large print.

A Seasonal Book of Hours

William G. Storey offers *A Seasonal Book of Hours* for Morning and Evening Prayer during Advent, Christmas, Lent, and Easter. This book will give your daily prayer the solemn and festive tone you yearn for during the solemn seasons of the Church's year. Like its predecessor, this seasonal book combines prayers from the Liturgy of the Hours and from the tradition's most eloquent authors to provide a simple and graceful order of prayer appropriate for individuals or groups.

Daily Lenten Meditations: Prayerful Reflections from John Paul II

This book contains excerpts taken from the homilies, addresses, and official letters of Pope John Paul II's long and generous evangelizing activity. These excerpts have been put together to form a kind of spiritual pilgrimage over the course of Lent. As Christ faced suffering, the Pope faced his own illness and infirmity with courage and fortitude walking his own Lenten pilgrimage every day with prayerful dignity and faith.

Resources for the Word of God

Living the Lectionary

Geoff Wood's reflections on the Sunday readings make visible scripture's perennial applicability to human experience. Through reference to Western literature as well as his life experiences, he engages our imagination and helps us to see the wisdom of the biblical word shine forth. Homilists will find this resource invaluable as will catechists, youth ministers, and RCIA teams. A separate volume is available for years A, B, and C.

Lectionary for Mass, Study Edition

This convenient and comprehensive paperback volume contains all of the readings for the sundays of Year A, Year B, and Year C and those for solemnities and feast days. All of the readings are from the New American Bible approved for use in the United States. Paperback.

Weekday Lectionary, Study Edition

Contains all the readings for weekdays, ritual Masses (such as weddings and funerals), votive Masses (such as Masses of the Blessed Virgin Mary), and Masses for various needs and occasions (such as Masses for peace). Paperback.

Workbook for Lectors and Gospel Readers

An annual book that contains the Sunday Mass readings for the current year, laid out as they appear in the Lectionary, with aids to help those who will proclaim the scriptures during the liturgy.

The Children's Version of *Daily Prayer!*

Children's Daily Prayer 2006–2007

This volume of LTP's popular annual resource for praying in the classroom just got better! It's still the clear, easy-to-follow format for classroom prayer for every day of the school year. It now includes the Gospel of the day, so children are praying along with the Church. Everything you need to pray on a given day can be found on one page!

The prayer includes

• Opening: Orients the students to the Gospel excerpt of the day—describes the story's background, explains any difficult vocabulary, and introduces the liturgy observed on this day.

• Psalm: The psalm is included on the spread so pages don't need to be turned. Psalm responses, which may be photocopied, are included.

• Gospel: Scripture reading is an excerpt from the Gospel read at daily mass—students are praying with the Church.

• For Silent Reflection: Questions for the individual student's "prayerful wondering."

• Closing Prayer: Collects the prayers of the students as the prayer concludes.

New for 2007!

• Author Suzanne M. Lewis

• Reproducible psalm response pages

• Many prayer services for feasts and special occasions

• Extra psalms and canticles